TOWARDS THE LIMITS OF FREUDIAN THINKING

FIGURES OF THE UNCONSCIOUS 21

TOWARDS THE LIMITS OF FREUDIAN THINKING

Critical Edition and Readings of *Beyond the Pleasure Principle*

Edited by

Herman Westerink,
Jenny Willner & Philippe Van Haute

LEUVEN UNIVERSITY PRESS

Minderbroedersstraat 4, B-3000 Leuven / Louvain (Belgium)

ISBN 978 94 6270 409 1
eISBN 978 94 6166 556 0 (ePDF)
eISBN 978 94 6166 586 7 (ePUB)
https://doi.org/10.11116/9789461665560
D/2024/1869/30
NUR: 770

Typesetting: Friedemann
Cover design: Daniel Benneworth-Gray
Cover images: (Right) The Development of Reconstructive Plastic Surgery during the First World War, Imperial War Museum Photograph Archive Collection. https://commons.wikimedia.org/wiki/File:The_Development_of_Reconstructive_Plastic_Surgery_during_the_First_World_War_Q30460.jpg. (Left) Crytoidea–Flaschenstrahlinge from Kunstformen der Natur (1904) by Ernst Haeckel. Original from Library of Congress. Digitally enhanced by rawpixel. https://www.rawpixel.com/image/2272986/free-illustration-image-haeckel-vintage-marine-life

GPRC
Guaranteed Peer Reviewed Content
www.gprc.be

Contents

Editors' Note and Acknowledgements

Herman Westerink & Jenny Willner

This volume uses the different versions of Freud's *Beyond the Pleasure Principle* as a starting point for a series of contributions that seek to re-actualise the classic text. It was Ilse Grubrich-Simitis who in her study *Zurück zu Freuds Texten* from 1993 drew attention to the pre-publication versions of the text in the Sigmund Freud Archives of the Library of Congress and presented some of their features. A further milestone followed 20 years later, when the German critical edition of all existing variants of the text was transcribed, edited and commented by Ulrike May and Michael Schröter and published in the journal *Luzifer-Amor: Zeitschrift zur Geschichte der Psychoanalyse* (2013, Volume 51). The achievement of May and Schröter was to include and present all six stages of revision of Freud's text, spanning from the first version from 1919 to Freud's last revisions for the edition in *Gesammelte Schriften* in 1925.

Our volume includes the English translation of this critical edition of *Beyond the Pleasure Principle*, which was generously made available to us for re-publication. The edition presented here was prepared by Matt ffytche, John Forrester and Michael Molnar and originally published in the journal *Psychoanalysis and History* (2015, Volume 17(2)), where a more detailed presentation of the English critical edition and editorial remarks can be found. Ffytche, Forrester and Molnar worked with the translation of *Beyond the Pleasure Principle* as found in the *Revised Standard Edition,* prepared by Mark Solms on behalf of the Institute of Psychoanalysis, London. The most important change in comparison to James Strachey's translation in the *Standard Edition* (Volume 18) concerns the translation of *Trieb* as 'drive' and not as 'instinct'. In all editorial matters we follow the edition in *Psychoanalysis and History.* This above all concerns the colour codings in the Freud text as introduced by Ffytche, Forrester and Molnar, allowing for an easy identification of the first version of the text from 1919 and the later added text parts and modifications in the various editions: 1920, 1921, 1923, 1925.

A: handwritten first version of the manuscript, 1919.
B: typed version of A with handwritten corrections and insertions, 1920.
C: first edition, 1920, published at Internationaler Psychoanalytischer Verlag, Leipzig, Vienna & Zurich.
D: second edition, 1921, same publisher.
E: third edition, 1923, same publisher.
F: edition in *Gesammelte Schriften Bd. 6*, 1925.

This means that the first version from 1919 (A), despite never being published during Freud's lifetime, is treated as a default version, making all insertions authorised by Freud easily recognisable as stemming from a later phase in the writing process. The footnotes without brackets are Freud's own notes, colour coded according to the version in which they first appeared. In all other footnotes the source is identified by the following abbreviations:

SE: notes inserted by James Strachey in the *Standard Edition.*
RSE: notes inserted by Mark Solms in the *Revised Standard Edition.*
LA: notes inserted by Ulrike May and Michel Schröter in the *Luzifer-Amor* edition of *Jenseits des Lustprinzips.*
PH: notes inserted by Matt ffytche, John Forrester and Michael Molnar in the *Psychoanalysis and History* edition of *Beyond the Pleasure Principle.*

The editors of the present volume are deeply indebted to both *Luzifer-Amor* and *Psychoanalysis and History* and all the above-mentioned editors and commentators. We are also thankful for the permission to re-publish Ulrike May's essay 'The Third Step in Drive Theory: On the Genesis of *Beyond the Pleasure Principle*', which is a detailed commentary of the findings of the critical edition and must be considered a major event in the scholarly reception of *Beyond the Pleasure Principle.*

Since it is customary to quote from the English edition as published in the *Standard Edition*, the editors of *Psychoanalysis and History* and of this volume decided to include the page numbers in Freud's text. They are the numbers between square brackets. References to contemporary secondary literature in the footnotes are listed in the bibliography to Ulrike May's essay.

The concept of this anthology, combining the critical edition, May's essay and a set of new commentaries, was designed by Philippe Van Haute and Herman

Westerink already in 2020, with Ulrike Kistner, Jenny Willner and Jakob Staberg as further contributors. In November 2022, Van Haute sadly passed away. Later, Willner joined Westerink as a co-editor. This means that the anthology, drafted and assembled by Van Haute and Westerink, was finished and retrospectively framed by Westerink and Willner. The publication of this volume honours the memory of Philippe Van Haute.

All three editors and the contributors – including Ulrike May – have over the years engaged in the Freud Research Group (FRG), which was founded by Philippe Van Haute in 2009. The research group brings together Freud scholars from several different countries and languages with diverging disciplinary backgrounds in psychoanalysis, philosophy, history of science, cultural and literary studies and religious studies. The present volume is one of several books and collected volumes that have come out of the cooperation in this lively forum. We are deeply thankful to all participants for the ongoing close readings and discussions.

We are also grateful for many fruitful comments from and discussions with colleagues on various occasions where we were able to present (parts of) our readings of *Beyond the Pleasure Principle*, notably the international conferences of the International Society of Psychoanalysis and Philosophy, the International Symposium in Phenomenology (Perugia), and the conferences organised at the Center for Contemporary European Philosophy (Nijmegen).

Different processes of translation have been crucial not only for the complex editorial history of *Beyond the Pleasure Principle* as drafted above, but also for specific contributions. Ulrike May's essay was translated into English for *Psychoanalysis and History* by Michael Molnar. For the current volume, we would like to thank Joey Kok, who translated parts of Van Haute's and Westerink's contribution from Dutch to English, Michael J. Taylor, who translated a previous version of Willner's contribution from German to English, and David Payne for the English-language editing of Staberg's contribution. Last but not least we thank Rebecca Bryan for meticulously proofreading the entire manuscript.

As regards institutional support, we want to thank the Faculty of Philosophy, Theology and Religious Studies, Radboud University Nijmegen for financial funding and Leuven University Press for supporting us all the way through this process, specifically for enabling us to present the colour codings of the variants of *Beyond the Pleasure Principle*. A special thank you goes to our peer-reviewers for their helpful and generous comments of the first version of this manuscript.

Dimensions of 'Beyond': An Introduction

Herman Westerink & Jenny Willner

Beyond the Pleasure Principle is likely the most commented of Freud's texts in philosophical literature. Notably the puzzling and intriguing concept of the death drive – even though Freud here only uses the plural: death drives – has been at the centre of reflections. This is no surprise. After all, this text has ever since its publication in 1920 been recognised as the zenith of Freud's metapsychology. Here, Freud dares to think beyond the limits of his own clinical practice, and beyond the theoretical 'shibboleths' of psychoanalysis.

In the title of the present volume, *Towards the Limits of Freudian Thinking*, the notion of limits stands in relation to the 'beyond' of the pleasure principle. It was the compulsion to repeat unpleasurable experiences, as observed most obviously in the recurring nightmares of shell-shocked soldiers, that forced Freud to engage with the limits of his theory of wish fulfilment. More than twenty years earlier, after the *Studies on Hysteria* (1895), published with Josef Breuer, Freud had proceeded from a theory of sexual trauma to a sexual aetiology of the neuroses focusing on infantile fantasy. While *The Interpretation of Dreams* (1900) was already a result of this shift, Freud undertook further inquiries into the question of sexual constitution, introducing the concepts of sexual drives and self-preservative drives in *Three Essays on the Theory of Sexuality* (1905). In the face of the First World War, the assumption that all neuroses were related to sexuality was challenged. Freud was confronted with the limits not only of his founding theoretical principles, but also of clinical practice: could severely traumatised patients ever be successfully treated?

In *Beyond the Pleasure Principle*, Freud approaches the limits of psychoanalysis in yet another sense. While reconsidering the notions of drive, repetition, trauma and pleasure, he registers, not without concern, that through these speculations, by approaching the last questions of life and of death, he has unwittingly steered his course "into the harbor of Schopenhauer's philosophy".[1] In fact he steered into the harbour of a whole history of Western

[1] S. Freud (1920g), *Beyond the Pleasure Principle*, *SE* 18, p. 50.

metaphysics.[2] And yet – despite some references to Kant, Schopenhauer and Nietzsche – he is far from seeking to systematically clarify the relation between psychoanalysis and philosophy. In terms of steering into different harbours, the striking feature of *Beyond the Pleasure Principle* is not the use of philosophical terms and concepts, but rather the many references to (evolutionary) biology and physiology (as physics). When Freud speaks of "far-fetched speculations"[3] pertaining to the origin of organic life, he seems to be announcing that he is about to abandon the realm of his own discipline, towards an inquiry into the – mechanical, chemical, somatic – sources of the drives, beyond the scope of psychoanalysis, as it were.

Is biology and physics the 'beyond' of psychoanalysis? Or are the natural sciences rather to be thought of as the basis of a theoretical superstructure? Frank J. Sulloway famously claimed that Freud, by engaging a set of outdated scientific theories, sought to provide his own theoretical edifice with a solid ground.[4] It is, however, highly questionable whether the biological references in *Beyond the Pleasure Principle* point towards any coherent set of theories. They can scarcely be said to form anything even resembling a solid basis for Freud's metapsychological speculations. Throughout the versions of his text, Freud refers to diverging and sometimes mutually opposing biological theories. Against this background, Freud's own statement that "biology truly is a land of unlimited possibilities" refers less to the status of his own biological references, and rather to a biology of the future, which may "blow away the whole of our artificial structure of hypothesis".[5]

An even more substantial question regarding the status of natural scientific concepts arises when Freud traces back the obscurity of his own speculation to the fact of "our being obliged to operate with the scientific terms, that is to say with figurative language, peculiar to psychology", only to add that this also holds true for "physiological or chemical" terms: "It is true that they too are only part of figurative language; but it is one with which we have long been familiar".[6] It may be argued that Freud's reading method does its best to defamiliarise the natural scientific concepts of his time.

---

2 R. Bernet (2020), *Force, Drive, Desire: A Philosophy of Psychoanalysis*. See for the following paragraphs on this subject also H. Westerink & P. Van Haute (2022), *Verleiding, drift en herhaling: Freuds metafysica van het trauma*, pp. 271ff.
3 Freud (1920g), *Beyond the Pleasure Principle*, p. 24.
4 F.J. Sulloway (1979), *Freud: Biologist of the Mind*.
5 Freud (1920g), *Beyond the Pleasure Principle*, p. 60.
6 Ibid.

In *Beyond the Pleasure Principle*, Freud dwells in the grey zones of his theory. Hence, the dimensions of 'beyond' are perhaps to be sought for less outside, and rather at the centre of the psychoanalytic edifice. If the drive is to be understood as a concept "on the frontier of the mental and the somatic",[7] the same applies to psychoanalysis itself, exploring the principles that structure the psychic life of embodied creatures and their symptoms. By engaging with resolutely material issues, Freud on the one hand speculates beyond the discourse founded by himself. On the other hand, he extends his own theory to encompass the entire natural world: he speculatively applies psychoanalytic libido theory to the fundamental reality of all organic life.

The relation between life and death occupies a central position in this text. Despite the religious connotations of the term of 'beyond', Freud does not connect this subject matter with theology, but rather with natural scientific debates. What is at stake in this interdisciplinary field is the unstable relation between biology and what no longer belongs to the realm of *bios*: inorganic matter, lifeless structures and the machine-like laws of physicalism.[8] Where does biology begin? Where does it end? Even today, the disciplinary limits of biology, linked to the precise moment at which organic life emerges from lifeless chemical structures of protein, remain undefined within the natural sciences and engender conflicting definitions. Freud's engagement with these issues touches upon the conflict between natural philosophic vitalism and mechanistic physicalism, two opposing paradigms with which he was more than familiar from working in the laboratories of both Carl Claus and Ernst Brücke. While the former had cooperated with Ernst Haeckel, the latter stood firmly within a mechanistic tradition of the Helmholtz school, which demarcated itself from the heritage of natural philosophy and from any kind of vitalism.[9] Freud's speculation on the primitive cell suggests that deadened matter structures organic life from within, that an inorganic element is necessary to life itself.

Freud's relation to the medical and natural sciences of his time has been subject to conflicting interpretations within both the psychoanalytic and the philosophical reception of his theory. His references to biology and physics were for a long time deemed highly problematic, as obstructing the reflection on the text's fundamental conceptuality. Jürgen Habermas famously

7 S. Freud (1915c), 'Instincts and Their Vicissitudes', *SE* 14, p. 122.

8 D. Wills (2016), *Inanimation: Theories of Inorganic Life*, pp. 55–79.

9 L.B. Ritvo (1990), *Darwin's Influence on Freud: A Tale of Two Sciences*, p. 10.

referred to Freud's engagement with biology in terms of a "scientistic self-misunderstanding".[10]

It goes without saying that Jacques Lacan has had a significant impact on several philosophical readings of Freud's work, currently most prominently in the writings of Mladen Dolar, Alenka Zupančič and Slavoj Žižek. The conclusion drawn by Lacan from the problem of the drives in relation to the somatic differs from the one presented by Freud. According to Lacan, the functioning of the unconscious can in no way be explained by referring to biological data.[11] Sexual psychogenesis is not to be understood from organic drive activity acting on the psychic apparatus, but from a 'lack' of the subject in relation to a limiting law. The subject is essentially characterised by a desire for the elimination of this 'lack'.[12] From the perspective of the theoretical tradition founded by Lacan, Freud's references to biology have caused significant unease: Lacan was particularly influential on the long-dominant view that Freud's interest in biology meant a regression in his theoretical development.[13] The most benevolent accounts of Freud's interest in phylogenesis from this perspective still suggest that Freud turned to evolutionary speculations because he lacked the Lacanian notion of a signifier.[14]

Jean Laplanche has most forcefully promoted a negative reading of Freud's references to biology. He viewed them as an error, the result of Freud succumbing to the temptation of biology, which led him astray from his own foundational insights.[15] According to Laplanche, sexuality is not a constitutional fact, but arises in early childhood when the drive becomes sexual in autoeroticism and at the same time becomes phantasmatic in relation to the sexual object.[16] In his theory of primal seduction, Laplanche argues that psychoanalysis should limit itself to a psychological theory of sexual trauma without reference to biology.

Over the last years, several different lines of reception have sought a possible other *retour à Freud*, one less negligent regarding the body and the organic. This can on the one hand be seen as part of a more general move away from the linguistic turn in contemporary continental philosophy. On the other hand, similar tendencies are already inherent in so-called poststructuralism,

10 J. Habermas (1968), *Knowledge & Human Interest*, pp. 300f.
11 J. Lacan (2006), *Écrits*, p. 575.
12 See P. Van Haute (2002), *Against Adaptation: Jacques Lacan's Subversion of the Subject*.
13 It can, however, be argued, that Lacan himself ought to be re-read in this respect, cf. L. Chiesa, 'The World of Desire: Lacan between Evolutionary Biology and Psychoanalytic Theory'.
14 D. Wilson (2018), 'Freud's Lamarckian Clinic', p. 262.
15 J. Laplanche (2015), *The Temptation of Biology: Freud's Theories of Sexuality*.
16 J. Laplanche (1987), *Nouveaux fondements pour la psychanalyse*.

where Lacan's impact can be traced even in the work of his critics, such as Deleuze and Guattari in *L'Anti-Oedipe* (1972), Foucault in *Histoire de la sexualité* (1976–1984) and Butler in *Gender Trouble* (1990) and *Bodies that Matter* (1993). Foucault's 'counterattack' on the primacy of law and desire from an experience of "bodies and pleasures" seems to be able to find support in Freud's non-oedipal theory of infantile sexuality.[17] And when Deleuze and Guattari speak of human beings as "desiring-machines", that is, as organic and psychic apparatuses, as forms, functions, relations and expressions of a productive force acting from within, they seem at first glance to be in line with Freud's view of the life drives as an energy which sets both the body and the psychic apparatus in motion from within and produces ever new forms.[18]

Within the much younger paradigm of new materialism, it has been Elizabeth Wilson in particular who has put forward the thesis that Freud becomes relevant for contemporary critical theory precisely where he refers to biology and physiology. Wilson disputes what she views as a common tendency of language-oriented, social-constructivist theory: the prioritisation of symbolic formations over biological conditions, of cultural anatomy over physiology. According to Wilson, neglecting biological data even comes close to an unacknowledged overestimation of biology, "as if such data reign over interpretative analysis or as if they enforce the final, factual limits of what can be imagined, elucidated, or craved."[19] Wilson argues that the psychoanalytic engagement with biology is relevant for understanding how the domains of the biogenetic and the psycho-cultural are "materially intertwined" and how biology can deliver a contribution to a feminist theory of "embodiment".[20]

Regarding the status of biology in psychoanalysis, a particularly fruitful line of enquiry has emerged from Jacques Derrida's readings of *Beyond the Pleasure Principle* in his posthumously published lecture series *La vie la mort*.[21] Introducing the term 'biodeconstruction', Francesco Vitale has demonstrated how closely Derrida's interest in the natural sciences is linked to his engagement with Freud: Derrida activates Freud's theory of the death drives in terms of a radical thinking of mortality and of biological life as constitutively inscribed

---

17 M. Foucault (1978), *The Will to Knowledge*, pp. 157, 159.

18 G. Deleuze & F. Guattari (1972), *L'Anti-Oedipe: Capitalisme et schizophrénie*. Already in his 1968 *Différence et répétition* Deleuze presents a critical reading of *Beyond the Pleasure Principle* focusing on the problematics of repetition and drive.

19 E. Wilson (2015), *Gut Feminism*, p. 46.

20 E. Wilson (2004), *Psychosomatic: Feminism and the Neurological Body*, pp. 3, 77.

21 J. Derrida (2020), *Life Death*, originally published as J. Derrida (2019), *La vie la mort: Séminaire* (1975–1976), Paris: Seuil. The four last lectures open up a new perspective on the role of biology in Derrida's most famous reading of *Beyond the Pleasure Principle*: J. Derrida (1987), *The Post Card: From Socrates to Freud and Beyond*.

by death, linking evolutionary theory to cybernetics in view of organic life as a kind of text.[22] Similarly, Robert Trumbull demonstrates how Derrida fleshes out a deconstructivist approach to resolutely material issues from Freud's engagement with biology.[23]

How can the present volume be located in relation to these lines of reception? We begin by redirecting the focus from conclusions drawn by later theorists to Freud's texts themselves, thoroughly re-reading them with both current philosophical debates and with the versions as presented in the critical edition in mind. We believe that Freud's references to biology can neither be replaced by symbolic structures, nor do they obstruct philosophical reflection: they enforce it. Regarding biology in *Beyond the Pleasure Principle*, we argue that questions pertaining to fundamental conceptualities lie at the core of the subject matter at stake – of the specific notions of organic and inorganic matter and of the principles and dynamics that structure life.

For philologically inclined readers, this raises a set of pragmatic questions regarding the genealogy of the biological speculation in *Beyond the Pleasure Principle* in view of Freud's earlier writings on both physics and biology, for instance in 'Project for a Scientific Psychology' (1895) and 'Instincts and Their Vicissitudes' (1915). How and why does a clinical practice focused on the narratives and verbal associations of patients engender a theory that seems to culminate in reflections on the nature of organic life and the status of the inanimate? In other words, where and why did the itinerary that made Freud steer into the harbour of metaphysics start?

One could argue that it began when Freud in the late 1890s questioned the exclusive role of accidental factors in the aetiology of the psychoneuroses. Questioning the determining role of individual traumatic experiences, he saw himself forced to – again – deal with the question of constitutional and hereditary factors.[24] He had previously distanced himself from the hereditary aetiology of neuroses, which remained the most common interpretative scheme available at the time.[25] Michel Foucault, despite his critique of Freud, praised the break with the prevalent neuropsychiatry of heredity and degeneration as the "political credit" of psychoanalysis.[26] With Freud's theory

22 F. Vitale (2018), *Biodeconstruction*.

23 R. Trumbull (2022), *Derrida, Freud, and the Future of Deconstruction*.

24 See Freud's Letter to Fliess from 21 September 1897: 'And with this the factor of a hereditary disposition regains a sphere of influence from which I had made it my task to expel it'. S. Freud (1985c), 'Extracts from the Fliess Papers', *SE* 1, p. 260.

25 On Freud's distancing from the hereditary aetiology of his teacher Jean-Martin Charcot, see E. Roith, 'Hysteria, Heredity and Anti-Semitism. Freud's Quiet Rebellion'.

26 Foucault (1978), *The Will to Knowledge*, p. 150. See also A. Davidson (2001), *The Emergence of Sexuality: Historical Epistemology and the Formation of Concepts*, pp. 66–92.

of the drive, it becomes obvious, however, that this is not a clean break. The status of constitution and heredity remains an open problem to which Freud never ceases to return from different angles, handling it in ambivalent ways: partly as an alien body, beyond the scope of psychoanalytic theory, but also suggesting its founding status within a post-Darwinian anthropology. Freud does not seem to be willing to leave the question of heredity to the prevailing neuropsychiatric discourses of degeneration. By means of his biological speculations he continues to foray into this territory.

As Freud himself noted, his own view of the hereditary and constitutional factors was radically different from that of his contemporaries. This holds true in particular regarding notions of normality and pathology.[27] While Freud does seek "the essential nature of sexuality" in "somatic processes", one crucial difference lies in his insistence that these processes are to be understood as constitutively polymorphous.[28] Another difference becomes obvious when he reconceptualises the "sexual constitution" as a "general neuropathic disposition".[29] This was the leading hypothesis of his inquiry into the general human sexual constitution and the sexual drives, and their aetiological role and significance – resulting in *Three Essays on the Theory of Sexuality*, where he contends that sexuality is an innate force already present and active in infantile life. The building blocks for his theory of infantile sexuality can already be traced in earlier writings, such as 'Project': the physiological and chemical processes, the mechanical excitations and muscular activities, the partial drives and their somatic sources, stimulus-receiving organs, autoerotic experience of pleasure at one's own body, organ pleasure, and organic repression.[30]

From *Three Essays* onwards Freud took his next steps. Sometimes inspired by and sometimes in opposition to his closest followers, he engaged with both academically accepted and abandoned, both with dominant and eccentric theories of evolution (embryology, palaeontology, zoology), as well as with the physicalist paradigm of his time. Regarding the status of phylogenetic inheritance, it is worth noting that Freud's application of models from one discourse to another goes in both directions. Not only does Freud apply (his version of) phylogenetics to case studies and works of cultural criticism, often enough his reformulation of biological heredity also proceeds in the other direction:

---

27 Because of this, Jacques Schotte has characterised psychoanalysis as patho-analysis: J. Schotte (1990), *Szondi avec Freud. Sur la voie d'une psychiatrie pulsionelle.*

28 S. Freud (1906a), 'My Views on the Part Played by Sexuality in the Aetiology of the Neuroses', *SE* 7, p. 277.

29 Ibid., p. 276.

30 For a detailed reading of *Three Essays* see, P. Van Haute & H. Westerink (2021), *From Pleasure to the Object: Reading Freud's Three Essays on the Theory of Sexuality.*

from clinical case material via psychoanalytic concepts into the discourse of phylogenetics. In *Totem and Taboo*, obsessional neurosis is the model at stake for reinterpreting the process of civilisation, which, in turn, is infused into a theory of repressed, displaced and phylogenetically inherited guilt.

According to Freud, constitutional and hereditary factors should be seen as the result of a long series of physiological and psychological modifications and adaptations under the influence of external and internal forces. In *Totem and Taboo*, in the case of the Wolf Man and notably also in 'A Phylogenetic Phantasy: Overview of the Transference Neuroses', Freud argues that the human constitution is the result of evolutionary and cultural-historical developments in which traumatic experiences and impressions in the primordial past have left indelible somatic and psychological traces. According to Sander L. Gilman, there is a specific historical reason why Freud located the trauma in such a speculative phylogenetic past: Freud's universalisation of the trauma served as a way of circumventing prevailing neurological theories according to which neurosis and hysteria were specific degenerative conditions typical for Eastern European Jews, who were assumed to be irreversibly marked by the hereditary consequences of diaspora and ghettoisation.[31]

Beginning with *Totem and Taboo*, concepts of phylogenetics and heredity became intertwined with cultural criticism in Freud's thought, famously culminating in *Moses and Monotheism*. We suggest that *Beyond the Pleasure Principle* can be situated firmly within this very development. Here, the history of the human species is incorporated into a theory of the fundamental forces and principles that characterise all organic life. The variety of species and innumerable individual variations is understood by Freud as the result of shocking and tension-inducing influences of external and internal forces and, as reactions to them, the acquired characteristics of species. The structure of the drive constitution is understood as the result of a series of traumatic events that have shaped the history of all organisms. The drives are conceived of as forces that illuminate both the phenomena faced in clinical practice and the basic characteristics of everything that lives.

In this way, trauma and drive become key concepts in Freud's metapsychology and tragic view of human life. In *Beyond the Pleasure Principle*, he explores and speculates on the relationship between the two. Are the drives aimed at change and development, perhaps even at 'perfection'? A first answer is that, on the contrary, the drives aim to restore a past state that was abandoned due to disturbing forces (traumas). The death drive is characterised by a manifest

[31] S. Gilman, 'Wandering Imaginations of Race and Hysteria. The Origins of the Hysterical Body in Psychoanalysis', p. 50.

compulsion to repeat, aiming to restore, at any cost, a previous inanimate state, to return to the inorganic. With the introduction of the life drives (Eros), Freud further radicalises this perspective: he insists that the life drives too are fundamentally regressive. They are spontaneously aimed at forming larger units, bringing back not inorganic states, but "earlier states of living substance".[32] Freud seems to suggest that development occurs even though the life drives strictly speaking do not aim for progress: a double setup of regressive aims paradoxically generates more differentiated and increasingly complex life forms. Development appears as a secondary effect, that is, as the result of life drives seeking to unite parts and the death drives aiming at dissolving units. While the death drives aim to restore the state before the union of parts and seek to return to the inanimate, the life drives aim to 'reunite' what has been fragmented and thus end up repeatedly re-producing the same detour, the developmental process from germ-cell to complex multicellular organism.

From here, we can bring Freud's clinical and metapsychological speculations into dialogue with a long tradition of philosophical reflection on the drives as causal and vital forces. This tradition starts with Aristotle and runs through Spinoza, Leibniz, Schopenhauer, Nietzsche and Bergson, among others, to Foucault, Deleuze and Guattari, and the new materialism of Elisabeth Grosz, Elisabeth Wilson and also Catherine Malabou. Freud's tragic vision of man, centred around trauma, drive, repetition and conflict, can be brought into critical dialogue with this tradition.

The present volume takes its starting point in what is known about the writing process and composition of *Beyond the Pleasure Principle*: Freud wrote a first version of the text in April 1919, decided not to publish it, started working on the text again in May 1920 and completed the manuscript for publication three months later. In reprints from the following years, short but often important changes and passages were added. Taking this into account is of crucial importance for philosophical readings since it is only in the version of 1920 that Freud introduces the new conceptuality of the death drives and life drives.

This very fact raises questions. Why did Freud leave the first version unpublished only to complete it a year later with a chapter introducing a new conceptuality? Could it perhaps be that the trains of thought he had developed in the first version led him towards conclusions that he could not accept or that he needed to fundamentally reconsider? And which, then, were the problems and questions that led Freud to new conclusions? By naming

32 Freud (1920g), *Beyond the Pleasure Principle*, p. 40.

and thematising the various editions of different texts, the additions and omissions, as much as possible, we get a better view of Freudian psychoanalysis as a field of interrelated problematics that also gives food for new theoretical thought. Only from such a perspective – and thus averse to any attempt to encapsulate Freudian thought once and for all in a set of dogmatic positions – can the Freudian corpus be fruitfully confronted with philosophical and psychoanalytic reflections on the drives, repetition, trauma, man's relationship to death, or the somatic traces of the history of the species.

Taking the critical edition into account, the role of biology in *Beyond the Pleasure Principle* gains even more relevance. Ulrike May argues that Sándor Ferenczi's input on biology was of vital importance during the months between the first (1919) and the second (1920) versions of the text.[33] Freud's cooperation with the Hungarian analyst indeed forms a decisive context for his phylogenetic speculation in general. This applies specifically to their unfinished work on what they alternatingly termed 'metabiology', 'deep biology', the 'Lamarck project' and 'bioanalysis'.[34] The relevance of this project for re-reading *Beyond the Pleasure Principle* is evident. Ferenczi defined bioanalysis as a speculative science which would "carry over into the field of the natural sciences in a systematic manner the knowledge gained and the technique used by psychoanalysis".[35] Biology is not the model at stake here; rather, it is remodelled from the point of view of psychoanalysis: Freud himself wrote in the preface to the third edition of *Three Essays* (1915) that Haeckel's recapitulation theory, expressing the idea that ontogeny repeats phylogeny, also made possible the study of phylogeny from ontogeny, i.e. from clinical and anthropological insights gained from psychoanalytic practice. The aim in *Three Essays* was then to "discover how far psychological investigation can throw light upon the biology of the sexual life of man".[36]

The interpretational sovereignty over biology was at stake: Freud and Ferenczi experimented with the idea of conquering biology from a psychoanalytic stance. This unfinished endeavour can be traced in a series of both canonical and less known writings, beginning with Ferenczi's 'Stages in the Development of the Sense of Reality' (1913) and Freud's 'A Phylogenetic Phantasy: Overview of the Transference Neuroses' (1915), via Ferenczi's *Thalassa: A Theory of Genitality*

[33] May, in this volume, p. 88.

[34] I. Grubrich-Simitis (1987), 'Trauma oder Trieb – Trieb und Trauma: Lektionen aus Sigmund Freuds phylogenetischer Phantasie von 1915', pp. 992–1023; for an extensive reconstruction, see U. May's 'Appendix I' in this volume, pp. 143–151; for further discussion, see the chapter by J. Willner, pp. 225–256.

[35] S. Ferenczi (1989 [1924]), *Thalassa: A Theory of Genitality*, p. 102.

[36] S. Freud (1905d), *Three Essays on the Theory of Sexuality*, *SE* 7, p. 131.

– drafted in 1914–1915, finalised and published in 1924 – and well into the biological speculation in *Beyond the Pleasure Principle* itself.

The plan, which never materialised, was to write a book about the French naturalist Jean-Baptiste Lamarck, whose theories had been refuted by August Weismann's germ-plasm theory. One reason for Freud and Ferenczi's untimely interest in Lamarck is connected to the concept of an inheritance of acquired characteristics: it shifts the focus from genetics to external forces, from the germ line to the (psycho)soma of the individual, exposed and susceptible to sensations from the external world.[37] At the same time, both Ferenczi and Freud undermine decisive features of Lamarckism, above all the idea of an innate progressive striving towards higher forms. According to Lamarck's vitalist concept, organs develop because fluids flow into the activated body part when stimulated and used. This curbs development, strengthening and growth. In Lamarck, the satisfaction of needs, efforts and intentions results in abilities and achievements which are passed on to future generations. In complete contrast, in the eccentric 'Lamarckism' developed by Ferenczi and Freud, the descendants are thought of as encumbered with burdens. Here, the object of transgenerational transference consists of displaced reaction formations in the face of forgotten, unknowable shocks that elude empirical knowledge.[38]

Focusing on Freud and Ferenczi's unfinished endeavour of a bioanalysis allows us to reframe the relation between natural sciences and psychoanalysis – beyond the deadlock of either ignoring the realm of the organic or declaring approaches oriented towards language, law and symbolic order obsolete. In *Thalassa* Ferenczi declares:

> It seems that we must familiarize ourselves with the idea of the over-determination of one and the same process, as psychoanalysis teaches us in the case of psychical processes, as well as in its explanation of physiological processes.[39]

Biology demands a theory of meaning and representation. In 'Freud's Influence on Medicine' (1933), drawing a methodological conclusion from the abandoned project of a bioanalysis, Ferenczi thematises the human as a psychosomatic being. He argues that the Freudian method avoids both a Cartesian dualism of body and soul and the methodological error of materialist-

---

[37] E. Slavet (2009), *Racial Fever: Freud and the Jewish Question*, pp. 68–97.

[38] J. Willner (2023), 'Catastrophes and Genitality: Ferenczi's Thalassa and the Politics of Bioanalysis', pp. 116–117.

[39] Ferenczi (1989), *Thalassa*, p. 32.

monism, which Ferenczi refers to as an overhasty unification of the psychic and the physical. Such a "unification is not possible at present, nor in the near future, and perhaps cannot be ever achieved completely."[40] Ferenczi, in other words, demarcates psychoanalytic thought from the concept of the human mind as an unbroken extension of the biological, and insists on what may be termed a methodological or perhaps even "strategic dualism"[41] as opposed to any ontological claim. The consequence is the primacy of language within the methodological approach, acknowledging a gap, a remainder within any form of scientific representation. The idea that there is no neutral language of natural science, no transparent language in which to represent the organic, is inherent to *Beyond the Pleasure Principle* too.[42]

The contributions in this volume in no way attempt to reconstruct a systematic, coherent and consistent theory of the drives or to definitively settle the relation between the discourses at work in *Beyond the Pleasure Principle*. The starting point is actually quite the opposite. Edward Said once characterised Freud's 'late style' in *Moses and Monotheism* as "episodic, fragmentary, unfinished (i.e. unpolished)", while producing a range of new ideas and exploring various trajectories.[43] The same can be said of several of Freud's texts that only reached their officially approved final form in the 1920s and 1930s.[44] They are compositions of different versions and later additions attempting to solve the unanswered questions and unresolved problems of the earlier versions. Having said this, the final versions authorised by Freud do not present coherent 'systems of thought', let alone *Weltanschauungen*. Quite the opposite, the published version of *Beyond the Pleasure Principle* is in several respects contradictory and inconsistent. Although Freud did make attempts to veil the sometimes radical changes in perspective, he never made the effort to reconsider – and hence to rewrite – the earlier written text parts from the perspective of the new drive theory introduced in the second (and published) version of the text.

---

40 S. Ferenczi (1994 [1933]), 'Freud's Influence on Medicine', pp. 146–147.

41 Willner (2023), 'Catastrophes and Genitality', p. 112.

42 Paul Ricoeur presents an analogous line of thought when he argues that a "mixed discourse" is constitutive for psychoanalysis. In Ricoeur's phrasing, *Beyond the Pleasure Principle* approaches biology through hermeneutics. P. Ricoeur (1970), *Freud and Philosophy*, pp. 65–67, 91–94.

43 E. Said (2014), *Freud and the Non-European*, p. 28.

44 *Beyond the Pleasure Principle* is one example, others are *The Interpretation of Dreams* and notably also *Three Essays on the Theory of Sexuality*.

For the reader's convenience, this volume includes the critical edition of Freud's *Beyond the Pleasure Principle* as it was published in the journal *Psychoanalysis and History* (2015, Volume 17(2)). This edition is based on the critical edition of the German text *Jenseits des Lustprinzips* prepared by Ulrike May and Michael Schröter and published in *Luzifer-Amor* (2013, Volume 51) together with a detailed commentary by May, which is also included in the present volume. In this historical exegesis, May discusses the context in which Freud's text was written, the contemporary debates he was engaged in and the insights into the development of his thought that can be gained from a close reading of the two main manuscript versions: the handwritten manuscript from 1919 and the published version from 1920. She highlights that Freud, when introducing his new drive theory in 1920, in fact abandoned his ideas on the conservative character of the sexual and self-preservative drives as articulated in the first version of the text. Together with the text edition, this commentary paves the way for the contributions of Philippe Van Haute and Herman Westerink, Ulrike Kistner, Jenny Willner, and Jakob Staberg in which various aspects of the two main versions of *Beyond the Pleasure Principle* are elaborated.

In their contribution 'From Repetition and Drive Monism to Binding and Conflict: Re-reading Freud's *Beyond the Pleasure Principle*', Philippe Van Haute and Herman Westerink argue that the text parts written in 1920, in which Freud introduces the concepts of life drives and death drives, can be seen as an attempt to find a way out of a deadlock Freud was confronted with after finishing the first version of the text. The second version of the text can be read as his own reply to the monistic consequences that followed from his line of reasoning in the first version. In this first version, Freud from his discussion of the compulsion to repeat argues that all drives are conservative, characterised by the principle of inertia, and ultimately aim at a return to an inanimate state. This ultimately implied that the aim of drives coincided with the pleasure principle, and consequently led to a monistic theory that Freud had always contested in favour of a drive conflict model. In the second version of the text, he associates the death drives with the pleasure principle as a principle of reduction of tension and excitation, while introducing the concept of life drives as drives aiming at coalescence of particles, cells, organs, bodies and individuals in the process of which there is increase of tension and excitation. It is these life drives that are eventually 'beyond' the pleasure principle. Taking the diverging trains of thought between the two main versions seriously allows for a better understanding of the inconsistencies and contradictions in the published version.

Ulrike Kistner, in her contribution 'Traumatic Neuroses and Psychoneuroses in (and) *Beyond the Pleasure Principle*', closely considers the 'war neuroses' in Freud's text. She shows that these 'war neuroses', mostly equated with 'traumatic neuroses', challenge the sexual aetiology of neuroses that Freud had articulated and defended since the second half of the 1890s. Ulrike Kistner argues that the urgent and relevant problem of the 'war neuroses' after the First World War confronted Freud with fundamental questions concerning pleasure and sexuality. In his clinical and theoretical writings on the psychoneuroses, Freud had to a large extent been able to dismiss these questions. They concern not only the apparent opposition between external blows and shocks triggering traumatic neuroses, and internal excitations producing transference neuroses. Instead, Freud also on the one hand seems to aim at the integration of the traumatic neuroses into a theory of the psychoneuroses, while on the other hand reasons that all psychoneuroses, seen from an evolutionary perspective, can be traced back to traumatic neurosis. Kistner also shows that the compulsion to repeat an unpleasurable experience, observed by Freud in clinical practice, which gave rise to the supposition of the conservative character of all drives, is no longer central in Freud's argumentations in the second version of the text. In the new drive dualism, the polarity of love and hate in relation to the object replaces the compulsion to repeat as the clinical phenomenon that manifests the character of the drives. It is this turn to the problem of aggression that has come to overshadow not only the first version of Freud's text, but also many of its readings.

In her contribution 'Neurotic Evolution: Bioanalysis against Biologism in *Beyond the Pleasure Principle*', Jenny Willner reads Freud's text in light of the uncompleted project of a 'bioanalysis' which he envisioned together with Sándor Ferenczi. In *Beyond the Pleasure Principle* Freud uses psychoanalytic notions as models (*Vorbilder*) for reframing the biological narrative of origin. His speculation about the "living organism in its most simplified possible form" uses the psychoanalytic concept of neurosis as a model for a counter-narrative of the origin and development of organic life. As Willner argues, Freud's speculation on the primitive cell demarcates itself from the ideologically freighted popular Darwinisms of his time, from the biologistic fantasies of progress, completion and purity, whose deadly effects would only become fully apparent in the decades following the essay's publication. The bioanalytic realm of *Beyond the Pleasure Principle* can be read both as a playful experiment with the relation between the theory of trauma and of the wish, and as a challenge to the biologistic worldview (*Weltanschauung*) which was formative for the generation that went to war in 1914. Against this background, Freud's references to Fechner, Haeckel and Lamarck are viewed not in terms of influence, but with the differences in mind which Freud's mode of reception inserts into the concepts coined by these thinkers. A major intervention lies in the inscription of death into the framework of his source material. As if following the final line of his 'Thoughts of the Time on War and Death' ("If you want to endure life, prepare yourself for death"), Freud's *Beyond the Pleasure Principle* inscribes the *thanatos* into the core of the *bios*. What is at stake is not only the ongoing tension between physicalism and evolutionism in natural sciences but also the status of what is living and what is dead.

In the last contribution, 'Ferenczi Thinking Beyond the Pleasure Principle', Jakob Staberg discusses the death drive as matrix for a theory of modernity structured around the notion of catastrophe. Reading *Beyond the Pleasure Principle* with Walter Benjamin and Roberto Calasso, Staberg discusses how nature and death are given a new meaning within the field of culture. By highlighting the repetition compulsion at work both in the wish to obtain order from the laws of nature and in the phobic relation to non-human origins, Freud approaches the symptoms of Western history: civilisation itself appears as a merely temporarily postponed death. Against this background, Staberg discusses the impact of Freud's notion of the death drive in Sándor Ferenczi's work. Towards the end of his life, Ferenczi collected disparate traces and entities that did not fit into Freud's speculative essay, although they belong to its main subject. Ferenczi's most famous paper, 'The Confusion of Tongues between the Adults and the Child', is the result of a much broader, unfinished project which Staberg explores in the fragments of Ferenczi's posthumously published *Clinical Diary*. According to Ferenczi, death appears as an ambivalent and unsettling notion constantly present in the psychoanalytic situation itself. A notion of something beyond the pleasure principle emanates from transference and countertransference, which Ferenczi elaborates in terms of an early analysis of authority and a dismantling of the father figure. Beyond Freud's ideal of a supposedly neutral analyst, and also beyond Ferenczi's own notion of a reciprocal analysis, Ferenczi here accounts for processes in which Freud's world of thought is at once challenged and taken to its extreme. Another dimension of Ferenczi's 'thinking beyond the pleasure principle' amounts to a radical re-reading of the bioanalytical speculations based on the question of survival, derived from an interpretation of organs as charged with meaning. According to Staberg, Ferenczi's unfinished metapsychology of splitting and psychic fragments paves the way for a psychoanalytical understanding of an archaic mother: life-giving and yet inseparable both from the threatening return of nature and from what Freud calls the death drive.

Bibliography

Bernet, Rudolf (2020), *Force, Drive, Desire: A Philosophy of Psychoanalysis*. Evanston (IL): Northwestern UP.

Chiesa, Lorenzo (2009), 'The World of Desire: Lacan between Evolutionary Biology and Psychoanalytic Theory', *Filozofski vestnik* 30(2), pp. 83–112.

Davidson, Arnold (2001), *The Emergence of Sexuality: Historical Epistemology and Formation of Concepts*. Cambridge (MA) & London: Harvard UP.

Deleuze, Gilles (1968), *Différence et répétition*. Paris: Presses universitaires de France.

Deleuze, Gilles & Guattari, Félix (1972), *L'Anti-Oedipe: Capitalisme et schizophrénie*. Paris: Éditions de minuit.

Derrida, Jacques (1987), *The Post Card: From Socrates to Freud and Beyond,* transl. Alan Bass. Chicago: University of Chicago Press.

Derrida, Jacques (2020 [1975–1976]), *Life Death*, transl. Pascale-Anne Brault & Michael Naas. Chicago: University of Chicago Press.

Ferenczi, Sándor (1989 [1924]), *Thalassa: A Theory of Genitality*. New York: The Psychoanalytic Quarterly Inc.

Ferenczi, Sándor (1994 [1933]), 'Freud's Influence on Medicine', in: Sándor Ferenczi, *Final Contributions to the Problems and Methods of Psycho-Analysis*. New York: Taylor & Francis, pp. 143–155.

Foucault, Michel (1978), *The Will to Knowledge. The History of Sexuality Vol. 1*. New York: Pantheon Books.

Freud, Sigmund (1905d), *Three Essays on the Theory of Sexuality*, in: *Standard Edition of the Complete Psychological Works of Sigmund Freud, Vol.* 7, ed. James Strachey. London: Hogarth Press, 1953–1966, pp. 130–243.

Freud, Sigmund (1906a), 'My Views on the Part Played by Sexuality in the Aetiology of the Neuroses', *SE* 7, pp. 271–279.

Freud, Sigmund (1915c), 'Instincts and Their Vicissitudes', *SE* 14, pp. 117–140.

Freud, Sigmund (1920g), *Beyond the Pleasure Principle*, *SE* 18, pp. 7–64.

Freud, Sigmund (1985c), 'Extracts from the Fliess Papers', *SE* 1, pp. 177–280.

Gilman, Sander L. (2020), 'Wandering Imaginations of Race and Hysteria. The Origins of the Hysterical Body in Psychoanalysis', in: ed. Johanna Braun, *Performing Hysteria. Images and Imaginations of Hysteria*. Leuven: Leuven UP, pp. 41–57.

Grubrich-Simitis, Ilse (1987), 'Trauma oder Trieb – Trieb und Trauma: Lektionen aus Sigmund Freuds phylogenetischer Phantasie von 1915', in: *Psyche. Zeitschrift für Psychoanalyse und ihre Anwendungen* 41(11), pp. 991–1023.

Habermas, Jürgen (1968), *Knowledge and Human Interest*. Frankfurt a.M.: Suhrkamp.

Lacan, Jacques (2006), *Écrits*, transl. Bruce Fink. New York & London: Norton.

Laplanche, Jean (1987), *Nouveaux fondements pour la psychoanalyse*. Paris: Presses universitaires de France.

Laplanche, Jean (2015), *The Temptation of Biology: Freud's Theories of Sexuality*, transl. Donald Nicholson-Smith. New York: The Unconscious in Translation.

Ricoeur, Paul (1970), *Freud and Philosophy*. New Haven & London: Yale UP.

Ritvo, Lucille B. (1990), *Darwin's Influence on Freud: A Tale of Two Sciences*. New Haven & London: Yale UP.

Roith, Estelle (2008), 'Hysteria, Heredity and Anti-Semitism. Freud's Quiet Rebellion', *Psychoanalysis and History* 10(2), pp. 149–168.

Said, Edward (2014), *Freud and the Non-European*. London & New York: Verso.

Schotte, Jacques (1990), *Szondi avec Freud. Sur la voie d'une psychiatrie pulsionelle*. Brussels: Editions universitaires De Boeck.

Slavet, Eliza (2009), *Racial Fever: Freud and the Jewish Question*. New York: Fordham UP.

Sulloway, Frank J. (1979), *Freud: Biologist of the Mind*. New York: Basic Books.

Trumbull, Robert (2022), *From Life to Survival. Derrida, Freud, and the Future of Deconstruction*. New York: Fordham UP.

Van Haute, Philippe (2002), *Against Adaptation: Jacques Lacan's Subversion of the Subject*. New York: Other Press.

Van Haute, Philippe & Westerink, Herman (2021), *From Pleasure to the Object: Reading Freud's Three Essays on the Theory of Sexuality*. New York: Routledge.

Westerink, Herman & Van Haute, Philippe (2022), *Verleiding, drift en herhaling: Freuds metafysica van het trauma*. Amsterdam: Boom.

Vitale, Francesco (2018), *Biodeconstruction. Jacques Derrida and the Life Sciences*, transl. Mauro Senatore. Albany: State University of New York Press.

Will, David (2016), *Inanimation: Theories of Inorganic Life*. Minneapolis: University of Minnesota Press.

Willner, Jenny (2023), 'Catastrophes and Genitality: Ferenczi's *Thalassa* and the Politics of Bioanalysis', in: ed. Raluca Soreanu, Jakob Staberg & Jenny Willner, *Ferenczi Dialogues: On Trauma and Catastrophe*. Leuven: Leuven UP, pp. 91–130.

Wilson, Daniel (2018), 'Freud's Lamarckian Clinic', in: ed. Joel Goldbach & James A. Godley, *Inheritance in Psychoanalysis*. Albany: State University of New York Press, pp. 255–273.

Wilson, Elisabeth (2004), *Psychosomatic: Feminism and the Neurological Body*. Durham & London: Duke UP.

Wilson, Elisabeth (2015), *Gut Feminism*. Durham & London: Duke UP.

Beyond the Pleasure Principle

Sigmund Freud

Edited by M. ffytche, J. Forrester and M. Molnar on the basis of the German critical edition by U. May and M. Schröter

I

[7] In the theory of psychoanalysis we have no hesitation in assuming that the course taken by mental events is automatically regulated by the pleasure principle. We believe, that is to say, that the course of those events is invariably set in motion by an unpleasurable tension, and that it takes a direction such that its final outcome coincides with a lowering or supension[1] of that tension – that is, with an avoidance of unpleasure or a production of pleasure. In taking that course into account in our consideration of the mental processes which are the subject of our study, we are introducing an *economic*[2] point of view into our work; and if, in describing those processes, we try to estimate this *economic* factor in addition to the *topographical* and *dynamic* ones, we shall, I think, be giving the most complete description of them of which we can at present conceive, and one which deserves to be distinguished by the term *metapsychological.*

It is of no concern to us in this connection to inquire how far, with this hypothesis of the pleasure principle, we have approached or adopted any particular, historically established, philosophical system.[3] We have arrived at these speculative assumptions in an attempt to describe and to account for the facts of daily observation in our field of study. Priority and originality are not among the aims that psychoanalytic work sets itself; and the impressions that underlie the hypothesis of the pleasure principle are so obvious that they

---

1 *LA*: 'or suspension' [Aufhebung] omitted in B – transcription error?

2 *LA*: F removes the emphasis from economic, topographical and dynamic, though retains it for metapsychological; *PH*: *SE* puts the same words in inverted commas.

3 *LA*: corrected from 'theory' in manuscript.

can scarcely be overlooked. On the other hand, we would readily express our gratitude to any philosophical or psychological theory which was able to inform us of the conditions[4] of the feelings of pleasure and unpleasure which act so imperatively upon us. But on this point we are, alas, offered nothing to our purpose. This is the most obscure and inaccessible region of the mind and, since we cannot avoid contact with it, the least rigid hypothesis, it seems to me, will be the best. We have decided to relate [8] pleasure and unpleasure to the quantity of excitation that is present in the mind but is not in any way 'bound'; and to relate them in such a manner that unpleasure corresponds to an increase[5] in the quantity of excitation and pleasure to a diminution. What we are implying by this is not a simple relation between the strength of the feelings of pleasure and unpleasure and the corresponding modifications in the quantity of excitation; least of all – in view of all we have been taught by psycho-physiology – are we suggesting any directly proportional ratio: the factor that determines the feeling is probably the amount of increase or diminution in the quantity of excitation in a given period of time. Experiment might possibly play a part here; but it is not advisable[6] for us analysts to go into the problem further so long as our way is not pointed by quite definite observations.

We cannot, however, remain indifferent to the discovery that an investigator of such penetration as G. T. Fechner held a view on the subject of pleasure and unpleasure which coincides in all essentials with the one that has been forced upon us by psychoanalytic work. Fechner's statement is to be found contained in a small work, *Einige Ideen zur Schöpfungs- und Entwicklungsgeschichte der Organismen*, 1873 (Part XI, Supplement, 94), and reads as follows:[7] 'In so far as conscious impulses always have some relation to pleasure or unpleasure, pleasure and unpleasure too can be regarded as having a psycho-physical relation to conditions of stability and instability. This provides a basis for a hypothesis into which I propose to enter in greater detail elsewhere. According to this hypothesis, every psycho-physical motion rising above the threshold of consciousness is attended by pleasure in proportion as, beyond a certain limit, it approximates to complete stability, and is attended by unpleasure in proportion as, beyond a certain limit, it deviates from complete stability; while between the two limits, which may be described as qualitative thresholds of pleasure and [9] unpleasure, there is a certain margin of aesthetic indifference….'

---

4 *LA*: B gives 'Bedeutungen' (meanings) – presumably transcription error in B.

5 *PH*: 'increase' and 'diminution' as well as 'in a given period of time' in the next sentence are all italicised in *SE*.

6 *LA*: corrected from 'there is no call for' in manuscript.

7 *LA*: paragraph break in B.

The facts which have caused us to believe in the dominance of the pleasure principle in mental life also find expression in the hypothesis that the mental apparatus endeavours to keep the quantity of excitation present in it as low as possible or at least to keep it constant. This latter hypothesis is only another way of stating the pleasure principle.[8] If the work of the mental apparatus is directed towards keeping the quantity of excitation low, then anything that is calculated to increase that quantity is bound to be felt as adverse to the functioning of the apparatus, that is as unpleasurable. The pleasure principle follows from the principle of constancy: actually the latter principle was inferred from the facts which forced us to adopt the pleasure principle. Moreover, a more detailed discussion will show that the tendency which we thus attribute to the mental apparatus is subsumed as a special case under Fechner's principle of the *tendency towards stability*,[9] to which he has brought the feelings of pleasure and unpleasure into relation.

It must be pointed out, however, that strictly speaking it is incorrect to talk of the dominance of the pleasure principle over the course of mental processes. If such a dominance existed, the immense majority of our mental processes would have to be accompanied by pleasure or[10] to lead to pleasure, whereas universal experience completely contradicts any such conclusion. The most that can be said, therefore, is that there exists in the mind a strong tendency[11] towards the pleasure principle, but that that tendency is opposed by certain other forces or circumstances, so that the final outcome cannot always be in harmony [10] with the tendency towards pleasure. We may compare what Fechner (1873, 90) remarks on a similar point: 'Since however a tendency towards an aim does not imply that the aim is attained, and since in general the aim is attainable only by approximations'....

If we turn now to the question of what circumstances are able to prevent the pleasure principle from being carried into effect, we find ourselves once more on secure and well-trodden ground and, in framing our answer, we have at our disposal a rich fund of analytic experience.

The first example of the pleasure principle being inhibited in this way is a familiar one which occurs with regularity. We know that the pleasure principle is proper to a primary[12] method of working on the part of the mental apparatus, but that, from the point of view of the self-assertion[13] of the organism among

8 *LA*: from C onwards the sentence follows on: 'pleasure principle; for if the work...' printer's error in C?
9 *PH*: these three words in inverted commas in *SE*.
10 *LA*: corrected from 'and' in manuscript.
11 *PH*: this word italicised in *SE*.
12 *PH*: italicised in *SE*.
13 *LA*: corrected from 'self-preservation' in manuscript.

the difficulties of the external world, it is from the very outset inefficient and even highly dangerous. Under the influence of the ego's self-preservative drives the pleasure principle is replaced by the *reality principle*. This latter principle does not abandon the intention of ultimately obtaining pleasure, but it nevertheless demands and carries into effect the postponement of satisfaction, the abandonment of a number of possibilities of gaining satisfaction and the temporary toleration of unpleasure as a step on the long indirect road to pleasure. The pleasure principle long persists, however, as the method of working employed by the sexual drives, which are so hard to 'educate', and, starting from those drives, or in the ego itself, it often succeeds in overcoming the reality principle, to the detriment of the organism as a whole.

There can be no doubt, however, that the replacement of the pleasure principle by[14] the reality principle can only be made responsible for a small number, and by no means the most intense, of unpleasurable experiences. Another occasion of the release of unpleasure, which occurs with no less regularity, is to be found in the conflicts and dissensions that take place in the mental apparatus while the ego is passing through its development into more highly composite organizations. Almost all the energy with which the apparatus is filled arises from its innate drive impulses. But these are not all allowed to reach [11] the same phases of development. In the course of things it happens again and again that individual drives or parts of drives turn out to be incompatible in their aims or demands with the remaining ones, which are able to combine into the inclusive unity of the ego. The former are then split off from this unity by the process of repression held back at lower levels of psychical development and cut off, to begin with, from the possibility of satisfaction. If they succeed subsequently, as can so easily happen with repressed sexual drives, in struggling through, by roundabout paths, to a direct or to a substitutive satisfaction, that event, which would in other cases have been an opportunity for pleasure, is felt by the ego as unpleasure. As a consequence of the old conflict which ended in repression, a new breach has occurred in the pleasure principle at the very time when certain drives were endeavouring, in accordance with the principle, to obtain fresh pleasure. The details of the process by which repression turns a possibility of pleasure into a source of unpleasure are not yet clearly understood or cannot be clearly represented; but there is no doubt that all neurotic unpleasure is of that kind – pleasure that cannot be felt as such.[15]

---

14 *LA*: 'the replacement of the pleasure principle by' inserted above the line in manuscript.

15 No doubt the essential point is that pleasure and unpleasure, being conscious feelings, are attached to the ego. [SE notes date of the addition].

The two sources of unpleasure which I have just indicated are very far from covering the majority of our unpleasurable experiences. But as regards the remainder it can be asserted with some show of justification that their presence does not contradict the dominance of the pleasure principle. Most of the unpleasure that we experience is perceptual[16] unpleasure. It may be perception of pressure by unsatisfied drives; or it may be external perception which is either distressing in itself or which excites unpleasurable expectations in the mental apparatus – that is, which is recognized by it as a 'danger'. The reaction to these drive demands and threats of danger, a reaction which constitutes the proper activity of the mental apparatus, can then be directed in a correct manner by the pleasure principle or the reality principle by which the former is modified. This does not seem to necessitate any far-reaching limitation of the pleasure principle. Nevertheless the investigation of the mental reaction to external danger is precisely in a position to produce new material and raise fresh questions bearing upon our present problem.

II

[12] A condition has long been known and described which occurs after severe mechanical concussions, railway disasters and other accidents involving a risk to life; it has been given the name of 'traumatic neurosis'. The terrible war which has just ended gave rise to a great number of illnesses of this kind, but it at least put an end to the temptation to attribute the cause of the disorder to organic lesions of the nervous system brought about by mechanical force.[17] The symptomatic picture presented by traumatic neurosis approaches that of hysteria in the wealth of its similar motor symptoms, but surpasses it as a rule in its strongly marked signs of subjective ailment (in which it resembles hypochondria or melancholia) as well as in the evidence it gives of a far more comprehensive general enfeeblement and disturbance of the mental capacity.[18] No complete explanation has yet been reached either of war neuroses or of the traumatic neuroses of peace. In the case of the war neuroses, the fact that the same symptoms could sometimes come about[19] without the intervention

16 *PH*: this word italicised in *SE*.

17 Cf. *On the Psychoanalysis of War Neuroses*. With articles by Ferenczi, Abraham, Simmel and E. Jones. Volume I, Internationale Psychoanalytische Bibliothek, 1919.

18 *LA*: corrected from 'capacities' in the manuscript of A. B onwards has 'capacities' – presumably transcription error.

19 *LA*: changed to 'came about' from D onwards.

of any gross mechanical force seemed at once enlightening and bewildering. In the case of the ordinary traumatic neuroses two characteristics emerge prominently: first, that the chief weight in their causation seems to rest upon the factor of surprise, of fright; and secondly, that a wound or injury inflicted simultaneously works as a rule against[20] the development of a neurosis.[21]

'Fright', 'fear' and 'anxiety' are improperly used as synonymous expressions; they are in fact capable of clear distinction in their relation to danger. 'Anxiety' describes a particular state of[22] expecting the danger or preparing for it, even though it may be an unknown one. 'Fear' requires a definite object of which to be afraid. 'Fright', however, is the name we give to the state a person gets into when he has run into danger without being prepared for it; it emphasizes the factor of surprise. I do not believe anxiety can produce a traumatic neuro-[13] sis. There is something about anxiety that protects its subject against fright and so against fright-neuroses. We shall return to this point later.

The study of dreams may be considered the most trustworthy method of investigating deep mental processes. Now dreams occurring in traumatic neuroses have the characteristic of repeatedly bringing the patient back into the situation of his accident, a situation from which he wakes up in another fright. This astonishes people far too little. They think the fact that the traumatic experience is constantly forcing itself upon the patient even in his sleep is a proof of the strength of that experience: the patient is, as one might say, fixated to his trauma. Fixations to the experience which started the illness have long been familiar to us in hysteria. Breuer and Freud declared in 1893 that 'hysterics suffer mainly from reminiscences'. In the war neuroses, too, observers like Ferenczi and Simmel have been able to explain certain motor symptoms by fixation to the moment at which the trauma occurred.

I am not aware, however, that patients suffering from traumatic neurosis are much occupied in their waking lives with memories of their accident. Perhaps they are more concerned with not[23] thinking of it. Anyone who accepts it as something self-evident that their dreams should put them back at night into the situation that caused them to fall ill has misunderstood the nature of dreams. It would be more in harmony with their nature if they showed the patient pictures from his healthy past or of the cure for which he hopes. If we are not to be shaken in our belief in the wish-fulfilling tenor of dreams by the dreams of traumatic neurotics, we still have one resource open

20 *PH*: 'against' italicised in *SE*.
21 *LA*: from C onwards this paragraph break omitted – presumably printer's error.
22 *LA*: B onwards has 'such as expecting' instead of 'of expecting' – presumably transcription error in B.
23 *PH*: 'not' italicised in *SE*.

to us: we may argue that the function of dreaming, like so much else, is upset in this condition and diverted from its purposes, or we [14] may be driven to reflect on the mysterious masochistic trends of the ego.[24]

At this point I propose[25] to leave the dark and dismal subject of traumatic neurosis and pass on to examine the method of working employed by the mental apparatus in one of its earliest[26] normal[27] activities – I mean in children's play.

The different theories of children's play have only recently been summarized and discussed from the psychoanalytic point of view by Pfeiffer[28] in 'Imago' (Vol. V/4),[29] to whose paper I would refer my readers. These theories attempt to discover the motives which lead children to play, but they fail to bring into the foreground the economic point of view,[30] the consideration of the yield of pleasure involved. Without wishing to include the whole field covered by these phenomena, I have been able, through a chance opportunity which presented itself, to throw some light upon the first game played by a little boy of one and a half and invented by himself. It was more than a mere fleeting observation, for I lived under the same roof as the child and his parents for some weeks, and it was some time before I discovered the meaning of the puzzling activity which he constantly repeated.

The child was not at all precocious in his intellectual development. At the age of one and a half he could say only a few comprehensible words; he could also make use of a number of sounds which expressed a meaning intelligible to those around him. He was, however, on good terms with his parents and their one servant girl, and tributes were paid to his being a 'good boy'. He did not disturb his parents at night, he conscientiously obeyed orders not to touch certain things or go into certain rooms, and above all he never cried when his mother left him for a few hours. At the same time, he was greatly attached to his mother, who had not only fed him herself but had also looked after him without any outside help. This good little boy, however, had an occasional disturbing habit of taking any small objects he could get hold of and throwing them away from him into a corner, under the bed, and so on, so that hunting for his toys and picking them up was often quite a business. As

---

24 *PH*: addition dated in *SE*. *SE* introduces a gap between the paragraphs here.
25 *LA*: corrected from 'intend' in manuscript.
26 *LA*: corrected from 'in a very [early]'.
27 *PH*: italicised in *SE*.
28 *LA*: later corrected to Pfeifer.
29 *PH*: Pfeifer (1919).
30 *PH*: *SE* has '*economic* motive'.

he did this he gave vent to a loud, long-drawn-out oooo,[31] accompanied by an expression of interest and satisfaction. His mother [15] and the writer of the present account were agreed in thinking that this was not a mere interjection but[32] represented the German word *fort*[33] ['gone']. I eventually realized that it was a game and that the only use he made of any of his toys was to play 'gone' with them.[34]

One day I made the[35] observation which confirmed my view. The child had a wooden reel with a piece of string tied round it. It never occurred to him to pull it along the floor behind him, for instance, and play at its being a carriage. What he did was to hold the reel by the string and very skilfully throw it over the edge of his curtained cot, so that it disappeared into it, at the same time uttering his expressive oooo.[36] He then pulled the reel out of the cot again by the string and hailed its reappearance with a joyful *da* ['there']. This, then, was the complete game – disappearance and return. As a rule one only witnessed its first act, which was repeated untiringly as a game in itself, though there is no doubt that the greater pleasure was attached to the second act.[37]

The interpretation of the game then became obvious. It was related to the child's great cultural achievement – the renunciation of a drive (that is, the renunciation of drive satisfaction) which he had made in allowing his mother to go away without protesting. He compensated himself for this, as it were, by himself staging the disappearance and return of the objects within his reach. It is of course a matter of indifference from the point of view of judging the affective[38] nature of the game whether the child invented it himself or took it over on some outside suggestion. Our interest is directed to another point. The child cannot possibly have felt his mother's departure as something agreeable or even indifferent. How then does his repetition of this distressing experience as a game fit in with the pleasure principle? It may perhaps be said in reply that her departure had to be enacted as a necessary preliminary to her

---

31 *LA*: B corrected to o-o-o-o; no emphasis in C; italicised in F; *SE* has 'o-o-o-o'.

32 *LA*: 'was not a mere interjection but' inserted above the line in manuscript.

33 *LA*: in C in spaced type; in F in inverted commas. *PH*: in *SE* this word italicised and in inverted commas.

34 *LA*: paragraph break in A and probably B (at the line-end); not carried over to C – presumably printer's error in C.

35 *LA*: corrected from 'an' in manuscript. *PH*: *SE* has 'an observation'.

36 *LA*: see note 31.

37 A further observation subsequently confirmed this interpretation fully. One day the child's mother had been away for several hours and on her return was met with the words 'Baby oooo!' [*LA*: in F: '*Baby o-o-o-o!*'] which was at first incomprehensible. It soon turned out, however, that during this long period of solitude the child had found a method of making *himself* disappear [*LA*: deleted: 'through']. He had discovered his reflection in a full-length mirror which did not quite reach to the ground, so that by crouching down he could make his mirror image 'gone'.

38 *RSE*: erroneously 'effective' in the *SE* (Mahoney (1987), *Freud as a Writer*, p. 52).

joyful return, and that it was in the latter that lay the true purpose [16] of the game. But against this must be counted the observed fact that the first act, that of departure, was staged as a game in itself and far more frequently than the episode in its entirety, with its pleasurable ending.

No certain decision can be reached from the analysis of a single case like this. On an unprejudiced view one gets an impression that the child repeated[39] his experience as a game[40] from another motive. At the outset he was in a passive[41] situation – he was overpowered by the experience; but, by repeating it, unpleasurable though it was, as a game, he took on an active part. These efforts might be put down to a drive for mastery that was acting independently of whether the memory was in itself pleasurable or not. But still another interpretation may be attempted. Throwing away the object so that it was 'gone' might satisfy an impulse of the child's, which was suppressed in his actual life, to revenge himself on his mother for going away from him. In that case it would have a defiant meaning: 'All right, then, go away! I don't need you. I'm sending you away myself.' A year later, the same boy whom I had observed at his first game used to take a toy, if he was angry with it, and throw it on the floor, exclaiming: 'Go to the fwont!' He had heard at that time that his absent father was 'at the front', and was far from regretting his absence; on the contrary he made it quite clear that he had no desire to be disturbed in his sole possession of his mother.[42] We know of other children who liked to express similar hostile impulses by throwing away objects instead of persons.[43] We are therefore left in doubt as to whether the impulse to work over in the mind some overpowering experience so as to make oneself master of it can find expression as a primary event, and independently of the pleasure principle. For, in the case we have been discussing, the child may, after all, only have been able to repeat his unpleasant experience in play because the repetition carried along with it a yield of pleasure of another sort but none the less a direct one.

Nor shall we be helped in our hesitation between these two views by further considering children's play. It is clear that in [17] their play children repeat everything that has made a great impression on them in real life, and

39 *LA*: in B corrected to 'turned his experience into a game'.

40 *LA*: 'as game' inserted above the line in manuscript.

41 *PH*: 'passive' and 'active' italicised in *SE*.

42 When this child was five and three-quarters, his mother died. Now that she was really 'gone' ('o-o-o') [*LA*: in F (*o-o-o*)], the little boy showed no signs of grief. It is true that in the interval a second child had been born and had roused him to violent jealousy.

43 Cf. my note on a childhood memory of Goethe's [Freud (1917b), 'A Childhood Recollection from Dichtung und Wahrheit', *SE* 17].

that in doing so they abreact the strength of the impression and, as one might put it, make themselves master of the situation. But on the other hand it is obvious that all their play is influenced by a wish that dominates them the whole time – the wish to be grown-up and to be able to do what grown-up people do. It can also be observed that the unpleasurable nature of an experience does not always unsuit it for play. If the doctor looks down a child's throat or does[44] some small operation on him, we may be quite sure that these frightening experiences will be the subject of the next game; but we must not in that connection overlook the fact that there is a yield of pleasure from another source. As the child passes over from the passivity of the experience to the activity of the game,[45] he hands on the disagreeable experience to one of his playmates and in this way revenges himself on a substitute.

Nevertheless, it emerges from this discussion that there is no need to assume the existence of a special imitative drive in order to provide a motive for play. Finally, a reminder may be added that the artistic play and artistic imitation carried out by adults, which, unlike children's, are aimed at an audience, do not spare the spectators (for instance, in tragedy) the most painful experiences and can yet be felt by them as highly enjoyable. This is convincing proof that, even under the dominance of the pleasure principle, there are ways and means enough of making what is in itself unpleasurable into a subject to be recollected and worked over in the mind. The consideration of these cases and situations, which have a yield of pleasure as their final outcome, should be undertaken by some system of aesthetics with an economic approach to its subject-matter. They are of no use for *our* purposes, since they pre-suppose the existence and dominance of the pleasure principle; they give no evidence of the operation of tendencies *beyond* the pleasure principle, that is, of tendencies more primitive than it and independent of it.

III

[18] Twenty-five years of intense work have had as their result that the immediate aims of psychoanalytic technique are quite other today than they were at the outset. At first the analysing physician could do no more than discover the unconscious material that was concealed from the patient, put it together, and, at the right moment, communicate it to him. Psychoanalysis was then first and foremost an art of interpreting. Since this did not solve

[44] *LA*: B onwards changed to 'carries out'.
[45] *LA*: C onwards 'of playing'.

the therapeutic problem, a further aim quickly came in view: to oblige[46] the patient to confirm the analyst's construction from his own memory. In that endeavour the chief emphasis lay upon the patient's resistances: the art consisted now in uncovering these as quickly as possible, in pointing them out to the patient and in inducing him by human influence – this was where suggestion operating as[47] 'transference' played its part – to abandon his resistances.

But it became ever clearer that the aim which had been set up – the aim that what was unconscious should become conscious – is not completely attainable by that method. The patient cannot remember the whole of what is repressed in him, and what he cannot remember may be precisely the essential part of it. Thus he acquires no sense of conviction of the correctness of the construction that has been communicated to him. He is obliged to *repeat* the repressed material as a contemporary experience instead of, as the physician would prefer to see, *remembering* it as something belonging to the past.[48] These reproductions, which emerge with such unwished-for exactitude, always have as their subject some portion of infantile sexual life – of the Oedipus complex, that is, and its derivatives; and they are invariably acted out in the sphere of the transference, of the patient's relation to the physician. When things have reached this stage, it may be said that the earlier neurosis has now been replaced by a fresh, 'transference neurosis'. It has [19] been the physician's endeavour to keep this transference neurosis within the narrowest limits: to force as much as possible into the channel of memory and to allow as little as possible to emerge as repetition. The ratio between what is remembered and what is reproduced varies from case to case. The physician cannot as a rule spare his patient this phase of the treatment. He must get him to re-experience some portion of his forgotten life, but must see to it, on the other hand, that the patient retains some degree of aloofness, which will enable him, in spite of everything, to recognize that what appears to be reality is in fact only a reflection of a forgotten past. If this can be successfully achieved, the patient's sense of conviction is won, together with the therapeutic success that is dependent on it.

In order to make it easier to understand this '*compulsion to repeat*' which emerges during the psychoanalytic treatment of neurotics, we must above all get rid of the mistaken notion that what we are dealing with in our struggle against

46 *LA*: corrected from 'induce' in manuscript.
47 *LA*: corrected from 'via' in manuscript.
48 See my paper on 'Remembering, Repeating and Working Through' (1914g [*SE* 12]).

resistances is 'resistance on the part of the unconscious'.[49] The unconscious – that is to say, the repressed[50] – offers no resistance whatever to the efforts of the treatment. Indeed, it itself has no other endeavour than to break through the pressure weighing down on it and force its way either to consciousness or[51] to a discharge through some real action. Resistance during treatment arises from the same higher strata and systems of the mind which originally carried out repression. But the fact that, as we know from experience, the motives of the resistances, and indeed the resistances themselves, are unconscious at first during the treatment, is a hint to us that we should correct a shortcoming in our terminology. We shall avoid a lack of clarity if we make our contrast not between the conscious and the unconscious but between the coherent ego and the repressed.[52] It may be that much of the ego is itself unconscious; only a part of it, probably, is covered by the term 'preconscious'.[53] Having replaced a purely descriptive [20] terminology by one which is systematic or dynamic, we can say that the patient's resistance arises from his ego, and we then at once perceive that the compulsion to repeat must be ascribed to the unconscious repressed. It seems probable that the compulsion can only express itself after the work of treatment has gone half-way to meet it and has loosened the repression.[54]

There is no doubt that the resistance of the conscious and unconscious ego operates under the sway of the pleasure principle: it seeks to avoid the unpleasure which would be produced by the liberation of the repressed. Our[55] efforts, on the other hand, are directed towards procuring the toleration of that unpleasure by an appeal to the reality principle. But how is the compulsion to repeat – the manifestation of the power of the repressed – related to the pleasure principle? It is clear that the greater part of what is re-experienced under the compulsion to repeat must cause the ego unpleasure, since it brings to light activities of repressed drive impulses. That, however, is unpleasure of a kind we have already considered and does not contradict the pleasure

49 *LA*: in B without any inverted commas; presumably transcription error. D onwards: on the part of the 'unconscious'. *SE*: on the part of the *unconscious*.

50 *LA*: B places inverted commas around 'the repressed'; C onwards the 'repressed'.

51 *LA*: corrected from 'and' in manuscript.

52 *LA*: D onwards 'ego' and the 'repressed'. *PH*: *SE* has 'ego' and the 'repressed'.

53 *LA*: D onwards 'It is certain that much of the ego is itself unconscious, and notably what we may describe as its nucleus; only a small part of it is covered by the term "preconscious"'. [*SE* notes the change].

54 I have argued elsewhere that what thus comes to the help of the compulsion to repeat is the factor of 'suggestion' in the treatment – that is, the patient's submissiveness to the physician, which has its roots deep in his unconscious parental complex. [Freud (1923c), 'Remarks on the Theory and Practice of Dream-Interpretation', *SE* 19].

55 *PH*: italicised in *SE*.

principle: unpleasure for one system and simultaneously satisfaction for the other. But we come now to a new and remarkable fact, namely that the compulsion to repeat also recalls from the past experiences which include no possibility of pleasure, and which can never, even long ago, have brought satisfaction even to drive impulses which have since been repressed.

The early efflorescence of infantile sexual life is doomed to extinction because its wishes are incompatible with reality and with the inadequate stage of development which the child has reached. That efflorescence comes to an end in the most distressing circumstances and to the accompaniment of the most painful feelings. Loss of love and failure leave behind them a permanent injury to self-regard in the form of a narcissistic scar, which in my opinion, as well as in Marcinowski's,[56] contributes more than anything to the 'sense of inferiority' [21] which is so common in neurotics. The child's sexual researches, on which limits were[57] imposed by his physical development,[58] lead to no satisfactory conclusion; hence such later complaints as 'I can't accomplish anything; I can't succeed in anything'. The tie of affection, which binds the child as a rule[59] to the parent of the opposite sex, succumbs to disappointment, to a vain expectation of satisfaction or to jealousy over the birth of a new baby – unmistakable proof of the infidelity of the object of the child's affections. His own attempt to make a baby himself, carried out with tragic seriousness, fails shamefully. The lessening amount of affection he receives, the increasing demands of education, hard words and an occasional punishment – these show him at last the full extent to which he has been *scorned*. These are a few typical instances, regularly to be found,[60] of the ways in which the love characteristic of the age of childhood is brought to a conclusion.

Patients repeat all of these unwanted situations and painful emotions in the transference and revive them with the greatest ingenuity. They seek to bring about the interruption of the treatment while it is still incomplete; they contrive once more to feel themselves scorned, to oblige the physician to speak severely to them and treat them coldly; they discover appropriate objects for their jealousy; instead of the passionately desired baby of their childhood, they produce a plan or a promise of some grand present – which turns out as a rule to be no less unreal. None of these things can have produced pleasure in the

56 Marcinowski, *The Erotic Sources of the Sense of Inferiority* [Marcinowski (1918), 'Die erotischen Quellen der Minderwertigkeitsgefühle'].

57 *LA*: changed to 'are' in F.

58 *LA*: corrected from 'constitution' in manuscript.

59 *LA*: 'as a rule' inserted above the line in manuscript.

60 *LA*: 'to be found' corrected from 'repeated' in manuscript. B onwards corrected to 'constantly recurring instances'.

past, and it might be supposed that they would cause less unpleasure today if they emerged as memories or dreams instead of taking the form of fresh experience. But a compulsion presses towards the latter.[61]

What psychoanalysis reveals in the transference phenomena of neurotics can also be observed in the lives of some normal people. The impression they give is of being pursued by a malignant fate or possessed by some daemonic[62] power; but psychoanalysis has always taken the view that their fate is for the most part arranged by themselves and determined by early infantile influences. The compulsion which is here in evidence differs in [22] no way from the compulsion to repeat which we have found in neurotics, even though the people we are now considering have never shown any signs of dealing with a neurotic conflict by producing symptoms. Thus we have come across people all of whose human relationships have the same outcome: such as the benefactor who is abandoned in anger after a time by each of his protégés, however much they[63] may otherwise differ from one another,[64] and who thus seems doomed to taste all the bitternesses[65] of ingratitude; or the man whose friendships all end in betrayal by his friend; or the man who time after time in the course of his life raises someone else into a position of great private or public authority and then, after a certain interval, himself upsets that authority and replaces him by a new one; or, again, the lover each of whose love affairs with a woman passes through the same phases and reaches the same conclusion, and so on and so on.[66] This 'perpetual recurrence of the same thing' causes us no astonishment when it relates to active[67] behaviour on the part of the person concerned and when we can discern in him an essential character trait which always remains the same and which is compelled to find expression in a repetition of the same experiences. We are much more impressed by cases where the subject appears to have a passive experience, over which he has no influence, but in which he meets with repetitions[68] of the same fatality. There is the case, for instance, of the woman who married three successive husbands each of whom fell ill soon afterwards and had to

61 *LA*: D replaces this sentence with the addition: 'They are of course the activities of drives intended to lead to satisfaction; but no lesson has been learnt from the old experience of these activities having led instead only to unpleasure. In spite of that, they are repeated, under pressure of a compulsion.' [Addition noted in *SE*].

62 *PH*: *SE* puts this word in inverted commas.

63 *LA*: E onwards revises to 'these'.

64 *LA*: this whole clause inserted above the line in manuscript.

65 *LA*: B onwards has 'bitterness' – transcription error in B?

66 *LA*: C onwards shortened to 'and so on' [usw.]. *PH*: The phrase is omitted in *SE*.

67 *PH*: *SE* italicises 'active' and 'passive' in the next sentence.

68 *LA*: B onwards has 'the repetition' (transcription error?); definite article added in writing (in another hand?). *PH*: *SE* has 'a repetition'.

be nursed by her on their death-beds.[69] The most moving poetic picture of a fate such as this is given by Tasso in his romantic epic *Gerusalemme Liberata*. Its hero, Tancred, unwittingly kills his beloved Clorinda in a duel while she is disguised in the armour of an enemy knight. After her burial he makes his way into a strange magic forest which strikes the Crusaders' army with terror. He slashes with his sword at this tall tree; but blood streams from the cut and the voice of Clorinda, whose soul is imprisoned in the tree, is heard complaining that he has wounded his beloved once again.

If we take into account observations such as these, based upon behaviour in the transference and upon the life histories of men and women, we shall find courage to assume that there really does exist in the mind a compulsion to repeat which overrides the pleasure principle. Now too we shall be inclined to [23] relate to this compulsion the dreams which occur in traumatic neuroses and the impulse which leads children to play.

But it is to be noted that only in rare instances can we observe the pure effects of the compulsion to repeat, unsupported by other motives. In the case of children's play we have already laid stress on the other ways in which the emergence of the compulsion may be interpreted; the compulsion to repeat and drive satisfaction which is immediately pleasurable seem to converge here into an intimate partnership. The phenomena of transference are obviously exploited by the resistance which the ego maintains in its pertinacious insistence upon repression; the compulsion to repeat, which the treatment tries to bring into its service is, as it were, called to its help by the ego,[70] clinging as it does to the pleasure principle. A great deal of what might be described as the compulsion of destiny seems intelligible on a rational basis; so that we are under no necessity to call in a new and mysterious motive force to explain it.[71] The least dubious instance[72] is perhaps that of traumatic dreams. But on maturer reflection we shall be forced to admit that even in the other instances the whole ground is not covered by the operation of the familiar motive forces. Enough is left unexplained to justify the hypothesis of a compulsion to repeat – something that seems more primitive, more elementary,[73] more driven than the pleasure principle which it overrides.[74] But if a compulsion to repeat does operate in the mind, we should be glad

69 Cf. the apt remarks on this subject by C.G. Jung (1909) ['Die Bedeutung des Vaters für das Schicksal des Einzelnen'].
70 *LA*: E onwards revised to 'drawn over by the ego to its side.' [Change noted in *SE*].
71 *PH*: paragraph break in *SE*.
72 *PH*: '[of such a motive force]' inserted in *SE*.
73 *LA*: in manuscript, deleted: 'than' before the comma.
74 *LA*: paragraph break omitted in C onwards, presumably printer's error.

to know something about it, to learn what function it corresponds to, under what conditions it can emerge and what its relation is to the pleasure principle – to which, after all, we have hitherto ascribed dominance over the course of the processes of excitation in mental life.

IV

[24] What follows is speculation, often far-fetched speculation, which the reader will consider or dismiss according to his individual predilection. It is further an attempt to follow out an idea consistently, out of curiosity to see where it will lead.

Psychoanalytic speculation takes as its point of departure the impression, derived from examining unconscious processes, that consciousness may be, not the most universal attribute of mental processes, but only one particular function amongst[75] them.[76] Speaking in metapsychological terms, it asserts that consciousness is a function of a particular system which it describes as Cs.[77] What consciousness yields consists essentially of perceptions of excitations coming from the external world and of feelings of pleasure and unpleasure which can only arise from within the mental apparatus; it is therefore possible[78] to assign to the system *Pcpt.-Cs.* a position in space. It must lie on the borderline between outside and inside; it must be turned towards the external world and must envelop the other psychical systems. It will be seen that there is nothing daringly new in these assumptions; we have merely adopted the views on localization held by cerebral anatomy, which locates the 'seat' of consciousness in the cerebral cortex – the outermost, enveloping layer of the central organ.[79]

Cerebral anatomy has no need to consider why, speaking anatomically, consciousness should be lodged on the surface of the brain instead of being safely housed somewhere in its inmost interior. Perhaps *we* shall be more successful in accounting for this situation in the case of our system *Pcpt.-Cs.*

Consciousness is not the only distinctive character which we ascribe to the processes in that system. On the basis of impressions derived from our psychoanalytic experience, we assume that all excitatory processes[80] that occur

75 *LA*: corrected from 'of' in manuscript.
76 *LA*: B onwards has 'function of them' – transcription error in B?
77 *LA*: italicised in F and *SE*.
78 *LA*: corrected from 'therefore a position… is assigned' in manuscript.
79 *LA*: paragraph break omitted C onwards – presumably printer's error in C.
80 *LA*: corrected from 'all processes' in manuscript.

in the other[81] systems leave [25] permanent traces behind in them which form the foundation of memory. Such memory-traces, then, have nothing to do with the fact of becoming conscious; indeed they are often most powerful and most enduring when the process which left them behind was one which never entered consciousness. We find it hard to believe, however, that permanent traces of excitation such as these are also left in the system *Pcpt.-Cs.* If they remained constantly conscious,[82] they would very soon set limits to the system's aptitude for receiving fresh excitations.[83] If, on the other hand, they were unconscious, we should be faced with the problem of explaining the existence of unconscious processes in a system whose functioning was otherwise accompanied by the phenomenon of consciousness. We should, so to say, have altered nothing and gained nothing by our hypothesis relegating the process of becoming conscious to a special system. Though this consideration is not absolutely conclusive, it nevertheless leads us to suspect that becoming conscious and leaving behind a memory-trace are processes incompatible with each other within one and the same system. Thus we should be able to say that the excitatory process becomes conscious in the system *Cs.* but leaves no permanent trace behind there; but that the excitation is transmitted to the systems lying next within[84] and that it is in them[85] that its traces, on which memory is based,[86] are left. I followed these same lines in the schematic picture which I included in the speculative section of my *The Interpretation of Dreams*. It must be borne in mind that little enough is known from other sources of the origin of consciousness; when, therefore, we lay down the proposition that *consciousness arises instead of a memory-trace*, the assertion deserves consideration, at all events on the ground of its being framed in fairly precise terms.

If this is so, then, the system *Cs.* is characterized by the peculiarity that in it (in contrast to what happens in the other psychical systems) excitatory processes do not leave behind any permanent change in its elements but expire, as it were, in the phenomenon of becoming conscious. An exception

81 *PH*: italicised in *SE*.

82 *LA*: The sentence originally ran: 'They would very soon set limits... fresh excitations.' Freud then began a new sentence: 'Even if this is not an absolutely compelling argument, it may' – which was then crossed out and replaced with 'if they remained constantly conscious; if on the other hand...' to run on from the previous sentence.

83 What follows is based throughout on J. Breuer's analysis in the theoretical section of 'Studies on Hysteria', 1895 (Breuer and Freud, 1895). [*LA*: this footnote written in the margin as if an afterthought.]

84 *LA*: inserted above the line in manuscript.

85 *PH*: italicised in *SE*.

86 *RSE*: this clause was omitted in the *SE* translation.

of this sort [26] to the general rule requires to be explained by some factor that applies exclusively to that one system. Such a factor, which is absent in the other systems, might well be the exposed situation of the system *Cs.*, immediately abutting as it does on the external world.

Let us picture a living organism in its most simplified possible form as an undifferentiated vesicle of a substance[87] that is susceptible to stimulation. Then the surface turned towards the external world will from its very situation be differentiated and will serve as an organ for receiving stimuli. Indeed embryology, in its capacity as a recapitulation of developmental history, actually shows us that the central nervous system originates from the ectoderm; the grey matter of the cortex remains a derivative of the primitive superficial layer of the organism and may have inherited some of its essential properties. It would be easy to suppose, then, that as a result of the[88] ceaseless impact of external stimuli on the surface of the vesicle, its substance to a certain depth may have become permanently modified, so that excitatory processes run a different course in it from what they run in the deeper layers. A crust would thus be formed which would at last have been so thoroughly 'baked through' by stimulation that it would present the most favourable possible conditions for the reception of stimuli and become incapable of any further modification. In terms of the system *Cs.*, this would mean that its elements could undergo no further permanent modification from the passage of excitation, because they had already been modified in the respect in question to the greatest possible extent: now, however, they would have become capable of giving rise to consciousness. Various ideas may be formed which cannot at present be verified as to the nature of this modification of the substance and of the excitatory process. It may be supposed that, in passing from one element to another, an excitation has to overcome a resistance, and that the diminution of resistance thus effected is what lays down a permanent trace of the excitation, that is, a facilitation. In the system *Cs.*, then, resistance of this kind to passage from one element to another would no longer exist. This picture can be brought into relation with Breuer's distinction between quiescent (or bound) and mobile cathectic energy in the elements [27] of the psychical systems;[89] the elements of the system *Cs.* would carry no bound energy but only energy capable of free discharge. For the present[90] it seems best, however, to express oneself as cautiously as possible on these points.

87 *LA*: corrected from 'living [substance]' in manuscript.

88 *LA*: D onwards 'result of ceaseless'.

89 What follows is based throughout on Breuer's analysis in [*SE*: the second section of] his theoretical contribution to *Studies on Hysteria* [Breuer & Freud (1895d), *Studies on Hysteria*].

90 *RSE*: omitted in the *SE* translation.

None the less, these speculations[91] will have enabled us to bring the origin of consciousness into some sort of connection with the situation of the system *Cs.* and with the peculiarities that must be ascribed to the excitatory processes taking place in it.

But we have more to say of the living vesicle with its receptive cortical layer. This little fragment of living substance is suspended in the middle of an external world charged with the most powerful energies; and it would be killed by the stimulation emanating from these if it were not[92] provided with a *protective shield* against stimuli. It acquires the shield in this way: its outermost surface ceases to have the structure proper to living matter, becomes to some degree inorganic and thence-forward functions as a special envelope or membrane resistant to stimuli. In consequence, the energies of the external world are able to pass into the next underlying layers, which have remained living, with only[93] a fragment of their original intensity; and these layers can devote themselves, behind the protective shield, to the reception of the amounts of stimulus which have been allowed through it. By its death, the outer layer has saved all the deeper ones from a similar fate – unless, that is to say, stimuli reach it which are so strong that they break through the protective shield. Protection against[94] stimuli is an almost more important function for the living organism than reception of stimuli. The protective shield is supplied with its own store of energy and must above all endeavour to preserve the special modes of transformation of energy operating in it against the effects threatened by the enormous energies at work in the external world – effects which tend towards a levelling out of them and hence[95] towards destruction. The main purpose of the reception[96] of stimuli is to discover the direction and nature of the external stimuli; and for that it is enough to take small specimens of the external world, to sample it in small quantities. In highly developed organisms the receptive cortical layer of the former vesicle has long been withdrawn into the depths of [28] the interior of the body, though portions of it have been left behind on the surface immediately beneath the general shield against stimuli. These are the sense organs, which consist essentially of equipment for the reception of certain specific effects of stimulation, but which also include special arrangements for further protection against excessive amounts of stimulation and for excluding

---

91 *LA*: F has 'this speculation'.
92 *LA*: inserted above the line in manuscript.
93 *LA*: F has 'now with' [from 'nur' to 'nun'] – printer's error?
94 *PH*: these words, and 'reception' all italicised in *SE*.
95 *LA*: 'towards a levelling out of them and hence' inserted below the line in manuscript.
96 *PH*: this word italicised in *SE*.

unsuitable kinds of stimuli. It is characteristic of them that they deal only with very small quantities of external stimulation and only take in samples[97] of the external world. They may perhaps be compared with feelers which are all the time making tentative advances towards the external world and then drawing back from it.

At this point I shall venture to touch for a moment upon a subject which would merit the most exhaustive treatment. As a result of certain psychoanalytic discoveries, we are today in a position to embark on a discussion of the Kantian theorem that time and space are 'necessary forms of thought'. We have learnt that unconscious mental processes are in themselves 'timeless'. This means in the first place that they are not ordered temporally, that time does not change them in any way and that the idea of time cannot be applied to them. These are negative characteristics which can only be clearly understood if a comparison is made with *conscious* mental processes. On the other hand, our abstract idea of time seems to be wholly derived from the method of working of the system *Pcpt.-Cs.* and to correspond to a perception on its own part of that method of working. This mode of functioning may perhaps constitute another way of providing a shield against stimuli. I know that these remarks must sound very obscure, but I must limit myself to these hints. (The other abstraction which can be linked to the functioning of Cs., however, is not space but matter, substance).[98]

We have pointed out how the living vesicle is provided with a shield against stimuli from the external world; and we had previously shown that the cortical layer next to that shield must be differentiated as an organ for receiving stimuli from without. This sensitive cortex, however, which is later to become the system *Cs.*, also receives excitations from *within*. The situation of the system between the outside and the inside and the differ-[29]ence between the conditions governing the reception of excitations in the two cases have a decisive effect on the functioning of the system and of the whole mental apparatus. Towards the outside it is shielded against stimuli, and the amounts of excitation impinging on it have only a reduced effect. Towards the inside there can be no such shield; the excitations in the deeper layers extend into the system directly and in undiminished amount, in so far as certain of their characteristics give rise to feelings in the pleasure-unpleasure series. The excitations coming from within are, however, in their intensity and in other,

97 *PH*: italicised in *SE*.

98 *LA*: this sentence deleted in B onwards. The opening bracket, corresponding to the closing one after 'substance', is missing in A. Another, less plausible, option is that the brackets were meant to enclose 'substance' alone.

qualitative, respects – in their amplitude, perhaps – more commensurate with the system's method of working than the stimuli which stream in from the external world. This state of things produces two definite results. First, the feelings of pleasure-unpleasure[99] (which are an index to what is happening in the interior of the apparatus) predominate over all external stimuli. And secondly, a particular way is adopted of dealing with any internal excitations which produce too great an increase of unpleasure: there is a tendency to treat them as though they were acting, not from the inside,[100] but from the outside, so that it may be possible to bring the shield against stimuli into operation as a means of defence against them. This is the origin of *projection*, which is destined to play such a large part in the causation of pathological processes.

I have an impression that these last considerations have brought us to a better understanding of the dominance of the pleasure principle; but no light has yet been thrown on the cases that contradict that dominance. Let us therefore go a step further.[101]

We describe as 'traumatic' any excitations from outside[102] which are powerful enough to break through the protective shield. It seems to me that the concept of trauma necessarily implies a connection of this kind with a breach in an otherwise efficacious barrier against stimuli. Such an event as an external trauma is bound to provoke a disturbance on a large scale in the functioning of the organism's energy and to set in motion every possible defensive measure. At the same time, the pleasure principle is for the moment put out of action. There is no longer any possibility of preventing the mental apparatus from being flooded with large amounts of stimulus, and another [30] problem arises instead – the problem of mastering the amounts of stimulus which have broken in and of binding them, in the psychical sense, so that they can then be disposed of.

The specific unpleasure of physical pain is probably the result of the protective shield having been broken through to a limited extent.[103] There is then a continuous stream of excitations from the part of the periphery concerned to the central apparatus of the mind, such as could normally arise only from within[104] the apparatus.[105] And how shall we expect the mind to react to this invasion? Cathectic energy is summoned from all sides to

[99] *LA*: B onwards has 'pleasure and unpleasure' – transcription error in B?
[100] *LA*: corrected from 'outside' in manuscript.
[101] *LA*: probably a paragraph break here in A – transcription error in B?
[102] *LA*: 'from outside' added below the line in manuscript.
[103] *LA*: corrected from 'in a single place' in manuscript. [*SE* has: 'in a limited area'].
[104] *PH*: italicised in *SE*.
[105] Cf. 'Drives and Their Vicissitudes' (1915c).

provide sufficiently high cathexes of energy in the environs of the breach. An 'anticathexis' on a grand scale is set up, for whose benefit all the other psychical systems are impoverished, so that the remaining psychical functions are extensively paralysed or reduced. We must endeavour to draw a lesson from examples such as this and use them as a basis for our metapsychological speculations. From the present case, then, we infer that a system which is itself highly cathected is capable of taking up an additional stream of fresh inflowing energy and of converting it into quiescent cathexis, that is of binding it psychically. The higher the system's own quiescent cathexis, the greater seems to be its binding force; conversely, therefore, the lower its cathexis, the less capacity will it have for taking up inflowing energy and the more violent must be the consequences of such a breach in the protective shield against stimuli. To this view it cannot be justly objected that the increase of cathexes[106] round the breach can be explained far more simply as the direct result of the inflowing masses of excitation. If that were so, the mental apparatus would merely receive an increase in its cathexes of energy, and the paralysing character of pain and the impoverishment of all the other systems would remain unexplained. Nor do the very violent phenomena of discharge to which pain gives rise affect our explanation, for they occur in a reflex manner – that is, they follow without the intervention of the mental apparatus. The indefiniteness of all our discussions on what we describe as metapsychology is of course due to the fact that we know nothing of the nature of the excitatory process that takes place in the elements of the [31] psychical systems, and that we do not feel justified in framing any hypothesis on the subject. We are consequently operating all the time with a large unknown factor, which we are obliged to carry over into every new formula. It may be reasonably supposed that this excitatory process can be carried out with energies that vary quantitatively;[107] it may also seem probable that it has more than one quality (in the nature of amplitude, for instance). As a new factor we have taken into consideration Breuer's hypothesis that charges of energy occur in two forms; so that we have to distinguish between two kinds of cathexis of the psychical systems or their elements – a freely flowing cathexis that presses on towards discharge and a quiescent cathexis. We may perhaps suspect that the binding of the energy that streams into the mental apparatus consists in its change from a freely flowing into a quiescent state.

106 *LA*: corrected from 'counterc[athexes]' in manuscript. F has 'cathexis'.
107 *PH*: 'quantitatively' and 'quality' italicised in *SE*.

We may, I think, tentatively venture to regard the common traumatic neurosis as a consequence of an extensive breach being made in the protective shield against stimuli. This would seem to reinstate the old, naive theory of shock, in apparent contrast to the later and psychologically more ambitious theory which attributes aetiological importance not to the effects of mechanical violence but to fright and the threat to life. These opposing views are not, however, irreconcilable; nor is the psychoanalytic view of the traumatic neurosis identical with the shock theory in its crudest form. The latter regards the essence of the shock as being the direct damage to the molecular structure or even to the histological structure of the elements of the nervous system; whereas what we[108] seek to understand are the effects produced on the organ of the mind by the breach in the shield against stimuli and by the problems that follow in its train. And we still attribute importance to the element of fright. It is caused by lack of any preparedness for anxiety, including lack of hypercathexis of the systems that would be the first to receive the stimulus. Owing to their low cathexis those[109] systems are not in a good position for binding the inflowing amounts of excitation and the consequences of the breach[110] in the protective shield follow all the more easily. It will be seen, then, that preparedness for anxiety and the hyper-cathexis of the receptive systems constitute the last line of defence of the shield against stimuli. In the case of quite a number of traumas, the [32] difference between systems that are unprepared and systems that are well prepared through being hypercathected may be a decisive factor in determining the outcome; though where the strength of a trauma exceeds a certain limit this factor will no doubt cease to carry weight.[111]

The fulfilment of wishes is, as we know, brought about in a hallucinatory manner by dreams, and under the dominance of the pleasure principle this has become their function. But it is not in the service of that principle that the dreams of patients suffering from traumatic neuroses lead them back with such regularity to the situation in which the trauma occurred. We may assume, rather, that dreams are here helping to carry out another task, which must be accomplished before the dominance of the pleasure principle can even begin. These dreams are endeavouring to master the stimulus retrospectively, by developing the anxiety whose omission was the cause of the traumatic neurosis. They thus afford us a view of a function of the mental apparatus

108 *PH*: 'we' italicised in *SE*.

109 *LA*: D onwards altered to 'the' systems.

110 *LA*: corrected from 'and the breach' in manuscript.

111 *LA*: paragraph break omitted in C onwards – presumably printer's error.

which, though it does not contradict the pleasure principle, is nevertheless independent of it and seems to be more primitive than the purpose of gaining pleasure and avoiding unpleasure.[112]

This would seem to be the place, then, at which to admit for the first time an exception to the proposition that dreams are fulfilments of wishes. Anxiety dreams, as I have shown repeatedly and in detail, offer no such exception. Nor do 'punishment dreams', for they merely replace the forbidden wish fulfilment by the appropriate punishment for it; that is to say, they fulfil the wish of the sense of guilt which is the reaction to the repudiated impulse. But it is impossible to classify as wish fulfilments the dreams we have been discussing which occur in traumatic neuroses, or the dreams during psychoanalyses which bring to memory the psychical traumas of childhood. They arise, rather, in obedience to the compulsion to repeat, though it is true that in analysis that compulsion is supported by the wish (which is not unconscious)[113] to conjure up what has been forgotten and repressed. Thus it would seem that the function of dreams, which consists in [33] setting aside any motives that might interrupt sleep, by fulfilling the wishes of the disturbing impulses, is not their *original* function. It would not be possible for them to perform that function until the whole of mental life had accepted the dominance of the pleasure principle. If there is a 'beyond the pleasure principle', it is only[114] consistent to grant that there was also a time before the purpose of dreams was the fulfilment of wishes.[115]

This would imply no denial of their later functions. Once this general rule has been broken, a further question now[116] arises. May not dreams which, with a view to the psychical binding of traumatic impressions, obey the compulsion to repeat – may not such dreams occur *outside* analysis as well? And the reply can only be a decided affirmative.

I have argued elsewhere[117] that 'war neuroses' (in so far as that term implies something more than a reference to the circumstances of the illness's onset) may very well be traumatic neuroses which have been facilitated by a conflict in the ego. The fact to which I have referred on page [p. 34], that a gross physical injury caused simultaneously by the trauma[118] diminishes the chances

112 *LA*: in A the sentence beginning 'I have argued elsewhere…' in the final paragraph of the section follows on directly.
113 *LA*: E onwards altered to 'which is encouraged by "suggestion"'. [Noted in *SE*].
114 *LA*: C onwards omits 'only' – printer's error in C?
115 *LA*: paragraph break omitted in C onwards – printer's error?
116 *LA*: E onwards altered to 'But if once this general rule… a further question arises' [from 'nun' to 'nur'].
117 See my introduction (1919d) to *Psychoanalysis and the War Neuroses*.
118 *LA*: 'by the trauma' inserted below the line in manuscript B.

that a neurosis will develop, becomes intelligible if one bears in mind two facts which have been stressed by psychoanalytic research: firstly, that mechanical agitation must be recognized as one of the sources of sexual excitation (cf. the remarks on the effect[119] of swinging and railway-travel in *Three Essays on the Theory of Sexuality*), and secondly, that painful and feverish illnesses exercise a powerful effect, so long as they last, on the distribution of libido. Thus, on the one hand, the mechanical violence of the trauma would liberate a quantity of sexual excitation which, owing to the lack of preparation for anxiety, would have a traumatic effect; but, on the other hand, the simultaneous physical injury, by calling for a narcissistic hypercathexis of the injured organ,[120] would bind the excess of excitation. It is also well known, though the libido theory has not yet made sufficient use of the fact, that such severe disorders in the distribution of libido as melancholia are temporarily brought to an end by intercurrent organic illness, and indeed that even a fully developed condition of dementia praecox is capable of a temporary remission in these same circumstances.

V

[34] The fact that the cortical layer which receives stimuli is without any protective shield against excitations from within must have as its result that these latter transmissions of stimulus have a preponderance in economic importance and often occasion economic disturbances comparable with traumatic neuroses. The most abundant sources of this internal excitation are what are described as the organism's 'drives' – the representatives of all the forces originating in the interior of the body and transmitted to the mental apparatus – at once the most important and the most obscure element of psychological research.

It will perhaps not be thought too rash to suppose that the impulses arising from the drives do not belong to the type of bound[121] nervous processes but of freely mobile processes which press towards discharge. The best part of what we know of these processes is derived from our study of the dream-work. We there discovered that the processes in the unconscious systems were fundamentally different from those in the preconscious (or conscious) systems.

[119] *LA*: corrected from 'influence' to 'effect' in manuscript B.

[120] See my paper on narcissism (1914c).

[121] *PH*: 'bound' and 'freely mobile' italicised in *SE*.

In the unconscious, cathexes can easily be completely[122] transferred, displaced and condensed. Such treatment, however, could produce only invalid results if it were applied to preconscious material; and this accounts for the familiar peculiarities exhibited by manifest dreams after the preconscious residues of the preceding day have been worked over in accordance with the laws operating in the unconscious. I described the type of process found in the unconscious as the 'primary' psychical[123] process, in contradistinction to the 'secondary' process which is the one obtaining in our normal waking life. Since all drive impulses have the unconscious systems as their point of impact, it is hardly an innovation to say that they obey the primary process. Again, it is easy to identify the primary psychical process with Breuer's freely mobile cathexis and the secondary process with the changes in his bound or tonic cathexis.[124] If so, it would be the task of the higher strata of the mental apparatus to bind the drive excitation reaching [35] the primary process. A failure to effect this binding would provoke a disturbance analogous to a traumatic neurosis; and only after the binding has been accomplished would it be possible for the dominance of the pleasure principle (and of its modification, the reality principle) to proceed unhindered. Till then the other task of the mental apparatus, the task of mastering or binding excitations, would have precedence – not, indeed, in opposition[125] to the pleasure principle, but independently of it[126] and to some extent in disregard of it.

The manifestations of a compulsion to repeat (which we have described as occurring in the early activities of infantile mental life as well as among the results[127] of psychoanalytic treatment) exhibit to a high degree a driven character and, when they act in opposition to the pleasure principle, give the appearance of some 'daemonic' force at work. In the case of children's play we seemed to see that children repeat unpleasurable experiences for the additional reason that they can master a powerful impression far more thoroughly by being active than they could by merely experiencing it passively. Each fresh repetition seems to strengthen the mastery they are in search of. Nor can children have their pleasurable[128] experiences repeated often enough, and they are inexorable in their insistence that the repetition shall be an identical one. This character trait disappears later on. If a joke is heard for a second time it

122 *LA*: added in the margin in manuscript.

123 *LA*: 'psychical' added above the line in manuscript.

124 Cf. my *The Interpretation of Dreams*, Chapter VII.

125 *PH*: italicised in *SE*.

126 *LA*: 'of it' inserted above the line.

127 *LA*: B onwards has 'experiences' – probably transcription error in B.

128 *PH*: italicised in *SE*.

produces almost no effect;[129] a theatrical production never creates so great an impression the second time as the first; indeed, it is hardly possible to persuade an adult who has very much enjoyed reading a book to re-read it immediately. Novelty is always the condition of enjoyment;[130] children will never tire of asking an adult to repeat a game that he has shown them or played with them, till he is too exhausted to go on. And if a child has been told a nice story, he will insist on hearing it over and over again rather than a new one; and he will remorselessly stipulate that the repetition shall be an identical one and will correct any alterations of which the narrator may be guilty – though they may actually have been made in the hope of gaining fresh approval. [36] None of this contradicts the pleasure principle; repetition, the re-experiencing of something identical, is clearly in itself a source of pleasure. In the case of a person in analysis, on the contrary, the compulsion to repeat the events of his childhood in the transference evidently disregards the pleasure principle in every[131] way. He[132] behaves in a purely infantile fashion and thus shows us that the repressed memory traces of his primaeval experiences are not present in him in a bound state and are indeed in a sense incapable of obeying the secondary process. It is to this fact of not being bound, moreover, that they owe their capacity for forming, in conjunction with the residues of the previous day, a wishful phantasy that emerges in a dream; this[133] same compulsion to repeat frequently meets us as an obstacle to our treatment when at the end of an analysis we try to induce the patient to detach himself completely from his physician. It may be presumed, too, that when people unfamiliar with analysis feel an obscure fear – a dread of rousing something that, so they feel, is better left sleeping – what they are afraid of[134] at bottom is the emergence of this compulsion with its hint of possession by some 'daemonic' power.

But how is the predicate of being 'driven' related to the compulsion to repeat? At this point we cannot escape a suspicion that we may have come upon the track of a universal attribute of drives and perhaps of organic life in general which has not hitherto been clearly recognized or at least not explicitly stressed.[135] It seems, then, that a drive is an urge inherent in organic life to restore an earlier state of things[136] which the living entity has been obliged to

129 *LA*: Freud originally continued 'the repetition', crossed out in manuscript.
130 *LA*: in B onwards corrected to 'enjoyment. But children'.
131 *LA*: in C–E 'in every' in spaced type; in F just 'every' is italicised.
132 *LA*: in B onwards corrected to 'The patient'.
133 *LA*: in B onwards corrected to 'dream. This same…'.
134 *LA*: 'are afraid of' is a correction from 'mean' in the manuscript.
135 *PH*: addition noted in *SE*.
136 *LA*: the first part of this sentence italicised in B.

abandon under the pressure of external disturbing forces; that is, it is a kind of organic elasticity, or, to put it another way, the expression of the inertia inherent in organic life.[137]

This view of drives strikes us as strange because we have become used to see in them a factor impelling towards change and development, whereas we are now asked to recognize in them the precise contrary – an expression of the conservative[138] nature of living substance. On the other hand we soon call to mind examples from animal life which seem to confirm the [37] view that drives are historically determined. Certain fishes, for instance, undertake laborious migrations at spawning-time in order to deposit their spawn in particular waters far removed from their customary haunts.[139] In the opinion of many biologists what they are doing is merely to seek out the localities in which their species formerly resided but which in the course of time they have exchanged for others. The same explanation is believed to apply to the migratory flights of birds of passage – but we are quickly relieved of the necessity for seeking for further examples by the reflection that the most impressive proofs of there being an organic compulsion to repeat lie in the phenomena of heredity and the facts of embryology. We see how the germ of a living animal is obliged in the course of its development to recapitulate (even if only in a transient and abbreviated fashion) the structures of all the forms from which it is sprung, instead of proceeding quickly by the shortest path to its final shape. This behaviour is only to a very slight degree attributable to mechanical causes, and the historical explanation cannot accordingly be neglected. So too the power of regenerating a lost organ by growing afresh a precisely similar one extends far up into the animal kingdom.

We shall be met by the plausible objection that it may very well be that, in addition to the conservative drives which impel towards repetition, there may be others which push forward towards progress and the production of new forms. This argument must certainly not be overlooked, and it will be taken into account at a later stage.[140] But for the moment it is tempting to pursue to its logical conclusion the hypothesis that all drives tend towards the restoration of an earlier state of things. The outcome may give an impression of mysticism or of sham profundity; but we can feel quite innocent of having had any such purpose in view. We seek only for the sober results of research

137 I have no doubt that similar notions as to the nature of 'drives' have already been put forward repeatedly.

138 *LA*: italicised in E onwards.

139 *LA*: F altered A's 'Wohnorten' to 'Aufenthalten'; *PH*: both translated here, following *SE* and *RSE*, as 'haunts'.

140 *PH*: the addition noted in *SE*.

or of reflection based on it; and we have no wish to find in those results any quality other than certainty.[141]

Let us suppose, then, that all the organic drives are conservative, are acquired historically and tend towards regression, the [38] restoration of an earlier state of things. It follows that all[142] phenomena of organic development must be attributed to external disturbing and diverting influences. The elementary living entity would from its very beginning have had no wish to change; if conditions remained the same, it would do no more than constantly repeat the same course of life. But in the external world everything was subject to change;[143] in the last resort, what has left its mark on the development of organisms must be the history of the earth we live in and of its relation to the sun. Every modification which is thus imposed upon the course of the organism's life is accepted by the conservative organic drives and stored up for further repetition. Those drives are therefore bound to give us[144] a deceptive appearance of being forces tending towards change and progress, whilst in fact they are merely seeking to reach an ancient goal by paths alike old and new.[145] Moreover it is possible to specify this final goal of all organic striving. It would be in contradiction to the conservative nature of the drives if the goal of life were a state of things which had never yet been attained. On the contrary, it must be an old[146] state of things, an initial state from which the living entity has at one time or other departed and to which it is striving to return by the circuitous paths along which its development leads. Since we take it as a truth that knows no exception[147] that everything living dies for internal[148] reasons – becomes inorganic once again – then we shall be compelled to say that *'the aim of all life is death'* and, looking backwards, that *'inanimate things existed before living ones'*.

The attributes of life were at some time evoked in inanimate matter by the action of a force of whose nature we can form no conception. It may perhaps have been a process similar in type to that which later caused the development of consciousness in a particular stratum of living matter. The tension which then arose in what had hitherto been an inanimate substance endeavoured to

141 The reader should not overlook the fact that what follows is the development of an extreme line of thought. Later on, when account is taken of the sexual drives, it will be found that the necessary limitations and corrections are applied to it. [Addition noted in *SE*].

142 *LA*: in E onwards 'the' substituted for 'all'.

143 *LA*: the first half of this sentence omitted in B onwards. Transcription error in B?

144 *LA*: in B onwards 'us' omitted. Transcription error in B?

145 *LA*: 'and new' added above the line in manuscript.

146 *PH*: italicised in *SE*.

147 *LA*: in B onwards revised to 'If we are to take it as a truth that knows no exception'.

148 *LA*: italics added to 'internal' in B onwards.

cancel itself out, the first drive came into being[149] in order to[150] return to the inanimate state. It was still an easy matter at that time for a living substance to die; the course of its life was probably only a brief one, whose direction was determined by the chemical structure of the young life. For a long time, perhaps, living substance was thus being constantly created afresh and easily dying, till decisive external influences altered in such a way as to oblige the still surviving[151] substance to diverge ever more widely from its original course [39] of life and to make ever more complicated *détours* before reaching its aim of death. These circuitous paths to death, faithfully kept to by the conservative drives, present[152] us today with the picture of the phenomena of life. If we firmly maintain the exclusively conservative nature of instincts, we cannot arrive at any other notions as to the origin and aim of life.

The implications in regard to the great groups of drives which, as we believe, lie behind the phenomena of life in organisms must appear no less bewildering. The hypothesis of self-preservative drives, such as we attribute to all living beings, stands in marked opposition to the idea that the life of the drives as a whole serves to bring about death. The theoretical importance of the drives of self-preservation, of self-assertion and of mastery greatly diminishes, so to speak.[153] They are component drives whose function it is to assure that the organism shall follow its own path to death, and to ward off any possible ways of returning to inorganic existence other than those which are immanent in the organism itself. We have no longer to reckon with the organism's puzzling determination (so hard to fit into any context) to maintain its own existence in the face of every obstacle. What we are left with is the fact that the organism wishes to die only[154] in its own fashion. Thus these guardians of life, too, were originally the myrmidons of death. Hence arises the paradoxical situation[155] that the living organism struggles most energetically against events (dangers, in fact) which might help it to attain its life's aim rapidly – by a kind of short-circuit. Such behaviour is, however, precisely what characterizes purely driven as contrasted with intelligent efforts. *A correction of this extreme view of the self-preservative instincts follows.*[156]

[149] *LA*: 'the first drive came into being' inserted below the line in manuscript.

[150] *LA*: corrected from B onwards to read: 'that of returning to…'. [*PH*: *SE* begins a fresh sentence after 'cancel itself out': 'In this way the first drive came into being, the drive to return…'].

[151] *LA*: 'still surviving' corrected from 'living' in manuscript.

[152] *LA*: in D onwards 'would thus present us'.

[153] *LA*: in B onwards 'so to speak' corrected to 'seen in this light'.

[154] *LA*: inserted above the line in the manuscript.

[155] *LA*: corrected from 'paradoxical behaviour' in the manuscript of B.

[156] *LA*: from C–E this last sentence becomes a footnote with the italics removed. Omitted in F. [Noted in *SE*].

But let us pause for a moment and reflect. It cannot be so. The sexual drives, to which the theory of the neuroses gives a quite special place, appear under a very different aspect. The external pressure which provokes a constantly increasing extent of development has not imposed itself upon every[157] organism. Many have succeeded in remaining up to the present time at their lowly level. Many, though not all, such creatures, which must resemble the earliest stages of the higher animals [40] and plants, are, indeed, living today. In the same way, the whole path of development to natural death is not trodden by all[158] the elementary entities which compose the complicated body of one of the higher organisms. Some of them, the germ cells, probably retain the original structure of living matter and, after a certain time, with their full complement of inherited and freshly acquired drive dispositions, separate themselves from the organism as a whole. These two characteristics may be precisely what enables them to have an independent existence. Under favourable conditions, they begin to develop – that is, to repeat the performance to which they owe their existence; and in the end once again one portion of their substance pursues its development to a finish, while another portion harks back once again as a fresh residual germ to the beginning of the process of development. These germ cells, therefore, work against the death of the living substance and succeed in winning for it what we can only regard as potential immortality, though that may mean no more than a lengthening of the road to death. We must regard as completely incomprehensible[159] the fact that this function of the germ cell is reinforced, or only made possible, if it coalesces with another cell similar to itself and yet differing from it.

The drives which watch over the destinies of these elementary organisms that survive the whole individual, which provide them with a safe shelter while they are defenceless against the stimuli of the external world, which bring about their meeting with other germ cells, and so on – these constitute the group of the sexual drives. They are conservative in the same sense as the other drives in that they bring back earlier states of living substance; but they are conservative to a higher degree in that they are peculiarly resistant to external influences; and they are conservative too in another sense in that they preserve[160] life itself for a comparatively long period.[161] They are the true life drives. They operate against the purpose of the other drives, which leads, by reason of

[157] *PH*: italicised in *SE*.

[158] *PH*: italicised in *SE*.

[159] *LA*: in B onwards corrected to: 'in the highest degree significant'.

[160] *LA*: corrected from 'endure/withstand' [aushalten] in manuscript.

[161] Yet it is to them alone that we can attribute an internal impulse towards 'progress' and towards higher development! (See below.) [1923 addition noted in *SE*].

their function, to death; and this fact indicates that there is an opposition between them and the other drives, an opposition whose importance was long ago recognized by the theory of the neuroses. It is as though the [41] life of the organism moved with a vacillating rhythm. One group of drives rushes forward so as to reach the final aim of life as swiftly as possible; but when a particular stage in the advance has been reached, the other group jerks back to a certain point to make a fresh start and so prolong the journey. But sexuality and the distinction between the sexes did not exist at the start of life, and the sequence just depicted appears to us to be a later complication of an originally simpler one. In fact it appears to repeat a moment (one unknown to us, but for certain a very important one in the history of living substance) which is the point from which, in order to prolong its life, it learned to develop a second goal, one that stood opposed to the first goal.[162]

Let us now hark back for a first time[163] ourselves and consider whether there is any basis at all for these speculations. Is it really the case that, apart from the sexual drives,[164] there are no drives that do not seek to restore an earlier state of things? that there are none that aim at a state of things which has never yet been attained? I know of no certain example from the organic world that would contradict the characterization I have thus proposed. There is unquestionably no universal drive towards higher development observable in the animal or plant world, even though it is undeniable that development does in fact occur in that direction. But on the one hand it is often merely a matter of opinion when we declare that one stage of development is higher than another, and on the other hand biology teaches us that higher development in one respect is very frequently balanced or outweighed by involution in another. Moreover, there are plenty of animal forms from whose early stages we can infer that their development has, on the contrary, acquired[165] a retrograde character.

---

162 *LA*: in manuscript B Freud began a handwritten correction of this sentence, then pasted the following reformulation over the previous one: 'And even though it is certain that sexuality and the distinction between the sexes did not exist when life began, the possibility remains that the drives which were later to be described as sexual ones [C alters to 'sexual' – printer's error?] may have been in operation from the very first, and it may not be true that it was only at a later time that they started upon their work of opposing the activities of the ego drives.' [In D 'ego drives' in inverted commas. At the end of the new formulation is an asterisk – obviously as the marker for an intended footnote, which wasn't written. This is supported by a blue question-mark, presumably the printer's, and a note, also in blue, written at the bottom of the page: note missing]. [Footnote added in F, and noted in *SE*]: It should be understood from the context that the term 'ego drives' is used here as a provisional description and derives from the earliest psychoanalytical terminology.

163 *PH*: SE reads 'for a moment'.

164 *LA*: these five words italicised in D onwards.

165 *LA*: in B onwards corrected to 'assumed' (in another hand?).

Both higher development and involution might well be the consequences of adaptation to the pressure of external forces; and in both cases the part played by drives might be limited to the retention (in the form of an internal source of power[166]) of an obligatory modification.[167]

[42] It may be difficult, too, for many of us, to abandon the belief that there is a drive towards perfection at work in human beings, which has brought them to their present high level of intellectual achievement and ethical sublimation and which may be expected to watch over their development into supermen. I have no faith, however, in the existence of any such internal drive and I cannot see how this benevolent[168] illusion is to be preserved. The present development of human beings requires, as it seems to me, no different explanation from that of animals. What appears in a minority of human individuals as an untiring impulsion towards further perfection can easily be understood as a result of the drive repression upon which is based all that is most precious in human civilization. The repressed drive never ceases to strive for complete satisfaction, which would consist in the repetition of a primary experience of satisfaction. No substitutive or reactive formations and no sublimations will suffice to remove the repressed drive's persisting tension; and it is the difference in amount between the pleasure of satisfaction which is demanded[169] and that which is actually achieved that provides the driving factor which will permit of no halting at any position attained, but, in the poet's words, '*ungebändigt immer vorwärts dringt*'.[170] The backward path that leads to complete satisfaction is as a rule obstructed by the resistances which maintain the repressions. So there is no alternative but to advance in the direction in which growth is still free – though with no prospect of bringing the process to a conclusion or of being able to reach the goal.[171] The processes involved in the formation of a neurotic phobia, which is nothing else than an attempt at flight from the satisfaction of a drive, present us with a model of the manner of origin of this supposititious 'drive towards perfection' – a drive

---

166 *LA*: in B onwards 'source of pleasure' – probably transcription error in B.

167 Ferenczi (1913, 137) has reached the same conclusion along different lines: 'If this thought is pursued to its logical conclusion, one must make oneself familiar with the idea of a tendency to perseveration or regression dominating organic life as well, while the tendency to further development, to adaptation, etc., would become active only as a result of external stimuli.' [*LA*: the phrase 'Ferenczi has reached, etc.' came after the citation in the manuscript, but was transposed to the beginning of the sentence].

168 *LA*: corrected from 'nice' in manuscript.

169 *PH*: 'demanded' and 'achieved' both italicised in *SE*.

170 *SE* ['Presses ever forward unsubdued'] Mephistopheles in *Faust, Part I* [Scene 4].

171 *LA*: in B there is an insertion mark, repeated in the margin with the addition: 'Ferenczi'. A note in blue pencil, presumably from the typesetter, says: 'missing'. Probably what is meant here is the comment introduced on the previous page.

which cannot possibly be attributed to every[172] human being. The dynamic[173] conditions for its development are, indeed, universally present; but it is only in rare cases that the economic situation appears to favour the production of the phenomenon.

I will add only a word to suggest that the efforts of Eros to [43] combine organic substances into ever larger unities can possibly provide[174] a substitute for this 'drive towards perfection' whose existence we cannot admit. The phenomena that are attributed to it seem capable of explanation by these efforts of Eros taken in conjunction with the results of repression.[175]

VI

[44] The upshot of our inquiry so far has been the drawing of a sharp distinction between the 'ego drives' and the sexual drives, and the view that the former exercise pressure towards death and the latter towards conservation of life.[176] But this conclusion is bound to be unsatisfactory in many respects even to ourselves. Moreover, it is actually only of the former group of drives that we can predicate a conservative, or rather retrograde, character corresponding to a compulsion to repeat. For on our hypothesis the ego drives arise from the coming to life of inanimate matter and seek to restore the inanimate state; whereas as regards the sexual drives, though it is true that they reproduce primitive states of the organism, what they are clearly aiming at by every possible means is the coalescence of two germ cells which are differentiated in a particular way. If this union is not effected, the germ cell dies along with all the other elements of the multicellular organism. It is only on this condition that the sexual function can prolong the cell's life and lend it the appearance of immortality. But what is the important event in the development of living substance which is being repeated in sexual reproduction, or in its forerunner, the conjugation of two protista? We cannot say; and we should consequently feel relieved if the whole structure of our argument turned out to be mistaken. The opposition between the ego or death drives[177] and the sexual or life drives would then cease to hold and the compulsion to repeat would no longer possess the importance we have ascribed to it.

---

172 *PH*: 'every' italicised in *SE*.
173 *PH*: 'dynamic' and 'economic' italicised in *SE*.
174 *LA*: F has 'probably provide'.
175 *PH*: 1923 addition noted in *SE*.
176 *LA*: E onwards has 'prolongation of life'.
177 *SE*: The first published appearance of the term.

Let us turn back, then, to one of the assumptions that we have already made, with the expectation that we shall be able to give it a categorical denial. We have drawn far-reaching conclusions from the hypothesis that all living substance is bound to die from internal causes. We made this assumption thus carelessly because it does not seem to us to be[178] an assumption. We are accustomed to think that such is the fact, and we [45] are strengthened in our thought by the writings of our poets. Perhaps we have adopted the belief because there is some comfort in it. If we are to die ourselves, and first to lose in death those who are dearest to us, it is easier[179] to submit to a remorseless law of nature, to the sublime *Ἀναγκη* [Necessity], than to a chance which might perhaps have been escaped. It may be, however, that this belief in the internal necessity of dying is only another of those illusions which we have created '*um die Schwere des Daseins zu ertragen*'.[180] It is certainly not a primaeval belief, for[181] the notion of 'natural death' is quite foreign to primitive races; they attribute every death that occurs among them to the influence of an enemy or of an evil spirit.[182] We must therefore turn to biology in order to test the validity of the belief.

If we do so, we may be astonished to find how little agreement there is among biologists on the subject of natural death and in fact that the whole concept of death melts away under their hands. The fact that there is a fixed average duration of life at least among the higher animals naturally argues in favour of there being such a thing as death from natural causes. But this impression is countered when we consider that certain large animals and certain gigantic arboreal growths reach a very advanced age and one which cannot at present be computed. According to the grand conception of W. Fliess [1906], all the phenomena of life exhibited by organisms – and also, no doubt, their death – are linked with the completion of fixed periods, which express the dependence of two kinds of living substance (one male and the other female) upon the solar year. When we see, however, how easily and how extensively the influence of external forces is able to modify the date of the appearance of vital phenomena (especially in the plant world) – to precipitate them or hold them back – doubts must be cast upon the rigidity of Fliess's formulas or at least upon whether the laws laid down by him are the sole determining factors.

---

178 *PH*: this word italicised in *SE*.

179 *LA*: corrected from 'one would at least want to submit…' in manuscript.

180 *SE*: 'To bear the burden of existence.' (Schiller, *Die Braut von Messina*, I, 8).

181 *LA*: C onwards reads 'the' instead of 'for' [den/denn] – presumably printer's error in C.

182 *LA*: This sentence added subsequently.

The greatest interest attaches from our point of view to the treatment given to the subject of the duration of life and the death of organisms in the writings of Weismann.[183] It was he who introduced the division of living substance into mortal and immortal parts. The mortal part is [46] the body in the narrower sense – the *soma*[184] – which alone is subject to natural death. The germ cells, on the other hand, are 'potentia[185] immortal, in so far as they are able, under certain favourable conditions, to develop into a new individual, or, in other words, to surround themselves with a new soma.' (Weismann, (1889 [1883]) 122).

What strikes us in this is the unexpected analogy with our own view, which was arrived at along such a different path. Weismann, regarding living substance morphologically, sees in it one portion which is destined to die – the soma, the body apart from the substance concerned with sex and inheritance – and an immortal portion – the germ plasm, which is concerned with the survival of the species, with reproduction. We, on the other hand, dealing not with the living substance but with the forces operating in it, have been led to distinguish two kinds of drives: those which seek to lead what is living to death, and others, the sexual drives, which are perpetually attempting and achieving a renewal of life. This sounds like a dynamic corollary to Weismann's morphological theory.

But the appearance of a significant correspondence is dissipated as soon as we discover Weismann's views on the problem of death. For he only relates the distinction between the mortal soma and the immortal germ plasm to *multicellular* organisms; in unicellular organisms the individual and the reproductive cell are still one and the same (Weismann, (1889 [1881]), 28). Thus he considers that unicellular organisms are potentially immortal, and that death only makes its appearance with the multicellular metazoa. It is true that this death of the higher organisms is a natural one, a death from internal causes; but it is not founded on any primal characteristic of living substance (Weismann, (1889 [1883]) 159) and cannot be regarded as an absolute necessity with its basis in the very nature of life (Weismann 1889 [1881]), 22). Death is rather a matter of expediency, a manifestation of adaptation to the external conditions of life; for, when once the cells of the body have been

[183] Über die Dauer des Lebens, 1882; Über Leben und Tod, [2. Aufl.] 1892; *Das Keimplasma*, 1892, amongst others.

[184] *LA*: italics omitted in F – printer's error? *PH*: *SE* has 'soma'.

[185] *LA*: barely legible inverted comma indicating the beginning of a citation, with closing mark at the end of the paragraph. Both inverted commas are left out from C onward; probably printer's error. F italicises this as a foreign word; *PH*: *SE* translates as 'potentially'.

divided into soma and germ plasm,[186] an unlimited duration of individual life would become a quite pointless luxury. When this differentiation had been made in the multicellular organisms, death became possible and expedient. Since then, the soma of the higher organisms has died at fixed periods for internal reasons, while the protista have remained immortal. It is not the case, on the other hand, that reproduc-[47]tion was only introduced at the same time as death. On the contrary, it is a primal characteristic of living matter, like growth (from which it originated), and life has been continuous from its first beginning upon earth (Weismann, 'Conclusion' (1889 [1883]) 159).

It will be seen at once that to concede in this way that higher organisms have a natural death is of very little help to us. For if death is a late[187] acquisition of organisms, then there can be no question of there having been death drives from the very beginning of life on this earth. Multicellular organisms may die for internal reasons, owing to defective differentiation or to imperfections in their metabolism, but the matter is of no interest from the point of view of our problem. An account of the origin of death such as this is moreover far less at variance with our habitual modes of thought than the strange assumption of 'death drives'.

The discussion which followed upon Weismann's suggestions led, so far as I can see, to no conclusive results in any direction.[188] Some writers returned to the views of Goette (1883), who regarded death as a direct result of reproduction. Hartmann (1906, 29) does not regard the appearance of a 'dead body' – a dead portion of the living substance – as the criterion of death, but defines death as 'the termination of individual development'. In this sense protozoa too are mortal; in their case death always coincides with reproduction, but is to some extent obscured by it, since the whole substance of the parent animal may be transmitted directly into the young offspring.

Soon afterwards research was directed to the experimental testing on unicellular organisms of the alleged immortality of living substance. An American biologist, Woodruff, experimenting with a ciliate infusorian, the 'slipper-animalcule', which reproduces by fission into two individuals, persisted until the 3029th generation (at which point he broke off the experiment), isolating one of the part-products on each occasion and placing it in fresh water. This remote descendant of the first slipper-animalcule was just as lively as its ancestor and showed no signs of ageing or degeneration. Thus, in so far

186 *LA*: singular in B and F. C–E have 'germ plasms' (printer's error).
187 *PH*: italicised in *SE*.
188 Cf. Hartmann (1906), Lipschütz (1914) and Doflein (1919).

as figures of this kind prove anything, the immortality of the protista seemed to be experimentally demonstrable.[189]

Other experimenters arrived at different results. Maupas, [48] Calkins and others, in contrast to Woodruff, found that after a certain number of divisions these infusoria become weaker, diminish in size, suffer the loss of some part of their organization and eventually die, unless certain recuperative measures are applied to them. If this is so, protozoa would appear to die after a phase of senescence exactly like the higher animals – thus completely contradicting Weismann's assertions that death is only[190] a late acquisition of living organisms.

From the aggregate of these experiments two facts emerge which seem to offer us a firm footing.[191] First: If two of the animalculae, at the moment before they show signs of senescence, are able to coalesce with each other, that is to 'conjugate' (soon after which they once more separate), they are saved from growing old and become 'rejuvenated'. Conjugation is no doubt the forerunner of the sexual reproduction of higher creatures; it is as yet unconnected with propagation and is limited to the mixing of the substances of the two individuals. (Weismann's 'amphimixis'.) The recuperative effects of conjugation can, however, be replaced by certain stimulating agents, by alterations in the composition of the fluid which provides their nourishment, by raising their temperature or by shaking them. We are reminded of the celebrated experiment made by J. Loeb, in which, by means of certain chemical stimuli, he induced segmentation in sea-urchins' eggs – a process which can normally occur only after fertilization.

Secondly: It is probable nevertheless that infusoria die a natural death as a result of their own vital processes. For the contradiction between Woodruff's findings and the others is due to his having provided each generation with fresh nutrient fluid. If he omitted to do so, he observed the same signs of senescence as the other experimenters. He concluded that the animalculae were injured by the products of metabolism which they extruded into the surrounding fluid. He was then able to prove conclusively that it was only the products of its *own* metabolism which had fatal results for the particular kind of animalcule. For the same animalculae which inevitably perished if they were crowded together in their own nutrient fluid flourished in a solution which was oversaturated with the waste products of a distantly related species. An infusorian, therefore, if it is left to itself, dies a natural death owing to

189 For this and what follows see Lipschütz (1914, 26 and 52 ff.).

190 *LA*: 'only' omitted in C onwards – presumably printer's error in C.

191 *PH*: *SE* introduces a paragraph break here.

its incomplete voidance of the products of its own metabolism. (It may be that the same [49] incapacity is the ultimate cause of the death of all higher animals as well).

At this point the question may well arise in our minds whether any object whatever is served by trying to solve the problem of natural death from a study of the protozoa. The primitive organization of these creatures may conceal from our eyes important conditions which, though in fact present in them too, only become *visible* in higher animals where they are able to find morphological expression. And if we abandon the morphological point of view and adopt the dynamic one, it becomes a matter of complete indifference to us whether natural death can be shown to occur in protozoa or not. The substance which is later recognized as being mortal[192] has not yet become separated in them from the immortal one. The drive forces which seek to conduct life into death may also be operating in protozoa from the first, and yet their effects may be so completely concealed by the life-preserving forces that it may be very hard to find any direct evidence of their presence. We have seen, moreover, that the observations and experiments[193] made by biologists allow us to assume that internal processes of this kind leading to death do occur also in protista. But even if protista turned out to be immortal in Weismann's sense, his assertion that death is a late acquisition would apply only to its manifest[194] phenomena[195] and would not make impossible the assumption of processes tending towards it.[196] Thus our expectation that biology would flatly contradict[197] the recognition of death drives has not been fulfilled. We are at liberty to continue concerning ourselves with their possibility, if we have other reasons for doing so.

The striking similarity between Weismann's distinction of soma and germ plasm and our separation of the death drives from the life drives persists and retains its significance.

We may pause for a moment over this pre-eminently dualistic view of the life of the drives. According to E. Hering's theory, two kinds of processes are constantly at work in living substance, operating in contrary directions, one constructive-assimilatory[198] and the other destructive-dissimilatory. May we

192 *LA*: in D onwards 'mortal' is changed to 'immortal' and vice versa.
193 *LA*: 'and experiments' omitted in C onwards – printer's error?
194 *PH*: 'manifest' and 'tending' italicised in *SE*.
195 *LA*: corrected from 'effects'.
196 *PH*: *SE* introduces paragraph break here.
197 *LA*: corrected from 'make impossible'.
198 *LA*: from C onwards the hyphens in this and the following combination are dropped and replaced by 'or', 'or'.

venture to recognize in these two directions taken by the vital processes the activity of our two groups of drives,[199] the life drives and the death drives? There is something else, at any rate, that we cannot remain blind to. We have unwittingly [50] steered our course into the harbour of Schopenhauer's philosophy. For him death is the 'true result and to that extent the purpose of life',[200] while the sexual drive is the embodiment of the will to live.

Let us make a bold attempt at another step forward. It is generally considered that the union of a number of cells into a vital association – the multicellular character of organisms – has become a means of prolonging their life. One cell helps to preserve the life of another, and the community of cells can survive even if individual cells have to die. We have already heard that conjugation, too, the temporary coalescence of two unicellular organisms, has a life-preserving and rejuvenating effect on both of them. Accordingly, we might attempt to apply the libido theory which has been arrived at in psychoanalysis to the mutual relationship of cells. We might suppose that the life drives or sexual drives which are active in each cell take the other cells as their object, that they partly neutralize the death drives (that is, the processes set up by them) in those cells and thus preserve their life; while the other cells do the same for *them*, and still others sacrifice themselves in the performance of this libidinal function. The germ cells themselves would behave in a completely 'narcissistic' fashion – to use the phrase that we are accustomed to use in the theory of the neuroses to describe a whole individual who retains his libido in his ego and pays none of it out in object cathexes. The germ cells require their libido, the activity of their life drives, for themselves, as a reserve against their later momentous constructive activity.[201] (The cells of the malignant neoplasms which destroy the organism should also perhaps be described as narcissistic in this same sense: pathology is prepared to regard their germs as innate and to ascribe embryonic attributes to them.)[202] In this way the libido of our sexual drives would coincide with the Eros of the poets and philosophers which holds all living things together.

Here then is an opportunity for looking back over the slow development of our libido theory. In the first instance the analysis of the transference neuroses forced upon our notice the opposition between the sexual drives,[203] which

199 *LA*: C onwards alters to 'drive impulses' – presumably printer's error in C.

200 Schopenhauer (1851; Sämtliche Werke, ed. Hübscher, 1938, 5, 236). *LA*: in C the quotation marks close after 'result' – presumably printer's error in C.

201 *LA*: the manuscript has a paragraph break here, which was then cancelled with a correction mark.

202 *PH*: addition dated in *SE*.

203 *LA*: 'sexual drives' and 'ego drives' placed in inverted commas in D onwards.

are[204] directed towards an object, and certain other drives, with which we were very insufficiently acquainted and which we described [51] provisionally as the ego drives. A foremost place among these was necessarily given to the drives serving the self-preservation of the individual. It was impossible to say what other distinctions were to be drawn among them. No knowledge would have been more valuable as a foundation for true psychological science than an approximate grasp of the common[205] characteristics and possible distinctive features of the drives. But in no region of psychology were we groping more in the dark. Everyone assumed the existence of as many drives or 'basic drives' as he chose, and juggled with them like the ancient Greek natural philosophers with their four elements – earth, air, fire and water. Psychoanalysis, which could not escape making *some* assumption about the drives, kept at first to the popular division of drives typified in the phrase 'hunger and love'. At least there was nothing arbitrary in this; and by its help the analysis of the psychoneuroses was carried forward quite a distance. The concept of sexuality,[206] and at the same time of the sexual drive, had, it is true, to be extended so as to cover many things which could not be classed under the reproductive function; and this caused no little hubbub in an austere, respectable or merely hypocritical world. The next step was taken when psychoanalysis felt its way closer towards the psychological ego, which it had first come to know only as a repressive, censoring agency, capable of erecting protective structures,[207] reactive formations. Critical and far-seeing minds had, it is true, long since objected to the concept of libido being restricted to the energy of the sexual drives directed towards an object. But they failed to explain how they had arrived at their better knowledge or to derive from it anything of which analysis could make use. Advancing more cautiously, psychoanalysis observed the regularity with which libido is withdrawn from the object and directed on to the ego (the process of introversion); and, by studying the libidinal development of children in its earliest phases, came to the conclusion that the ego is the true and original reservoir of libido, [52] and that it is only from that reservoir that libido is extended on to objects. The ego now found its position among sexual objects and was at once given the foremost place among them. Libido which was in this way lodged in the ego was described as '*narcissistic*'.[208] This narcissistic libido was of course

204 *LA*: corrected from 'become'.
205 *LA*: inserted below the line.
206 *LA*: inverted commas added from D onwards.
207 *PH*: *SE* has 'and reactive formations' – this may be due to the omission of a comma after 'reactive formations' in C – presumably printer's error.
208 See my paper on narcissism (1914c) [Section I]. *LA*: italics removed from 'narcissistic' in C onwards.

also a manifestation of the force of the sexual drive in the analytical sense of those words, and it had necessarily to be identified with the 'self-preservative drives' whose existence had been recognized from the first. Thus the original opposition between the ego drives and the sexual drives proved to be inadequate. A portion of the ego drives was seen to be libidinal; sexual drives – probably alongside others – operated in the ego. Nevertheless we are justified in saying that the old formula which lays it down that psychoneuroses are based on a conflict between ego drives and sexual drives contains nothing that we need reject today. It is merely that the distinction between the two kinds of drives which was originally regarded as in some sort of way *qualitative*, must now be characterized differently – namely as being *topographical*. And in particular it is still true that the transference neuroses, the essential subject of psychoanalytic study, are the result of a conflict between the ego and the libidinal cathexis of objects.

But it is all the more necessary for us to lay stress upon the libidinal character of the self-preservative drives now that we are venturing upon the further step of recognizing the sexual drive as Eros, the preserver of all living[209] things, and of deriving the narcissistic libido of the ego[210] from the stores of libido by means of which the cells of the soma are attached to one another. But we now find ourselves suddenly faced by another question. If the self-preservative drives too are of a libidinal nature, are there perhaps no other drives whatever but the libidinal ones? At all events there are none other visible. But in that case we shall after all be driven to agree with the critics who suspected from the first that psychoanalysis explains *everything* by sexuality, or with innovators like Jung who, making a hasty judgement, have used the word libido to mean 'drive force'[211] in general. Must not this be so?

It was not[212] our intention[213] at all events to produce such a result. Our argument had as its point of departure a sharp distinction between ego drives, which we equated with death drives, [53] and sexual drives, which we equated with life drives. (We were prepared at one stage to include the so-called self-preservative drives of the ego among the death drives; but we must now correct ourselves on this point and withdraw it.)[214] Our views have from the very first been *dualistic* and today they are even more definitely dualistic than

209 *LA*: C onwards omits 'living' – printer's error in C?

210 *LA*: 'of the ego' added in at the beginning of a line.

211 *PH*: *SE* places 'libido', not 'drive force', in inverted commas.

212 *LA*: corrected to 'It would not be' from C onwards.

213 *PH*: italicised in *SE*.

214 *LA*: in D onwards the last clause altered to 'but we subsequently corrected ourselves on this point and withdrew it'.

before – now that we describe the opposition as being, not between ego drives and sexual drives but between life drives and death drives. Jung's libido theory is on the contrary monistic;[215] the fact that he has called his one drive force 'libido' is bound to cause confusion, but need not affect us otherwise.[216] We suspect that drives other than the libidinal ones of self-preservation operate in the ego, and it ought to be possible for us to point to them. Unfortunately, however, the analysis of the ego has made so little headway that it is very difficult for us to do so. It is possible, indeed, that the libidinal drives in the ego may be linked in a peculiar manner ('interlocked', to borrow a term from Alfred Adler)[217] with these other ego drives which are still strange to us. Even before we had any clear understanding of narcissism, psychoanalysts had a suspicion that the 'ego drives' had libidinal components attached to them. But these are very uncertain possibilities, to which our opponents will pay very little attention. The difficulty remains that psychoanalysis has not enabled us hitherto to point to any drives[218] other than the libidinal ones. That, however, is no reason for our falling in with the conclusion that no others in fact exist.

In the obscurity that reigns at present in the theory of the drives, it would be unwise to reject any idea that promises to throw light on it. We started out from the great opposition between the life and death drives. Now object love itself presents us with a second example of a similar polarity – that between love (or affection) and hate (or aggressiveness). If only we could succeed in relating these two polarities to each other and in deriving one from the other! From the very first we recognized the presence of a sadistic component in the sexual drive.[219] As we know, it can make itself independent and can, in the form of a perversion, dominate an individual's entire [54] sexual activity. It also emerges as a predominant component drive in one of the 'pregenital organizations', as I have named them. But how can the sadistic drive, whose aim it is to injure the object, be derived from Eros, the preserver of life? Is it not plausible to suppose that this sadism is in fact a death drive which, under the influence of the narcissistic libido, has been forced away from the ego and has consequently only emerged in relation to the object? It now enters the service of the sexual function. During the oral stage of organization of the libido, the act of obtaining erotic mastery over an object coincides with that object's destruction; later, the sadistic drive separates off, and finally, at

215 *PH*: italicised in *SE*.
216 *PH*: *SE* notes the date of the addition.
217 *LA*: the phrase concerning Adler omitted in D onwards. *RSE*: In the first edition only: '– by drive "confluence", to borrow a term used by Adler [1908] – '.
218 *PH*: *SE* inserts 'ego-' in square brackets.
219 This was already so in the first edition of *Three Essays on the Theory of Sexuality* in 1905.

the stage of genital primacy, it takes on, for the purposes of reproduction, the function of overpowering the sexual object to the extent necessary for carrying out the sexual act. It might indeed be said that the sadism which has been forced out of the ego has pointed the way for the libidinal components of the sexual drive, and that these follow after it to the object. Wherever the original sadism has undergone no mitigation or intermixture, we find the familiar ambivalence of love and hate in erotic life.[220]

If such an assumption as this is permissible, then we have met the demand that we should produce an example of a death drive – though, it is true, a displaced one. But this way of looking at things is very far from being easy to grasp and creates a positively mystical impression. It looks suspiciously as though we were trying to find a way out of a highly embarrassing situation at any price. We may recall, however,[221] that there is nothing new in an assumption of this kind. We put one forward on an earlier occasion, before there was any question of an embarrassing situation. Clinical observations led us at that time to the view that masochism, the component drive which is complementary to sadism, must be regarded as sadism that has been turned round upon the subject's own ego.[222] But there is no difference in principle between a drive turning from an object to the ego and its turning from the ego to an object – which is the new point now under discussion. Masochism,[223] the turning round of the drive upon the subject's own ego, would [55] in that case be a return to an earlier phase of the drive's history, a regression. The account that was formerly given of masochism requires emendation as being too sweeping in one respect: there *might* be such a thing as primary masochism – a possibility which I had contested at that time.[224]

Let us, however, return to the self-preservative sexual drives. The experiments upon protista have already shown us that conjugation – that is, the coalescence of two individuals which separate soon afterwards without any subsequent cell-division occurring – has a strengthening and rejuvenating effect upon both of them.[225] In later generations they show no signs of

220 *LA*: the last two sentences pasted into the manuscript as an insertion.

221 *LA*: 'however' omitted in C – printer's error?

222 See my *Three Essays* (1905d); and 'Instincts and Their Vicissitudes' (1915c).

223 *LA*: crossed out 'Sadism'.

224 A considerable portion of these speculations have been anticipated by Sabina Spielrein (1912) in an instructive and interesting [*LA*: 'and interesting' inserted below the line] paper which, however, is unfortunately not entirely clear to me. She there describes the sadistic components of the sexual drive as 'destructive'. A. Stärcke (1914), again, has attempted to identify the concept of libido itself with the biological concept (assumed on theoretical grounds) of an impetus towards death. See also Rank (1907). All these discussions, like that in the text, give evidence of the demand for a clarification of the theory of the drives such as has not yet been achieved.

225 See the account quoted above from Lipschütz (1914).

degenerating and seem able to put up a longer resistance to the injurious effects of their own metabolism. This single observation may, I think, be taken as typical of the effect produced by sexual union as well. But how is it that the coalescence of two only slightly different cells can bring about this renewal of life? The experiment which replaces the conjugation[226] of protozoa by the application of chemical or even of mechanical stimuli (cf. Lipschütz, 1914) enables us to give what is no doubt a conclusive reply to this question. The result is brought about by the influx of fresh amounts of stimulus. This tallies well with the hypothesis that the life process of the individual[227] leads for internal reasons to an abolition of chemical tensions, that is to say, to death, whereas union with the living substance of a different individual increases those tensions, introducing what may be described as fresh 'vital differences' which must then be lived off. As regards this dissimilarity there must of course be one or more optima. The dominating tendency of mental life, and perhaps of nervous life in general, is the effort to reduce, to keep constant or to remove internal tension due to [56] stimuli (the 'Nirvana principle', to borrow a term from an English author[228] Barbara Low [1920, 73]) – a tendency which finds expression in the pleasure principle; and our recognition of that fact is one of our strongest reasons for believing in the existence of death drives.

But we still feel our line of thought appreciably hampered by the fact that we cannot ascribe to the sexual drive the characteristic of a compulsion to repeat which first put us on the track of the death drives. The sphere of embryonic developmental processes is no doubt extremely rich in such phenomena of repetition; the two germ cells that are involved in sexual reproduction and their life history are themselves only repetitions of the beginnings of organic life. But the essence of the processes to which sexual life is directed is the coalescence of two cell bodies. That alone is what guarantees the immortality of the living substance in the higher organisms.

In other words, we need more information on the origin of sexual reproduction and of the sexual drives in general. This is a problem which is calculated to daunt an outsider and which the specialists themselves have not yet been able to solve. We shall therefore give only the briefest summary of whatever seems relevant to our line of thought from among the many discordant assertions and opinions.

226 *LA*: C onwards has 'copulation'.

227 *LA*: 'of the individual' inserted above the line.

228 *LA*: 'English author' omitted in C onwards.

One of these views deprives the problem of reproduction of its mysterious fascination by representing it as a part manifestation of growth. (Cf. multiplication by fission, sprouting or gemmation.) The origin of reproduction by sexually differentiated germ cells might be pictured along sober Darwinian lines by supposing that the advantage of amphimixis, arrived at on some occasion by the chance conjugation[229] of two protista, was retained and further exploited in later development.[230] On this view 'sex' would not be anything very ancient; and the extraordinarily violent drives whose aim it is to bring about [57] sexual union would be repeating something that had once occurred by chance and had since become established as being advantageous.

The question arises here, as in the case of death, whether we do right in ascribing to protista those characteristics alone which they actually exhibit, and whether it is correct to assume that forces and processes which become visible only in the higher organisms originated in those organisms for the first time. The view of sexuality we have just mentioned is of little help for our purposes. The objection may be raised against it that it postulates the existence of life drives already operating in the simplest organisms; for otherwise conjugation,[231] which works counter to the course of life and makes the task of ceasing to live more difficult, would not be retained and elaborated but would be avoided. If, therefore, we are not to abandon the hypothesis of death drives, we must suppose them to be associated from the very first with life drives. But it must be admitted that in that case we shall be working upon an equation with two unknown quantities.[232]

Apart from this, science[233] has so little to tell us about the origin of sexuality that we can liken the problem to a darkness into which not so much as a ray of a hypothesis has penetrated. In quite a different region, it is true, we do[234] meet with such a hypothesis; but it is of so fantastic a kind – a myth rather than a scientific explanation – that I should not venture to produce it here, were it not that it fulfils precisely the one condition whose fulfilment we desire. For it traces the origin of a drive to *a need to restore an earlier state of things.*

229 *LA*: C onwards has 'copulation'.

230 Though Weismann (1892) denies this advantage as well: 'In no case does fertilization correspond to a rejuvenescence or renewal of life, nor is its occurrence necessary in order that life may endure: it is merely an arrangement which renders possible *the intermingling of two different hereditary tendencies.*' [English translation, 1893, 231.] He nevertheless believes that an intermingling of this kind leads to an increase in the variability of the organism concerned.

231 *LA*: C onwards has 'copulation'.

232 *LA*: paragraph break omitted in C onwards – presumably printer's error.

233 *LA*: corrected from 'the literature' in manuscript.

234 *PH*: italicised in *SE*.

What I have in mind is, of course, the theory which Plato put into the mouth of Aristophanes in the *Symposium*, and which deals not only with the origin[235] of the sexual drive but also with the most important of its variations in relation to its object.

'The original human nature was not like the present, but different. In the first place, the sexes were originally three in number, not two, as they are now; there was man, woman, and the union of the two '[236] Everything about these primaeval men was double: they had four hands and four feet, two paces, two privy parts, and so on. Eventually Zeus decided to cut these men in two, 'like a sorb apple which is halved for pickling'. After the division had been made, 'the two parts of man, [58] each desiring his other half, came together, and threw their arms about one another eager to grow into one'.[237]

Shall we follow the hint given us by the poet-philosopher, and venture upon the hypothesis that living substance at the time of its coming to life was torn apart into small particles, which have ever since endeavoured to reunite through the sexual drives? that these drives, in which the chemical affinity of inanimate matter persisted, gradually succeeded, as they developed through the kingdom of the protista, in overcoming the difficulties put in the way of that endeavour by an environment charged with dangerous stimuli – stimuli which compelled them to form a protective cortical layer? that these splintered fragments of living substance in this way attained a multicellular

---

235 *PH*: italicised in *SE*.

236 *LA*: in B Freud used Rudolf Kassner's translation for this and the following quotation from Plato. In E onwards this was exchanged for a rendering by Ulrich von Wilamowitz-Moellendorff and a footnote was added with the citation '*Platon* I, p. 366'.

237 [*SE*: Jowett's translation. Footnote added 1921:] I have to thank Professor Heinrich Gomperz, of Vienna, for the following discussion on the origin of the Platonic myth, which I give partly in his own words. It is to be remarked that what is essentially the same theory is already to be found in the Upanishads. For we find the following passage in the *Brihadâranyaka-upanishad*, 1, 4, 3 [Max Müller's translation, 2, 85 f.], where the origin of the world from the Atman (the Self or Ego) is described: 'But he felt no delight. Therefore a man who is lonely feels no delight. He wished for a second. He was so large as man and wife together. He then made this his Self to fall in two, and then arose husband and wife. Therefore Yagñavalkya said: "We two are thus (each of us) like half a shell." Therefore the void which was there, is filled by the wife.'
The *Brihadâranyaka-upanishad* is the most ancient of all the Upanishads, and no competent authority dates it later than about the year 800 B.C. In contradiction to the prevailing opinion, I should hesitate to give an unqualified denial to the possibility of Plato's myth being derived, even if it were only indirectly, from the Indian source, since a similar possibility cannot be excluded in the case of the doctrine of transmigration. But even if a derivation of this kind (through the Pythagoreans in the first instance) were established, the significance of the coincidence between the two trains of thought would scarcely be diminished. For Plato would not have adopted a story of this kind which had somehow reached him through some oriental tradition – to say nothing of giving it so important a place – unless it had struck him as containing an element of truth.
In a paper devoted to a systematic examination of this line of thought before the time of Plato, Ziegler (1913) traces it back to Babylonian origins.

condition and finally transferred the drive for reuniting, in the most highly concentrated form, to the germ cells? – But here, I think, the moment has come for breaking off.

[59] Not, however, without the addition of a few words of critical reflection. It may be asked whether and how far I am myself convinced of the truth of the hypotheses that have been set out in these pages. My answer would be that I am not convinced myself and that I do not seek to persuade other people to believe in them. Or, more precisely, that I do not know how far I believe in them. There is no reason, as it seems to me, why the emotional factor of conviction should enter into this question at all. It is surely possible to throw oneself into a line of thought and to follow it wherever it leads out of simple scientific curiosity, or, if the reader prefers, as an advocatus diaboli, who is not on that account himself sold to the devil. I do not dispute the fact that the third step in the theory of drives, which I have taken here, cannot lay claim to certainty[238] in the same way as the two earlier ones – the extension of the concept of sexuality and the hypothesis of narcissism. These two innovations were a direct translation of observation into theory and were no more open to sources of error than is inevitable in all such cases. It is true that my assertion of the regressive character of drives also rests upon observed material – namely on the facts of the compulsion to repeat. It may be, however, that I have over-estimated their significance. And in any case it is impossible to pursue an idea of this kind except by repeatedly combining factual material with what is purely speculative and thus diverging widely from empirical observation. The more frequently this is done in the course of constructing a theory, the more untrustworthy, as we know, must be the final result. But the degree of uncertainty is not assignable. One may have made a lucky hit or one may have gone shamefully astray. I do not think a large part is played by what is called 'intuition' in work of this kind. From what I have seen of intuition, it seems to me to be the product of a kind of intellectual impartiality. Unfortunately, however, people are seldom impartial where ultimate things, the great problems of science and life, are concerned. Each of us is governed in such cases by deep-rooted internal prejudices, into whose hands our speculation unwittingly plays. Since we have such good grounds for being distrustful, our attitude towards the results of our own deliberations cannot well be other than one of cool benevolence. I hasten to add, however, that self-criticism such as this is far from binding one to any special tolerance towards dissentient opinions. It is [60] perfectly legitimate to

[238] *LA*: in D onwards amended to 'the same degree of certainty as the two…'.

reject remorselessly theories[239] which are contradicted by the very first steps in the analysis of observed facts, while yet being aware at the same time that the validity of one's own theory is only a provisional one.[240]

I[241] need not feel greatly disturbed in judging our speculation upon the life and death drives by the fact that so many bewildering and obscure processes occur in it – such as one drive being driven out by another or a drive turning from the ego to an object, and so on. This is merely due to our being obliged to operate with the scientific terms, that is to say with the figurative language, peculiar to psychology (or, more precisely, to depth psychology). We could not otherwise describe the process in question at all, and indeed we could not have become aware of them. The deficiencies in our description would probably vanish if we were already in a position to replace the psychological terms by physiological or chemical ones. It is true that they too are only part of a figurative language; but it is one with which we have long been familiar and which is perhaps a simpler one as well.

On the other hand it should be made quite clear that the uncertainty of our speculation has been greatly increased by the necessity for borrowing from the science of biology. Biology is truly a land of unlimited possibilities. We may expect it to give us the most surprising information and we cannot guess what answers it will return in a few dozen years to the questions we have put to it. They may be of a kind which will blow away the whole of our artificial structure of hypotheses. If so, it may be asked why I have embarked upon such a line of thought as the present one, and in particular why I have decided to make it public. Well – I cannot deny that some of the analogies, correlations and connections which it contains seemed to me to deserve consideration.[242]

---

239 *LA*: corrected from 'teachings' in manuscript.

240 *LA*: paragraph break omitted in C onwards – presumably printer's error in C.

241 *LA*: amended to 'we' in C onwards.

242 I will add a few words to clarify our terminology, which has undergone some development in the course of the present work. We came to know what the 'sexual drives' were from their relation to the sexes and to the reproductive function. We retained this name after we had been obliged by the findings of psychoanalysis to connect them less closely with reproduction. With the hypothesis of narcissistic libido and the extension of the concept of libido to the individual cells, the sexual drive was transformed for us into Eros, which seeks to force together and hold together the portions of living substance. What are commonly called the sexual drives are [*LA*: amended to 'were' in D onwards] looked upon by us as the part of Eros [61] which is directed towards objects. Our speculations have suggested that Eros operates from the beginning of life and appears as a 'life drive' in opposition to the 'death drive' which was brought into being by the coming to life of inorganic substance. These speculations seek to solve the riddle of life by supposing that these two drives were struggling with each other from the very first. [*RSE*: This footnote does not appear in the manuscript. Freud evidently added it while correcting the proofs (Grubrich-Simitis (1996), *Back to Freud's texts*, p. 187 n. 13)]. It is not so easy, perhaps, to follow the transformations through which the concept of the 'ego drives' has passed. To begin with we applied that name to all drive trends (of which we had no closer knowledge) which could be distinguished from the sexual drives directed towards an object; and we opposed the

VI[243]

[62] If it is really the case that seeking to restore an earlier state of things is such a universal characteristic of drives, we need not be surprised that so many processes take place in mental life independently of the pleasure principle. This characteristic would be shared by all the component drives and in their case would aim at returning once more to a particular stage in the course of development. These are matters over which the pleasure principle has as yet no control; but it does not follow that any of them are necessarily opposed to it, and we have still to solve the problem of the relation of the drive processes of repetition to the dominance of the pleasure principle.

We have found that one of the earliest and most important functions of the mental apparatus is to bind the drive impulses which impinge on it, to replace the primary process prevailing in them by the secondary process and convert their freely mobile cathectic energy into a mainly quiescent (tonic) cathexis. While this transformation is taking place no attention can be paid to the development of unpleasure; but this does not imply the suspension of the pleasure principle. On the contrary, the transformation occurs on *behalf* of the pleasure principle; the binding is a preparatory act which introduces and assures the dominance of the pleasure principle.

Let us make a sharper distinction than we have hitherto made between function and tendency. The pleasure principle, then, is a tendency operating in the service of a function whose business it is to free the mental apparatus entirely from excitation or to keep the amount of excitation in it constant or to keep it as low as possible. We cannot yet decide with certainty in favour of any of these ways of putting it; but it is clear that the function thus described would be concerned with the most universal endeavour of all living substance – namely to return to the quiescence of the inorganic world. The pleasure drive, which governs all psychical life, is in this respect no different from the other organic drives, which somatic excitation conveys to the psychical.[244]

---

ego drives to the sexual drives of which the libido is the manifestation. Subsequently we came to closer grips with the analysis of the ego and recognized that a portion of the 'ego drives' is also of a libidinal character and has taken the subject's own ego as its object. These narcissistic self-preservative drives had thenceforward to be counted among the libidinal sexual drives. The opposition between the ego drives and the sexual drives was transformed into one between the ego drives and the object drives, both of a libidinal nature. But in its place a fresh opposition appeared between the libidinal (ego and object) drives and others, which must be presumed to be present in the ego and which may perhaps actually be observed in the destructive drives. Our speculations have transformed this opposition into one between the life drives (Eros) and the death drives. [62] [*PH*: the dating of the second half of the footnote noted in *SE*].

243 *LA*: corrected to 'VII' in B onwards.

244 *LA*: this sentence is deleted from B onwards.

We have all experienced how the greatest pleasure attainable by us, that of the sexual act,[245] is associated with a momentary extinction of a[246] highly intensified excitation. The binding of a drive impulse would be a preliminary function designed to prepare the excitation for its final elimination in the pleasure of discharge.

[63] This raises the question of whether feelings of pleasure and unpleasure can be produced equally from bound and from unbound excitatory processes. And there seems to be no doubt whatever that the unbound or primary processes give rise to far more intense feelings in both directions than the bound or secondary ones. Moreover the primary processes are the earlier in time; at the beginning of mental life there are no others, and we may infer that if the pleasure principle had not already been operative in them[247] it could never have been established for the later ones. We thus reach what is at bottom no very simple conclusion, namely that at the beginning of mental life the pleasure drive[248] was far more intense than later but not so unrestricted: it had to submit to frequent interruptions. In later times the dominance of the pleasure principle is very much more secure, but the drive[249] itself has no more escaped the process of taming than the other drives in general.[250]

In any case, whatever it is that causes the appearance of feelings of pleasure and unpleasure in processes of excitation must be present in the secondary process just as it is in the primary one. Perhaps the so-called feelings of tension that our consciousness mediates internally, along with feelings of pleasure and unpleasure, should actually be attributed to the bound processes, whereas the direct feelings of pleasure and unpleasure should be attributed to the unbound processes and the processes of discharge. Perhaps the occurrence of pleasurable and unpleasurable tension will be rendered more comprehensible to us by means of this distinction.

I consider it superfluous to try to excuse either the timidity or the uncertainty of these speculations. Whoever wishes to isolate the actuality behind them should turn his attention to the phenomenon of the *compulsion to repeat.*[251]

---

245 *LA*: this phrase inserted below the line.

246 *LA*: before this word, crossed-out: 'any' in manuscript.

247 *PH*: italicised in *SE*.

248 *LA*: corrected to 'struggle for pleasure' in B onwards.

249 *LA*: 'it' substituted for 'the drive' in B onwards.

250 *LA*: 'in general' inserted by hand, and 'other' crossed out at the same time, but the deletion was perhaps mistakenly not carried over into C. Paragraph break removed in B onwards.

251 *LA*: in B the whole passage running from 'Perhaps the so-called feelings…' to '… compulsion to repeat' was crossed out. There follows a handwritten addition, which was crossed out in turn: 'There is a competing view, however, which would aim to correlate feelings of tension with the absolute quantity

Here might be the starting-point for fresh investigations.[252] Our consciousness communicates to us feelings from within not only of pleasure and unpleasure but also of a peculiar tension which in its turn can be either pleasurable or unpleasurable. Should the difference between these feelings enable us to distinguish between bound and unbound processes of energy? or is the feeling of tension to be related to the absolute magnitude, or perhaps to the level, of the cathexis, while the pleasure and unpleasure series indicates a change in the magnitude of the cathexis within a given unit of time? Another striking fact is that the life drives have so much more contact with our internal perception – emerging as breakers of the peace[253] and constantly producing tensions whose release is felt as pleasure – while the death drives seem to do their work unobtrusively. The pleasure principle seems actually to serve the death drives. It is true that it keeps watch upon stimuli from without, which are regarded as dangers by both kinds of drives; but it is more especially on guard against increases of stimulation from within, which would make the task of living more difficult. This in turn raises a host of other questions to which we can at [64] present find no answer. We must be patient and await fresh methods and occasions of research. We must be ready, too, to abandon a path again[254] that we have followed for a time, if it seems to be leading to no good end. Only believers, who demand that science shall be a substitute for the catechism they have given up, may[255] blame an investigator for developing or even transforming his views. We may take comfort, too, for the slow advances of our scientific knowledge in the words of the poet:

> Was man nicht erfliegen kann, muss man erhinken.
> … … … .
> Die Schrift sagt, es ist keine Sünde zu hinken.[256]

and level of cathected energy, while correlating pleasure and unpleasure with changes in quantity over time. The two possibilities are not compatible with each other and…'. [See the reproduction of the original typescript in *Psychoanalysis and History* 2015 (2), Figure 1, p. 204].

252 *PH*: see reproduction of the original handwritten paragraph in *Psychoanalysis and History* 2015 (2), p. 272.

253 *LA*: 'emerging as breakers of the peace' added subsequently.

254 *RSE*: this word was omitted in the *SE* translation.

255 *LA*: amended to 'will' in F.

256 *SE*: ['What we cannot reach flying we must reach limping… The Book tells us it is no sin to limp.' The last lines of 'Die beiden Gulden', a version by Rückert of one of the *Maqâmât* of al-Hariri.].

The Third Step in Drive Theory: On the Genesis of *Beyond the Pleasure Principle*[1]

Ulrike May

Thirty years ago Ilse Grubrich-Simitis reported a find in the Freud Archive[2] of the Library of Congress.[3] She had discovered there two manuscript versions of Freud's *Beyond the Pleasure Principle*.[4] Grubrich-Simitis's report would be referred to in reviews of her book and in several articles;[5] however, nobody to date has followed up this indication and subjected these versions to closer examination. It is my intention to do that here.

This will begin with an attempt at identifying and dating the two manuscripts. After that I shall briefly present the main thesis of *Beyond the Pleasure Principle*, sketch the context of the work, and finally, concentrate on the main theme of this study: a comparison of the two versions with each other and with the text subsequently published in several editions. Whether or not my interpretation carries conviction, at all events it will be evident that the long-drawn-out process from which *Beyond the Pleasure Principle* emerged, and which is revealed here for the first time, offers us an insight into the driving forces of Freud's theory formation.

In this present work I shall refer only very selectively to the literature on *Beyond the Pleasure Principle*, and I regret that I cannot discuss numerous contributions on the death drive and on Freud's text; and neither its controversial early reception nor later articles and books.[6] I hope I shall be able to make up for that elsewhere.

---

1 [Translated by Michael Molnar] I am grateful to the participants of *Freudianische Liebhabereien II* (St. Gilgen 2012), to friends in the Alpine Forum for the History of Psychoanalysis, to members of the Berlin Freud Group, as well as to Friedl Früh, Thomas Aichhorn and Jean-Daniel Sauvant for their interest in my work. I owe particular thanks to Dr Leonard Bruno (Library of Congress) for his committed support of my research.

2 The collection of Sigmund Freud Papers at the Library of Congress in Washington will henceforth be abbreviated to SFP/LoC.

3 I. Grubrich-Simitis (1996), *Back to Freud's Texts: Making Silent Documents Speak*, pp. 182–191.

4 S. Freud (1920g), *Beyond the Pleasure Principle*, *SE* 18, pp. 1–64.

5 See, for example, M. Solms (1994), 'Review'; L. Schacht (1995), 'Review'; F.-W. Eickhoff (1995), 'Review'; T. Aichhorn (2006), 'Jenseits des Lustprinzips', p. 159; E. Falzeder (2007), 'Is there still an unknown Freud?', p. 207; P.-L. Assoun (2009), *Dictionnaire des oeuvres psychanalytiques*, p. 223.

6 As representative examples I would name the volume *On Freud's "Beyond the Pleasure Principle"* in

I. Two manuscript versions of Beyond the Pleasure Principle

The published text of *Beyond the Pleasure Principle*, hitherto the only one known, appeared in late November 1920.[7] It was corrected and slightly enlarged by Freud himself for the second (1921) and third (1923) editions, as well as for its publication in the *Gesammelte Schriften* (1925). Alterations to the text on these occasions were, with some exceptions, documented in the *Standard Edition*, as also in the *Studienausgabe*, which was based upon it. But the content of the two above-mentioned manuscript versions of *Beyond the Pleasure Principle* from the Washington archive was not previously known in any detail, nor how they relate to the published version. Only now can the versions be compared, using the critical edition published here (pp. 29–80), which reflects every definable stage of textual production.

It is certain that both manuscripts of *Beyond the Pleasure Principle* were composed at different times.[8] In the earlier version, henceforth referred to as the 'first version', we are dealing with a final copy in Freud's handwriting; in the catalogue of the Sigmund Freud Papers at the Library of Congress, which is available on the internet, it is entered as "holograph manuscript".[9] It consists of 34 sides and is divided into six chapters; the script contains few corrections.[10] Title and author head the first page. Preceding it is a cover page, obviously added later, on which "*Beyond the Pleasure Principle*. 1920" has been noted in Freud's handwriting. A cursory glance at the title may have led to the supposition that the manuscript originated in 1920 – which is, however, not the case.

---

the series *Contemporary Freud* (edited by S. Akhtar & M.K. O'Neil, 2011) with recent contributions on this work. Further, O. Kernberg (2009), 'The Concept of the Death Drive'; J. Laplanche (1986), 'Der Todestrieb in der Theorie des Sexualtriebes'; J. Laplanche (2004), 'The so-called "Death Drive": A Sexual Drive'; C. Schmidt-Hellerau (2006), 'Surviving in Absence'; F.J. Sulloway (1979), *Freud: Biologist of the Mind*; in German, among much else: Aichhorn (2006), 'Jenseits des Lustprinzips'; H. Beland (2008), 'Erklärungs- und arbeitswert der Todestriebhypothese'; J.F. Danckwardt (2011), 'Die Verleugnung des Todestriebs'; C. Frank (2011), 'Zum Ringen mit Manifestationen des Todestriebes'; F. Früh (2011), 'Zu Todestrieb und Wiederholungszwang in Freuds "Jenseits des Lustprinzips"'; U. Hock (2000), *Das Unbewußte Denken*; G. Kimmerle (1988), *Verneinung und Wiederkehr*; C. Kirchhoff (2011), 'Von der Wiederkehr des unbewußten Wunsches als Todestrieb'; R. Krause (2012), 'Psychodynamische Aspekte der Gedächtnisfunktion'; H. Müller-Pozzi (2008), *Eine Triebtheorie für unsere Zeit*; B. Reiter (1996), 'Dunkel is das Leben, ist der Tod'.

7 S. Freud & G. Groddeck (2008), *Briefwechsel*, p. 134.

8 As to their provenance, it is to be noted that the first version must have entered the Library of Congress as a result of the transfer of Freud's estate in 1986. The second version was handed over to the Freud Archive in 1970. It came from the estate of Max Eitingon, who had been given it as a present. Presumably he had it bound in the form it is today. Grubrich-Simitis (1996), *Back to Freud's Texts*, p. 90; E. Gumbel (1995), 'Über mein Leben mit der Psychoanalyse', p. 61; S. Freud & M. Eitingon (2004), *Briefwechsel 1906–1939*, p. 884 (Letter 782 E).

9 A. Teichroew & F. Bauman (2011), *Sigmund Freud Papers*. Location of both earlier versions: Box OV 7, Reel 3.

10 For a facsimile of the opening page, see Grubrich-Simitis (1996), *Back to Freud's Texts*, p. 184.

The second manuscript version of *Beyond the Pleasure Principle*, described in the Sigmund Freud Papers at the Library of Congress catalogue as "holograph and typewritten manuscript, bound", is a bound volume that includes both entirely handwritten (31) and also typed (42) pages.[11] This manuscript is also inscribed "*Beyond the Pleasure Principle* / by / Sigm. Freud". It has seven chapters, that is, one chapter more than the first version. The typed pages include glued handwritten interpolations and handwritten corrections.

Comparing the first and second versions, one soon realises that the typed part of the latter is identical with the former. Freud therefore wrote a first version by hand, had it typed, and worked over the typescript again by hand, presumably over several periods of work.[12] In this way he wrote an entire new chapter for the second version and inserted it between the fifth and sixth chapters of the first version. The new chapter was given the number 6, while the previous sixth chapter became chapter 7 in the second version.

To clarify the difference between the first and second versions: the former consists of ca. 74,000 characters, the latter ca. 120,000 (including spaces and footnotes). Therefore the first version constitutes only about 60% of the text of the second version. I concur with Grubrich-Simitis's evaluation that the first and second versions differ so sharply that they can be considered "two manifestations of a work in progress".[113] As will later become clear, the differences relate not only to the length, but above all to the content.

While the first and second versions differ extensively, the difference between the second manuscript and the first printed version, i.e. the first edition, are comparatively limited; they are more or less equal in number to the differences between the four printed editions. In terms of both quantity and content, the difference between the first and second versions is by far the most significant.

Below I shall set out what we know about the genesis of *Beyond the Pleasure Principle*. Since the extensive studies by Jones (1962), Schur (1973) and Grubrich-Simitis (1993), new sources have become accessible which have a bearing on Freud's work on *Beyond the Pleasure Principle*; above all his complete correspondences with Abraham, Ferenczi and Eitingon, as well as with his daughter Anna.

---

11 Ibid., p. 183.

12 See also ibid., p. 186; ink and/or writing instruments vary.

13 Ibid., p. 186. Grubrich-Simitis points out that apart from *Beyond the Pleasure Principle* there is only one other Freud text – namely *Moses and Monotheism* (1939a) – of which an earlier version survives that differs so sharply from the published text. Ibid., p. 182; see also I. Grubrich-Simitis (1997), 'Freud's Study of Moses as a Day-dream'.

1. On the dating of the first version: mid-March to mid-April 1919

The start of setting down the first version is well documented. On 17 March 1919, in a letter to Ferenczi, Freud mentioned the project for the first time: "I finished a [...] paper on the genesis of masochism, which bears the title 'A child is being beaten'. A second one with the mysterious heading Beyond the Pleasure Principle is in process".[14] Subsequently, in further letters to Ferenczi in late March, we hear that Freud was "amusing myself greatly" and wanted to have the work "copied in order to hear your opinion about it";[15] in it he was "saying many things that are quite unclear, out of which the reader has to make the right thing. Sometimes one can't do otherwise".[16] Presumably he finished writing out *Beyond the Pleasure Principle* before 18 April, since on that day Freud mentioned it in the past tense to Jones. He thanked him for a fountain pen that he had received from him, and continued: "My last two productions, 'Ein Kind wird geschlagen' and *Jenseits des Lustprinzips* which you will have to criticise one day, were written under bodily pain caused by a bad pen".[17] My assumption as to the time when the writing down was completed is based on this remark. I consider it significant, because Freud always expressed himself with precision. If he had not ended the manuscript by 18 April, he would not have used "were written" in the past tense.[18]

The reference to the pen provides another clue on dating when it was written down. In March 1919, Jones travelled to Switzerland, where he met Rank and Sachs. On 17 March, he wrote to Freud from Bern that he had brought him a pen from London.[19] Rank returned to Vienna on 11 April;[20] on 18 April Freud thanked Jones for the pen, which Rank must have delivered to him.[21] Thus Freud could have written the final pages of *Beyond the Pleasure Principle* between 11 and 18 April with the new pen. A first impression, which would need verifying by comparison with the holograph, argues against this. The handwriting of the manuscript appears uniform, and in fact seems rather

14 S. Freud & S. Ferenczi (1993–2000), *The Correspondence of Sigmund Freud and Sándor Ferenczi, Vol. 2*, p. 335 (Letter 794 F).

15 Ibid., p. 340 (Letter 799 F).

16 Ibid., p. 341 (Letter 800 F).

17 S. Freud & E. Jones (1993), *The Complete Correspondence of Sigmund Freud and Ernest Jones 1908–1939*, p. 341 (Letter 237 F).

18 In contrast to Strachey and Grubrich-Simitis, who date the completion of the manuscript to 'May' or 'early May', here it is attributed to a few weeks earlier. Both authors clearly base themselves on Freud's letter to Ferenczi quoted in the next paragraph but one. Freud (1920g), *Beyond the Pleasure Principle*, p. 3; Grubrich-Simitis (1996), *Back to Freud's Texts*, p. 185.

19 Freud & Jones (1993), *Complete Correspondence*, p. 337 (Letter 234 J).

20 Freud & Ferenczi (1993–2000), *Correspondence, Vol. 2*, p. 345 (Letter 805 F).

21 Freud & Jones (1993), *Complete Correspondence*, p. 341 (Letter 237 F).

to have been written with a 'bad pen' and as if against some mechanical resistance, so that one can justify the assumption that the writing was, at the latest, finished by 18 April. At all events, Freud committed the first version to paper in the course of no more than a few weeks. One may marvel how that was possible, while involved in a full-time practice; I will return to this question later (see Appendix I).

On 12 May, Freud informed Ferenczi of an inhibition to his productivity, which had begun on 6 May after he had found out from Lajos Lévy that Anton von Freund's cancer had broken out again. He added: "I had not only completed the draft of *Beyond the Pleasure Principle*, which is being copied out for you, but I also took up the little thing about the 'uncanny' again, and, with a simple-minded idea [*Einfall*], I attempted a Ψa foundation for group psychology".[22] Here Freud is not only confirming that the draft of *Beyond the Pleasure Principle* was already finished by 6 May, but is also noting that the manuscript would be transcribed for Ferenczi, an intention that he had announced in late March. Clearly this 'draft' is identical with the first version presented here, of which there was not only a handwritten but also a typed version that survives in the glued manuscript of the second version.[23]

The fact that the manuscript was for Ferenczi and not for another pupil, and that Freud wanted an exchange of opinions with him above all and hoped for his "understanding" that he had "not yet abandoned me in any situation",[24] relates to projects that preoccupied both of them. I will discuss these in depth in Appendix I.[25]

---

22 Freud & Ferenczi (1993–2000), *Correspondence, Vol. 2*, p. 354 (Letter 813 F).

23 Since the postal service to Budapest was particularly unreliable during the spring of 1919 and functioned best by means of messengers, Freud would not have mailed the typescript to Ferenczi. There were no visits on either side during the spring and summer of 1919. Ferenczi probably did not see the typescript until autumn when he visited Vienna. Hence it is understandable why he made no comment on *Beyond the Pleasure Principle* between May and September 1919. See, for example, ibid., pp. 330, 342, 368; A. Huppke & M. Schröter (2011), 'IPV-Sekretär und Mäzen', pp. 91f.

24 Freud & Ferenczi (1993–2000), *Correspondence, Vol. 2*, p. 341 (Letter 800 F).

25 The first version itself includes two remarks that have a bearing upon the date of its origin and can thus serve as a control for the dating. The first is Freud's reference to the volume on the war neuroses, which is already mentioned in the first version with all bibliographical details (in this volume, p. 33). Since the volume was distributed in May 1919, but was already in print in early April 1919, no contradiction to the above-assumed date exists. The second remark concerns an essay on children's games that had "recently been published by S. Pfeifer in *Imago*" (in this volume, p. 35). Freud had read this essay in June 1918 and had already at the time stated that "something else, something more comprehensive remains to be said about children's games". The text was then printed in the fourth issue of the fifth volume of *Imago*, dated 1919. Exactly when this issue appeared is not known. It was definitely not yet in print in February, because Freud asked Ferenczi on 13 February to check Pfeifer's contribution for its style. This means the announcement that the journal had "recently" appeared could well refer to March or April, and would also be consistent with the period of origin posited here. Freud (1920g),

Freud's letter to Ferenczi on 12 May shows that, having completed the first version of *Beyond the Pleasure Principle*, he wrote 'The Uncanny',[26] which was completed by 10 July 1919, while he was still in practice.[27] After that, from 15 July, he went on holiday to Bad Gastein, taking with him the first version of *Beyond the Pleasure Principle*.[28] Then began months of rethinking and reworking.

2. On the dating of the second version: July 1919 to July 1920

While one can date the beginning and completion of the first version fairly accurately, there are few reliable indications as to the genesis of the second version. Above all, we have no references to when exactly the various insertions and the new sixth chapter came into being. The question must therefore remain open of when Freud decided to introduce the term 'death drive', which appears in print in the new chapter for the first time.

At the same time, it is worth bearing in mind when and how Freud commented on his work on *Beyond the Pleasure Principle* during the period from July 1919 to July 1920, and what questions occupied his attention. That year he was working on new editions of several publications and preparing the next great theme, the *Group Psychology*,[29] but only wrote one new article, namely 'The psychogenesis of a case of homosexuality in a woman' (more on this context below).[30] In my view this indicates how deeply his thoughts were preoccupied by *Beyond the Pleasure Principle*.

I shall now proceed to document Freud's comments on the projects he pursued from July 1919 to July 1920. In four letters during the summer holidays of 1919, Freud reported what he was working on at the time, and each time it was *Beyond the Pleasure Principle*. On 21 July he wrote to Anna from Bad Gastein that he was devoting his time "to the manuscript of *Beyond the Pleasure Principle*, which I brought with me and which is developing well here".[31] A week later he wrote to her that he was now reading Schopenhauer's works, having requested Rank to send him them. The reading was helping him

Beyond the Pleasure Principle, pp. 12, 224; Freud & Eitingon (2004), *Briefwechsel*, p. 151 (Letter 137 F); S. Freud & K. Abraham (2002), *Complete Correspondence*, p. 395; Freud & Ferenczi (1993–2000), *Correspondence, Vol. 2*, pp. 289, 332 (Letters 751 F, 790 F).

26 S. Freud (1919h), 'The Uncanny', *SE* 17.

27 Freud & Ferenczi (1993–2000), *Correspondence, Vol. 2*, pp. 354, 363 (Letters 813 F, 817 F).

28 Ibid., p. 363.

29 S. Freud (1921c), *Group Psychology and the Analysis of the Ego*, *SE* 18.

30 S. Freud (1920a), 'The Psychogenesis of a Case of Homosexuality in a Woman', *SE* 18.

31 S. Freud & A. Freud (2013), *Correspondence 1904–1938*, p. 152.

"with the work that I have brought with me".[32] At this time he also told Jones and Andreas-Salomé that he was working on *Beyond the Pleasure Principle.*[33] To the latter he said he had "chosen the theme of death for my old age" and now had to "read whatever goes with that e.g. for the first time Schopenhauer". In the first version of *Beyond the Pleasure Principle*, Schopenhauer was not mentioned, so Freud was here too referring to the second version.[34]

On 13 August 1919, Freud left Gastein.[35] He continued his holidays in Badersee (near Garmisch-Partenkirchen), from where he thanked Pfister for sending a book, which he was reading at that time because he "was having a quiet rest".[36] Eitingon, who with his wife had rented accommodation in the vicinity, had a "look" at the manuscript of *Beyond the Pleasure Principle.*[37] He thus became the first pupil to read the new essay, in the form of its first version. Later he would speak a number of times about the work, which corresponded to his own philosophical inclinations. Perhaps this was why Freud gave him the original of the second version (see footnote 8).

On 9 September 1919, Freud and the Eitingons left Badersee; Freud for Hamburg to visit his daughter Sophie. On the return journey he stopped over in Berlin on 23 September, met Abraham and Eitingon, and spent the afternoon in Abraham's house, leaving in the evening to return to Vienna by sleeper car.[38] He later told Wittels that at the time he gave "several friends in Berlin" a manuscript of *Beyond the Pleasure Principle* to read; the text was not yet finished: "the only missing part was on the mortality or immortality of protozoa".[39] This suggests that it was the first version, in which the sixth chapter is missing, which deals with single- and multicellular organisms. Therefore, on the journey to Hamburg, or perhaps only on the return journey, Freud handed to his Berlin colleagues the typescript of the first version of *Beyond the Pleasure Principle*, perhaps a carbon copy of the transcript prepared for Ferenczi. At any rate Abraham also took the opportunity to read the text. This is of relevance, because neither his private correspondence with Freud nor his later *Rundbriefe* from Berlin include any reference to *Beyond the Pleasure*

---

32 Ibid., p. 163.

33 Freud & Jones (1993), *Complete Correspondence*, p. 353 (Letter 248 F); S. Freud & L. Andreas-Salomé (1972), *Letters*, p. 99.

34 Freud (1920g), *Beyond the Pleasure Principle*, p. 50.

35 Freud & Freud (2013), *Correspondence*, p. 173.

36 S. Freud & O. Pfister (1963), *Psychoanalysis and Faith: the Letters of Sigmund Freud and Oskar Pfister*, p. 72. The book was *The Erotic Motive* (1919) by Albert Mordell: it has no discernible connection to the themes of *Beyond the Pleasure Principle.* See E. Jones (1957), *The Life and Work of Sigmund Freud, Vol. 3*, p. 473.

37 Freud & Eitingon (2004), *Briefwechsel*, p. 209 (Letter 180 F).

38 Ibid., p. 160; Freud & Abraham (2002), *Complete Correspondence*, pp. 403f. and n. 1.

39 S. Freud (1924g), 'Letter to Fritz Wittels', *SE* 19, p. 287 n. 1.

Principle, not even during the months when the work was being intensively and contentiously discussed within the committee.[40]

With Ferenczi it was another matter. After Freud had returned to Vienna and resumed his practice on 1 October 1919, the travel ban between Hungary and Austria was lifted. Ferenczi visited Freud in late September for a few days, possibly even longer, and in early November for at least a week.[41] A letter of 20 November indicates that the conversation was very enlivening for Ferenczi. He and Freud "were able to exchange such a wealth of insights as perhaps never before". He had already written the two reviews of the "biological works" that Freud had requested from him.[42] This refers to an essay by Schaxel on the basic questions of theoretical biology[43] and Lipschütz's book *Die Pubertätsdrüse und ihre Wirkungen* [Puberty Glands and their Function] (1919); Ferenczi had reviewed them both for the *Internationale Zeitschrift* für Psychoanalyse.[44]

The remarks quoted above offer a clue to Freud's interests at the time. Together with Ferenczi, he was preoccupied by the question of the relationship between psychoanalysis and biology, an interest that they had shared for a long time (see Appendix I). The choice of works reviewed by Ferenczi is indicative. In his book, Alexander Lipschütz, a pupil of Eugen Steinach in Vienna and at that time *Privatdozent* in Bern, presented the latest state of affairs in biological sex research, and in doing so based his work primarily upon the sensational research of Steinach, who had managed to change the manifest sex of animals and men through operatively transplanting testicles and ovaries; among other things he had 'feminized' male homosexuals. More or less in passing, Lipschütz also gave credit to Freud's sexual theory, to which Ferenczi naturally referred in his review.[45] For his part, on the last two pages of 'The psychogenesis of a case of homosexuality in a woman', Freud mentioned Steinach's work, which could not leave him indifferent because it touched upon the fundamental suppositions of the theory of sexuality, namely that of constitutional bisexuality.[46] Here then lies one link between that article – the only work that Freud wrote during the months in which he was pondering the

---

40 Naturally, it must remain an open question whether that is not simply because the relevant sources have not survived. What can be stated with certainty, however, is that *Beyond the Pleasure Principle* left no mark on Abraham's theoretical work; he could not or would not use it for his own thought.

41 Freud & Ferenczi (1993–2000), *Correspondence, Vol. 2*, pp. 368–369 (Letter 821 Fer); Freud & Pfister (1963), *Letters*, p. 72; S. Freud (2010), *Unterdeß halten wir zusammen*, p. 549; K. Fallend (1995), *Sonderlinge, Träumer, Sensitive*, p. 183.

42 Freud & Ferenczi (1993–2000), *Correspondence, Vol. 2*, p. 368 (Letter 821 Fer).

43 J. Schaxel (1919), *Über die Darstellung allgemeiner Biologie*.

44 S. Ferenczi (1920a), 'Rezension Lipschütz'; S. Ferenczi (1920b), 'Rezension Schaxel'.

45 A. Lipschütz (1919), *Die Pubertätsdrüse und ihre Wirkungen*, pp. 125, 127; Ferenczi (1920a), 'Rezension Lipschütz', pp. 136f.

46 Freud (1920a), 'The Psychogenesis of a Case of Homosexuality in a Woman', pp. 171f.

first version of *Beyond the Pleasure Principle* – and his overriding conceptual interests at the time.

On the publications of Julius Schaxel, the evolutionary biologist and University Chair at Jena, suffice to say that they were of great interest to Ferenczi and Freud because of their emphasis on sexuality and because of their understanding of life and death.[47]

In passing, it is worth noting that the preoccupation with sexual biology also left an impression on the fourth edition of *Three Essays on the Theory of Sexuality*, which Freud was working on in May 1920. He added a new section ('Chemical theory') as well as two long additions to footnotes, in which he discusses Lipschütz and Steinach on the biological bases of sexual difference.[48] But it is above all in *Beyond the Pleasure Principle* that references to Lipschütz's work occur.[49] His comprehensive presentation of biological research on mortality and immortality, death and life is an important point of reference for the new, sixth chapter.[50] In some passages Freud follows him surprisingly closely, as is documented in Appendix II.[51] There, I also discuss the other biologists that Freud deals with in the sixth chapter of *Beyond the Pleasure Principle*.

Ferenczi's remarks in his letter of 20 November 1919 support the assumption that in the autumn of 1919, Freud was continuing to pursue the questions he had posed in the first version of *Beyond the Pleasure Principle*. I consider it probable that conversations with Ferenczi gave him new impetus to rework the text, and above all to compose the sixth, 'biological' chapter.[52]

In early December, there is more news from Freud himself. In a letter to Eitingon he writes: "I am very slowly studying drive and group psychology".[53] This appears to refer to reading biological and sociological works. It is certain that at that time Freud was reading Ferenczi's reviews of Schaxel and Lipschütz

---

47 Julius Schaxel (1887–1943), a pupil of Ernst Haeckel and at that time Professor of Zoology and Botany at Jena, took part as a guest at the new founding of the Swiss Society of Psychoanalysis on 24 March 1919, at which Jones, Rank and Sachs were also present (*Internationale Zeitschrift* für Psychoanalyse 6 [1920], p. 104). His first marriage was to Hedwig Schaxel, who later became a psychoanalyst. In the work reviewed by Ferenczi (1920b), he, like Freud, adopted a strictly mechanical, materialist point of view. E. Mühlleitner (1992), *Biographisches Lexikon der Psychoanalyse*, pp. 155f.; C. Reiss (2007), 'No Evolution, no Heredity, just Development'. On his life, which was marked by his commitment to socialism, see C. Reiss et al. (2008), 'Das autobiographische Manuskript des Entwicklungsbiologen Julius Schaxel'.

48 S. Freud (1905d), *Three Essays on the Theory of Sexuality*, *SE* 7, pp. 215–216, 146–147, 177.

49 Freud (1920g), *Beyond the Pleasure Principle*, pp. 47, 55.

50 A. Lipschütz (1914), *Warum wir sterben*.

51 Later, in a letter to Lipschütz, Freud remembers his book on puberty glands, from which he had "gained so much knowledge". S. Freud (1960), *The Letters of Sigmund Freud*, pp. 406–407.

52 See also Grubrich-Simitis (1996), *Back to Freud's Texts*, p. 190.

53 Freud & Eitingon (2004), *Briefwechsel*, p. 176 (Letter 154 F).

"with complete approval".[54] In January 1920 he wrote the study of female homosexuality to which we have referred.[55] In late January 1920, close together, came the deaths of Anton von Freund (on 20 January) and Freud's daughter Sophie (on 25 January). It is only one and a half months later, on 8 March 1920, that we once again hear something of Freud's projected work. In similar words to those he used in December, he informed Eitingon: "Meanwhile I am still working on group psychology and death drives, which will probably provide the contents for the still completely mysterious summer".[56] The term 'death drives' appears at this point for the first time in a letter, and this is also the first time since early August 1919 that Freud explicitly mentions *Beyond the Pleasure Principle*, or more exactly one of its central concepts – apart from the ambiguous mention of 'drive psychology' to Eitingon in December 1919. Not that the term 'death drives' was new, as will be shown. However, the letter referred to above is clear evidence that in March 1920 Freud was working on the topic of *Beyond the Pleasure Principle*.[57]

As mentioned, in mid-May he was working on *Three Essays on the Theory of Sexuality* for the fourth edition, into which he inserted the passages on Lipschütz and in the foreword referred to Schopenhauer and Plato's Eros, that is, to authors and concepts that play a part in *Beyond the Pleasure Principle* – in the second, not the first, version, and in its new sixth chapter. Since Freud is now mentioning the cornerstones and central referents of the second version and its corresponding print edition – Lipschütz, Schopenhauer, Plato – I am assuming that he had by then more or less completed the new theoretical orientation that marks the sixth chapter of *Beyond the Pleasure Principle*. It was on 24 May 1920 that he informed Jones, who was visiting Vienna, that after having prepared the new edition of *Three Essays on the Theory of Sexuality*, he was now turning to *Beyond the Pleasure Principle*.[58] A little later Eitingon would receive the same announcement: "I am now correcting and completing 'Beyond', namely the pleasure principle, and find myself once again in a productive phase".[59]

Hence it is certain that in late May 1920 Freud began his final work on the manuscript of *Beyond the Pleasure Principle*.[60] A few weeks later he was

54 Freud & Ferenczi (1993–2000), *Correspondence, Vol. 2*, p. 371 (Letter 824 F).
55 Jones (1957), *The Life and Work, Vol. 3*, p. 42.
56 Freud & Eitingon (2004), *Briefwechsel*, p. 194 (Letter 168 F).
57 In both letters to Eitingon, "group psychology" and "death drives", or "drive psychology", appear next to each other, a relationship that gives food for thought.
58 Freud & Jones (1993), *Complete Correspondence*, pp. 382–383 (Letter 277 F).
59 Freud & Eitingon (2004), *Briefwechsel*, p. 207 (Letter 178 F).
60 The assertion that on 16 June Freud read a résumé of *Beyond the Pleasure Principle* to the Vienna Group comes from Jones. But no such presentation is recorded on this or any other evening around this

feeling "quite well and capable of accomplishment".[61] He was planning on completing the text in June and July: it had "yielded some strange sequels".[62] On 18 July 1920, Freud had finally reached the point at which he could announce that the work was finished to Ferenczi and Eitingon, who were the ones most interested in the topic of *Beyond the Pleasure Principle*: "The 'Beyond' is finished".[63]

In a letter to Eitingon one finds the remark: "You will be able to confirm that it [the manuscript; U.M.] was half ready when Sophie was alive and blooming".[64] Freud was thus himself positing a link between *Beyond the Pleasure Principle* and his daughter's death, which would later be suspected by Fritz Wittels and others. Jones is among those who found his objection to this interpretation "not valid". He considers that Freud "did not want to admit" that the new ideas about mortality and immortality, which are central to the sixth chapter, were "influenced by his depression over losing his daughter".[65] In contrast, I consider that Freud's presentation is correct. For in the summer of 1919 at Badersee, Eitingon did in actual fact have a 'look' at the draft of *Beyond the Pleasure Principle* and read it in September 1919; and this draft, i.e.

---

period in the protocols of the Vienna Society. Jones (1957), *The Life and Work, Vol. 3*, p. 42; Fallend (1995), *Sonderlinge, Träumer, Sensitive*, pp. 202ff.

61 Freud & Ferenczi (1993–2000), *Correspondence, Vol. 3*, p. 29 (Letter 848 F).

62 Ibid.

63 Ibid., p. 32; cf. Freud & Eitingon (2004), *Briefwechsel*, p. 213 (Letter 184 F). Grubrich-Simitis questions whether this message might not refer to an abbreviated draft of the sixth chapter. If this were the case, Freud would have had to have written out a ready copy of this extensive and weighty chapter in a short time, since the entire manuscript of *Beyond the Pleasure Principle* was already with the typesetter on 3 August. Grubrich-Simitis (1996), *Back to Freud's Texts*, p. 191 n. 22; Freud & Eitingon (2004), *Briefwechsel*, p. 215 (Letter 185 F).
No control of the dating similar to that of the first version is possible for the second and print versions, because the mention of Sophie's death (in the print version) or the new edition of *Three Essays* (in the second version) and other remarks do not permit any convincing conclusions to be drawn as to the dating. This applies also to the insertion of the name Barbara Low, known to have suggested the term 'Nirvana principle', into the print version, in place of the anonymous "English author". Freud had received Low's *Psycho-Analysis* (1920) from Jones, who had written a foreword for it dated 30 August 1919. Low was a member of the English group and had various private, analytic and professional relationships with Jones, Ferenczi and Freud. It should be pointed out that Low's Nirvana principle meant something different from Freud's. She writes: "It is possible that deeper than the Pleasure-principle lies the Nirvana-principle, as one may call it – the desire of the newborn creature to return to that stage of omnipotence, where there are no non-fulfilled desires, in which it existed within the mother's womb". Thus she relates the Nirvana principle to the wish to return to the womb, to a state of (prenatal) omnipotence, similar to that described by Ferenczi (1913). As in other cases (Groddeck's 'Id'; Näcke's 'Narcissism', see U. May[-Tolzmann] (1991), 'Zu den Anfängen des Narzißmus'), Freud thus took over solely the term 'Nirvana principle', but not its meaning. Freud (1920g), *Beyond the Pleasure Principle*, p. 56; Freud & Jones (1993), *Complete Correspondence*, p. 383 (Letter 277 F); P. King & R. Steiner (1992), *The Freud-Klein Controversies*, p. xvii; Freud & Ferenczi (1993–2009), *Correspondence, Vol. 3*, p. 21 (Letter 845 F); B. Low (1920), *Psycho-Analysis*, p. 73.

64 Freud & Eitingon (2004), *Briefwechsel*, p. 213 (Letter 184 F).

65 Jones (1957), *The Life and Work, Vol. 3*, p. 42.

the first version, already contains the fundamentals of the death drive concept, although the term 'death drive' does not occur there (see below).

I also view the course of the year in question (July 1919–July 1920) differently from Jones. He explains that Freud was "not satisfied" with the first draft and seemed to have let his work on *Beyond the Pleasure Principle* drop "until the following summer".[66] In contrast, I suspect that *Beyond the Pleasure Principle* was Freud's main interest between July 1919 and July 1920, and that he composed the second version between May and July 1920, perhaps even earlier. As will be described later, the alterations in the second version, namely the introduction of the third drive theory, were so radical that it must have taken considerable time for Freud to commit himself to them.[67]

Incidentally, I consider that the renewal of 'bioanalytic' conversations with Ferenczi in the autumn of 1919 played an important role in the reworking of *Beyond the Pleasure Principle*, for it is only in the second version that Freud deals at length with authors like Weismann, Lipschütz or Doflein – known representatives of the biological sciences. Possibly Jones was not aware how close the relationship between Freud and Ferenczi was at that time and how intensively they had been exchanging views for years on the connections between biology and psychoanalysis, during the course of which neither of them hesitated about following trains of thought that Jones himself considered "highly speculative" and "transmuted from some personal and profound source".[68] This might have influenced his conclusion that Freud had let the matter drop.

3. On the dating of the print version: July and/or August 1920

There are only insignificant differences between the second manuscript and the first print version of *Beyond the Pleasure Principle*.[69] I suspect that the alterations in question were added relatively late on, no doubt after 18 July when Freud described the manuscript as already finished. Early August is likely. At that time the work was already "with the typesetters".[70] When Freud wrote to Anna on 7 August that he was correcting the "old" work, he was

66 Ibid.

67 The numbering of the drive theories is managed in different ways. Some authors take the theory of death drive and Eros as the third, for example, Fenichel, others as the second drive theory, for example Quinodoz, according to what degree of autonomy is accorded to the theory of narcissism. O. Fenichel (1945), *The Psychoanalytic Theory of the Neuroses*); J.-M. Quinodoz (2011), *Freud lesen*, p. 313.

68 Jones (1957), *The Life and Work, Vol. 3*, pp. 43, 287.

69 In this article 'print version' always refers to the first edition.

70 Freud & Eitingon (2004), *Briefwechsel*, p. 215 (Letter 185 F).

referring to *Beyond the Pleasure Principle* – namely to the page proofs, which shortly afterwards would be mentioned by Jones.[71] Hence I am assuming that during his holidays, which he again took in Bad Gastein from 29 July to the end of August 1920, Freud added to the proofs those corrections by which the print differs from the second version. In early October, *Beyond the Pleasure Principle* was at the printer; it appeared in late November as a booklet [*Beiheft II*] accompanying the *Internationale Zeitschrift*.[72]

So much for the genesis of *Beyond the Pleasure Principle*. In all it took nearly one and half years, from March 1919 to July/August 1920 until the text had reached the stage when it was ready for publication. Freud did not just sit at his desk and write down his texts in one go, as the fair copy of his manuscripts might suggest. In the case of *Beyond the Pleasure Principle*, it seems to me rather that he was preoccupied by the theme for months – actually, as we will later see, for years – and worked his way thoroughly through the relevant literature before he even began to set down the first draft.[73]

Before I depict the different versions of *Beyond the Pleasure Principle* and compare them to each other, it is worth glancing at the reactions of some of Freud's pupils. They reveal, as I see it, the main reason for the controversial reception of the text, namely the shaky (empirical) foundation of Freud's principal thesis.

II. The clinical impetus for the third drive theory

The question of the origins of *Beyond the Pleasure Principle* has preoccupied the psychoanalytic community from the very beginning, starting with Wittels, who in his Freud biography first voiced the suspicion that Freud had written it as a reaction to the death of his daughter Sophie in January 1920.[74] Freud's previously mentioned objection to this had no effect. Further speculation on the biographical background of *Beyond the Pleasure Principle* followed – possibly determined by the particular character of the work which, from the

71 Freud & Freud (2013), *Correspondence*, p. 186 and n. 7; Freud & Jones (1993), *Complete Correspondence*, p. 389.

72 G. Wittenberger & C. Tögel (1999–2006), *Rundbriefe des Geheimen Komitees, Bd. 1*, p. 57; Freud & Groddeck (2008), *Briefwechsel*, p. 134.

73 This also applied to *Group Psychology*. In May 1919, Freud mentions a first idea; during the autumn and winter of 1919 and the spring of 1920 he was "studying" works on group psychology, and in August 1920 he wrote the first draft. Freud & Ferenczi (1993–2009), *Correspondence, Vol. 2*, p. 354 (Letter 813 F); *Vol. 3*, p. 33 (Letter 853 F); Freud & Jones (1993), *Complete Correspondence*, pp. 369, 373 (Letters 266 F, 269 F); Freud & Eitingon (2004), *Briefwechsel*, pp. 176, 194 (Letters 154F, 168 F).

74 F. Wittels (1924), *Sigmund Freud*, p. 251.

moment it was composed, disturbed and alienated even the most faithful students, and which remains controversial today, both for its introduction of the death drive and for the very manner of its introduction.[75]

Ferenczi, who was most easily able to follow the development of Freud's theories, expressed the fear that *Beyond the Pleasure Principle* would release a "philosophico-speculative tidal wave", which would be detrimental to psychoanalysis.[76] Freud found this prediction confirmed when in September 1922 he wrote to Eitingon after the Berlin IPA Congress that during some "speculative talks he felt "intensely haunted" by the thought that he was "the one to blame because of *Beyond the Pleasure Principle*".[77] Apart from that, Ferenczi stressed that he found that in *Beyond the Pleasure Principle* Freud had not distanced himself sufficiently from Jung.[78] The Jungian school could triumph and represent their master as "persecuted innocence", because Freud had equated libido with the life drives, or a "life-preserving principle", and thus defined it in a similar way to Jung. Jones expressed the same reservations, as did the Dutch analyst August Stärcke.[79] Even Eitingon did not keep to himself the problems that *Beyond the Pleasure Principle* was causing, and let Freud know that this text gave him "a lot to work on".[80] Though he could comprehend the difference between the death and life drives, "what founds the regressive character of the drives, the compulsion to repeat, remains as unclear to me now as it was at Badersee, when I first heard of it, or in Holland [i.e. at the Congress in The Hague]. In each of the three mentioned areas, in traumatic neuroses, in children's play and in the phenomenon of transference, I still see it as too much in the realm of the pleasure principle".[81] Similarly Jones, who read *Beyond the Pleasure Principle* "with mixed feelings":

75 For my own first assessment of the text, see U. May (2013), 'Freud's Beyond the Pleasure Principle: The end of psychoanalysis or its new beginning?'.

76 Wittenberger & Tögel (1999–2006), *Rundbriefe des Geheimen Komitees, Bd. 2*, p. 124.

77 Freud & Eitingon (2004), *Briefwechsel*, pp. 301f. (Letter 257 F).

78 Wittenberger & Tögel (1999–2006), *Rundbriefe des Geheimen Komitees, Bd. 2*, p. 124.

79 Ibid., p. 133. Freud reacted with several letters between September and November 1922 to discussions on this theme in the Dutch group (SFP/LoC, Box 47, Folder 7). He took the reservations of Ferenczi and Jones into account, by inserting two sentences into the second edition of *Beyond the Pleasure Principle* which he was preparing in May 1921, and in which he stressed that his conception was of a dualistic character, since he was postulating both death and life drives. Freud (1920g), *Beyond the Pleasure Principle*, p. 53; in this volume, p. 70).

80 Freud & Eitingon (2004), *Briefwechsel*, p. 217 (Letter 187 E).

81 Ibid., p. 229. In an extract several pages long from *Beyond the Pleasure Principle*, Eitingon inscribed two question marks in the left margin, at the very passage that deals with Freud's core proposition on the compulsion to repeat. See Freud (1920g), *Beyond the Pleasure Principle*, pp. 19–20; Eitingon Bequest, Israel State Archives, Jerusalem; with thanks to M. Schröter.

> 'Of the two main ideas, one is quite clear to me: the tendency of the instincts to repeat an old situation and if possible restore an equilibrium [...]. The second idea, that this is independent of the Lustprinzip, I have so far only imperfectly digested.'[82]

As far as I can see, the differentiation from Jung and from vitalism is no longer of any relevance. But, like Eitingon and Jones, do we not also find it difficult to accept the core ideas of *Beyond the Pleasure Principle*: namely that there are primary psychical processes or forces that do not obey the pleasure principle, as had been accepted for libidinal activity? According to Freud's new assumption, they would not strive towards pleasure and satisfaction, but in the last resort to the inorganic state, to death. Unerringly, impervious to influence, they repeat unpleasurable experiences, seeking no change but a return to previous stages of development. These psychical processes, modes of functioning, or forces could well underlie psychical symptoms, but do not operate according to the familiar pattern of the search for pleasure/satisfaction and the avoidance of unpleasure, and thus elude analytical intervention.

In my view, *Beyond the Pleasure Principle* deals with problems 'beyond' the scope of analysis – in other words, with the limits of psychoanalysis, about which, like Eitingon and Jones at the time, we are reluctant to hear. In studies of this work it is often stressed that in the course of time we have acquired a better understanding of phenomena like acting out and self-destructive behaviour, which left Freud helpless. We have, supposedly, made great progress in theory and technique since then, and, unlike Freud, are perfectly capable of

82 Freud & Jones (1993), *Complete Correspondence*, p. 389 (Letter 284 J). Jones retained his scepticism, or rejection, of anything 'beyond' the pleasure principle, and took the matter up again in letters to Freud during 1930 and 1935, but in terms of the tensions caused by differences between the so-called British and Viennese schools (ibid., pp. 667ff., 740ff.). As mentioned, no traces of Abraham's reaction survive. We only know that he gratefully acknowledged reception of *Beyond the Pleasure Principle*. However, it is not completely out of the question that the following passage in a letter of 19 October 1919 refers to *Beyond the Pleasure Principle* (in its first version): "A word about your last paper! I am most enthusiastic about it. It seems to me that you have never before penetrated so deeply into the uttermost depths of a problem. Moreover, the presentation is so beautifully comprehensible and clear that reading it is an outstanding intellectual and aesthetic pleasure". The editors of the correspondence identify this paper as 'The Uncanny', which is possible, since it appeared in issue 5/6 of *Imago*, which came out in autumn 1919. Apart from that, the description "beautifully comprehensible and clear" applies better to 'The Uncanny' than *Beyond the Pleasure Principle*. The only indication that Abraham might have had the latter in mind is a letter of 13 March 1920. He writes there: "I found 'The Uncanny' very gripping". This makes it seem as if he first read the text at this point, and not in October 1919. Wittenberger & Tögel (1999–2006), *Rundbriefe des Geheimen Komitees, Bd. 2*, p. 23; Freud & Abraham (2002), *Complete Correspondence*, pp. 405, 418. On Andreas-Salomé's reaction, see Freud & Andreas-Salomé (1972), *Letters*, pp. 105–106.

treating serious disturbances.[83] I must leave the question open as to whether this is indeed the case. At any rate, in *Beyond the Pleasure Principle*, Freud, as I understand him, was reworking his experiences of failed analyses, and trying to anchor them in theory.[84]

The experience of the limits of psychoanalysis was not new. Freud had always paid attention to which psychical disturbances were amenable to psychoanalysis and which were not, and he posited the criterion of accessibility to psychical influences as the prime marker in his classification of these disturbances. Moreover, he was thus defending himself against the accusation that he considered his method of treatment to be universally applicable. In the 1890s he categorised phenomena not to be treated by psychical methods as somatically conditioned disturbances,[85] and after the turn of the century as narcissistic disturbances, which he contrasted with the transference neuroses, which could be treated. I believe that in *Beyond the Pleasure Principle* he found a further answer to the question of inaccessibility to analysis, and condensed the forces opposing it into the concept of the death drive, which soon afterwards led to the concept of the negative therapeutic reaction.[86] Freud's increasing therapeutic pessimism is probably most marked in 'Analysis Terminable and Interminable'.[87] Here, the forces that defend themselves against the cure and bring about the failure of the analysis are derived from the death drive.[88] This is, as Strachey termed it in his editorial note, "the most powerful impeding factor of all and one totally beyond any possibility of control".[89]

83 See, for example, B. Joseph (1982), 'Addiction to Near-death'; M. Feldman (2011), 'Manifestations of the Death Instinct'.

84 M. Schur, too, was of the opinion that *Beyond the Pleasure Principle* could be traced back not least to the analyses of severely disturbed patients such as the Wolf Man, who after over a thousand hours of analysis (1910–1914) sought Freud out again in the spring of 1919, and from November 1919 to March 1920 underwent a short follow-up analysis: see S. Freud (1918b), 'From the History of an Infantile Neurosis', *SE* 17, pp. 121f.; S. Freud (1937c), 'Analysis Terminable and Interminable', *SE* 23, pp. 217f.; M. Schur (1972), *Sigmund Freud*, pp. 320f.; U. May (2008), 'Nineteen patients in analysis with Freud', pp. 67–69. Another serious case, among others, described by him as suffering from a "masochistic" problem, was Viktor von Dirsztay, whose many years of analysis, also more than a thousand sessions, ended in early 1920. See ibid., pp. 66–67; U. May (2011b), 'Fourteen Hundred Hours of Analysis with Freud'; U. May (2011c), 'Ein Ungarischer Baron in Analyse bei Freud'. Finally, the many years of Elfriede Hirschfeld's analysis ended in 1914 in "incurability", as Freud himself wrote. See E. Falzeder (1995), 'My Grand-Patient, my Chief Tormentor'; May (2008), 'Nineteen patients in analysis with Freud', pp. 69–70; S. Freud & L. Binswanger (1992), *The Sigmund Freud-Ludwig Binswanger Correspondence 1908–1938*, p. 132.

85 U. May[-Tolzmann] (1996), *Freuds frühe klinische Theorie.*

86 S. Freud (1923b), *The Ego and the Id*, *SE* 19.

87 Freud (1937c), 'Analysis Terminable and Interminable'.

88 Ibid., pp. 242–243.

89 Ibid., p. 212.

Incidentally, returning from my last visit to the Freud Archive in Washington, where I read a great number of unpublished letters from the period 1920 to 1939, I brought back a strong and unexpected impression – of Freud's sobering judgement of the limited prospects of analysis. When I subsequently worked on the early versions of *Beyond the Pleasure Principle*, this empirical aspect of the text struck me more forcibly, and I maintain that in *Beyond the Pleasure Principle* Freud published a theoretical turning point, at whose core lies a new conceptualisation of the efficacy of psychoanalysis, even though the work fulfils other, equally significant functions in terms of the tasks and projects that Freud pursued all his life.[90]

III. Beyond the Pleasure Principle in the context of Freud's contemporaneous publications

Over the period just before he began writing out the first version of *Beyond the Pleasure Principle*, during his work on the text and after completing the print version, Freud composed in all six further works.[91] The first two of these were produced in the weeks before the first version: the 'Introduction' to the booklet on the war neuroses, as well as 'A Child is Being Beaten',[92] which was first mentioned in late January and already finished by 17 March.[93] In early May, after Freud finished the first version of *Beyond the Pleasure Principle*, 'The Uncanny' makes its first appearance, and it was finished on 10 July 1919. During the years of work on the theme and manuscript of *Beyond the Pleasure Principle*, Freud wrote, as mentioned, only one single article: 'On the

90 See U. May (2012b), *Trauma und Konflikt in "Jenseits des Lustprinzips"*.

91 According to the Freud bibliography of I. Meyer-Palmedo & G. Fichtner (1999), *Freud-Bibliographie mit Werkkonkordanz*. This figure does not take into account obituaries, introductions or shorter pieces of no relevance to theory. In the new editions, too, that Freud worked on between January 1919 and August 1920 (for example, the sixth and seventh editions of *Psychopathology of Everyday Life*), there are no new commentaries relevant to theory, with the exception of the fourth edition of *Three Essays*, produced in May 1920. See Freud & Ferenczi (1993–2009), *Correspondence, Vol. 3*, p. 20 (Letter 844 F); Freud & Jones (1993), *Complete Correspondence*, pp. 382–383 (Letter 277 F).

92 S. Freud (1919d), 'Introduction to *Psycho-Analysis and the War Neuroses*', *SE* 17; S. Freud (1919e), 'A Child is being Beaten', *SE* 17.

93 On the dating of the introduction to the war neuroses, no exact information is available, nor is any to be found in Strachey's introduction to that text. Since Freud took up exactly the same position with regard to the aetiology of the war neuroses on 2 February in the Vienna Psychoanalytic Society as he did in the introduction, the text may well have been produced shortly before or after this date. Fallend (1995), *Sonderlinge, Träumer, Sensitive*, pp. 158f. On the dating of 'A child is being beaten': Freud & Ferenczi (1993–2000), *Correspondence, Vol. 2*, pp. 329, 335 (Letter 787 F, 794 F); Freud (2012a), 'Briefe an Kata und Lajos Lévy', p. 29.

Psychogenesis of a Case of Homosexuality in a Woman', which he finished in January 1920.[94] Until the completion of the print version of *Beyond the Pleasure Principle*, he produced nothing new, apart from the insertions into the fourth edition of *Three Essays*.[95] In the weeks after finishing *Beyond the Pleasure Principle*, two further works were written: the first draft of *Group Psychology and the Analysis of the Ego*, which was completed by 20 August 1920, as was 'Supplements to the Theory of Dreams'.[96]

There are close connections to *Beyond the Pleasure Principle* in all these texts. It could hardly be otherwise, for in writing them Freud could not have disregarded the present state of his research. In general, Freud's expositions are not comprehensible out of the context in which they originated. They do not represent firm, unchangeable 'findings' or a sum total of impressions and conclusions abstracted from the development of his theoretical thinking. They are stages in a chain of insights, which do not follow one another arbitrarily, but which are, from the author's viewpoint, evidence of a continual, well-grounded increase in knowledge. The following connections can be seen between *Beyond the Pleasure Principle* and other works of that period:

— in *Beyond the Pleasure Principle* Freud continues his reflections on the causes of traumatic neurosis. He had already in his early publications considered the place of trauma in the aetiology of neuroses. In the 'Introduction' to the booklet on the war neuroses he stated the most recent state of his thinking on the subject; in *Beyond the Pleasure Principle* it is taken a small step further.[97]

---

94 Freud (1920a), 'The Psychogenesis of a Case of Homosexuality in a Woman'.

95 Freud (1905d), *Three Essays on the Theory of Sexuality*.

96 Freud (1921c), *Group Psychology and he Analysis of the Ego*; S. Freud (1920f), 'Supplements to the Theory of Dreams'; Freud (1920g), *Beyond the Pleasure Principle*, pp. 4–5. On dating 'The Uncanny': Freud & Ferenczi (1993–2000), *Correspondence, Vol. 2*, pp. 354, 363 (Letters 813 F, 817 F). On 'Psychogenesis': ibid., *Vol. 3*, p. 4 (Letter 830 F). On *Three Essays*: Freud & Jones (1993), *Complete Correpondence*, pp. 382–383 (Letter 277 F). On *Group Psychology*: Freud & Ferenczi (1993–2000), *Correspondence, Vol. 2*, p. 354 (Letter 813 F); Freud & Freud (2013), *Correspondence*, p. 195; Freud & Ferenczi (1993–2000), *Correspondence, Vol. 3*, p. 33 (Letter 852 F).

97 In doing so in *Beyond the Pleasure Principle*, the approach to war and traumatic neuroses developed in the war neuroses 'Introduction' is left to one side. According to that, so to speak, 'structural' approach, war neurosis was a narcissistic neurosis, i.e. a disturbance of the ego, since its origin "has been made possible or has been promoted" by a conflict between an 'old' and a 'new' ego ideal. Freud (1919d), 'Introduction to *Psycho-Analysis and the War Neuroses*', p. 209; cf. also Freud & Ferenczi (1993–2000), *Correspondence, Vol. 2*, p. 305 (Letter 768 F); Fallend (1995), *Sonderlinge, Träumer, Sensitive*, p. 159.

— While working on the text, a modification of the view of masochism, which he had recently developed in 'A Child is Being Beaten', imposed itself upon him. The new view would be taken further in *The Ego and the Id* and above all in 'The Economic Problem of Masochism'.[98]
— In *Beyond the Pleasure Principle*, Freud further developed the concept of the compulsion to repeat, and differently from in 'Remembering, Repeating and Working-Through'.[99] In 'The Uncanny', which was completed after the first version of the text, he presented a preliminary stage of his new view. Here he depicted the compulsion to repeat in a particularly graphic form and referred to *Beyond the Pleasure Principle* as "another work, already completed, in which this has been gone into in detail".[100] The concept was consolidated in the second and print versions of the text.
— The link between *Beyond the Pleasure Principle* and 'On the Psychogenesis of a Case of Homosexuality in a Woman' is weaker, but no less tangible. As previously shown, in this article and in the fourth edition of *Three Essays*, Freud made references to biological aspects, which predominate in long passages of *Beyond the Pleasure Principle*, above all in the sixth chapter. This widening of the viewpoint better to take in 'life' and the organism takes up the tendency to found psychoanalytic concepts on a biological basis which can be seen from the very beginning in Freud's work. In this respect, *Beyond the Pleasure Principle*, with its new drive theory and new views on the theory of the psychical apparatus, represents a significant extension of the metapsychological studies of 1915,[101] which in turn, evidently, have their precedents, for example in the 'Two Principles', the first edition of *Three Essays*, the seventh chapter of *The Interpretation of Dreams* and the 'Project'.[102]

98 S. Freud (1923d), 'A Neurosis of Demoniacal Possession in the Seventeenth-Century', *SE* 19; S. Freud (1924c), 'The Economic Problem of Masochism', *SE* 19.

99 S. Freud (1914g), 'Remembering, Repeating and Working-Through', *SE* 12.

100 Freud (1919h), 'The Uncanny', p. 238.

101 Particularly, S. Freud (1915c), 'Instincts and Their Vicissitudes', *SE* 14; S. Freud (1915e), 'The Unconscious', *SE* 14; S. Freud (1985a), *A Phylogenetic Fantasy: Overview of the Transference Neuroses.*

102 S. Freud (1911b), 'Formulations on the Two Principles of Mental Functioning', *SE* 12; Freud (1905d), *Three Essays*; S. Freud (1900a), *The Interpretation of Dreams*, *SE* 4 & 5; S. Freud (1950c), 'Project for a Scientific Psychology', *SE* 1. In these publications perhaps Freud was dealing with various aspects of one complex of themes: the complexes of masochism and the compulsion to repeat. Just as he previously represented normal anal eroticism in 'Character and Anal Eroticism' and a neurotic variant in the 'Rat man' case, so he described a neurotic aspect of masochism and the compulsion to repeat in 'A Child is Being Beaten', and in 'The Uncanny' the normality of this compulsion, subsequently to include the metapsychological aspect in *Beyond the Pleasure Principle*, and to incorporate it into the general theory. S. Freud (1908b), 'Character and Anal Eroticism', *SE* 9; S. Freud (1909d), 'Notes upon a Case of Obsessional Neurosis', *SE* 10.

Just as *Beyond the Pleasure Principle* takes up earlier threads and lines of theory development and continues them, the writing that followed extends the thoughts contained in this work.

> — Thus 'Supplements to Dream Theory', Freud's lecture at the IPA Congress at The Hague, which has only survived in the form of the author's abstract, presents a first clinical application of the views Freud had arrived at in *Beyond the Pleasure Principle.* A continuation can be found in 'Remarks on the Theory and Practice of Dream-Interpretation' and in *The Ego and the Id,* above all in the concept of the super-ego as "a kind of gathering-place for the death instincts".[103]
> — The relationship between *Beyond the Pleasure Principle* and *Group Psychology and the Analysis of the Ego* remains obscure. It seems to me that Freud's ideas on the origins of multicellular organisms and the function of Eros are akin to his conception of the formation of groups and the cohesive function of identification.

This brief sketch is an attempt at drawing up the relevant connections between works from 1919 to 1921. *Beyond the Pleasure Principle* does not stand on its own, nor is it an aberration of Freud's that one should do one's best to ignore: it represents a step forward in his continual theorising, and one that he himself considered unavoidable. The alterations suggested there were of various types, and applied equally to clinical and to metapsychological theory, as well as to concepts drawn from practice, such as the compulsion to repeat. They furthered the state of theory at which Freud had arrived in early 1919, and formed a basis for changes that then followed.

IV. The first version: "far-fetched speculation", or a Beyond the Pleasure Principle *with neither death drive nor Eros*

One can read Freud's works as responses to questions that concerned him all his life. A first such question is the aetiology of neuroses and psychoses. It gave rise to the so-called clinical theory.[104] A second project that Freud pursued with equal persistence was metapsychology, i.e. an overall theory

103 S. Freud (1923c), 'Remarks on the Theory and Practice of Dream-Interpretation', *SE* 19; Freud (1923b), *The Ego and the Id,* p. 54.

104 See May[-Tolzmann] (1996), *Freuds frühe klinische Theorie.*

of psychical functioning, embracing both pathology and normality. A third project was aimed at elevating psychoanalysis to a fundamental discipline ranking above other sciences, to which it could contribute decisive input or at least collaboration, for example psychiatry, biology, psychology, sociology, literature, studies of religion and art, or philosophy.

In the light of these projects, *Beyond the Pleasure Principle* was a contribution to clinical theory, insofar as traumatic neurosis and the phenomenon of a compulsion to repeat that was inaccessible to therapy required the introduction of a new way of understanding them.[105] In addition, the text then became, in the first instance, a contribution towards metapsychology, since Freud had developed new ideas on the mode of functioning of the psychical apparatus and on the fate and hallmarks of energies and drives. In his reworking of the first version, *Beyond the Pleasure Principle* also became a contribution towards the conquest of biology, as part of the third project. There is probably no other Freud publication in which the human being is so positively presented as a biological entity that transmits life and dies itself – though one must bear in mind that more or less at the same time Freud sees humans primarily as social beings, namely in *Group Psychology*.

The most significant difference between the first and second versions of *Beyond the Pleasure Principle*, as I have stressed, is that the first version contains only six chapters and the second and the print versions seven. The chapter in which both the 'death drive' and its opponent 'Eros' appear for the first time is lacking in the first version. Equally, there is nothing on sadism or masochism in the first version; they are first mentioned in the second version. Thus the first version constitutes a *Beyond the Pleasure Principle* without death drive or Eros.

From the reader's viewpoint, the first version appears quieter and more considered, but is as dramatically scripted as the second and print versions. Freud takes great pains to awaken our curiosity and interest: he announces new principles and connections, and reveals them at the culmination of his discussion. In contrast to the second version, in the first one Freud is still

105 Recently Krause has drawn attention to the fact that *Beyond the Pleasure Principle* contains the very modern notion that psychical processes linked to traumatisation bore the characteristics of "freestanding self-regulating processes" not subject to the pleasure-unpleasure principle. Similarly Fernando, with his concept of "zero processes", links it explicitly to Freud's ideas in *Beyond the Pleasure Principle* of the existence of psychical processes that correspond neither to primary nor secondary processes. Both studies seem to me so significant that I have chosen to mention them, although I cannot otherwise address the secondary literature on *Beyond the Pleasure Principle*. Krause (2012), 'Psychodynamische Aspekte der Grundfunktion', p. 14; J. Fernando (2012), 'Trauma und der Zeroprozess'.

alone, by himself. He names only a few works by colleagues and pupils,[106] and does not yet refer to biology and philosophy: in the first version there is no mention of Schopenhauer, Plato, Fechner, Weismann, Lipschütz, Doflein, Max Hartmann or Fliess. It is, for the time being, only concerned with Freud's own thoughts and observations.

Nevertheless, it is in the first version that the great turning point is accomplished, abandoning a cornerstone of the metapsychological theorising that had to date prevailed – namely the assumption that the origins and primitive strata of mental life were ruled by the pleasure-unpleasure principle. All Freud's work to date without exception was marked by, and founded upon, this assumption; it underlaid neurosis theory, dream theory, the theory of relations to reality, and the theory of technique.

The turning point was accompanied by a great effort to bring the new into effect alongside the old, that is, to find a way of reconciling the changes with what had been asserted to date, or to bring about the transition without giving up previous views. In that respect it was not a correction, a case of a new theory replacing the old. Freud was, rather, trying to integrate new views and assumptions into previous theory in such a way that it would remain valid. At the end of the discussion, he himself admits that he has not succeeded in doing this to his own satisfaction.

It is true that in the first version of *Beyond the Pleasure Principle* (as in the manuscript and print versions), Freud makes contradictory claims. That does not mean he was not concerned about a conceptual integration of his presuppositions. He did not leave contradictions in place because the psyche is contradictory, but attempted to solve the contradictions, sometimes succeeding, sometimes not. More to the point: Freud cannot be co-opted to support the viewpoint that diminishing theoretical aspirations and reconciling oneself to the unexplained are evidence of the psychoanalytical spirit. Confusion and lack of theory were not the aim of his efforts to establish a theory of neuroses and psychoses, or a model of psychic functioning.

I shall now sketch out the overall lines of thought in the first version of *Beyond the Pleasure Principle*. In so doing, I shall name and briefly refer to the most important corrections that Freud undertook in the later reworkings. The great intervention into the first version – the new chapter – will be dealt with separately at the end.

---

106 The authors of *Psychoanalysis and the War Neuroses*: Ferenczi, Abraham, Simmel and Jones; S. Pfeifer (1919), 'Äußerungen infantil-erotischer Triebe im Spiel'; C.G. Jung (1909), 'Die Bedeutung des Vaters für das Schicksal des Einzelnen'; J. Breuer & S. Freud (1895), *Studies on Hysteria*, *SE 1*. Freud (1920g), *Beyond the Pleasure Principle*, pp. 12 n. 1, 14, 22 n. 1, 25 n. 1, 31.

In advance it must be said that, as my title proclaims, I shall be concentrating on Freud's ideas concerning the drives; anything to do with psychical energy will remain in the background. Deliberately and on purely pragmatic grounds, the focus of my study will be on the dynamic aspect.[107]

1. *The first chapter*

It begins cautiously, with a reminder of the basic assumption that had held good until then: that in the life of the mind there is a strong tendency towards pleasure – the pleasure principle – which is in opposition to other forces. The pleasure principle gives way to the reality principle – this, too, is nothing new, for Freud had been working with this basic scheme of mental and psychical functioning since 'Two principles' (1911b) at the latest, but of course, in essence, even earlier, since *The Interpretation of Dreams* (1900a) and the 'Project' (1950c).

In mental life, Freud continues, severe unpleasure results when repressed drive demands overcome the defences. These demands have once been repressed because they could not be borne, and if in spite of that they find their way into consciousness, once again unpleasure will be experienced. Freud repeats this in his previous terms, so that after reading the first chapter of the first version, one has learnt nothing that contradicts earlier views. One can still form no clear impression of what might lie 'beyond' the pleasure principle, as the title proclaims.

It should be noted that the second and print versions of the first chapter differ only marginally from the first version, namely in the three passages that Freud inserted on reworking it.[108] They relate to discussions by Fechner (1873) of the significance of pleasure and unpleasure, and their relationship to quantitative changes of arousal, and also to the "tendency towards stability".[109] In my opinion these insertions are only there to support Freud's observations; they do not alter the conceptual content of the first chapter.

---

[107] On the economic aspect, see for example, R.R. Holt (1962), 'A Critical Examination of Freud's Concept of Bound vs. Free Cathexis'; R.R. Holt (1968), 'Beyond Vitalism and Mechanism'; Sulloway (1979), *Freud: Biologist of the Mind*; Hock (2000), *Das Unbewußte Denken*; Früh (2011), 'Zu Todestrieb und Wiederholungszwang in Freuds "Jenseits des Lustprinzips"'.

[108] Freud (1920g), *Beyond the Pleasure Principle*, pp. 8–9; in this volume, pp. 30–31.

[109] Sulloway is of the opinion that Freud did not offer an adequate representation of Fechner's theory. Sulloway (1979), *Freud: Biologist of the Mind*, pp. 404–406.

2. *The second chapter*

Similar comments apply to the second chapter. The first, second and print versions are nearly identical, apart from two footnotes Freud inserted on reworking the first version.[110]

Freud begins the chapter with a description of the war neuroses and the traumatic neuroses. He emphasises the peculiar feature that in the dreams of those suffering from traumatic neuroses the accident is repeated. The exposition breaks off at this point, and he turns to the repetitions that characterise children's play. When what has been endured passively is actively repeated in play, the repetition often serves to satisfy desire for revenge. In that respect these repetitions lead to a gain in pleasure and confirm the old proposition of the dominance of the pleasure principle. The tendency to repetition intrinsic in children's play is, therefore, not so troubling as the repetitions of the accident in the dreams of traumatic neurosis.[111]

In the second chapter Freud goes no further. We are still on familiar ground. However, he begins preparing us for what is to come. He presents the phenomena that he considers to need explanation, which trouble him and should trouble us. It troubles him that the trauma reappears in the dreams of traumatic neurosis. It is evident in the second chapter that this type of repetition is something fundamentally different from the repetitions of repressed libidinal drive impulses.

3. *The third chapter*

This chapter too differs only marginally in the second and print versions. On reworking the first version Freud adds a reference to a work by Marcinowski (1918): an act of friendship towards a colleague whom, it seems, he wanted to bind closer to the psychoanalytical movement.[112] Apart from that nothing is changed.

At the beginning of the third chapter Freud reminds us that repetitions also occur in analysis. They are necessary because they furnish the opportunity

[110] Both footnotes relate to Freud's grandson Ernst, and give a vivid and touching depiction of two '*fort-da*' episodes, but do not in the slightest alter the course of the argument. The first footnote was added in the second version; the second, which mentions the death of Ernst's mother (Sophie), only in the print version. Freud (1920g), *Beyond the Pleasure Principle*, pp. 15, 16; in this volume, pp. 36, 37.

[111] Children's play is frequently adduced as evidence of the compulsion to repeat – in my opinion in clear contrast to Freud's exposition here and elsewhere. Thus, further below, on repetitions in play: "None of this contradicts the pleasure principle". Ibid., p. 36.

[112] Ibid., p. 20. See H. Bernhardt (2011), 'Johann Jaroslaw Marcinowski'.

of adequately working through conflicting drive impulses. Of course, this too is not new. The significance and function of repetitions were comprehensively treated in 'Remembering, Repeating and Working-Through'.[113] However, it is stressed that the compulsion to repeat in analysis is something peculiar, for the reason that – like the dreams of accident neuroses – experiences are also repeated that "include no possibility of pleasure, and which can never, even long ago, have brought satisfaction even to drive impulses which have since been repressed".[114] Freud now becomes categorical. He has reached the first point towards which he was steering.

His assertion is: there are psychically relevant 'impelling' processes that cannot be derived from libidinal impulses. They also have an impelling nature, and in 'Instincts and their vicissitudes' Freud stated this was characteristic of the drive.[115] But these other impelling processes are not identical with libidinal impulses. This was the point where Jones, Eitingon and others could not follow. Their reaction is understandable, for Freud was demanding a radical alteration of the analytical viewpoint. When confronted by symptoms, one had become accustomed to looking out for repressed gratification. That was now obsolete. There were apparently significant events and fantasies of infantile life that led to the formation of symptoms, yet whose driving force was not derived from libidinal wishes, naturally including pleasurable and sadistic ones. The concept of the compulsion to repeat suddenly acquired another, novel, meaning. Because of the resistance to this switch, Freud inserted into the second edition of 1921 a sentence intended to make it clear that he meant this innovation to be taken seriously.[116]

At the end of the chapter, Freud emphasises again how important the factor of the compulsion to repeat is for him. In children's play the compulsion to repeat is bound together with other, libidinal (sadistic, i.e. pleasurable) motives, and here it cannot be grasped in its pure form. In analysis too, it never emerges in action in its pure form, yet the repetitions of what is unpleasurable force upon us the impression during the analysis that something peculiar is taking place. Finally, in dreams of accident neuroses, the compulsion manifests itself most clearly and compellingly. The urge to repeat what is unpleasurable is – and now the decisive words – "more primitive, more elementary, more driven [*triebhafter*] than the pleasure principle which it overrides".[117]

---

[113] Freud (1914g), 'Remembering, Repeating and Working-Through'.
[114] Freud (1920g), *Beyond the Pleasure Principle*, p. 20.
[115] Freud (1915c), 'Instincts and Their Vicissitudes'.
[116] Freud (1920g), *Beyond the Pleasure Principle*, p. 21; in this volume, p. 42.
[117] Ibid., p. 23.

Here Freud describes the compulsion to repeat as 'drive-like', and thereby implies that he was working towards a new way of defining the drives, and of bringing other drives into consideration, apart from the libidinal and self-preservative drives.

4. The fourth chapter

One must read the fourth and fifth chapters (in the first, second and print versions) together, since the most significant message, the "far-fetched speculation", extends across both of them.[118] Freud introduces the fourth chapter by announcing it. Thus speculation is already the topic of the first version. Freud warns us of it in advance, yet neither in the fourth nor the following chapters of the first version is there any mention of a death drive. What then is meant by this far-fetched speculation?

First of all Freud deals with consciousness and memory in a manner already familiar to us, above all from the 'Project'.[119] He himself refers to his discussion in *The Interpretation of Dreams*, and then breaks off, in order to depict the evolution of the organism from "an undifferentiated vesicle of a substance that is susceptible to stimulation",[120] which gradually forms a crust, i.e. a part that no longer changes and serves as a protective layer: this part has died and is inorganic. Freud experimentally transfers this model onto the origins of consciousness, but this too is not the announced speculation. He continues pondering the evolution of the sense organs, and defines trauma as a breach in the "protective shield".[121] But we have still not reached the "far-fetched speculation". Rather, Freud is only heading towards something new. Part of it is in the assertion that trauma puts the pleasure principle out of operation. Trauma shows that the organism has duties to perform that are more important than the search for pleasure and the avoidance of unpleasure. Stimulation must be psychically bound before it can be channelled. Psychical binding involves a change into quiescent cathexis. Hence, only when the incoming stimuli have been bound do they become subordinate to the pleasure-unpleasure principle. Binding obeys a principle that is "independent"

118 Ibid., p. 24.
119 Freud (1950c), 'Project for a Scientific Psychology'.
120 Freud (1920g), *Beyond the Pleasure Principle*, p. 26.
121 Ibid., p. 27. Laplanche and Pontalis point to the concept of 'protective apparatuses' in the 'Project' as precursors of the protective shield. Whether Freud's definition of trauma was current or innovative cannot be examined here. A. Menninger points out that authors before Freud were already defining trauma as an excess of sudden arousal. J. Laplanche & J.-B. Pontalis (1973), *The Language of Psycho-Analysis*, p. 357; A. Menninger (2011), *Sigmund Freud als Autor*, pp. 137f., 156f.

of the pleasure principle and is "more primitive" than it.[122] Any more than that is not stated in this chapter.

In order to follow Freud, one must not be distracted by the fact that he uses the concept of 'binding' in the fourth chapter of *Beyond the Pleasure Principle* differently than before.[123] He no longer means the act of transforming from a primary to a secondary process, or turning impulse energy seeking release into bound energy. These processes had hitherto been regarded as a later gain, as a mode of functioning of the psychical apparatus that only develops gradually. Now, however, this 'binding' describes a transformation (into 'quiescent' cathexis), which is a prerequisite of the primary processes. It facilitates understanding of this new conceptualisation if one considers the empirical reference or the clinical core of the metapsychological explanation, which is: traumata have particular psychical effects; the task of controlling them has primacy over the urge to gain pleasure and avoid unpleasure. From this angle, the new concept of binding appears cogent, even if it is not identical to the old version.

While Freud was reworking the fourth chapter of the first version, he added two longer passages at the end.[124] They repeat the new theses and reinforce them: the traumatic neuroses are to be categorised as belonging to a sphere beyond the pleasure principle, because the dreams of traumatised neurotics have nothing to do with wish fulfilment. Also the dreams of analysands who reproduce the traumas of childhood do not fit into wish fulfilment theory.[125] Therefore, the 'beyond' of the pleasure principle is valid also in the case of dreams. They too serve other functions than wish fulfilment, namely the psychical overcoming of traumatic experiences. Such dreams also occur, as Freud hesitantly agreed, outside analysis.[126]

Freud hesitated, because he had reached the conclusion that he would have to change dream theory; a cautious approach was necessary. It was not as if he had never before had the idea that dreams can primarily serve the psychical working through of (traumatic) experiences. As early as September 1918, in

122 Freud (1920g), *Beyond the Pleasure Principle*, p. 32.

123 For example, Freud (1911b), 'Formulations on the Two Principles', p. 221; Freud (1915e), 'The Unconscious', p. 188. Holt was among the first to point this out. Perhaps he read Freud's work too closely, with too fine a toothcomb, so to speak, as he himself later noted. Much of what we today understand as a 'concept', for example 'binding', was not always so. Freud uses the term at times as it were colloquially, as denoting various things according to context. Holt (1962), 'A Critical Examination', p. 92; R.R. Holt (1989), *Freud Re-appraised*, pp. 108f.

124 Freud (1920g), *Beyond the Pleasure Principle*, pp. 32–33; in this volume, pp. 52–53. There is a further insertion at the beginning of the chapter. Ibid., p. 24; in this volume, p. 44.

125 Ibid., p. 33.

126 Ibid.

his Budapest lecture on the war neuroses, Ferenczi had stated that he was following "a hint of Freud's" in seeing the fright dreams of traumatic neuroses as "spontaneous attempts at cure".[127] But Freud hesitated. He had to reflect and decide how this tendency, the attempt to heal or gain control, might be integrated into the theory. It was not an empirical question. From the analysis of traumatic neuroses alone came no resolution. Thus, in *Beyond the Pleasure Principle* Freud decided to incorporate the new function into dream theory, by means of the supposition that there was a 'prehistory' of the dream, which served to gain control of trauma. It was chronologically and logically prior to the wish fulfilment, i.e. it occurred before wish fulfilment and formed its precondition. In this way, Freud saved the (old) tendency towards wish fulfilment, and had at the same time introduced a new tendency – an example of his procedure in modifying his theory.

In the first of the two passages added in the reworking of the first version, punishment dreams are also briefly mentioned.[128] Here Freud gives the impression that they represent no problem for the theory. In August 1920, after he had completed *Beyond the Pleasure Principle*, he distanced himself from this in his talk at the congress at The Hague, in which he explained punishment dreams as fulfilment of the wishes of the critical instances in the ego (ego ideal, censor, conscience).[129] Soon afterwards, Freud went a step further in his revision of dream theory, which is explicitly linked to the arguments in *Beyond the Pleasure Principle*.[130]

Before approaching the fifth chapter, I should like to draw attention to the fact that there has not yet been any mention in the text of drives similar to what would later be the death drive, nor of sexual and self-preservative drives. In only one place and in passing does Freud compare the quantity of stimuli from the trauma with the equally threatening stimuli "from within".[131] Apart from that, the first four chapters deal exclusively with trauma.

The phenomenon of trauma had concerned Freud from his first attempt at constructing a theory onwards, i.e. at least since his encounter with Charcot. It played a central part in all theoretical advances, both in clinical theory and

[127] S. Ferenczi (1919a), 'Die Psychoanalyse der Kriegsneurosen', p. 20.

[128] Freud (1920g), *Beyond the Pleasure Principle*, p. 32; in this volume, p. 52.

[129] Freud (1920f), 'Supplements to the Theory of Dreams', p. 4.

[130] Freud (1923c), 'Remarks on the Theory and Practice of Dream-Interpretation'. In the second supplement at the end of the chapter Freud refers to his postulate in *Three Essays*, that mechanical shocks can release sexual arousal. He now points out that real injuries that occur at the same time as shocks do not have a traumatic effect, because the arousal thus caused is 'bound' by narcissistic cathexis of the affected part of the body. Freud (1920g), *Beyond the Pleasure Principle*, p. 33; in this volume, p. 53.

[131] Ibid., p. 29.

metapsychology. In *Beyond the Pleasure Principle*, Freud made another attempt at understanding trauma clinically and incorporating it into theory; but this was not a matter of those traumas that, as he often said, formed the core of analysable transference neuroses.[132] These have been psychically taken up or 'bound'. In *Beyond the Pleasure Principle* it is more a matter of the traumas that arouse traumatic neuroses, including war neuroses, i.e. clinical configurations in which the unalterable return of the traumatic situation constitutes the main symptomatic indication, and which to a large extent resist treatment.[133] As often, the trauma was the riddle that needed to be solved, and the drive was the answer (or one of various possible answers).

5. *The fifth chapter*

As in chapters one to four, Freud corrects little of substance in reworking the first version of the fifth chapter – with one exception, to which I shall return. Thus, his thought process remains almost the same through all the versions.

In this chapter, Freud took the step that he himself considered the most speculative of all. In the fourth chapter he had arrived at the conclusion that there must be a principle that precedes the primary and secondary processes, and the pleasure-unpleasure (and also the reality) principle – one that regulates the course of psychical processes, before the pleasure principle can come into operation. As mentioned, this alone signifies a massive change in his previous fundamental ideas of how the mind functions. Now, however, Freud returned to the phenomena that gave him no rest: children's play and repetitions in analysis. The former did not necessitate the assumption of a compulsion to repeat, but the "obstacle to our treatment" of the compulsion to repeat

132 See, for example, Freud's letter to Jones on 18 February 1919, immediately before writing *Beyond the Pleasure Principle*: "a traumatic neurosis [is] thus to be found at the bottom of every case of Übertraggs-neurose". Freud & Jones (1993), *Complete Correspondence*, p. 334.

133 Surprisingly, Freud repeatedly expressed curt and negative views on the analysability of traumatic neuroses. For example, in 1909 he wrote to Abraham that traumatic neurosis was "difficult to tackle". A similar remark can be found in the *Introductory Lectures* or in *Inhibitions, Symptoms and Anxiety* where Freud asserts that "not a single analysis of a traumatic neurosis of any value is extant" – and this after the attempt to claim the war neuroses for analysis. In a similar sense in the late *Outline of Psychoanalysis* he writes of traumatic neuroses that "their relations to determinants in childhood have hitherto eluded investigation". Freud's insistence on the exceptionality of traumatic neuroses and the autonomy of traumatic events, and his emphasis on the 'beyond' a pleasure principle, seem to me to prepare an approach to a new mental domain. The history of psychoanalytic theory after Freud has shown how 'modern' his grasp of this 'beyond' was, even though many pupils could or would not follow him (see above, n. 105). S. Freud (1916–1917a), *Introductory Lectures*, *SE* 16, p. 274; S. Freud (1926d), *Inhibitions, Symptoms and Anxiety*, *SE* 20, p. 129; S. Freud (1940a), *Outline of Psychoanalysis*, *SE* 23, p. 184; Freud & Abraham (2002), *Complete Correspondence*, p. 82.

in analysis did.[134] There follows a further revelation towards which the text had been steering, namely the compulsion to repeat may exist 'beyond' the pleasure principle, but is itself the mark of a drive, and more than that: of all drives. The drives are differently constituted from what had previously been assumed; they do not only urge discharge, nor do they only strive towards pleasure and satisfaction, as was depicted shortly before in 'Instincts and Their Vicissitudes' or in the *Introductory Lectures*.[135] Rather the drives tend in the first instance to re-establish a previous state: they wish, so to speak, not to be drives, but strive to return to a state of inertia.[136]

But this is not yet the culmination of the argument. Freud breaks off to refer to the biological principle of ontogenesis repeating phylogenesis. After that he proposes the speculation itself.[137] He wants to pursue it to its "logical conclusion", even at the risk of "an impression of mysticism or of sham profundity": life arose although it did not want to arise; organisms evolved higher forms although they did not want to; life and evolution were "imposed", the consequence of external influences. What organisms actually wanted was – death: "the aim of all life is death [...] inanimate things existed before living ones".[138] Freud emphasises both phrases by underlining or spaced type. With the origin of life there came into existence the first 'drive', which wished to return to the inanimate state; life was only a detour towards death; the entire life of the drives served to bring about death.

After communicating this "far-fetched speculation", Freud turns to the state of his theory and inquires how it can be reconciled with those new ideas. Hitherto the sexual and self-preservative drives had been at the centre of his ideas of mental life, or more precisely, of the aetiology of the neuroses and psychoses. Now he had allowed his speculations to bring him to a point where he was envisaging the origin of life from inorganic matter, and the tendency, implicit therein as he saw it, to revert to an inorganic state. How could the sex and self-preservative drives be conceived in conjunction with these new ideas?

It was immediately apparent that the sex drives could not be treated as equivalent to drives that urged death. That would be too great a contradiction with the previous concept. Thus Freud was left no alternative other than to categorise the drives leading to death among the self-preservative drives – a daring decision that gained a certain degree of plausibility if supplemented by the assumption that the self-preservative drives were charged with assuring

134 Freud (1920g), *Beyond the Pleasure Principle*, p. 36.
135 Freud (1915c), 'Instincts and Their Vicissitudes'; Freud (1916–1917a), *Introductory Lectures.*
136 Freud (1920g), *Beyond the Pleasure Principle*, p. 36.
137 Ibid., pp. 37f.
138 Ibid., p. 38.

what was, as it were, the death most suitable for that organism, the one closest to its constitutionally predicated optimal duration of life.[139] It should be noted here that this idea, which nowadays might appear off-beat, would have been understood differently at the time, for there was a current expression in biology that a living being died 'from internal causes'; or one spoke of the 'right death', meaning a death where the being's life was not cut short by accidental adverse circumstances.

If the sexual drives could not therefore be treated as equivalent to the new drives which strove towards an inorganic state, according to Freud they still had specific characteristics in common with them. The sexual drives, too, strove to return to an earlier state. They were in a certain sense even more 'conservative' than the death-seeking drives.[140] The phenomena that Freud had in mind here were the relative resistance of the sexual drives to outside influence, and the regressive undertow or adhesion of the libido, to be observed in analyses, i.e. all those tendencies that oppose changes, the resistance in analyses which cannot be resolved, the 'force' that stands 'behind' the repetition of unpleasurable, traumatic situations. On the one hand, the sexual drives presented characteristics of the drives that strove for death, and on the other hand they worked against death, because they were concerned with multiplying and reproduction, and in this manner they preserved life "for a comparatively long period".[141]

At this point, in the middle of the fifth chapter, Freud stumbled on a serious problem, as I see it, which he himself did not indicate as such, but which in my opinion had far-reaching consequences. I deduce this from the small but significant correction mentioned above, which was made during the reworking of the first version. It relates to a point at which he mentions reproduction, i.e. the preservation of life, which arises from the fusion of germ-cells. In the first version of *Beyond the Pleasure Principle* Freud wrote:

> We must regard as completely incomprehensible the fact that this function of the germ cell [i.e. the preservation of life] is reinforced, or only made possible, if it coalesces with another cell similar to itself and yet differing from it.

Reading this sentence, one stops short and wonders why Freud found the fusion of germ-cells to be "incomprehensible". Evidently he was not happy

139 Ibid., pp. 38f.
140 Ibid., p. 40.
141 Ibid., p. 40.

with this expression, for he corrected it in the reworking of the first version. Afterwards it read: "We must regard as *in the highest degree significant* the fact that this function of the germ cell etc.".[142]

Thus, in the second and print versions, the initial turn of phrase, "completely incomprehensible", becomes "in the highest degree significant". I assume that Freud first described the fusion of germ-cells as incomprehensible because there was no place for it in his previous conception of infantile sexuality. Naturally he kept in view the fact that, among other things, sexuality had to serve the function of reproduction, but this aspect was allotted to adult life and not to the epitome of sexuality – infantile sexuality – which was characterised by autoerotism and the search for pleasure.[143] Freud had held to that view in the 1915 drive theory, in terms of the formula that the relationship of the drive to the object' is loose, and that the object is interchangeable; it is what is "most variable about a drive", and primarily of interest because of the possibility of satisfaction that it presents.[144] Seen from the viewpoint of infant sexuality, the object is therefore anything but an entity with which one wishes to coalesce. However one may choose to understand Freud's conception of infantile sexuality, the idea that it deals with a wish or drive towards 'coalescence' with another entity is the opposite of what Freud had hitherto had in mind. I think that is why, in the first version, he described that union as "completely incomprehensible". Coalescence did not match with the core notion of what Freud understood as sexuality; his concept of it was not orientated towards adult sexuality, where genital-sexual union is central.

Union or coalescence becomes something 'in the highest degree significant' in the second version, and that was possible because here, in the new sixth chapter, Freud had introduced 'Eros'.[145] I would go so far as to say that he introduced Eros because he wanted to maintain the concept of infantile sexuality. In the second version, the tendency towards coalescence is ascribed to Eros. In this way, coalescence (of cells, of organisms, of humans) is, as it were, bracketed off from the conceptualisation of the sexual drives. However, in the first version of *Beyond the Pleasure Principle* there is still no Eros.[146] Not only does Freud not use the word, but everything that would later characterise Eros, was, as shown, still ascribed in the first version to the sexual drives.

---

142 Ibid., p. 40; in this volume, p. 59 n. 159, italics U.M.

143 Freud (1905d), *Three Essays*, pp. 181–182.

144 Freud (1915c), 'Instincts and Their Vicissitudes', p. 122.

145 Freud (1920g), *Beyond the Pleasure Principle*, p. 50.

146 The final paragraph of the fifth chapter, where 'Eros' occurs, was only inserted into the third edition in 1923. Ibid., pp. 42–43; in this volume, p. 62.

To recap: in the first version of *Beyond the Pleasure Principle*, Freud still does not use the term 'death drive', but he introduces a new definition of the drives, its central defining characteristic being the urge to return to a previous state, and he speaks at length about those drives, whose aim is to lead the organism to its death. In that respect I consider his response to Wittels accurate: that he had already had the most important ideas of *Beyond the Pleasure Principle* while his daughter Sophie was "healthy and blooming". Eros, on the other hand, is not to be found, either as word or idea, in the first version. Here it is still an un-separated constituent of the sexual drives. Only in the second version is it bracketed off from the sexual drives, as not belonging to the sexual in its narrow sense, and introduced as an autonomous drive or group of drives.

In many passages in the first, second and print versions of *Beyond the Pleasure Principle*, particularly in the fifth chapter, we sense Freud worrying over the question of how one should understand coalescence or the conjoining of several entities into a "higher" organism, and "higher development" in general, including that of humans.[147] It is with a conspicuously strong affect, one could perhaps speak of a conceptual predilection, that Freud rejects an 'urge' towards higher development, and emphasises that in organic life higher development only takes place against the will of the organism, and only by means of disturbing influences from outside.[148] In the case of humans too, there is no real urge towards advancement; all cultural achievements are only, so to speak, mechanical results of repression and sublimation.[149]

Having reached the end of the fifth chapter, one can hardly remember what Freud actually set out to do. To recapitulate: he wanted to explain the apparently incorrigible repetition of unpleasurable experiences, as it appeared in the dreams of the traumatic neuroses, in analysis (and in life), in line with some inner compulsion. In the first version, his answer is that the repetition is to be attributed to a drive. It is not only the consequence of a trauma that makes it impossible psychically to work through "masses of stimulus" streaming in, nor just is it a consequence or expression of a defect in the

147 Ibid., pp. 41f.

148 In this connection Freud refers to Ferenczi, who had also spoken of a "persistent" or "regressive" tendency in organic life, and like Freud attributed all higher development to the necessity of adapting to external circumstances. Ibid., p. 41 n. 3; S. Ferenczi (1913), 'Stages in the development of the sense of reality'; see Appendix I.

149 In the third edition of *Beyond the Pleasure Principle* (1923) Freud amended this and suggested, in an addition to the end of the fifth chapter, that Eros could be seen as a sort of "substitute for this 'drive towards perfection' whose existence we cannot admit". That means: higher and further development cannot be attributed to the activity of the sex drives, but only to the involvement of Eros which strives to combine "organic substances into ever larger unities". This confirms my assumption that the concept of Eros was created for the purpose of taking over those functions that Freud did not want to link to the sexual. Freud (1920g), *Beyond the Pleasure Principle*, p. 43; in this volume, p. 62.

functioning of the psychical apparatus, but, at one and the same time, in some manner the expression or function of a drive, or 'serving' a drive whose aim is to bring any functioning to a stop.

I see here a trend of thought leading from trauma to drive. What was first a weakness of the apparatus, the organism or the ego, turns by reversal into the satisfaction of a drive impulse towards self-destruction. A similar dynamic can be observed in Freud's reworking of the text for the second edition of 1921. Here in the second chapter he inserted half a sentence, which proposed a relationship between the compulsion to repeat and the "mysterious masochistic trends of the ego".[150] This small insertion also shows the above-mentioned characteristic of Freud's theory formation: a weakness of the psychical apparatus, which results in the emergence of unpleasurable memories, becomes, in the next stage of theory, a drive event or a drive wish. Perhaps it is an essential feature of Freud's thought that it circles trauma, takes trauma into its sights, and then, at some periods of theory development, moves away from it to the topic of conflict, or, at other periods, to previous and inherited traumas, or, at yet other periods, to the drive or the drives, whether that be sexual or death drives. And as soon as Freud comes to the drive, its basically or potentially overwhelming and traumatic character forces itself upon him: what Andreas-Salomé called "the 'passive drive'", after having read *Beyond the Pleasure Principle*, thus bringing us back to trauma.[151]

In the first version of *Beyond the Pleasure Principle*, the movement begins with trauma and leads to the compulsion to repeat, which is defined as a drive and seen as representing a group of drives that resist change and in the end strive towards death. Their effort is to bring about the destruction and immobility of their own life, not its reproduction. In the first version, Freud made them equivalent to the self-preservative drives, but would correct that in the second and print versions. I assume he initially wanted to retain the old theory, in which the sex drives are in opposition to the self-preservative drives, and here there was no place for the drives urging death, other than that of the self-preservative drives. Freud was uneasy about this solution. He explicitly distanced himself from it in reworking the first version, and treated the question of the placing of the drives urging death at length in the new sixth chapter, where he also proposed an alternative solution: the so-called third drive theory.[152]

150 Ibid., p. 14; in this volume, p. 35.

151 Freud & Andreas-Salomé (1972), *Letters*, p. 105. On the relationship between trauma and drive in Freud's theory, see, above all, I. Grubrich-Simitis (1987a), 'Trauma oder Trieb – Trieb und Trauma'; I. Grubrich-Simitis (2007), 'Trauma oder Trieb –Trieb und Trauma: Wiederbetrachtet'.

152 Freud (1920g), *Beyond the Pleasure Principle*, p. 37, 40; in this volume, pp. 56, 59.

6. *The sixth (= seventh) chapter*

The sixth and last chapter of the first version, which becomes the seventh in the print version, is short – in the typescript it consists of only two and a half sides. Freud was particularly dissatisfied with it, for in the reworking he crossed out the last two paragraphs of the first version, began replacing them with a new text, which he again crossed out, and only then wrote the final conclusion.[153] It is not only in the many corrections, but also in the text itself, that one senses the author's discomfort. He felt he had not managed to bring the work to a good ending.

At the beginning of the chapter, Freud summarises where his thoughts on the traumatic neuroses have led him, and repeats his most important conclusion, a revision of the concept of the drive: that all drives are primarily distinguished by a striving to return to previous states, and only secondarily – i.e. only when the circumstances for the pleasure-unpleasure principle have been established – by their striving for pleasurable satisfaction. Such is the new definition of the drives. Freud himself found it problematic. As he saw it, the question of how the pleasure-unpleasure principle related to the "drive processes of repetition" remained "still to solve".[154] By this I consider that he meant that the pleasure principle and the compulsion to repeat could not be reconciled with metapsychological theory.[155]

As he continued, Freud tried one last time to incorporate the new ideas into the old theory, this time with the formulation that the pleasure-unpleasure principle serves the principle of constancy of stimuli, or the principle that maintains the level of stimuli as low as possible, and to this extent it is subordinate to the principles or drives that lead to death.[156] But he was dissatisfied with that too. He made some more observations and then abruptly broke off. The chapter suddenly ends with the words (later crossed out): "I consider it superfluous to try to excuse either the timidity or the uncertainty of these speculations. Whoever wishes to isolate the real factor behind them should devote his attention to the *compulsion to repeat*".[157]

153 Ibid., pp. 63–64; in this volume, pp. 79–80. See reproduction of the handwritten paragraphs in *Psychoanalysis and History* 2015 (2), pp. 204, 272.
154 Freud (1920g), *Beyond the Pleasure Principle*, p. 62.
155 The capitulation in the face of the metapsychological formulation of the new drive definition is easily overlooked, although Freud himself makes the admission. Another example of the failure of the metapsychology is identification. Although it is among the most important clinical and practical concepts and can be incorporated without any problem into clinical theory, it resists metapsychological formulation. Freud (1921c), *Group Psychology and the Analysis of the Ego*, pp. 106, 120f.
156 Freud (1920g), *Beyond the Pleasure Principle*, p. 62.
157 See in this volume, pp. 79–80.

The first version of *Beyond the Pleasure Principle* ends with this admission: that he had not managed to reconcile the pleasure-unpleasure principle with the drives urging death. This does not mean Freud was declaring that the phenomenon that was proving such an obstacle to his deliberations – the compulsion to repeat – was invalid. On the contrary: Freud held fast to the phenomenon, to the peculiarity and resistance to the theory of the compulsion to repeat. This too seems to me a characteristic of his thinking: that in a critical case he would give up, or declare unviable, the theoretical level, speculation and theorising, rather than ignore troublesome phenomena. Hence Freud insists that there is a curious compulsion to repeat that reproduces unpleasure, that does not obey the pleasure-unpleasure principle and cannot be incorporated into the theory.

V. The second and print versions: from speculation to the third drive theory

Freud wrote a new chapter for the second and print versions, which he inserted between the penultimate and final chapters of the first version. This sixth chapter has a particular status because Freud comments here on his discussions in the previous chapters, and states which thoughts, speculations and 'findings' he wishes to maintain and which ones to discard. At first sight this may not be recognised, since he plays down the reversal he accomplishes in the new chapter. It is already concealed in the first sentences and contains the key to understanding the chapter and, I believe, the entire work of *Beyond the Pleasure Principle.*

Freud begins with the following statement:

> The upshot of our inquiry so far has been the drawing of a sharp distinction between the 'ego-drives' and the sexual drives, and the view that the former exercise pressure towards death and the latter towards a prolongation of life. But this conclusion is bound to be unsatisfactory in many respects even to ourselves.[158]

He gives no reason why the contrast that he has just emphatically represented should be "unsatisfactory even to ourselves". Initially, one understands the sentence as referring to the trouble caused by his expositions in the fifth

[158] Ibid., p. 44.

chapter, and preparing the ground for making what he had in mind more plausible. But I believe the case is different. *He* was the one who had become dissatisfied during the months that passed between the last line of the fifth and the first line of the sixth chapters, and had struggled through to a new definition and grouping of the drives. This cannot be deduced from the first lines of the new chapter.

The same thing holds for the following sentence in which Freud asserts without any evidence that "actually" only the ego or self-preservative drives are subject to the compulsion to repeat[159] – whereas a few pages earlier, in the fifth chapter, he had said that the compulsion to repeat is a characteristic of all the drives, and that the sexual drives are even more 'conservative' than the ego drives.[160] Once again, Freud confronts us with a conclusion that he has drawn in the interim without informing us of the reasons for the revision of his thesis. The disputation is not really backed up in the later text either. At any rate, in the sixth chapter Freud takes back the main thesis of the fifth chapter – that all drives are subject to the compulsion to repeat – and substitutes a new one for it. In addition, a second one – that the ego drives press towards death, but the sexual drives do not – is in part given up, in part profoundly modified.

I would therefore say that after Freud had finished the first version, his doubts about his most important theses had become so strong that he decided largely to withdraw them. But he does not allow us to share the process that brought him to this reversal; instead he sets up in their place new theses that explicitly contradict the preceding ones, thereby suggesting that we would experience the same dissatisfaction, the previous ideas not having convinced us either.

This way of reading will resolve many of the contradictions between statements in the sixth and the previous chapter. They result from Freud having changed his mind, but not wanting to set aside the old text, i.e. the first version. He did not want to write a new text, but rather hoped he could save the old manuscript through such remarks as those quoted above, and carry on working with it. At a relatively late point in the sixth chapter, he states openly that he had "corrected" and "withdrawn" a main thesis (the ego or self-preservative drives = death drive), but it is already, so to speak, too late for this reference.[161] It confuses the reader more than it helps him or her through the text. Apart from that, Freud inserted a footnote into the fifth chapter, which is meant to prepare the reader for the reversal that will come

159 Ibid.
160 Ibid., p. 40.
161 Ibid., p. 53; in this volume, p. 70 n. 214.

in the sixth chapter. It states: "A correction of this extreme view of the self-preservative instincts follows".[162] Later (1925) Freud brought the footnote in earlier, immediately after stating his great speculation, formulating it thus:

> The reader should not overlook the fact that what follows is the development of an extreme line of thought. Later on, when account is taken of the sexual drives, it will be found that the necessary limitations and corrections are applied to it.[163]

Despite these explanations, until now it has not been possible to work out from the text the dynamic on which it is founded: that central theses which Freud had expounded in the first chapters, above all in the fifth, and which formed part of his "far-reaching speculation", would simply be dropped in the sixth, because he no longer advocated them. Only now that we know the sixth chapter was written long after completion of the first version has a new reading of *Beyond the Pleasure Principle* become possible.

At the same time, one must bear in mind that the speculations or theses that Freud sometimes – for example in the opening lines of the sixth chapter – designates as 'findings' are of a purely theoretical nature. That means their plausibility is hardly, or not at all, founded on observation, empirical facts, impressions, or however else one might term the relation of mental to objective reality. As Freud himself says near the end of the work, there is only one empirical anchorage for the theses in *Beyond the Pleasure Principle*, "namely on the facts of the compulsion to repeat", meaning those repetitions of the unpleasurable which cannot be attributed to disappointment, frustration, denial, etc. of drive wishes.[164] The task that he faced was to integrate them into the theory. He tried out several solutions, and these are by their very nature theoretical; they are no more or less than thought experiments. Any author will in the end hold fast to the thought experiment or formulation that best suits, and that suits him or her best. If one calls such decisions 'findings', one fails to take sufficiently into account the fictional or subjective factor inherent in the construction of all theory (see below).

There is more going on in the sixth chapter. Freud not only separates himself from the main theses of the first version; he also accomplishes the switch to the so-called third drive theory, or more exactly, "third step in the

162 Ibid., p. 39 n. 1.
163 Ibid., p. 37 n. 2.
164 Ibid., p. 59.

theory of the drives".[165] He introduces two new drives or drive groups, the death drives and Eros, whereby the 'old' drive groups, namely the ego or self-preservative drives and the sexual drives, are subsumed under Eros. What that means in detail will be examined below. Firstly, some remarks on the concept of the death drive, which counts as the most important innovation and core factor of *Beyond the Pleasure Principle.*

1. *The death drives and the death drive*

The death drive and the death drives were no novelty for Freud. He had used the expression, already with a certain naturalness, in a letter to Eitingon of 8 March 1920.[166] Apart from that it was used in a note, presumably written in 1918.[167] Stekel and other members of the Vienna Society had already spoken even earlier of death drives, to which Freud himself refers.[168] The term was therefore not new; what was new was the high rank accorded to the concept in the reworking of the first version of *Beyond the Pleasure Principle.*

The note referred to above, belonging to a small series of notes on the leaves of a Hungarian calendar, is of particular interest for *Beyond the Pleasure Principle.* The point at which "death drives" occurs reads: "Sex. union repeats *in nuce* the primal event of bringing the lifeless to life. / Death drives masked as life drives. Sextr. [sexual drives] seem to lead to death. In fact the opposite".[169]

165 Ibid.

166 Freud & Eitingon (2004), *Briefwechsel*, p. 194 (Letter 168 F). Whether the letter was written before or after writing the sixth chapter cannot be determined.

167 A photo of the undated note, which is part of a group of similar pages, is reproduced in M. Molnar (1992), *The Diary of Sigmund Freud 1929–1939.* Molnar, the editor, proposes July 1918 as its date, which seems plausible to me (see footnote 169). Grubrich-Simitis on the other hand brings the notes forward to 1920, the time when Freud was writing the sixth chapter of *Beyond the Pleasure Pinciple.* She also mentions 1919 as a year of origin, but rejects this with the argument that the notes related to the "mortality or immortality of protozoa", the theme which, as Freud asserted to Wittels, he had first dealt with after Sophie's death. The bulk of Freud's notes (his '*Notizenwerk*' in Grubrich-Simitis's term) have not yet been published. See Grubrich-Simitis (1996), *Back to Freud's Texts*, p. 191 n. 22. A preliminary impression can be gained from ibid., pp. 92–130 and G. Fichtner & A. Hirschmüller (2011), 'Gedankensplitter – Gedankenkeime'.

168 Freud (1920g), *Beyond the Pleasure Principle*, p. 55 n. 1. Freud names O. Rank (1981), *The Artist*, and S. Spielrein (1994), 'Destruction as the Cause of Coming into Being', and Stärcke (1914), 'Inleiding'; with thanks to Harry Stroeken. He does not mention, however, Stekel, with whom he was at odds at that point. In this connection, Ferenczi's concept of the 'tendencies to death', which he spoke of to Andreas-Salomé in 1913, should also be mentioned (see Appendix I). See also H. Nunberg & E. Federn (1962–1975), *The Minutes of the Vienna Psychoanalytic Society, Vol. 1*, pp. 175–182; *Vol. 3*, pp. 329–335.

169 Molnar (1992), *The Diary of Sigmund Freud.* With thanks to Stefan Marianski of the Freud Museum London, who put copies of the notes at my disposal, and to Michael Schröter for his help with the transcription. In question are eleven leaves from a Hungarian calendar (11.6 x 15.5 cm) bearing only the printed day and month, but not the year. The first seven leaves bear the inscriptions 'Április 9',

The following should be noted: the question of which event in phylogeny is repeated in sexual union is also taken up and mentioned in *Beyond the Pleasure Principle*,[170] and we are already familiar with the thought of 'death drives masked as life drives' from the first version. This refers to the self-preservative drives, which look as if they served life in the sense of self-preservation, but actually lead to the 'right' death. The idea that sexual union is a life-bringing factor ("In fact the opposite") can also be found in *Beyond the Pleasure Principle*.[171] The next but one note is about the "striving of the drives against increase of tension", which follows from "the nature of the drives", which "work towards the abolition of tension"; there is a preceding mention of "vital differences".[172] These formulations appear in part in the first and above all in the second and print versions of *Beyond the Pleasure Principle*.[173] In the same sense Freud refers in the text to the booklet *Warum wir sterben* ['Why We Die'], whose author (Lipschütz) is also mentioned in the calendar notes (on a page in the May series) (see Appendix II).[174]

If the notes I am referring to here date from 1918, this would mean that Freud had been preoccupied for some time by the questions he deals with in *Beyond the Pleasure Principle*. Nevertheless one must concur with Strachey

'Április 10', etc. up to 'Április 15'; the remaining four 'Május 12' up to 'Május 15'. According to Marianski (email: 8 February 2012) the calendar leaves appear to have come from a single calendar block. How it came into Freud's possession is not known (perhaps Hungarian friends gave it to him). The April series of notes differs from the May series. In the former Freud is primarily noting clinical ideas (on homosexuality, on the father complex, etc.) and explicitly mentions three patients: Anton von Freund, Rudolf Kriser and N.N. At the end of the last note of the April series there is a date written in his handwriting: '29.6.1918'. Since we know from Freud's patient calendar that these three patients were only together at the same time with Freud during the period from February to late June 1918, one is drawn to the assumption that these notes relate to the same period; the handwritten date would fit (on 29 June all three patients had their last hour before the summer break). May (2008), 'Nineteen Patients in Analysis with Freud'. The overall dating of the seven April leaves is therefore certain: the notes stem from the period between February and June 1918, the last note presumably 29 June. On the four May calendar pages Freud's notes are exclusively about ideas belonging to the realm of *Beyond the Pleasure Principle*. Among other things they deal with the sexual and death drives, regulation of drive tension, uni- and multicellular organisms, and Lipschütz. On the May series pages Freud wrote three dates: '15 July', '16 July' and '17 July': unfortunately with no year. If the impression that all the pages come from one single calendar is correct, then the May series is also likely to be from 1918. The notes in the April series would then end on 29 June 1918, the May group continue from 15 July 1918. During these days between 5 July and late September 1918, Freud was staying in Hungary; first in Budapest, then in Csorbató; assuming the notes are from 1918, they could also then be preparation for work on the Lamarck project that Freud and Ferenczi planned for the summer (see Appendix I). The question why Freud used the calendar pages both in Vienna (April series) and in Budapest (May series) remains open, as well as the dating of the May series, and with it the appearance of the term 'death drives', which cannot be established with absolute certainty.

170 Freud (1920g), *Beyond the Pleasure Principle*, pp. 44, 55–56, 58.

171 Ibid., pp. 48, 50, 55–56.

172 Copy in Molnar (1992), *The Diary of Sigmund Freud*.

173 Freud (1920g), *Beyond the Pleasure Principle*, p. 55.

174 Lipschütz (1914), *Warum wir sterben*.

when he footnotes "the ego or death drives" on the first page of the sixth chapter of *Beyond the Pleasure Principle* with the remark that this is the first published appearance of the term.[175] It is indeed the first published use – albeit not in the canonical form, but disguised as "ego or death drives" (*Ich(Todes-) Triebe*), and not in the singular, but the plural. A few pages later it appears for the first time in its exact form, but again in the plural and set in inverted commas: "'death drives'".[176] The term is introduced almost casually, as if it were only a convenient abbreviation of the more awkward "ego or death drives". The inconspicuous terminological alteration naturally contains the great theoretical decision: away from the ego–death drives of the fifth to the new death drives of the sixth chapter, which are no longer defined as guarantors, but as opponents, of self-preservation.

Before going into the question of how the 'death drives' of the sixth chapter relate to the 'drives, which strive towards death' of the fifth, I should like to stress the fact that in both instances Freud uses the plural 'drives' or 'death drives' and not the singular 'death drive'.[177] This holds good for the entire sixth chapter: the plural form appears seventeen times, a true singular only once, in the long explanatory footnote at the end, which was only inserted during proof corrections, after finishing the second version.[178] It is here that Freud speaks of the 'death drive' in the singular for the first time and contrasts it with Eros. The narrowing down of death drives to death drive was therefore a late decision, so that strictly speaking one should not talk of 'the death drive' but of 'the death drives' in relation to *Beyond the Pleasure Principle.* In publications after *Beyond the Pleasure Principle*, Freud still frequently uses the plural, only later preferring the singular, as in *The Ego and the Id*, the explicit sequel and clinical application of *Beyond the Pleasure Principle.*[179]

In what follows, an attempt will be made to reproduce the thought processes of the sixth chapter. It leads into an "intellectual hell", to borrow an expression from Freud's letters to Fliess.[180] As I see it, this effect can be largely traced back to Freud confronting the reader with an implicit further theoretical development, without clearly acknowledging it as such.

---

175 Freud (1920g), *Beyond the Pleasure Principle*, p. 44 n. 2.

176 Ibid., p. 47.

177 See also S. Akhtar (2011), 'Introduction', p. 8.

178 Freud (1920g), *Beyond the Pleasure Principle*, pp. 60–61 (in this volume, p. 77). Such figures can easily be obtained using the search function on Freud's *Gesammelte Werke* on the PEP-Archive. The death drive occurs three times in the singular. But in two of these cases Freud is speaking of sadism as 'a' death drive, that is, one of several. Ibid., pp. 53–54.

179 Freud (1923b), *The Ego and the Id*, p. 12.

180 S. Freud (1985b), *The Complete Letters of Sigmund Freud to Wilhelm Fliess*, p. 421.

2. The new sixth chapter

The distinctive feature of the new chapter is that Freud enters into conversation with writers on biology and evolutionary biology,[181] in order to find out from them what they have to say about his speculations. He refers most frequently to August Weismann (*Über die Dauer des Lebens* ['The Duration of Life'], 1882; *Über Leben und Tod* ['On Life and Death'], 1884; *Das Keimplasma* ['The Germ Plasm'], 1892), then to Max Hartmann (*Tod und Fortpflanzung* ['Death and Reproduction'], 1906), Alexander Goette (*Über den Ursprung des Todes* ['On the Origin of Death'], 1883), and Wilhelm Fliess (*Der Ablauf des Lebens* ['The Course of Life'], 1906), and in passing to Ewald Hering (*Zur Lehre vom Lichtsinn* ['On the Theory of Visual Sense'], 1878). From the recent literature he uses above all Theodor Lipschütz's booklet *Warum wir sterben* ['Why we die'](1914) and Franz Doflein's book *Das Problem des Todes und der Unsterblichkeit bei den Pflanzen und Tieren* ['The Problem of Death and Immortality in Plants and Animals'] (1919), which summarised the latest state of research on Weismann's theses. Apart from that, he mentions experimental work by Loeb, Woodruff, Maupas, Calkins and Hertwig.[182]

In passing, a disturbing peculiarity of the way these authors are used should be mentioned: Freud incorporates not only scattered phrases but also long passages from the biological literature, nearly always referring to the source in a footnote, but in the text the inverted commas are frequently missing, so that one thinks one is reading Freud, whereas the sentences or turns of phrase are from Weismann, Hartmann, etc. Thus the voices of other authors mix in the sixth chapter, and cannot be distinguished from Freud's voice. I go into further detail on this strange discovery in Appendix II.

Before beginning my commentary on the chapter, I should like to emphasise that, as before, my concern is to accentuate the lines of thought and focal points, and in doing so much must remain undiscussed. I shall hardly go into the aforementioned biological works. The passages on sadism and masochism in the middle of the chapter will be treated separately later on.[183]

At the beginning of the sixth chapter, Freud sets out the two speculations that he abandoned after writing the fifth chapter, and poses the question whether, according to biology, all living entities must die.[184] I should explain

[181] Freud (1920g), *Beyond the Pleasure Principle*, pp. 45–50, 55–56.

[182] I shall not be going into the experimental works. Freud might have already studied Lipschütz's *Warum wir sterben* (1914) during the summer of 1918 (see the remarks on Freud's calendar notes above).

[183] Freud (1920g), *Beyond the Pleasure Principle*, pp. 54–55.

[184] Ibid., p. 44.

that this question is posed because he is setting out to formulate a generally applicable theory: only if all living entities must die does it seem to him meaningful to speak of drives that urge death. The first expert he invokes is Fliess, with whom he had once exchanged opinions on such questions. He speaks of his 'large conception' to determine mathematically the time of death and reproduction, only to reject the system in a few words immediately afterwards as unconvincing owing to its rigidity.[185]

Freud turns afterwards to August Weismann, and his distinction between the mortal and the immortal part of the organism.[186] Weismann called the former "soma", the latter "germ-plasm", and postulated that mortality only affects higher organisms, unicellular ones being, as it were, immortal.[187] Freud follows this up, postulating that the distinction between soma and germ-plasm could be seen as an analogy to his own opposition of the life or sexual drives and the ego or death drives; this is his "dynamic corollary to Weismann's morphological theory".[188] Freud dismisses, however, the assumption of a later origin of mortality, simply because, according to his view, mortality and death drives must have been present "from the very beginning of life on this earth".[189] No further reasons are given.

After having rejected Fliess and Weismann, Freud reports the discussion in biology that had arisen over Weismann's claim that unicellular organisms are immortal. He cites the discoveries and thoughts of Hartmann, Lipschütz, Doflein and Goette, only to reject them at the end: they lead "to no conclusive results in any direction".[190] Only two contributions engage his interest: the first of which shows that under certain circumstances the coalescence of unicellular organisms has a rejuvenating effect, and the second of which provides evidence of the mortality of unicellular organisms.[191] Neither work remained un-contradicted in the discussion. Freud presumably highlighted them because they suited his own presuppositions. In the sixth chapter he returns several times to the idea of rejuvenation through conjugation. It

185 Ibid., p. 45. It should be noted that Fliess was at the time preoccupied with similar questions to Freud: namely mortality, immortality and the origin of sexual reproduction. In his booklet *Vom Leben und vom Tod* [*On Life and Death*] (1909), which appeared in its fourth edition in 1919, he mentions the same authors as Freud does in *Beyond the Pleasure Principle* (Loeb, Hartmann, Maupas, Woodruff). That indicates that in the sixth chapter we are involved in a familiar discussion of that time, on the boundaries between medicine and biology. See W. Fliess (1919), *Vom Leben und vom Tod*, pp. 77f., 86f., 92f.

186 Freud (1920g), *Beyond the Pleasure Principle*, p. 45.

187 E.g. A. Weismann (1882), *Über die Dauer des Lebens*.

188 Freud (1920g), *Beyond the Pleasure Principle*, p. 46.

189 Ibid., p. 47.

190 Ibid.

191 Ibid., pp. 48f.

forms part of his own conceptual preferences, which he himself says play an unavoidable part in the formation of theory.[192]

Freud ends the first part of the sixth chapter, which deals with the mortality of organisms, with a dismissive comment on the work of biologists.[193] In the end, it is "a matter of complete indifference" what conclusions they reach, since everything may be different from what biology holds.[194] He admits that biology provides no grounds for contrasting life and death drives, nor that one could speak of life and death (or death and life drives) from the beginning of organic development, but he maintains that this is irrelevant. For if we adopt the 'dynamic' point of view, i.e. tracing phenomena back to the effects of drive forces, then one drive force can be 'covered' or concealed by another, so that we cannot make out whether a drive force is involved or which one it might be.[195] Later on in the same chapter, in relation to the origin of the sexual drives, Freud again adopts this unsettling attitude towards the biological sciences, attributing some *a priori* primacy to psychoanalysis.[196]

Before continuing my summary of the sixth chapter, I should like to draw attention to the fact that until now Freud has continued to follow the line of the first version: he is still contrasting the sexual drives with the drives that strive towards death, and he is still equating the sexual with the life drives and those tending to death with the ego or self-preservative drives.[197] Only one small shift of terminology is so far to be recognised: Freud now frequently uses the term 'death drives' (but meaning the 'old' death drives, i.e. those drives from the first version which urge death and are ascribed to the group of self-preservation), and he also begins to call the sexual drives more frequently 'life drives' (but still meaning the sexual drives of the first version).

To return to the text: Freud now turns his attention to multicellular organisms. Once more he is fascinated by the aspect of rejuvenation and extending life through conjugation,[198] about which it should be remarked that in the discussions of the time both assumptions were current: that the

192 Ibid., p. 59. This partiality would be converted into action in the case of rejuvenation. As is known, Freud submitted to a Steinach operation in November 1923. According to Steinach, vasectomy should activate hormone production, thereby leading to rejuvenation and keeping the cancer in abeyance. As Schur records, after the diagnosis of cancer Freud also received regular injections of male hormones, chiefly for its reconstructive effect. Jones (1957), *The Life and Work, Vol. 3*, p. 104; Schur (1972), *Sigmund Freud*, p. 450.

193 Freud (1920g), *Beyond the Pleasure Principle*, pp. 44–49.

194 Ibid., p. 49.

195 Ibid.

196 Ibid., p. 57.

197 One must distinguish between self-preservation on the one hand, and reproduction, or preservation of life, on the other. The former is ascribed to the ego drives, the latter to the sexual drives.

198 Ibid., pp. 50, 55–56.

coalescence of two or more cells into a group of cells was harmful and led to death, and that it prolonged life. Freud agrees with the latter view and continues by setting out a new 'bold' speculation.[199] It concerns Eros – and thereby unsettles the basic conception of the first version. From here onwards, the text of *Beyond the Pleasure Principle* becomes more difficult and less transparent than previously. All that is clear is that in the further course of the chapter, Freud explicitly renounces two central theses of the first version: the equating of the death drives with the self-preservative or ego drives, and the assumption that the compulsion to repeat is a characteristic of all the drives.

As I see it, Eros is the pinnacle of this new theoretical construction. In my opinion, it provided the strongest impetus to renew the theory developed in the first version. But what was the 'bold' new speculation that incited Freud to introduce Eros into the theory, and allot it the foremost place? It involved Freud applying "the libido theory which has been arrived at in psychoanalysis to the mutual relationship of cells".[200] He imagined that the cells related to each other as human beings or psychical forces in humans do. The speculation was that death and life drives are 'active' in the cell; the life drives of one cell 'neutralise' the death drives of other cells (not its own) and thus render them harmless; in this manner cells keep one another alive. Cells (or their sexual drives, or their energy), which carry out the work of neutralisation, can perish in the process. Not all cells take part in neutralising; some behave "in a completely 'narcissistic' fashion", namely germ-cells. They transmit no energy or force to other cells; do not, so to speak, bother about them, as the narcissistic ego "pays none of it out in object-cathexes". The germ-cells require their force or energy "as a reserve against their later momentous constructive activity". Freud ends this speculative-fictive series of ideas with the statement: "In this way the libido of our sexual instincts would coincide with the Eros of the poets and philosophers which holds all living things together".[201]

In this way, Eros is introduced into the theory with no preliminary, very unexpectedly and without exactly determining the relation between it and libido, or the sex drives. From the quotation we can only conclude that Eros, conceived in the first instance as a biological force, has the duty of keeping cells and organisms alive, and that it is close to the sex drives, if not identical with them.

Immediately after the first mention of Eros, Freud breaks off this train of thought, changes the subject, and in the following pages recapitulates the

199 Ibid., p. 50.
200 Ibid.
201 Ibid.

development of his libido theory, beginning with the opposition of the sexual drives and the self-preservative drives, which he had for the first time explicitly formulated in 1910.[202] It seems to me that this retrospective insert can be explained by the fact that in mentioning Eros a historical step had been taken: the switch to the new, third drive theory had begun. Freud may not announce it very clearly or explicitly, but during that retrospective he was already moving towards the new theory and distancing himself from the theses of the first version of *Beyond the Pleasure Principle*. The first great revision concerned the equation of the ego/self-preservative drives with the death drives. Regrettably, this is not easy to make out in the familiar version of *Beyond the Pleasure Principle*, since at this point the second printed version made a correction to the text, which concealed the process.[203] Whereas in the first edition Freud was still writing that he would "now" give up equating death drives and ego/self-preservative drives, from the second edition onwards it reads that he *has* already given up this notion.[204] However, Freud revised it only "now", at this point in the text – it was not until here that he explicitly withdrew it. For what reason?

My answer would be as follows: in the period between the first and the second manuscript version, Freud had become convinced that what he had imagined to be self-preservation had, in fact, an overwhelmingly libidinal character. Alternatively: after he had turned his attention to Eros and come up with the idea of declaring it responsible for self-preservation, it then seemed to him that his previous notion of seeing self-preservation as a detour to death was no longer tenable. Or: Freud was so taken by his speculation as to how cells kept each other alive with the help of libidinal forces that he wanted to make it a component of his theory, even though it postulated the exact opposite of what he had held in the fifth chapter. I would put it this way: once again the priority of the libidinal had asserted itself in his thinking.

Now the self-preservative instincts are restored (from p. 53 on) to what they had been before *Beyond the Pleasure Principle*. They are liberated from the function of death and again pronounced to be primarily libidinal forces, which bear a close relation to Eros. This reconstruction of the theory had

---

[202] Ibid., pp. 50–52; S. Freud (1910i), 'Psychogenic Visual Disturbance according to Psychoanalytical Conceptions', *SE* 11, p. 214.

[203] Freud (1920g), *Beyond the Pleasure Principle*, pp. 52–53.

[204] In the final received version (1925) it reads: "We were prepared at one stage [...] to include the so-called self-preservative drives of the ego among the death drives: but we *subsequently* [...] corrected ourselves on this point and withdrew it". In the first edition (1920), however, the last phrase still read: "but we must now correct ourselves"; italics U.M. This is an important text variant, which is not documented in the German *Studienausgabe* [or the *Standard Edition*]. See ibid., p. 53; in this volume, p. 70.

one consequence that Freud does not mention at this particular point: the striving towards death was no longer bound to any group of drives. In the old theory, the death drives had had no place. If one wanted to keep them, a new place would have to be found for them. Freud found this place: he created a new place for the death drives by introducing them as a new, autonomous group of drives. This is how it is set out in the footnote at the end of the sixth chapter, which was attached at the last moment, namely in the proofs of the first edition.[205]

I shall now turn to the second great revision of the theoretical position as established in the first version – a revision that Freud had already signalled at the beginning of the sixth chapter, and which he carried out in the course of the chapter.[206] It concerns the sexual drives and their relationship to the compulsion to repeat. While he asserted in the fifth chapter that the compulsion to repeat was a general characteristic of the drives, now he states that the sexual drives are not subject to it. Their essential factor is sexual union, continuation of life;[207] the compulsion to repeat characterises only the death drives. Thus the central thesis of the previous chapter and of the first version of *Beyond the Pleasure Principle* is swept aside. Freud presents no reasons for the revision. He restricts himself to the statement that he "could not ascribe to the sexual drive the characteristic of a compulsion to repeat" – without any clue in the text that he had looked anywhere for evidence.[208]

In this connection, Freud turns one last time to biology for information on what it has to say about the origin of life and sexual union.[209] In brief: Weismann and others hold what must be the dominant view: that unicellular organisms or protista reproduce non-sexually by cell division, and that sexual reproduction only takes place later in the evolutionary process. Freud takes a similar stand to the one he took on the question of mortality. He writes: "The question arises here, as in the case of death [...] whether we do right in ascribing to protista those characteristics alone which they actually exhibit" or whether one can assume that "forces and processes which become visible only in the higher organisms" are already present among the simpler ones.[210] That means: even if forces like the sexual drives can only be recognised in higher organisms, they could or should be already present in lower ones – an argument typical for Freud, which, for all his interest in historical and

[205] Ibid., pp. 60–61; in this volume, pp. 77–78.
[206] Interposed thoughts on sadism will be discussed below. Ibid., pp. 53–54.
[207] Ibid., pp. 56f.
[208] Ibid., p. 56.
[209] Ibid.
[210] Ibid., p. 57.

genetic factors, denies the idea of development itself.[211] To this must be added the fact that the assumption that sexual reproduction is a later acquisition of phylogenesis was, as it were, on principle unacceptable to Freud, as also, for example, to Fliess, who held that our "instinct" tells us "that the answer of our biologists *cannot* be right".[212]

After biology had failed several times as a support in the sixth chapter, in the end only Plato's fable of the origin of the two sexes seemed to be suitable as proof.[213] The fable had been familiar to Freud for a long time: it is to be found in the first pages of *Three Essays*.[214] In the foreword of the fourth edition of this book, dating from May 1920, the proximity of the sexual drives to the Eros of 'divine Plato' is mentioned, perhaps to prepare the readership for *Beyond the Pleasure Principle*, the next publication.[215] Ferenczi too, in his congress lecture on the war neuroses, describes Plato's Eros, encompassing all tender and sensual urges, as a proximate concept to that of the sexual.[216]

Finally, Freud extends the fable: it is not sexual reproduction and the sexes that originated as Plato described, but life itself.[217] One could regard the sexual drives as a type of continuation of chemical affinity. As various chemical substances strive to merge, the sexual drives are the bearers of a wish for reunion – and thereby to re-establish a previous state. To that extent, according to Freud, Plato's myth corresponds to his own theory. The general characteristic of the drives is not the compulsion to repeat but the regressive "need to restore an earlier state of things".[218] The actual and true compulsion to repeat applies, as stated, only to the death drives.

Freud ends the sixth chapter with self-critical remarks. He has not sold himself to the devil, but has just given himself over to a line of thought. Certainly the new drive theory "cannot lay claim to the same degree of certainty as the two earlier ones". In setting up the death and life drives, it is a case of speculation and "borrowing from the science of biology", whereas

211 Cf. Sulloway (1979), *Freud: Biologist of the Mind*, pp. 365ff.; also my remarks on the 'early stage' category, U. May (2011a), 'Auf dem Weg zu Karl Abrahams "Versuch einer Entwicklungsgeschichte der Libido"', pp. 135f.

212 Fliess (1919), *Vom Leben und vom Tod*, p. 77; on this see Appendix II.

213 Freud (1920g), *Beyond the Pleasure Principle*, p. 57. In the *Outline*, Freud does however distance himself from it. See also my remarks on the note of September 1938 on the origin of Eros and death, which shows that Freud did not consider that he had definitively answered the questions thrown up in *Beyond the Pleasure Principle*. Freud (1940a), *Outline*, p. 148; Grubrich-Simitis (1996), *Back to Freud's Texts*, p. 93.

214 Freud (1905d), *Three Essays*, p. 136.

215 Ibid., p. 134.

216 Ferenczi (1919a), 'Die Psychoanalyse der Kriegsneurosen', p. 17.

217 Freud (1920g), *Beyond the Pleasure Principle*, p. 58.

218 Ibid., p. 57.

the first two drive theories emerged from "a direct translation of observation into theory".[219] At any rate, however, the third drive theory also "rests upon observed material – namely on the facts of the compulsion to repeat".[220]

Before I turn to a discussion of the third drive theory, a few words on the final, seventh chapter. As shown above, the first three paragraphs of the print version derive from the first version; the fourth was newly written in the reworking. Here Freud introduces further thoughts on the relationship of pleasure and unpleasure to the life and death drives, and points out, among other things, that the death drive is not as accessible to internal perception as the "breakers of the peace", the life drives, for the death drives manifest themselves less in tension or pleasure and unpleasure. But "a host of other questions to which we can at present find no answer" remain open.[221]

3. The way from the first to the second and the print versions

a. Deradicalisation, conservation of the old, addition of the new drive theory

The third drive theory emerged during the course of Freud's reworking of the first version of *Beyond the Pleasure Principle*. While writing out the first version he had already found that he had gone too far in his "far-fetched speculation". For he had asserted that all drives strive towards death, i.e. all of them are subject to the compulsion to repeat. He had been obliged to partly withdraw this radical formulation, since it could not be integrated into the old (i.e. first and second) drive theories. Thus, already within the first version, he had to delimit the area of validity of the death urge to the self-preservative drives, and to moderate the radical version of the great speculation with respect to the sexual drives. What remained was only that the sexual drives showed an urge to return to a previous state; not, however, an urge towards death. Even though Freud had corrected all this in the first version, he was not satisfied with the text and amended it again in the second and print versions. He now took almost everything back: the death urge was no longer attributed to the self-preservative drives, and neither self-preservative nor sexual drives were subject to the compulsion to repeat. This signified a complete about-turn. The speculation at the centre of the first version of *Beyond the Pleasure Principle* now seemed in every respect untenable.

219 Ibid., pp. 59, 60.
220 Ibid., p. 59.
221 Ibid., pp. 63–64.

The situation in which Freud found himself with the manuscript of the first version may have been similar to his 'overthrow of all values' in the 1890s, when he realised that his analysands' stories of sexual abuse were often fantasies and not memories of real abuse. At the time he faced the threat of the collapse of his theory, as he now did of his great speculation in *Beyond the Pleasure Principle*. Then, as now, however, Freud found a solution. In the case of *Beyond the Pleasure Principle*, it was the third drive theory. It was presented in the new sixth chapter written for the second and print versions. The new theory allowed Freud to retain the old theory and accommodate the new one, the core of his far-reaching speculation. Hence he spoke of "the third step in the theory of the drives".[222] This third step was a new step, but did not signify doing away with the first and second. In other words, the third drive theory did not take over, or take the place of, the first and second theory, but took them further – just as the seduction theory was never totally abandoned, but retained a place in the aetiological theory of mental disturbances. This is the approach that Freud generally adopted in constructing his theories. For *Beyond the Pleasure Principle* that meant the first and second drive theory retained their validity; they only received a new frame, that of the death drive and Eros.[223]

The death drives, or the death *drive* as it would be called in Freud's last addition to the proofs before typesetting (see above), was therefore a separate drive. It was no longer subordinated to the self-preservative drives, but together with Eros was given a place above the two drive groups (sexual and self-preservative drives) of the old theory. Freud wanted to hold on to the death drive because he had the impression that in analyses (and in dreams of the traumatic neuroses) the unpleasurable returned in a manner that was not to be understood as the return of the repressed. He wanted to raise this phenomenon, or more exactly, the phenomenon as he saw it, to the level of theory. Or rather, the phenomenon of the compulsion to repeat that was not bound to the pleasure-unpleasure principle seemed so significant that he wanted to create a place in theory for it. That he attempted to derive the compulsion to repeat from a drive, the death drive, is founded, as I see it, on his fundamental conviction that unchanging, immutable mental phenomena could only be derived from a drive. Thus, in the theory, the death drive would be set above the old pair – the self-preservative and sexual drives – and above

222 Ibid., p. 59.

223 A similar situation pertains to the revision of the first theory of anxiety. Freud renounced it explicitly, only to come subsequently to the conclusion that it was "not so much a question of taking back our earlier findings as of bringing them into line with more recent discoveries". Freud (1926d), *Inhibitions, Symptoms and Anxiety*, pp. 109, 141.

narcissism, and allotted a partner or opponent: Eros or the 'life drives'. This is how I see the main approach to the reworking of the first version of *Beyond the Pleasure Principle*. This approach can only be made out because the first version of the text has survived and we can, by comparing it with the second and print versions, form a new image of the genesis and place of the third drive theory.

One could say that the print version of *Beyond the Pleasure Principle* is the result of a process of deradicalisation, perhaps in the sense of the dictum – a "succession of daringly playful fantasy and relentlessly realistic criticism", as Freud once described the "mechanism of production" in a letter to Ferenczi.[224] For this reason I am not of the opinion that the sixth chapter represents the core or heart of the whole work.[225] In my view the heart of the work is the far-reaching speculation of the fifth chapter of the first version: the idea that the entire drive system serves to bring the organism to death. Perhaps Freud left the text of the first version largely unchanged in the reworking because of that, and put the new ideas into the newly written chapter, because he wanted to leave the first venture, the great speculation, intact in all its radicality – even though he would have to partly abandon it in the sixth chapter.

Freud's assertion that he did not first introduce the death drive after the death of his daughter Sophie holds good, insofar as the basic insight of *Beyond the Pleasure Principle* was already contained in the first version of spring 1919. Presumably its theoretical incorporation, namely its elaboration in terms of the third drive theory, which was the final result of working out this insight, would only come after February 1920. If this is correct, that would mean that Eros was introduced after Sophie's death, and hence, if one wants to engage in such considerations, this theoretical step would have had more to do with his daughter's death than did the conceptualisation of the death drive.

b. On the introduction of Eros

At the point in the text where Freud announces the lesser new speculation quoted above, about the process of exchange between cells, which he sees as the direct action of Eros, one positively senses his relief.[226] Why was he relieved? I believe there were several rational grounds and a less rational one. The less rational one was that the idea of Eros corresponded to a conceptual preference of Freud's, namely the conviction or vision of the priority of the

---

224 Freud & Ferenczi (1993–2000), *Correspondence, Vol. 2*, p. 55 (Letter 542 F).
225 See Grubrich-Simitis (1996), *Back to Freud's Texts*, p. 191.
226 Freud (1920g), *Beyond the Pleasure Principle*, p. 50.

libidinal, which had dominated his theorising from the outset.[227] The idea that the function of cells was controlled by Eros seemed halfway to revoking the dark thought of the death urge. But this led to the new problem: that now all forces with which the theory dealt possessed a libidinal character, as Freud himself indicated.[228] I shall return later to this question.

One ground that seems more rational has already been presented, and I shall repeat it here: I suspect that Freud was relieved by his idea because Eros was a concept or force that was close to the sexual drives, without being identical to them. According to the lesser speculation, what Eros represented (at first) was the biological aspect of cohesion and conglomeration, the union of cells into cell groups and their coagulation, the union of germ-cells and the construction of new organisms, setting up connections, assimilation,[229] neutralisation and rendering harmless the forces that strive towards death and self-destruction. This motley collection of functions, which Freud brings together with Eros in *Beyond the Pleasure Principle*, was an innovation in the history of his theorising. As far as I can see, it had hitherto not been an explicit component of the theory, neither in the first version of *Beyond the Pleasure Principle* nor in his work before 1920.[230]

Freud had, of course, always spoken of the reproductive function (and preservation of the species), and attributed it to adult sexuality.[231] In the first version he described it as "completely incomprehensible" that reproduction, seen biologically, results quite concretely from a matter of 'union' or 'coalescence' (of cells). In the reworking, as shown, he corrected this statement, and in the second and print versions wrote in its place "in the highest degree significant".[232] This is the one really important correction of the content that Freud undertook in the first version – apart from the complete sixth chapter, of course. It indicates what might have occurred to him during the reworking of this version. I think he found a way of giving significance to sexual union: it became significant when and because it was a function of Eros. Previously it had been "incomprehensible" because it did not fit into the sexual theory,

227 May[-Tolzmann] (1996), *Freuds frühe klinische Theorie.*

228 Freud (1920g), *Beyond the Pleasure Principle*, p. 52.

229 In *Beyond the Pleasure Principle*, Freud briefly refers to Ewald Hering (1878), who distinguished between assimilation/construction and dissimilation/destruction. Ibid., p. 49.

230 An electronic search through Freud's *Gesammelte Werke* by means of PEP results in one single mention of 'Eros' before 1920: in the Leonardo study. S. Freud (1910c), 'Leonardo da Vinci and a Memory of his Childhood', *SE* 11, p. 70.

231 In *Three Essays* one reads about puberty: "The sexual drive has hitherto been predominantly auto-erotic; it now finds a sexual object" and "[t]he sexual drive is now subordinated to the reproductive function; it becomes, so to say, altruistic". Freud (1905d), *Three Essays*, p. 207.

232 Freud (1920g), *Beyond the Pleasure Principle*, p. 40; in this volume, p. 59 n. 159

for Freud considered the sexual drives predominantly autoerotic, egoistic, narcissistic; in his understanding there was no question of their seeking union and coalescence with an object. Thus I think that the introduction of Eros gave Freud the possibility of attributing to Eros the urge for union that is a function of adult life, so that the old conception of infantile sexuality could be retained, and at the same time a way could be opened up of theoretically integrating these processes for which there had hitherto been no place; that is, actions to do with coalescence, fusion and connection, perhaps also with identification, higher development and formation of groups.

In introducing Eros, Freud emphasised its biological aspect, and he did the same thing with the death drive: I see this as a hallmark of the third drive theory. Only after completing *Beyond the Pleasure Principle* did Freud attempt to find the psychical corollaries of Eros and the death drive. As is known, he did find them, and not simply in terms of a plain analogy, i.e. transposing the description of the supposedly biological events into psychical terms. In *Beyond the Pleasure Principle* he began seeking a way back to the psychical when he tentatively incorporated sadism and masochism into the new theory (see below).[233] Nevertheless, the basic conception of *Beyond the Pleasure Principle* was in fact biological. In the long footnote at the end of the sixth chapter, Freud himself says that the third drive theory was attempting to solve "the riddle of life" by accepting these two drives "struggling with each other from the very first".[234] Similarly he wrote to Arthur Schnitzler that he had "tried to reveal Eros and the death instinct as the motivating powers whose interplay dominates all the riddles of life".[235] In 'Analysis Terminable and Interminable' we read that his schema of Eros and the death drive "claim[s] biological validity", just as in the *Outline* Freud states that "in biological functions" the two drives work together and in opposition, and this "gives rise to the whole variegation of the phenomena of life".[236]

I have emphasised several times that the introduction of Eros relates to a wish to widen psychoanalytical theory into the biological. From this viewpoint, *Beyond the Pleasure Principle* belongs to a series of great projects that Freud was furthering, together with Ferenczi (see Appendix 1). Nowadays we are

---

233 Other formulations also extend the somatic into the psychical, such as "deriving the narcissistic libido of the ego from the stores of libido by means of which the cells of the soma are attached to one another", or the idea that "the life drives or sexual drives [...] partly neutralize the death drives". Ibid., pp. 50, 52. The term a 'way back' is taken from a Ferenczi letter to Freud: "I got lost in *biological* problems and can't find my way back to psychology!" Freud & Ferenczi (1993–2000), *Correspondence, Vol. 2*, p. 46 (Letter 535 Fer).

234 Freud (1920g), *Beyond the Pleasure Principle*, p. 61.

235 Freud (1960), *The Letters of Sigmund Freud*, p. 339.

236 Freud (1937c), 'Analysis Terminable and Interminable', p. 245; Freud (1940a), *Outline*, p. 149.

unwilling to acknowledge this aspect of Freud's thought, because it does not correspond to contemporary trends in theory. We would like to have a Freud who did not believe in the inheritance of acquired characteristics, in innate primal phantasies or in the significance of the phylogenetic heritage. Yet Freud worked with these ideas because he felt that the functioning of the psychical could not be explained in any other way.[237]

c. On the death drives of the second and print versions

As shown, in the sixth chapter the death drives become a separate group of drives. This constitutes the clearest difference between the drives that strive towards death, as they are described in the first version, and the death drives of the second version. The former should be identical with self-preservation; the latter were conceived as their opponents. Thus, in the second and print versions they represent, so to speak, in the pure form, the dark tendency to zero level, and this in several respects: the mechanical-physical, the biological, and, rudimentarily, the psychical. Freud had always had this tendency in view, at least since the 'Project' of 1895. What was new was the way it was set out and made concrete. It now stood for the (physical and biological) tendency to return to an inorganic state, and also, in a mitigated form, for the psychical tendency to return to earlier states, i.e. to regress, as well as standing for everything that resists change (also psychical) and prefers unchanging repetition, i.e. that is subject to the compulsion to repeat. As Freud emphasises in the print version of *Beyond the Pleasure Principle*, the sexual drives, the self-preservative drives and Eros were free from the compulsion to repeat (but not from the tendency towards regression). In this respect too, the print version of *Beyond the Pleasure Principle* represents a mitigated variant of the first version: what was new, the compulsion to repeat, and its source of power, the death drive, were retained, but their area of activity restricted.

Consequently, in the second and print versions the massive impulse of the first version was restrained, all valuable acquisitions were secured and the innovations, brought more or less into agreement, were integrated into the theory. In other words: the threatening insight of the first version, envisaging the end of the primacy of both the pleasure principle and the sexual drives, had been subjected to a reworking and led to the third drive theory. Nevertheless, in the seventh chapter of *Beyond the Pleasure Principle*, Freud wrote that the

[237] This is particularly impressively set out in 'The Uncanny', where the 'echo' is discussed, which lends to a number of psychical events (fear of castration, the Oedipus complex, etc.) a peculiar effect that does not stem from individual development.

task of linking the old with the new remained "still to solve".[238] As I see it, he means here the economic presentation. Even apart from that, the new theory had become more complex, less manageable, less clear-cut – among other reasons, because Eros and the sexual drives were very similar and at the same time fundamentally different, a fact that Freud did not explicitly mention.

A second problem was to make the concept of the death drives concrete. They seemed to Freud indispensable – yet for the time being he only had little to say about them. It was not even certain that they 'strive' or 'urge' like the other drives: Freud found rather that they worked "unobtrusively".[239] In addition, as previously mentioned, the question of their relationship to pleasure and unpleasure remained open. Hence they had little in common with what had hitherto been designated as drives, and yet were held to be valid drives, and incorporated as such into the theory, because they stood for the human (psychical and biological) tendency towards regression, rigidity, inalterability and unwillingness to change, as well as for mortality or for the course of life which, as Freud wrote to Ferenczi in 1917, was not straight, but showed an "unambiguous downward direction" towards death.[240]

It is probable that Freud's conviction of the empirical grounding of the death drive was conjoined to other motives that had little to do with observation or clinical practice. A remark made to Andreas-Salomé is indicative of this. In the summer of 1919, Freud told her of his work on *Beyond the Pleasure Principle* and asserted that he had "stumbled on a remarkable notion based on my theory of the instincts", as if purely thinking about the drives had brought him to the idea of the death drives.[241]

The notes referred to earlier, dating (probably) from July 1918, also support this assumption. They state that by their nature the drives "struggle against" an increase in tension, work towards "the abolition of tension" and that the death drives "mask" themselves as life drives.[242] This was actually already the core idea of the first version of *Beyond the Pleasure Principle*.[243] Perhaps it was at that time that Freud began increasingly to extract something other than he had previously from the drives' struggle against increase in tension.

238 Freud (1920g), *Beyond the Pleasure Principle*, p. 62.
239 Ibid., p. 63.
240 Freud & Ferenczi (1993–2000), *Correspondence, Vol. 2*, p. 251 (Letter 717 F).
241 Freud & Andreas-Salomé (1972), *Letters*, p. 99.
242 Molnar (1992), *The Diary of Sigmund Freud*.
243 This corresponded to Freud's continual striving to reveal the fine appearance – in this case, self-preservation – as deceptive, and to unmask what was seemingly harmless and benevolent as its opposite. Thus in 'The theme of the three caskets', a sort of precursor of *Beyond the Pleasure Principle*, he spoke of the distracting substitution of the love goddess in place of the goddess of death. S. Freud (1913f), 'The Theme of the Three Caskets', *SE* 12, p. 191.

Until now he had been fascinated by the drives and by their epitome: the sexual drives that strive towards satisfaction by all possible means, conflict with the ego's interests, and contribute decisively towards the formation of symptoms. They were the "breakers of the peace", bringing movement and dynamism into the psychical processes, and manifesting themselves in various disguised and symbolical ways and forms.[244] In the years around 1918, a shift of emphasis may have occurred, consisting 'only' in the fact that Freud now took more account of the fact that the striving for pleasure brought with it a striving for rest from pleasure, or that the peak of pleasure is at the same time the end of pleasure. The so-called 'problem of excitation' that continually concerned Freud had always to do with the meshing of pleasure and unpleasure, i.e. with the fact that an increase of excitation is both pleasurable and unpleasurable, and that the peak of pleasure is immediately followed by its end. In *Beyond the Pleasure Principle*, Freud focused for the first time on the 'other' side of the drive; he had "stumbled on" the other side, the striving towards the zero point, whose significance came to seem ever greater to him, until he finally (and only for a moment) in the first version found the entire organism and all drive forces to be ruled by this striving.

d. The problem of aggression

The introduction of Eros as a force that maintains life came, as Freud himself admitted, with a serious disadvantage: it now seemed as if all psychically relevant drive forces were of a libidinal nature.[245] Freud hoped to have found a way out when, in the sixth chapter, he classified sadism among the death drives, i.e. when he defined the psychical driving force of sadism as a possible vicissitude of the death drive. Until now I have ignored this step, because it appears like a foreign body in the text. For, from the moment when trauma was examined in the fourth chapter of *Beyond the Pleasure Principle* onwards, the text related primarily to biological and not psychical phenomena.

The classification of aggression is known to have been a problem that beset Freud from the very beginning.[246] His fundamental conception of the primacy of the sexual/libidinal excluded a leading role for aggression. Yet he

244 Freud (1920g), *Beyond the Pleasure Principle*, p. 63.

245 Ibid., p. 52. Incidentally, this confirms the assumption that Freud first saw the death drive as a biological force. Freud had confronted the same problem on the introduction of narcissism, i.e. with the formulation of the second drive theory (ibid.). As far as I can see, this problem is of his own making, so to speak, since Freud himself decided to define self-preservation as a predominantly libidinal function.

246 U. May (2010), 'Karl Abrahams Revolution'; (2012a), 'Zur Frühgeschichte der Analerotik'.

kept encountering aggression, or more specifically, the question of whether aggressive wishes had a primary character; that is, whether they could be the 'ultimate' foundation of psychical processes. It began with the Oedipus complex in its first, simple version, introduced in *The Interpretation of Dreams*, via death wishes against parents or siblings that relate back to the disappointment of love wishes – not the contrary.[247] The examination of the status of aggression ends in the *Outline*, where the question is brought up of whether the satisfaction of aggressive wishes is experienced as pleasurable in the same way as the satisfaction of libidinal wishes; Freud leaves the question more or less open.[248] He is similarly reticent on the question of whether aggressive wishes have a pathogenic effect, i.e. can be repressed. Here, there is, he says, "an interesting discrepancy between theory and experience":[249] theoretically all drive impulses can be repressed, yet observation shows that the pathogenic impulses regularly "arise from the component drives of sexual life".[250] They occur in an alloy with aggressive/destructive impulses, but it is indubitable that "the drives which manifest themselves physiologically as sexuality play a prominent, unexpectedly large part in the causation of the neuroses – whether it is an exclusive one remains to be decided".[251]

Without going into the history of the concept of aggression, I would like to draw attention to the fact that until *Beyond the Pleasure Principle*, sadism had qualified as a "component of the sexual drives", i.e. as a libidinal partial drive with an "admixture" of aggression, domination or self-assertion. In the sixth chapter of *Beyond the Pleasure Principle*, Freud tried another location, and attributed it to the death drives, with the qualification that it was a case of a death drive "driven out" of the ego and thereby becoming sadistic.[252] The driving out would, incidentally, be accomplished by narcissistic forces: in self-protection the death drive would be detached from ego/self/organism, its actual 'object' or its actual place of action and residence, and diverted outwards. In other words: in order not to destroy oneself, one destroys others. Thereby a new approach to the clinical understanding of aggression has been opened up: it is not yet carried out in *Beyond the Pleasure Principle* and only in retrospect recognisable as a beginning.[253]

---

247 Freud (1900a), *The Interpretation of Dreams*.
248 Freud (1940a), *Outline*, p. 154 n. 1.
249 Ibid., pp. 185–186.
250 Ibid., p. 186.
251 Ibid.
252 Freud (1920g), *Beyond the Pleasure Principle*, p. 54.
253 See, above all, A. Kris (1994), 'Freud's Treatment of a Narcissistic Patient'.

What is already recognisable in *Beyond the Pleasure Principle* is that the new location of aggression brings the death drive in the psychical into relation with masochism, which satisfied Freud for two reasons. Firstly, sadism once again became a secondary, derivative phenomenon. That was in contrast to the position he had only just formulated in 'A Child is Being Beaten', but corresponded to his conviction of the primacy of the libidinal.[254] Secondly, it confirmed what could be called the tragic human constitution, encompassing both inherent impulses that strive for pleasure and satisfaction, and others that counteract these wishes from the outset, and have other aims. That presaged on the one hand a primary masochism, which Freud introduced a few years later; and on the other it pointed in the direction of constitutionally given, phylogenetically reinforced forces, repressive of, and hostile to, drives, such as Freud had always assumed, beginning with the 1890s trinity of shame, disgust and morality, and continuing after 1900 with inner agents of the prohibition of drives – conscience, self-observation and self-criticism – and the two egos from 1914–1915 onwards, which, after *Beyond the Pleasure Principle* and the interim stage of group psychology, led to innovation in ego theory, in the form of the concept of the superego in *The Ego and the Id*. In these respects, the new positioning of sadism and masochism seemed to fit well into the theory and texture of Freud's conceptual preferences.

VI. Concluding remarks

1. On the procedural nature of Freud's theory formation

Now that we know the sixth chapter and other parts of *Beyond the Pleasure Principle* came into being long after the rest of the text had been written, a new interpretation presents itself, which resolves many flagrant contradictions. One can now say that these contradictions are a consequence of the work, displaying, side by side, various stages of Freud's thought processes. In other words, in *Beyond the Pleasure Principle*, Freud was pondering the question of how particular clinical phenomena, namely repetitions connected with strong unpleasure and which could not be referring back to anything previously pleasurable, might be reconciled with the theory developed up to 1919, and he came to conclusions that he revised already within the first version, and later, again, in the sixth chapter written for the second version.

[254] Freud (1919e), 'A Child is Being Beaten', p. 194.

Freud himself indicated the continual changes in his views, convictions or insights, but these indications were so brief, casual or unclear that, as far as I know, no reader has hitherto entertained the idea of taking them seriously, or of reading the text not as the 'result' of Freud's reflections but as a documentation of his thought processes. To repeat: the first to the fifth chapter represent the first stage of his reflections, while the next stage is to be found mainly in the sixth chapter, including some later passages inserted into the preceding text. The sixth chapter contains largely a commentary on, or correction of, previously held views. Such self-corrections are in general typical for Freud's theory development, but he seldom revised basic assumptions within a text in which he had already expounded them. In that respect, *Beyond the Pleasure Principle* occupies a special place, since Freud expresses, with full conviction, a sequence of views that contradict one another, and, moreover, without allowing the reader to follow the process.

This procedure raises questions, among them that of the extent to which one can appeal to Freud, i.e. to call oneself or others Freudian. The process-based nature of Freud's theory formation appears to stand in the way of that.[255] To call every stage of theory development 'Freudian' is formally correct, but practically impossible, since one would have to say of contradictory positions that they are Freudian. To thus designate only the chronologically final stage would not suit the spirit of the enterprise, which aims at keeping open and advancing the process of discovery. How can someone who advances it further than the last stage reached by Freud claim to do so in Freud's sense? Which interpretation is Freudian and which not, and who decides? Should one not conclude that Freudian theory only existed as long as Freud was alive and seen as an authority, whereby the 'valid' theory would always have been the latest one? And that with the end of Freud's authority, i.e. at the latest, the time of his death, no one else could seriously consider themselves Freudian?

Or is there a part of the theory that one can 'keep hold of', which does not come apart in the further development of the theory, which does not disappear and is not subject to transience? Can this be applied to the so-called cornerstones, which Freud repeatedly mentioned (with some slight variation: the acceptance of the unconscious, repression, infantile sexuality, the Oedipus complex)? And what would their relation be to the theory? Or is it not the cornerstones themselves but other elements of theory to which we

[255] The observation that, after the revisions of his theory that Freud undertook from 1914 on, it was no longer clear what counted as 'Freudian', thus offering psychoanalysis the opportunity of a new and fruitful pluralism, is a central idea of Makari's *Revolution in Mind* (2008).

could attribute a certain constancy? I know no answers to these questions, but am certain that one should consider anew which parts of the theory can be altered, disposed of or corrected, and which not, assuming there are such.[256]

The procedural nature of Freud's theory formation is too seldom considered, so long as single steps in the process are seen as 'findings', 'results' or 'frequently confirmed observations'. Freud was generally aware of the fragile and subjective nature of his theory, or more exactly, when he was aware of it, he could present it convincingly, as in the final pages of the sixth chapter of *Beyond the Pleasure Principle*, where he writes that the thought of every author is "governed [...] by deep-rooted internal prejudices, into whose hands our speculation unwittingly plays".[257] This procedural, fluid and highly subjective understanding of science has been largely forgotten by Freud's followers. In the texts of his pupils, the theory, with all its components, becomes a firmly established matter, exalted above doubt.[258]

2. *Proposal for a new interpretation of* Beyond the Pleasure Principle

This insight into the procedural character of Freud's theory formation presented me with the key to a new understanding of *Beyond the Pleasure Principle.* It is now my view that Freud expounded his main idea, which he termed "far-reaching speculation", in the first half of the fifth chapter, which belongs in the first version of spring 1919. Here he affirms that everything living strives towards an inorganic state and all drives urge towards death. In the second half of the fifth chapter, in the same work phase, he attempted to bring this insight into accord with his previous ideas on drives, and arrived at the conclusion that he could not sustain it. Above all, it could not be reconciled with the sexual drives. Freud held that in many respects one could attribute a conservative character to the sexual drives, but that they were not actually aiming at a return to an inorganic state or death. Furthermore, it seemed to him that the sexual drives were not wholly subject to the compulsion to repeat. Thus, already in the first version, he took back half of his fundamental idea: the "far-fetched speculation", namely its extension to the sexual drives. This correction can be relatively clearly inferred from the text.

It is easy to understand why Freud was not satisfied with this. For the great speculation now seemed to have more or less broken down. Once more,

256 In an earlier work I argued that the realm of intrapsychic processes (among others, the defence mechanisms) is one such 'firm' component. May[-Tolzmann] (1996), *Freud frühe klinische Theorie.*

257 Freud (1920g), *Beyond the Pleasure Principle*, p. 59.

258 Cf. May (2011a), 'Auf dem Weg', p. 148.

the attempt to do justice to the self-destructive character of the unchanging repetition of unpleasurable events and to trace it back to a general striving against change and towards lifelessness, death or the inorganic did not tally with the impression made on him by the functioning of the sexual drives. Insight was countered by insight. The only remaining solution was to attribute the striving for death to the self-preservative drives. Naturally, this too was not convincing, even though the paradoxical nature of the conception – to see the living as only seemingly alive and simply a masquerade of death – also had something in its favour. So much for the first version and for Freud's effort to integrate processes beyond the pleasure principle into the theory.

After completing the first version in April 1919, Freud continued to think about how he could integrate into the theory both the compulsion to repeat, which could not be reduced to a pleasurable experience, and the striving towards death – two instances that were closely bound together in his mind. The result of this reconsideration was the sixth chapter, which he wrote in the early summer of 1920. Firstly he gave up the assumption that the self-preservative drives were working towards death. Secondly, and also in contrast to the first version, he took the view that neither the sexual nor the self-preservative drives were subject to the compulsion to repeat. The phenomenon of the compulsion to repeat, as it appeared to Freud in the early summer of 1920, lay not only beyond the pleasure principle but in general beyond the hitherto presupposed groups of drives and psychical processes. It resisted integration into the theory, but was, as Freud now found out, a psychical process *sui generis*, i.e. something totally different from the hitherto presupposed primary and secondary processes (subordinate to the pleasure principle). Likewise, the drive to which Freud ascribed the compulsion to repeat – namely the death drive – showed no sufficiently strong similarity to the sexual and self-preservative drives. Nevertheless, it was, together with the new psychical process of the compulsion to repeat, of such great significance for Freud that he could not leave it out of his account. The compulsion to repeat and the death drive that 'explained' it had to have their place in the theory. The only possibility that remained was to bring in the death drive (including the compulsion to repeat) as a separate drive. Freud set up Eros alongside it, to include the 'old' drive groups, namely the sexual and self-preservative drives.

Even though he altered details, until his final theoretical writings Freud held to this conception of the psychical driving forces, which he had developed during the final stage of theory formation in the sixth chapter of *Beyond the Pleasure Principle*.

3. *The interrelation of the drive theories*

The procedural nature of Freud's theory formation was, to some extent, held back by another factor, which is that later stages of his thought processes do not do away with the earlier ones. The first drive theory (sexual vs. self-preservative drives) is not invalidated by the second (narcissism theory), any more than the third drive theory (death drive vs. Eros) replaces the preceding ones. This particular interrelationship of the theories seems to me to be a hallmark of Freud's thought. The stages of theory formation do not exclude one another; rather it is a case of a process in which the 'old' stages of knowledge are integrated into the newer ones – or at least, such was the intention. To that extent there are no true and false theories here, rather just partial truths of a provisional character, where the later theories are more complex than the earlier ones, and in Freud's eyes represent a more advanced stage of knowledge.[259]

It has been observed that Freud did not give up the seduction theory, but incorporated it into his later theories; in the same way his first theory of anxiety becomes a component of the second. As far as the drive theories are concerned, the prevailing opinion seems to me to have been different to date: it is generally accepted that the later ones replace the older ones. In contrast to that, I would state that Freud intended the first and second drive theories to be subsumed under the third. I infer this from *Beyond the Pleasure Principle*, and in my view Freud held to this until the end, as one sees in *An Outline of Psychoanalysis*, where he writes that the first and second drive theories "fall within Eros",[260] or, more exactly, that sexual and self-preservative drives, as well as ego and object love, are subordinated to Eros, whereas the death drives are situated on the same level as Eros. They are "completely different" and have little or no similarity to the sexual and self-preservative drives or to narcissism.

What also speaks for the validity of all the drive theories is that Freud linked them to well-defined spheres of phenomena. The first drive theory, according to his conception, applied largely to the transference neuroses or to the neurotic aspect of mental disturbances, the second to the so-called narcissistic neuroses (and psychoses), or, alternatively, to narcissistic aspects of mental disturbances, and the third to psychical events and disturbances in which the unpleasurable repetition of what had never been pleasurable,

[259] Jeanne Lampl-de Groot reports that Freud once compared his theory to an "Italian renaissance church" that "in the course of time (centuries) is so altered that the original church becomes a transept and a nave is built onto it. Thus the space is enlarged, but the original church remains in place". S. Freud (2012b), *Brieven aan Jeanne Lampl-De Groot*, p. 204; original text in Dutch.

[260] Freud (1940a), *Outline*, p. 148.

i.e. traumatic aspects, played an important part. Again, when looked at in this way, the single drive theories do not take over from one another, but encompass different clinical phenomena.

4. *The traumatic as a sui generis psychical process*

To conclude, I should like to emphasise that a new psychical sphere was opened up by Freud's claim that psychical processes existed which did not follow the pattern of the search for pleasure and the avoidance of unpleasure, and which were therefore not amenable to analysis as it was being practised. On the one hand, the realm of the traumatic was not new, for Freud had been interested in trauma from the very beginning and continued to be so until his last works.[261] For him it was mostly a riddle to be solved, and the drive was often the solution, as it also is in *Beyond the Pleasure Principle*, where the examination begins with trauma and leads to the death drive, which was meant to explain traumatic repetition. On the other hand, in *Beyond the Pleasure Principle* the traumatic was for the first time interpreted as a separate function, which is fundamentally different from the functions that Freud had previously interpreted. Now, many years later, we can maintain that we have approached a deeper understanding of the traumatic.[262] From this angle, Freud's *Beyond the Pleasure Principle* turns out in the end to be a truly modern work, even though at the time and ever since, it has provoked controversy and rejection.

Appendix I: Freud, Ferenczi and the early history of the psychical (1913–1919)

In this Appendix I shall briefly explain why *Beyond the Pleasure Principle* is one of a series of works on the 'conquest' of biology, in which Freud was attempting to shed light on the prehistory and early history of the psychical.[263] Ferenczi participated in this project: after the friendship with Wilhelm Fliess ended, he was Freud's main interlocutor on questions of the application of psychoanalysis to biology. Freud and Ferenczi had many interests in common:

---

261 S. Freud (1939a), *Moses and Monotheism*, *SE* 23; Freud (1940a), *Outline*.

262 Cf. W. Bohleber (2000), *Die Entwicklung der Traumatheorie in der Psychoanalyse*.

263 On Freud's interest in biology and the close links between his theory and theories of the biological sciences, see above all Sulloway (1979), *Freud: Biologist of the Mind*; Grubrich-Simitis (1987c), 'Trauma oder Trieb'; L.B. Ritvo (1990), *Darwin's Influence on Freud*; R. Burkholz (1995), *Reflexe der Darwinismus-Debatte in der Theorie Freuds*.

for example, paranoia, homosexuality, narcissism, the development of the ego, hypochondria, telepathy – and, as it happened, the pre- and early history of the psychical, i.e. developmental biology, the history of mankind and of the earth. With no other pupil did Freud exchange ideas so intensively and continually; neither Abraham, nor Jones, nor Eitingon, and presumably not with Rank either. With the exception of his works on technique, Ferenczi's role in the development of Freud's work has to date been little studied.[264] His own contribution to the question of the paleobiological sources of the psychical is his *Thalassa* (1924), which refers explicitly to *Beyond the Pleasure Principle* and likewise aims to determine the phylogenetic source and significance of the sexual drive forces and, in particular, of sexual union.[265]

Totem and Taboo can be considered Freud's first contribution to the early history of the psychical.[266] At its centre is the derivation of conscience, morality and religion, as well as magical thinking and the omnipotence of thought from the early history of mankind. A second attempt at shedding light on the psychical as the product of a long prehistory is the 'Overview of the Transference Neuroses'.[267] Clinical examples, i.e. formations of fixation and disposition of libido and ego development, modalities of regression and defence processes, are traced back to a multi-phasal 'struggle with the exigencies of the Ice Age' and subsequently to various forms of increasing 'oppression by the father';[268] the Oedipus complex together with cultural acquisitions rooted in it (morality and religion) are presented in the wider context of the history of mankind. In my opinion, Freud's third contribution to this project of seeing the psychical, and above all the drive forces, from a viewpoint that transcends individual development was *Beyond the Pleasure Principle.* Here the perspective was widened even further and extended back to the origin of life on earth. Ferenczi took part in all this research and accompanied it with his own work and insights. A few stages on the journey will be briefly depicted below, beginning with his work on the sense of reality.[269]

264 A. Haynal (1989), *Die Technik-Debatte in der Psychoanalyse.* See, however, Grubrich-Simitis (1987c), 'Trauma oder Trieb'.

265 Grubrich-Simitis has also pointed out that there is "a wealth of implicit and explicit cross-references" between *Beyond the Pleasure Principle* and Ferenczi's genital theory. Freud (1985a), *A Phylogenetic Fantasy*, p. 95 n. 30; cf. also Grubrich-Simitis (1987c), 'Trauma oder Trieb'. On *Thalassa*, see also R.J. Butzer & R. Burkholz (1991), 'Urvater und Eiszeit', and Burkholz (1995), *Reflexe der Darwinismus-Debatte*, pp. 174f.

266 S. Freud (1912–1913a), *Totem and Taboo, SE* 13.

267 Freud (1985a), *A Phylogenetic Fantasy.*

268 Ibid., p. 19.

269 Ferenczi (1913), 'Stages in the Development of the Sense of Reality'.

In this work, Ferenczi is already freely and independently in command of the historic-phylogenetic approach. Thus he speaks of how the development of reality testing, as he had proposed it, could come to be understood some day as the residue of periods of the historical descent of humankind, and as reactions to "geological changes in the surface of the earth".[270] Exactly like Freud, he also saw development as a process that did not occur "spontaneously", but was simply a reaction to influences from outside, to hardship and deprivation. This also meant that 'life' was to be conceived of as resisting change; in Ferenczi's words, it was ruled by a "tendency to persist or to regress".[271] Ferenczi definitely meant this tendency to be a "tendency to death", as is shown by a September 1913 diary entry of Andreas-Salomé.[272] Furthermore Andreas-Salomé clearly recognised that the "tendency to death and rest" was also included in Freud's theory from the beginning; for him living organisms were "reluctant to be disturbed".[273] This shows that in 1913 the concept of death tendencies or death drives in terms of psychobiological speculation was already seen as being inherent in Freud's thought.[274]

In 1914, it is known that Freud spent the Easter holiday with Rank and Ferenczi in Brioni, and there, as Freud later wrote, they "had such a good time with fantasies about Ψa prehistory".[275] Afterwards Ferenczi reported ideas on his genital and coitus theory and, after his first brief analysis with Freud in October 1914, he continued this work, reading up on "embryological, zoological, and comparative physiological material".[276] Freud kept the prehistory of the psychical firmly in his sight. In October 1914, in the preface to the third edition of *Three Essays*, he stressed the significance of phylogenetic determinants and defined psychical dispositions in Lamarckian terms as "the precipitate of earlier experiences of the species";[277] similarly in his Wolf Man study, which he completed in November 1914, he had claimed the existence of phylogenetically acquired schemata, forming the basis of the experience of

[270] Ibid., p. 237.
[271] Ibid.; cf. Freud (1920g), *Beyond the Pleasure Principle*, p. 41.
[272] L. Andreas-Salomé (1965), *In der Schule bei Freud*, p. 155 n. 80.
[273] The entry reads: "I cannot escape the idea that the tendency to death and rest – which Freud attributes to every living being as its essential being, inborn, and from which it is reluctant to be disturbed – is itself a rather neurotic estimation of life". Ibid., p. 172.
[274] Burkholz (1995), *Reflexe der Darwinismus-Debatte*, pp. 144f. He points out that the 'conservatism' of the drives, and the idea that every higher development was imposed from outside, were close to the views of Ewald Hering and August Pauly.
[275] Freud & Ferenczi (1993–2000), *Correspondence, Vol. 2*, p. 56 (Letter 542 F).
[276] Ibid., p. 60 (546 Fer); *Vol. 1*, p. 553 (Letter 473 Fer); *Vol. 2*, pp. 44–45, 46–47, 54 (Letters 532 Fer, 535 Fer, 541 Fer).
[277] Freud (1905d), *Three Essays*, p. 131.

the Oedipus complex.[278] Ferenczi seized on these indications in his review of *Three Essays* (whose third edition he translated into Hungarian), and pointed out that Freud was attempting to "overturn all accepted ideas", for nobody before had thought that a "psychological method, and an introspective one at that, could help to explain a biological problem".[279] Freud rightly held the view that psychoanalysis was capable of 'working out' a part of biology, namely the background to the sexual function. Perhaps one would someday "experience the final step too [...]: the exploitation of knowledge of the psychical mechanisms in organic and inorganic events in general".[280] In this manner, Ferenczi indicated the direction in which Freud, and he himself, intended psychoanalysis to develop further.

After writing the Wolf Man case, Freud began work on the (twelve) metapsychological studies. In July 1915, he prepared the final piece, the previously mentioned 'Overview of the Transference Neuroses', in which he set out his palaeobiological views at length.[281] The second part of the text connects with the remarks of Ferenczi cited above, on the sense of reality, to which direct reference was made, and which was elaborated into an overarching theory.[282] Freud wrote to Ferenczi that his "priority" in the work was "evident".[283] At first Freud "was thinking of alluding only briefly to the phylogenetic series with reference to your work and with fitting commendation of your fruitful and original idea about the influence of the geological vicissitudes". But then Ferenczi's reaction gave him "the desire for a more extensive presentation".[284] In late July he completed the text (he decided against publication in November 1917).[285] Ferenczi was happy that his sense of reality article had found a 'phylogenetic' sister in Freud's text, and he contributed some of his own thoughts and objections, which Freud in part took into account.[286] In October 1915, Ferenczi was planning his own series with the title 'Bioanalytical Essays', but did not make any progress.[287]

---

278 Freud (1918b), 'From the History of an Infantile Neurosis', pp. 86f., 119f.

279 S. Ferenczi (1915), 'Die wissenschaftliche Bedeutung von Freuds "Sexualtheorie"', pp. 239f.

280 Ibid., p. 241. It is against this background that one should read Freud's 'bold' attempt in *Beyond the Pleasure Principle* to 'work out' the function of the cell. Freud (1920g), *Beyond the Pleasure Principle*, p. 50.

281 See Grubrich-Simitis (1987c), 'Trauma oder Trieb'; Grubrich-Simitis (2007), 'Trauma oder Trieb: Wiederbetrachtet'.

282 Ferenczi (1913), 'Stages in the Development of the Sense of Reality'; Freud (1985a), *A Phylogenetic Fantasy*, pp. 11–13, 16.

283 Freud & Ferenczi (1993–2000), *Correspondence, Vol. 2*, p. 66 (Letter 551).

284 Ibid., p. 68 (Letter 554 F).

285 Ibid., p. 249 (Letter 715 F).

286 Ibid., pp. 70, 74 (Letters 556 Fer, 559 F).

287 Ibid., pp. 84–85 (Letter 572 Fer).

In April 1916, further ideas came to Ferenczi.[288] Freud encouraged him: the "biological speculations" were his "real field of study" in which he would be "without peer".[289] In July and October of that year, Ferenczi had two further periods of analysis with Freud: from time to time he reported new thoughts on the prehistory of the psychical.[290] In late December 1916, Freud made another attempt and told Ferenczi he had ordered "the Lamarck" from the library, "and our project, 'Lamarck and ΨA,' suddenly came to mind as hopeful and rich in content. I am predicting all kinds of things there and am actually already convinced about it". Now he wanted Ferenczi's assurance: "that you will maintain your collaboration and do something serious in the near future".[291]

In the following year too, Freud and Ferenczi held to their plan. In January 1917, Freud wrote out a project, detailed the division of labour, began reading Lamarck and other relevant works and drew up a bibliography.[292] Ferenczi sent his first notes, fell ill and spent several months' convalescence on the Semmering.[293] In late May, Freud called off the Lamarck work they had planned for the summer, saying he "would prefer to relinquish the whole thing" to Ferenczi.[294] But a few days later he received the first letter from Groddeck: "the most interesting letter from a German physician" that he had ever received, and its contents had numerous points of contact with the Lamarck idea.[295] Groddeck began with the assumption that the 'It' had a formative influence on the entire person, body and soul, just as one could say of the unconscious; that in Lamarck's sense, it constituted the 'missing link' between the physical and the psychical.[296] Freud was motivated by the closeness of Groddeck's idea to his own Lamarckian ideas to continue the project. In summer he spent two weeks in Hungary with Ferenczi;[297] it is possible they tried to collaborate. After the holiday Freud wrote: "Perhaps I will even grab hold of our big Lamarck work", which sounds as if he had now decided to take the initiative and develop the theme alone.[298] He asked Ferenczi for a "benevolent review" of a publication of Groddeck's, which

288 Ibid., p. 125 (Letter 606 Fer).
289 Ibid., p. 126 (Letter 607 F).
290 E.g. ibid., p. 133 (Letter 613 Fer).
291 Ibid., p. 167 (Letter 635 Fer).
292 Ibid., pp. 169, 175 (Letters 636 F, 642 F).
293 Ibid., pp. 170, 172 (Letters 637 Fer, 639 Fer).
294 Ibid., p. 210 (Letter 676 F).
295 Ibid., p. 212. On Lamarckism and psycho-Lamarckism see especially M. Giefer (2008), 'Zur Einführung'; Burkholz (1995), *Reflexe der Darwinismus-Debatte*, pp. 172ff.
296 Freud & Groddeck (2008), *Briefwechsel*, p. 62.
297 Freud & Abraham (2002), *Complete Correspondence*, p. 355.
298 Freud & Ferenczi (1993–2000), *Correspondence, Vol. 2*, p. 240 (Letter 708 F).

coincided with their "Lamarck idea", and Ferenczi once again sent his own thoughts.[299]

A letter from Freud to Abraham in November 1917 makes it clear what the two of them were planning with their Lamarck project:

> Have I really not told you about the Lamarck idea? It arose between Ferenczi and me, but neither of us has the time or spirit to tackle it at present. The idea is to put Lamarck entirely on our ground and to show that his 'need', which creates and transforms organs, is nothing but the power of *Ucs.* ideas over one's own body, of which we see remnants in hysteria, in short the 'omnipotence of thoughts'. This would actually supply a Ψa explanation of expediency; it would put the coping stone on ΨA. Two big principles of change (of progress) would emerge; the change through adaptation of one's own body and the subsequent change through transformation of the external world (autoplastic and heteroplastic), etc.[300]

In late 1917, Ferenczi was working on an adjunct problem in a Lamarckian way, namely the formation of hysterical symptoms, but his interest soon waned again. Freud too stated he could not make his mind up "about getting back to Lamarck".[301]

In May 1918, Ferenczi suggested they should again try working on Lamarck.[302] Freud agreed, but was concerned because, owing to luggage restrictions, he could not "take along the literature about Lamarck-Darwin".[303] Ferenczi assured him that they could find what they needed in the local libraries.[304] Freud's last day of work was on 29 June; afterwards he travelled first to the von Freund family villa in Budapest, where Ferenczi paid him frequent visits.[305] A study had been set up especially for him, and it may have been there that he wrote the notes on leaves of a Hungarian calendar. On 1 August, with Ferenczi, he drove to Csorbató, where they spent much time

299 Ibid., pp. 241, 242–243, 244 (Letters 709 F, 710 Fer, 711 Fer).

300 Freud & Abraham (2002), *Complete Correspondence*, pp. 361–362. Another instance where one senses Freud's desire to trace biology, i.e. the development of organs, back to psychical processes.

301 S. Ferenczi (1919b), 'The Phenomena of Hysterical Materialization'; Freud & Ferenczi (1993–2000), *Correspondence, Vol. 2*, p. 256 (Letter 720 F).

302 Ibid., p. 282 (Letter 743 Fer).

303 Ibid., p. 289 (Letter 751 F).

304 Ibid., p. 290 (Letter 752 Fer).

305 See Huppke & Schröter (2011), 'IPV-Sekretär und Mäzen', pp. 63–69; K. Lévy (2012), 'Erinnerungen an den Sommer 1918', p. 54.

together.[306] A letter of October 1918 records Ferenczi's disappointment "that the planned collaborative work was left undone", and that this was (as he wrote to Freud) on account of his own "ridiculous little irritations".[307] He compared the holiday in Csorbató with the one in Palermo in 1910, when their mutual paranoia project failed owing to personal incompatibility, but insisted: "The ground on which we will certainly always find ourselves, is, of course, science".[308]

This is not yet the end of the story. Though it seemed to Freud and Ferenczi in the summer of 1918 (perhaps as in 1917) that they had not reached an understanding on a common approach, both of them continued to follow the Lamarck theme. After Ferenczi's departure, Freud wrote on 13 September 1918: "Today, unsuspected, a 'thought' [*Einfall*] about our Lamarckian fantasies, the first impulse of its kind in two months".[309] The thought that had occurred two months previously might have been one of those on the calendar leaves, above all the one already quoted, about the 'masking' of death drives as life drives, and sexual union as repetition of the primeval bringing the lifeless to life. As I have indicated, these notes may be the first evidence of the basic ideas of *Beyond the Pleasure Principle*. One can probably disregard the fact that Freud speaks of "Lamarckian fantasies", whereas the notes do not exactly merit this description. My impression is that Freud considered 'Lamarckian' any ideas that related the prehistory of the psychical to the effect of primeval events.

For several months after September 1918, Freud did not return to the Lamarck project. Instead he informed Ferenczi of the "dream formation" of the two egos, his first response to the question of the aetiology of the war neuroses.[310] In October 1918, he also began the analysis of his daughter Anna, which probably stimulated him to write his essay on masochism in early 1919, and after ending it in mid-March, he mentions for the first time a new work "with the mysterious heading Beyond the Pleasure Principle".[311]

I consider it possible that this text emerged from similar circumstances to 'Overview of the Transference Neuroses' in summer 1915. At that time Freud took up suggestions from Ferenczi, who had published them two years

[306] See Kata Lévy's memoir of this period. How long Ferenczi stayed in Csorbató is unknown; a letter from Freud to his brother Alexander on 13 August 1918 (SFP/LoC) shows that it was at least two weeks. Ibid., esp. pp. 55f.; also Freud (2012a), 'Briefe an Kata und Lajos Lévy', p. 20.

[307] Freud & Ferenczi (1993–2000), *Correspondence, Vol. 2*, p. 297 (Letter 760 Fer).

[308] Ibid.

[309] Ibid., p. 293 (Letter 755 F).

[310] Ibid., p. 305; Freud (1919d), 'Introduction to *Psycho-Analysis and the War Neuroses*'.

[311] Freud & Ferenczi (1993–2000), *Correspondence, Vol. 2*, p. 335 (Letter 794 F).

previously, and now he had "the desire for a more extensive presentation".[312] The paranoia project planned for Palermo had followed a similar course: there too, no workable collaboration was achieved, so that Freud constructed his own version of the aetiology of paranoia, which he published in his study of the Schreber case.[313] Equally, after the renewed failure to cooperate with Ferenczi, he could have decided in early 1919 to realise the Lamarck project alone and find his own answer to the question of the prehistory of the psychical. The result would be *Beyond the Pleasure Principle*, with its theory of the origin of the drives, to which Ferenczi would react a few years later with his *Thalassa* (1924). In his obituary of Ferenczi, Freud characterised this work as the application of psychoanalysis "to the biology of the sexual processes and, beyond them, to organic life in general", and added: "It was perhaps the boldest application of psychoanalysis that was ever attempted".[314] Ferenczi had laid stress "on the conservative nature of the drives", recognised symbols "as evidence of ancient connections", and shown "how the characteristics of what is psychical preserve traces of primeval changes in the bodily substance".[315]

One gathers from this what it was that bound Freud and Ferenczi: their interest in the derivation of the psychical from a historical period that preceded ontogenetic development. Ferenczi was perhaps 'bolder' than Freud, if not with regard to genital theory, then on the relationship of psychoanalysis to biology. As already shown, Freud, too, did not really treat biology as an interlocutor of equal rank. For his part, Ferenczi left behind comments based on the idea that psychoanalysis has primacy over all other sciences. In one circular letter, for example, he wrote: "I am convinced that psychoanalysis is the catalyst of a new world view, that will unify all natural and human sciences".[316] Freud would probably not have expressed himself so imperiously, or at least not in a publication. But Ferenczi's attitude towards the biological sciences is not dissimilar to that represented by Freud in *Beyond the Pleasure Principle.*

---

312 Ibid., p. 68 (Letter 554 F).

313 S. Freud (1911c), 'Psycho-Analytic Notes on an Autobiographical Account of a Case of Paranoia', *SE* 12. Ferenczi also published his thoughts on paranoia independently: S. Ferenczi (1911a), 'Stimulation of the Anal Erotogenic Zone as a Precipitating Factor in Paranoia'; S. Ferenczi (1911b), 'On the Part played by Homosexuality in the Pathogenesis of Paranoia'.

314 S. Freud (1933c), 'Sandor Ferenczi', *SE* 22, p. 228. Grubrich-Simitis states that Freud and Ferenczi's "literary interests" differed in the summer of 1918. Grubrich-Simitis (1987b), 'Metapsychology and Metabiology', p. 95. Burkholz believes the Lamarck project was abandoned. Burkholz (1995), *Reflexe der Darwinismus-Debatte*, p. 174. By contrast I emphasise the long-term continuity of their common interests.

315 Freud (1933c), 'Sandor Ferenczi', p. 228.

316 Wittenberger & Tögel (1999–2006), *Rundbriefe des Geheimen Komitees, Bd. 1*, p. 200.

So much for the early history of *Beyond the Pleasure Principle.* I trust I have made it clear that this text deals with themes that had already preoccupied Freud for years. He and Ferenczi already had many failed attempts behind them, beginning with the 'Overview of the Transference Neuroses', which he himself withdrew from publication, surely because he was not persuaded that it carried conviction. There followed several years of initially fruitless discussions over the question of the nature and origin of drive impulses. That also explains how, in March 1919, after this long period of preparatory work, Freud only needed a few weeks to write out the first version of *Beyond the Pleasure Principle.*

Appendix II: On Freud's use of sources in the sixth chapter

In the sixth chapter of *Beyond the Pleasure Principle,* Freud refers to a number of writers who had worked upon the mortality and immortality of living organisms and on the origin of sexual reproduction. Mostly he mentions their work and provides the reference (year and page number). The impression is thus created that he paraphrased the ideas of the writers, i.e. presented them in his own words. However, when one consults the sources, one finds out that Freud has taken word for word, or closely followed, the formulations, phrases and entire sentences of other writers without making this adequately clear. This will be shown in some examples that follow (and the number could be increased), with reference to the work of August Weismann, Max Hartmann, Alexander Lipschütz and Richard Avenarius.[317]

It should be noted at the outset that the fine formulation concerning sexual reproduction lending life "the appearance of immortality" – Freud uses it on the first page of the sixth chapter – originates with Johannes Müller (1801–1858).[318] It was often quoted, for example, among the writers mentioned here: by Weismann, by Hartmann and also by Franz Doflein.[319] The "simple, but meaningful dictum", as Weismann called it, comes from Müller's *Handbuch der Physiologie des Menschen.* In order to give an impression of the style of the biological science of the time, the formulation should be quoted in context. Müller writes:

317 Most of the writers mentioned here – namely Müller (*Handbuch der Physiologie des Menschen,* 1837); Weismann (1882, 1884, 1892); Lipschütz (1919) – are to be found in Freud's library. See J.K. Davies & G. Fichtner (2006), *Freud's Library.*

318 Freud (1920g), *Beyond the Pleasure Principle,* p. 44.

319 Weismann (1882), *Über die Dauer des Lebens,* p. 5; M. Hartmann (1906), *Tod und Fortpflanzung,* p. 37; and also by F. Doflein (1919), *Das Problem des Todes,* p. 3.

> While life is continued, with an appearance of immortality, from one individual to another, the individuals themselves perish: but if *all* the individuals of a species are destroyed, the species itself, whether of animals or plants, becomes extinct, as the history of the earth proves. The *vital* or *organic force* flows, as it were, in a stream from the producing parts into those ever newly produced, while the old parts perish.[320]

Here Freud borrowed a formulation whose author he did not have to name since he was commonly known. It is another matter with the publications of August Weismann. Freud refers to him most in the sixth chapter, and to three works: *The Duration of Life* (1889 [1882]), *On Life and Death* (1889 [1884]) and *The Germ-Plasm. A Theory of Heredity* (1893 [1892]).[321] The first of the references reads:

> It was he [Weismann] who introduced the division of living substance into mortal and immortal parts. The mortal part is the body in the narrower sense – the 'soma' – which alone is subject to natural death. The germ cells, on the other hand, are potentially immortal, in so far as they are able, under certain favourable conditions, to develop into a new individual, or, in other words, to surround themselves with a new soma.[322]

In the handwritten manuscript of *Beyond the Pleasure Principle*, in the sixth chapter in particular, one finds inverted commas before "*potentia*" ("potentially") and after "*umgeben*" ("to surround themselves") as well as a complete reference to the source, namely: "Über Leben und Tod, 2. Aufl. 1892, p. 20".[323] But in the print version of *Beyond the Pleasure Principle* the inverted commas have been omitted, perhaps forgotten by the printer and overlooked during correction of the proofs. It is no longer clear that a long quotation ends where a source reference occurs, so that the text with which we are familiar gives the impression that these are all Freud's words. But they are Weismann's. In his text one reads:

[320] Müller (1837), *Handbuch der Physiologie des Menschen*, p. 40.
[321] See Freud (1920g), *Beyond the Pleasure Principle*, pp. 45–49, 56.
[322] Ibid., pp. 45–46; in this volume, p. 64.
[323] See ibid. This precision is lost in the *Studienausgabe*, where there is a reference only to the differently paginated 1884 first edition of the work, with no page reference (*Studienausgabe* Bd. III, S. 255, Anm. 1).

> It is necessary to distinguish between the mortal and immortal part of the individual – the body in its narrower sense (*soma*) and the germ-cells. Death only affects the former; the germ-cells are potentially immortal, in so far as they are able, under favourable circumstances, to develop into a new individual, or, in other words, to surround themselves with a new body (*soma*).[324]

Whereas in this case it may have been carelessness in the typesetting, Freud himself inserts no inverted commas in the next but one paragraph of *Beyond the Pleasure Principle*, where he refers four times to Weismann.[325] He correctly cites the sources with publication year and page number, e.g. Weismann 1882, p. 38 in the footnotes [of the German edition: in the *Standard Edition* the references are in brackets in the text – Tr.]. Yet one is surprised that so many of Weismann's formulations appear, which Freud repeats basically unaltered. In this single paragraph alone, one reads, for example, that "in unicellular organisms the individual and the reproductive cell are still one and the same";[326] that death "cannot be regarded as an absolute necessity with its basis in the very nature of life";[327] that "[d]eath is rather a matter of expediency", because "an unlimited duration of individual life would become a quite pointless luxury".[328] The paragraph ends thus:

> It is not the case, on the other hand, that reproduction was only introduced at the same time as death. On the contrary, it is a primal characteristic of living matter, like growth (from which it originated) [...] (Weismann, 1884, 84f.).[329]

In Weismann one reads "that also, the other way round, reproduction was not first introduced at the same time as death, that on the contrary it is a primal characteristic of living matter, like growth from which it originated".[330] Although Freud's footnotes show that he cites Weismann, one would not have thought that he followed him so closely and extensively.

---

324 A. Weismann (1889 [1882]), *On The Duration of Life*, p. 122.
325 Freud (1920g), *Beyond the Pleasure Principle*, pp. 46–47.
326 Weismann (1882), *Über die Dauer des Lebens*, p. 38; Freud (1920g), *Beyond the Pleasure Principle*, p. 46.
327 Weismann (1882), *Über die Dauer des Lebens*, p. 33; Freud (1920g), *Beyond the Pleasure Principle*, p. 46.
328 Ibid.
329 Ibid., pp. 46f.
330 A. Weismann (1884), *Über Leben und Tod*, p. 84.

A little later Freud refers to the work *Tod und Fortpflanzung* (1906) by Max Hartmann, briefly summarises his position, and in doing so cites in inverted commas two formulations typical of Hartmann, and provides the exact source reference with year and page number. But the textual correspondence goes further than one might expect. In *Beyond the Pleasure Principle* he writes:

> Hartmann (1906, p. 29) does not regard the appearance of a 'dead body' – a dead portion of the living substance – as the criterion of death, but defines death as 'the termination of individual development'. In this sense protozoa too are mortal; in their case death always coincides with reproduction, but is to some extent obscured by it, since the whole substance of the parent animal may be transmitted directly to the young offspring.[331]

In Hartmann one reads at the referenced point (whose formulation in part refers back to a previous passage):

> In the last mentioned cases reproduction to some extent obscures death, since the whole substance of the parent animal may be transmitted directly to the young offspring. Consequently, what is to be regarded as the essential feature of individual death is not the dead body, but the termination of individual development.[332]

Following this, Freud refers to Alexander Lipschütz (1883–1980), whom he had discussed at length elsewhere, in the fourth edition of *Three Essays* (see above). In a footnote he refers to his booklet *Warum wir sterben* (1914): "For this and what follows see Lipschütz".[333] The reference is no more than justified. The following passages from *Beyond the Pleasure Principle* consist in part of word for word borrowings, in part of paraphrasings of Lipschütz's exposition. I have selected two examples.

> — *Freud:* If two of the animalculae, at the moment before they show signs of senescence, are able to coalesce with each other, that is to "conjugate" (soon after which they once more separate), they are saved from growing old and become "rejuvenated".[334]

331 Freud (1920g), *Beyond the Pleasure Principle*, p. 47.

332 See Hartmann (1906), *Tod und Fortpflanzung*, p. 22.

333 Freud (1920g), *Beyond the Pleasure Principle*, p. 47 n. 2; Lipschütz (1914), *Warum wir sterben*, pp. 26 and 52ff.

334 Freud (1920g), *Beyond the Pleasure Principle*, p. 48.

— *Lipschütz:* If two creatures coalesce together, "copulate", at a moment before "signs of senescence" can be detected, in order to separate again after a time, they become "rejuvenated", they are saved from "growing old".[335]

Or:

— In *Beyond the Pleasure Principle* one reads that the "recuperative effects of conjugation can, however, be replaced by certain stimulating agents, by alterations in the composition of the fluid which provides their nourishment, by raising their temperature or by shaking them."[336]
— In Lipschütz we find "that not only copulation allows creatures to overcome the bad situation, but also various simple stimulating agents, such as alterations in the composition of the fluid which provides their nourishment, raising their temperature or shaking them."[337]

Finally Richard Avenarius (1843–1896) should be cited, a German philosopher known as the founder of empirio-criticism. Avenarius (1888) sketched a bio-mechanical and strictly logical outline of the processes of life, and coined, among others, the terms 'vital differences' and their 'optimum'. According to him, vital differences arise from the union of different organisms; they must be "lived off" and "levelled out". In *Beyond the Pleasure Principle* Freud employs these concepts – vital differences, that arise from union, their optimum and levelling out – as an explanation of the striving towards a zero point, but without naming the author, which in this case, as in that of Müller's "appearance of immortality", could be attributable to the fact that the origin of the term was generally known.[338]

I will make do with these examples. They show how close Freud's thought was to ideas in the biology of the time. They speak of life, death and reproduction in the same tone, and some of the poetic or pithy formulations that we have come to ascribe to Freud originate in contemporaneous writers

335 Lipschütz (1914), *Warum wir sterben*, p. 56.
336 Freud (1920g), *Beyond the Pleasure Principle*, p. 48.
337 Lipschütz (1914), *Warum wir sterben*, p. 56. On pp. 59f., 64f., 80f. of *Warum wir sterben*, one finds further descriptions of findings in research on protista, which Freud repeats in similar words. Freud (1920g), *Beyond the Pleasure Principle*, pp. 47f., 50.
338 Freud (1920g), *Beyond the Pleasure Principle*, p. 55. The terms 'optimum of vital difference' and 'equalising' tensions also appear, as stated, in the Hungarian calendar notes of July 1918 (?), and so does Lipschütz's name, in the note: "Immortality of substance in general does not exist. Lipschütz". This could refer to *Why We Die*: "there is no immortality in the sense of an unchanging continuity of the living substance". Lipschütz (1914), *Warum wir sterben*, p. 29.

on the biological sciences or philosophy, without this being visible in the text of *Beyond the Pleasure Principle* as we know it from the *Gesammelte Werke*, the *Studienausgabe* or the *Standard Edition*.

Bibliography

Aichhorn, Thomas (2006), 'Jenseits des Lustprinzips (1920)', in: ed. Hans-Martin Lohmann & Joachim Pfeiffer, *Freud-Handbuch. Leben – Werk – Wirkung*. Stuttgart & Weimar: Metzler, pp. 158–162.

Akhtar, Salman (2011), 'Introduction', in: ed. Salman Akhtar & Mary Kay O'Neil, *On Freud's Beyond the Pleasure Principle*. London: Karnac, pp. 1–10.

Andreas-Salomé, Lou (1965), *In der Schule bei Freud. Tagebuch eines Jahres 1912 1913*. Munich: Kindler.

Assoun, Paul-Laurent (2009), *Dictionnaire des oeuvres psychanalytiques*. Paris: Presses universitaires de France.

Avenarius, Richard (1888), *Kritik der reinen Erfahrung*. Leipzig: Fues.

Beland, Hermann (2008), 'Erklärungs- und Arbeitswert der Todestriebhypothese. Diskussion anhand klinischer und theoretischer Beispiele', *Jahrbuch der Psychoanalyse* 56, pp. 23–47.

Bernhardt, Heike (2011), 'Johann Jaroslaw Marcinowski (1868–1935) und sein Sanatorium Haus Sielbeck am Uklei. Psychoanalyse im klinischen Setting'. Mit einem Anhang: Freuds Briefe an Marcinowski, ed. Gerhard Fichtner & Michael Schröter, *Luzifer-Amor* 24(47), pp. 133–168.

Bohleber, Werner (2000), 'Die Entwicklung der Traumatheorie in der Psychoanalyse', *Psyche. Zeitschrift für Psychoanalyse und ihre Anwendungen* 54, pp. 797–839.

Breuer, Josef & Freud, Sigmund (1895d), *Studies on Hysteria*, in: *Standard Edition of the Complete Psychological Works of Sigmund Freud, Vol. 2*, transl. James Strachey. London: Hogarth Press, 1953–1974.

Burkholz, Roland (1995), *Reflexe der Darwinismus-Debatte in der Theorie Freuds*. Stuttgart & Bad Cannstatt: Frommann-Holzboog.

Butzer, Ralph J. & Burkholz, Roland (1991), 'Urvater und Eiszeit. Biologischevolutionäres und psycholamarckistisches Denken', *Luzifer-Amor* 4(8), pp. 24–49.

Danckwardt, Joachim F. (2011), 'Die Verleugnung des Todestriebs', *Jahrbuch der Psychoanalyse* 62, pp. 137–116.

Davies, J. Keith & Fichtner, Gerhard (eds.) (2006), *Freud's Library. A Comprehensive Catalogue – Freuds Bibliothek. Vollständiger Katalog*. London & Tübingen: Freud Museum & Edition Diskord.

Diercks, Christine & Schlüter, Sabine (2011), *Psycho-Sexualität. Grundlagen, infantile Sexualität, Libido, Todestrieb*, Sigmund-Freud-Vorlesungen 2010. Vienna: Mandelbaum.

Doflein, Franz (1919), *Das Problem des Todes und der Unsterblichkeit bei den Pflanzen und Tieren.* Jena: G. Fischer.

Eickhoff, Friedrich-Wilhelm (1995), 'Review: Grubrich-Simitis, I., Zurück zu Freuds Texten', *Psychoanalytic Quarterly* 64, pp. 762–769.

Fallend, Karl (1995), *Sonderlinge, Träumer, Sensitive. Psychoanalyse auf dem Weg zur Institution und Profession. Protokolle der Wiener Psychoanalytischen Vereinigung und biographische Studien.* Vienna: Jugend & Volk.

Falzeder, Ernst (1994), 'My Grand-Patient, my Chief Tormentor: A hitherto Unnoticed Case of Freud's and the Consequences', *Psychoanalytic Quarterly* 63, pp. 297–233.

Falzeder, Ernst (2007), 'Is there still an unknown Freud? A Note on the Publication of Freud's Texts and on Unpublished Documents', *Psychoanalysis and History* 9, pp. 201–232.

Fechner, Gustav Theodor (1873), *Einige Ideen zur Schöpfungs- und Entwickelungsgeschichte der Organismen.* Leipzig: Breitkopf & Härtel; new edition: Tübingen: Edition Diskord, 1985.

Feldman, Michael (2011), 'Manifestations of the Death Instinct in the Consulting Room', in: ed. Salman Akhtar & Mary Kay O'Neil, *On Freud's Beyond the Pleasure Principle.* London: Karnac, pp. 206–229.

Fenichel, Otto (1945), *The Psychoanalytic Theory of Neurosis.* New York: Norton.

Ferenczi, Sándor (1911a), 'Stimulation of the Anal Erotogenic Zone as a Precipitating Factor in Paranoia', in: Sándor Ferenczi, *Final Contributions to Psycho-Analysis*, ed. Michael Balint, transl. Eric Mosbacher et al. London: Hogarth Press, 1955, pp. 295–298.

Ferenczi, Sándor (1911b), 'On the Part played by Homosexuality in the Pathogenesis of Paranoia', in: Sándor Ferenczi, *First Contributions to Psychoanalysis*, transl. Ernest Jones. London: Hogarth Press, 1952, pp. 154–186.

Ferenczi, Sándor (1913), 'Stages in the Development of the Sense of Reality', in: Sándor Ferenczi, *First Contributions to Psychoanalysis*, transl. Ernest Jones. London: Hogarth Press, 1952, pp. 213–239.

Ferenczi, Sándor (1915), 'Die wissenschaftliche Bedeutung von Freuds "Sexualtheorie"', in: Sándor Ferenczi, *Bausteine zur Psychoanalyse, Vol. 1.* Frankfurt a.M., Berlin & Vienna: Ullstein, 1984, pp. 237–242.

Ferenczi, Sándor (1919a), 'Die Psychoanalyse der Kriegsneurosen', in: Sándor Ferenczi, *Bausteine zur Psychoanalyse, Vol. 3.* Frankfurt a.M., Berlin & Vienna: Ullstein, 1984, pp. 95–118.

Ferenczi, Sándor (1919b), 'The Phenomena of Hysterical Materialization', in: Sándor Ferenczi, *Further Contributions to the Theory and Technique of Psycho-Analysis.* London: Hogarth Press, 1950, pp. 89–104.

Ferenczi, Sándor (1920a), 'Rezension Lipschütz, A.: Die Pubertätsdrüse und ihre Wirkungen', *Internationale Zeitschrift für Psychoanalyse* 6, pp. 84–89; also in: Sándor Ferenczi, *Bausteine zur Psychoanalyse, Vol. 4.* Frankfurt a.M., Berlin & Vienna: Ullstein, 1984, pp. 130–139.

Ferenczi, Sándor (1920b), 'Rezension Schaxel, A.: Über die Darstellung allgemeiner Biologie (1919)', *Internationale Zeitschrift für Psychoanalyse* 6, pp. 82–84; also in: Sándor Ferenczi, *Bausteine zur Psychoanalyse, Vol. 4*. Frankfurt a.M., Berlin & Vienna: Ullstein, 1984, pp. 126–130.

Ferenczi, Sándor (1924), *Thalassa: A Theory of Genitality*. New York: The Psychoanalytic Quarterly Inc., 1938; reprinted London: Karnac, 1989.

Fernando, Joseph (2012), 'Trauma und der Zeroprozess', *Psyche. Zeitschrift für Psychoanalyse und ihre Anwendungen* 66(11), pp. 1043–1073.

Fichtner, Gerhard & Hirschmüller, Albrecht (2011), 'Gedankensplitter – Gedankenkeime. Freuds Notizbüchlein aus den Jahren 1901 bis 1910', *Luzifer-Amor* 24(48), pp. 140–155.

Fliess, Wilhelm (1906), *Der Ablauf des Lebens. Grundlegung zur exakten Biologie*. Leipzig & Vienna: Deuticke, 1923.

Fliess, Wilhelm (1909), *Vom Leben und vom Tod. Biologische Vorträge*. Jena: Diederichs, 1919.

Frank, Claudia (2011), 'Zum Ringen mit Manifestationen des Todestriebes – theoretische und klinische Aspekte', *Jahrbuch der Psychoanalyse* 62, pp. 75–96.

Freud, Sigmund (1900a), *The Interpretation of Dreams*, in: *Standard Edition of the Complete Psychological Works of Sigmund Freud, Vol. 4–5*, transl. James Strachey. London: Hogarth Press, 1953–1974.

Freud, Sigmund (1905d), *Three Essays on the Theory of Sexuality*, *SE* 7, pp. 130–243.

Freud, Sigmund (1908b), 'Character and Anal Eroticism', *SE* 9, pp. 169–175.

Freud, Sigmund (1909d), 'Notes upon a Case of Obsessional Neurosis', *SE* 10, pp. 155–249.

Freud, Sigmund (1910c), 'Leonardo da Vinci and a Memory of his Childhood', *SE* 11, pp. 63–137.

Freud, Sigmund (1910i), 'The Psycho-analytic View of Psychogenic Disturbance of Vision', *SE* 11, pp. 211–218.

Freud, Sigmund (1911b), 'Formulations on the Two Principles of Mental Functioning', *SE* 12, pp. 218–226.

Freud, Sigmund (1911c), 'Psychoanalytic Notes on an Autobiographical Account of a Case of Paranoia (Dementia Paranoides)', *SE* 12, pp. 9–82.

Freud, Sigmund (1912–1913a), *Totem and Taboo*, *SE* 13, pp. 1–161.

Freud, Sigmund (1913f), 'The Theme of the Three Caskets', *SE* 12, pp. 291–301.

Freud, Sigmund (1914c), 'On Narcissism: An Introduction', *SE* 14, pp. 73–102.

Freud, Sigmund (1914g), 'Remembering, Repeating and Working-Through', *SE* 12, pp. 147–156.

Freud, Sigmund (1915c), 'Instincts and Their Vicissitudes', *SE* 14, pp. 117–140.

Freud, Sigmund (1915e), 'The Unconscious', *SE* 14, pp. 166–204.

Freud, Sigmund (1916–1917a), *Introductory Lectures on Psycho-Analysis*, *SE* 15 & 16.

Freud, Sigmund (1917b), 'A Childhood Recollection from *Dichtung und Wahrheit*', *SE* 17, pp. 147–156.

Freud, Sigmund (1918b), 'From the History of an Infantile Neurosis', *SE* 17, pp. 7–122.
Freud, Sigmund (1919d), 'Introduction to *Psycho-Analysis and the War Neuroses*', *SE* 17, pp. 207–210.
Freud, Sigmund (1919e), 'A Child is Being Beaten', *SE* 17, pp. 179–204.
Freud, Sigmund (1919h), 'The Uncanny', *SE* 17, pp. 219–252.
Freud, Sigmund (1920a), 'The Psychogenesis of a Case of Female Homosexuality', *SE* 18, pp. 147–172.
Freud, Sigmund (1920f), 'Supplements to the Theory of Dreams', *SE* 18, pp. 4–5.
Freud, Sigmund (1920g), *Beyond the Pleasure Principle*, *SE* 18, pp. 7–64.
Freud, Sigmund (1921c), *Group Psychology and the Analysis of the Ego*, *SE* 18, pp. 69–143.
Freud, Sigmund (1923b), *The Ego and the Id*, *SE* 19, pp. 12–66.
Freud, Sigmund (1923c), 'Remarks on the Theory and Practice of Dream-Interpretation', *SE* 19, pp. 109–121.
Freud, Sigmund (1924c), 'The Economic Problem of Masochism', *SE* 19, pp. 159–170.
Freud, Sigmund (1924g [1923]), 'Letter to Fritz Wittels', *SE* 19, pp. 286–288.
Freud, Sigmund (1926d), *Inhibitions, Symptoms and Anxiety*, *SE* 20, pp. 87–172.
Freud, Sigmund (1933c), 'Sándor Ferenczi', *SE* 22, pp. 227–229.
Freud, Sigmund (1937c), 'Analysis Terminable and Interminable', *SE* 23, pp. 216–253.
Freud, Sigmund (1939a), *Moses and Monotheism*, *SE* 23, pp. 7–137.
Freud, Sigmund (1940a), *An Outline of Psycho-Analysis*, *SE* 23, pp. 144–207.
Freud, Sigmund (1940e), 'Splitting of the Ego in the Process of Defence', *SE* 23, pp. 275–278.
Freud, Sigmund (1950c [1895]), 'Project for a Scientific Psychology', *SE* 1, pp. 295–387.
Freud, Sigmund (1960), *The Letters of Sigmund Freud*, ed. Ernst L. Freud, transl. Tania Stern & James Stern. London: Hogarth Press.
Freud, Sigmund (1985a [1987]), *A Phylogenetic Fantasy. Overview of the Transference Neuroses*, ed. Ilse Grubrich-Simitis, transl. Axel Hoffer & Peter T. Hoffer. Cambridge (MA): The Belknap Press of Harvard UP.
Freud, Sigmund (1985b [1986]), *The Complete Letters of Sigmund Freud to Wilhelm Fliess, 1877–1904*, transl. & ed. Jeffrey Masson. Cambridge (MA) & London: The Belknap Press of Harvard UP.
Freud, Sigmund (2010), *Unterdeß halten wir zusammen. Briefe an die Kinder*, ed. Michael Schröter in collaboration with Ingeborg Meyer-Palmedo & Ernst Falzeder. Berlin: Aufbau.
Freud, Sigmund (2012a), 'Briefe an Kata und Lajos Lévy (1918–1926)', in: ed. Thomas Aichhorn & Michael Schröter, *Luzifer-Amor* 25(50), pp. 7–61.

Freud, Sigmund (2012b), *Brieven aan Jeanne Lampl-de Groot (1921–1939), met fragmenten uit brieven aan haar ouders (1921-1923)*, ed. Gertie Bögels. Amsterdam: Sjibbolet.

Freud, Sigmund & Abraham, Karl (2002), *The Complete Correspondence of Sigmund Freud and Karl Abraham 1907–1925: Completed Edition*, transcr. and ed. Ernst Falzeder, transl. Caroline Schwarzacher et. al., introduction by André Haynal & Ernst Falzeder. London: Karnac.

Freud, Sigmund & Andreas-Salomé, Lou (1972 [1966]), *Letters*, ed. Ernst Pfeiffer, transl. William Robson-Scott & Elaine Robson-Scott. London: Hogarth.

Freud, Sigmund & Binswanger, Ludwig (2003 [1992]), *The Sigmund Freud-Ludwig Binswanger Correspondence 1908–1938*. New York & London: Other Press.

Freud, Sigmund & Eitingon, Max (2004), *Briefwechsel 1906–1939, 2 Vols.*, ed. Michael Schröter, Tübingen: Edition Diskord.

Freud, Sigmund & Ferenczi, Sándor (1993–2000), *The Correspondence of Sigmund Freud and Sándor Ferenczi, 3 Vols.*, eds. Eva Brabant, Ernst Falzeder & Patrizia Giampieri-Deutsch under the supervision of André Haynal, transcr. Ingeborg Meyer-Palmedo, transl. Peter T. Hoffer. Cambridge (MA) & London: The Belknap Press of Harvard UP.

Freud, Sigmund & Freud, Anna (2013 [2006]), *Correspondence 1904–1938*, ed. Ingeborg Meyer-Palmedo, transl. Nick Somers. Cambridge: Polity.

Freud, Sigmund & Groddeck, Georg (2008), *Briefwechsel*, ed. Michael Giefer in collaboration with Beate Schuh. Frankfurt a.M. & Basel: Stroemfeld.

Freud, Sigmund & Jones, Ernest (1993), *The Complete Correspondence of Sigmund Freud and Ernest Jones 1908–1939*, ed. R. Andrew Paskauskas. Cambridge (MA) & London: The Belknap Press of Harvard UP.

Freud, Sigmund & Pfister, Oskar (1963), *Psychoanalysis and Faith: the Letters of Sigmund Freud and Oskar Pfister*, ed. Heinrich Meng & Ernst L. Freud, transl. Eric Mosbacher. London: Hogarth Press.

Früh, Friedl (2011), 'Zu Todestrieb und Wiederholungszwang in Freuds "Jenseits des Lustprinzips" – mit Jean Laplanche gelesen', in: Christine Diercks & Sabine Schlüter, *Psycho-Sexualität. Grundlagen, infantile Sexualität, Libido, Todestrieb*, Sigmund-Freud-Vorlesungen 2010. Vienna: Mandelbaum, pp. 189–198.

Giefer, Michael (2008), 'Zur Einführung', in: Sigmund Freud & Georg Groddeck (2008), *Briefwechsel*, ed. Michael Giefer in collaboration with Beate Schuh. Frankfurt a.M. & Basel: Stroemfeld, pp. 9–41.

Goette, Alexander (1883), *Über den Ursprung des Todes*. Hamburg: Voss.

Grubrich-Simitis, Ilse (1987a), 'Trauma oder Trieb – Trieb und Trauma. Lektionen aus Freuds phylogenetischer Phantasie von 1915', *Psyche. Zeitschrift für Psychoanalyse und ihre Anwendungen* 41, pp. 992–1023.

Grubrich-Simitis, Ilse (1987b), 'Metapsychology and Metabiology', in: Sigmund Freud, *A Phylogenetic Fantasy. Overview of the Transference Neuroses*, ed. Ilse Grubrich-Simitis, transl. Axel Hoffer & Peter T. Hoffer. Cambridge (MA): The Belknap Press of Harvard UP, 1987, pp. 85–119.

Grubrich-Simitis, Ilse (1996 [1993]), *Back to Freud's Texts. Making Silent Documents Speak*, transl. Philip Slotkin. New Haven & London: Yale UP.

Grubrich-Simitis, Ilse (1997 [1991]), 'Freud's study of Moses as a Day-dream: A Biographical Essay', in: Ilse Grubrich-Simitis, *Early Freud and Late Freud. Reading Anew Studies on Hysteria and Moses and Monotheism*. London: Routledge, pp. 53–89.

Grubrich-Simitis, Ilse (2007), 'Trauma oder Trieb – Trieb und Trauma: Wiederbetrachtet', *Psyche. Zeitschrift für Psychoanalyse und ihre Anwendungen* 61, pp. 637–656.

Gumbel, Erich (1995), 'Über mein Leben mit der Psychoanalyse', *Jahrbuch der Psychoanalyse* 34, pp. 7–63.

Hartmann, Max (1906), *Tod und Fortpflanzung*. Munich: Reinhardt.

Haynal, André (1989 [1987]), *Die Technik-Debatte in der Psychoanalyse. Freud, Ferenczi, Balint*. Frankfurt a.M.: S. Fischer.

Hering, Ewald (1878), *Zur Lehre vom Lichtsinn. Sechs Mittheilungen an der Kaiserlichen Akademie der Wissenschaft in Wien*. Vienna: Gerolds.

Hock, Udo (2000), *Das Unbewußte Denken. Wiederholung und Todestrieb*. Frankfurt a.M.: S. Fischer.

Holt, Robert R. (1962), 'A critical examination of Freud's concept of bound vs. free cathexis', in: Robert R. Holt, *Freud Re-appraised. A fresh look at psychoanalytic theory*. New York & London: Guilford Press, 1989, pp. 71–113.

Holt, Robert R. (1968), 'Beyond vitalism and mechanism. Freud's concept of psychic energy', in: Robert R. Holt, *Freud Re-appraised. A fresh look at psychoanalytic theory*. New York & London: Guilford Press, 1989, pp. 141–168.

Holt, Robert R. (1989), *Freud Re-appraised. A fresh look at psychoanalytic theory*, New York & London: Guilford Press.

Huppke, Andrea & Schröter, Michael (2011), 'IPV-Sekretär und Mäzen – Freuds Patient, Vermögensverwalter und Freund. Die Briefe Anton v. Freunds an Sigmund Freud (1916–1919)', *Luzifer-Amor* 24(48), pp. 53–98.

Jones, Ernest (1957), *The Life and Work of Sigmund Freud. Vol. 3. The Last Phase 1919–1939*. London: Hogarth Press.

Joseph, Betty (1982), 'Addiction to Near-death', *International Journal of Psychoanalysis* 63, pp. 449–456.

Jung, Carl Gustav (1909), 'Die Bedeutung des Vaters für das Schicksal des Einzelnen', *Jahrbuch für psychoanalytische und psychopathologische Forschung* 1, pp. 155–173.

Kernberg, Otto (2009), 'The Concept of the Death Drive. A Clinical Perspective', *International Journal of Psychoanalysis* 90, pp. 1009–1023.

Kimmerle, Gerd (1988), *Verneinung und Wiederkehr. Eine methodologische Lektüre von Freuds »Jenseits des Lustprinzips«*. Tübingen: Edition Diskord.

King, Pearl & Steiner, Ricardo (eds.) (1991), *The Freud-Klein Controversies 1941–1945*. London: Tavistock & Routledge.

Kirchhoff, Christine (2011), 'Von der Wiederkehr des unbewußten Wunsches als Todestrieb und der Nachträglichkeit in der Theorie', *Jahrbuch der Psychoanalyse* 62, pp. 97–119.

Krause, Rainer (2012), 'Psychodynamische Aspekte der Gedächtnisfunktion', *Forum Psychoanalyse* 28, pp. 11–25.

Kris, Anton (1994), 'Freud's Treatment of a Narcissistic Patient', *International Journal of Psychoanalysis* 75, pp. 649–664.

Laplanche, Jean (1986), 'Der Todestrieb in der Theorie des Sexualtriebs', in: Jean Laplanche, *Die allgemeine Veführungstheorie*. Tübingen: Edition Diskord, pp. 178–198.

Laplanche, Jean (2004), 'The so-called "Death Drive": A Sexual Drive', *British Journal of Psychotherapy* 20(4), pp. 455–471.

Laplanche, Jean & Pontalis, Jean-Bertrand (1973), *The Language of Psycho-Analysis*. London: Hogarth Press.

Lévy, Kata (2012), 'Erinnerungen an den Sommer 1918', *Luzifer-Amor* 25(50), pp. 52–60.

Lipschütz, Alexander (1914), *Warum wir sterben*. Stuttgart: Franckh.

Lipschütz, Alexander (1919), *Die Pubertätsdrüse und ihre Wirkungen*. Bern: Bircher.

Low, Barbara (1920), *Psycho-Analysis. A Brief Account of the Freudian Theory*. London: Allen & Unwin.

Mahoney, Patrick J. (1987), *Freud as a Writer*. New Haven & London: Yale UP.

Makari, George (2008), *Revolution in Mind. The Creation of Psychoanalysis*. London: Harper Collins.

Marcinowski, Johannes (1918), 'Die erotischen Quellen der Minderwertigkeitsgefühle', *Zeitschrift für Sexualwissenschaft* 4, pp. 313–321.

May[-Tolzmann], Ulrike (1991), 'Zu den Anfängen des Narzißmus: Ellis – Näcke – Sadger – Freud', *Luzifer-Amor* 4(8), pp. 50–88.

May[-Tolzmann], Ulrike (1996), *Freuds frühe klinische Theorie (1894–1896). Wiederentdeckung und Rekonstruktion*. Tübingen: Edition Diskord.

May, Ulrike (2008 [2007]), 'Nineteen Patients in Analysis with Freud (1910–1920), *American Imago* 65: 41–105.

May, Ulrike (2010), 'Karl Abrahams Revolution: Vom Wonnesaugen zum oralaggressiven Vernichtungswunsch', *Luzifer-Amor* 23(46), pp. 58–85.

May, Ulrike (2011a), 'Auf dem Weg zu Karl Abrahams "Versuch einer Entwicklungsgeschichte der Libido" (1924). Der Beitrag August Stärckes zur Theorie der Oralität', in: ed. Christine Diercks & Sabine Schlüter, *Psycho-Sexualität. Grundlagen, infantile Sexualität, Libido, Todestrieb*, Sigmund-Freud-Vorlesungen 2010. Vienna: Mandelbaum, pp. 131–153.

May, Ulrike (2011b [2010]), 'Fourteen Hundred Hours of Analysis with Freud: Viktor von Dirsztay: A Biographical Sketch', *Psychoanalysis and History* 13(1), pp. 91–138.

May, Ulrike (2011c), 'Ein ungarischer Baron in Analyse bei Freud', in: ed. Agnes Berger et al., *Der psychoanalytische Aufbruch Budapest – Berlin 1918–1920.* Frankfurt a.M.: Brandes & Apsel, pp. 25–33.

May, Ulrike (2012a), 'Zur Frühgeschichte der Analerotik', *Psyche. Zeitschrift für Psychoanalyse und ihre Anwendungen* 66, pp. 213–246.

May, Ulrike (2012b), *Trauma und Konflikt in Jenseits des Lustprinzips. Der Todestrieb und die Grenzen der Psychoanalyse.* Gießen: Psychosozial-Verlag.

May, Ulrike (2013), 'Freud's Beyond the Pleasure Principle: The end of psychoanalysis or its new beginning?', *International Forum of Psychoanalysis* 22, pp. 208–216.

Menninger, Anneliese (2011), *Sigmund Freud als Autor in Villarets Handwörterbuch der Gesamten Medizin von 1888–1891*, Hamburg: Kovač.

Meyer-Palmedo, Ingeborg & Fichtner, Gerhard (1999 [1989]), *Freud-Bibliographie mit Werkkonkordanz. Second ed., revised and expanded.* Frankfurt a.M.: S. Fischer.

Molnar, Michael (ed.) (1992), *The Diary of Sigmund Freud, 1929–1939. A Chronicle of Events in the Last Decade.* London: Hogarth Press.

Mordell, Albert (1919), *The Erotic Motive in Literature.* London: Kegan Paul, Trench Trubner & Co., Ltd.

Mühlleitner, Elke (1992), *Biographisches Lexikon der Psychoanalyse. Die Mitglieder der Psychologischen Mittwoch-Gesellschaft und der Wiener Psychoanalytischen Vereinigung 1902–1938.* Tübingen: Edition Diskord.

Müller, Johannes (1837), *Handbuch der Physiologie des Menschen für Vorlesungen, Vol. 1*, Koblenz: Hölscher. Available at: http://reader.digitalesammlungen.de/resolve/display/bsb10369073.html [Accessed 1 February 2015].

Müller-Pozzi, Heinz (2008), *Eine Triebtheorie für unsere Zeit. Sexualität und Konflikt in der Psychoanalyse.* Bern: Huber.

Nunberg, Herman & Federn, Ernst (1962–1975), *The Minutes of the Vienna Psychoanalytic Society. 4 Volumes.* New York: International Universities Press.

Pfeifer, Sigmund (1919), 'Äußerungen infantil-erotischer Triebe im Spiel', *Imago* 5, pp. 243–282.

Quinodoz, Jean-Michel (2011 [2004]), *Freud lesen. Eine chronologische Entdeckungsreise durch sein Werk.* Gießen: Psychosozial-Verlag.

Rank, Otto (1981 [1907]), *The Artist*, transl. E. Saloman & E.J. Lieberman, *Journal of the Otto Rank Association* 15(1).

Reiss, Christian (2007), 'No Evolution, no Heredity, just Development – Julius Schaxel and the End of Evo-Devo Agenda in Jena, 1906–1933. A Case Study', *Theory in Biosciences* 126(4), pp. 155–164.

Reiss, Christian et al. (2008), 'Das autobiographische Manuskript des Entwicklungsbiologen Julius Schaxel (1887–1943) vom 24. Juli 1943. Versuch einer Kontextualisierung', *Annals of the History and Philosophy of Biology* 13, pp. 4–52.

Reiter, Bernard (1996), 'Dunkel ist das Leben, ist der Tod. Zu Freuds Todestriebtheorie', *Zeitschrift für Psychoanalytische Theorie und Praxis* 11, pp. 27–47.

Ritvo, Lucille B. (1990), *Darwin's Influence on Freud. A Tale of Two Sciences.* New Haven & London: Yale UP.

Schacht, L. (1995), 'Review. Grubrich-Simitis, I., Zurück zu Freuds Texten', *Journal of the American Psychoanalytic Association* 43, pp. 583–585.
Schaxel, Julius (1919), Über die Darstellung allgemeiner Biologie. Berlin: Bornträger.
Schmidt-Hellerau, Cordelia (2006), 'Surviving in Absence – on the Preservative and Death Drives and their Clinical Utility', *Psychoanalytic Quarterly* 79, pp. 1057–1095.
Schur, Max (1972), *Sigmund Freud: Living and Dying*. New York: International Universities Press.
Solms, Mark (1994), 'Review. Grubrich-Simitis, I.: Zurück zu Freuds Texten', *International Journal of Psychoanalysis* 75, pp. 153–159.
Spielrein, Sabina (1994 [1912]), 'Destruction as the Cause of Coming into Being', *Journal of Analytical Psychology* 39, pp. 155–186.
Stärcke, August (1914), 'Inleiding' [Einleitung zur holländischen Übersetzung von Sigmund Freud: I. Die »kulturelle« Sexualmoral und die moderne Nervosität; II. Zwangshandlungen und Religionsübung]. Baarn: Hollandia, pp. 2–8.
Steinach, Eugen (1920), *Verjüngung durch experimentelle Neubelebung der alternden Pubertätsdrüse*. Berlin: Springer.
Sulloway, Frank J. (1979), *Freud. Biologist of the Mind*. London: Burnett Books.
Teichroew, Allan & Bauman, Fred (2011), *Sigmund Freud Papers. A Finding Aid to the Papers in the Sigmund Freud Collection in the Library of Congress. Revised and expanded by Margaret McAleer*. Washington: Manuscript Division, Library of Congress. Weismann, August (1882), Über die Dauer des Lebens. Ein Vortrag. Jena: Fischer (published in English in 1889: *On Life and Death*, in: A. Weismann, *Essays upon Heredityand Kindred Biological Problems*. Oxford: Clarendon Press, pp. 107–160).
Weismann, August (1882), *Über die Dauer des Lebens: Ein Vortrag*. Jena: Fischer (published in English in 1889: *The Duration of Life*, in: A. Weismann, *Essays upon Heredity and Kindred Biological Problems*. Oxford: Clarendon Press, pp. 1–66).
Weismann, August (1884), *Über Leben und Tod. Eine biologische Untersuchung*. Jena: Fischer.
Weismann, August (1892), *Das Keimplasma. Eine Theorie der Vererbung*. Jena: Fischer (published in English in 1893: *The Germ-Plasm. A Theory of Heredity*. New York: Scribner's).
Wittels, Fritz (1924), *Sigmund Freud. His Personality, His Teaching, & His School.* London: George Allen & Unwin.
Wittenberger, Gerhard & Tögel, Christfried (1999–2006), *Die Rundbriefe des "Geheimen Komitees", Vols. 1–4*. Tübingen: Edition Diskord.

From Repetition and Drive Monism to Binding and Conflict: Re-reading Freud's Beyond the Pleasure Principle*

Philippe Van Haute & Herman Westerink

In most literature in which *Beyond the Pleasure Principle* is discussed, this text is read as if it were a – more or less – monolithic unity in which Freud attempts to systematically introduce a new coherent drive theory that solves the problem of the compulsion to repeat unpleasurable experiences. In this new drive theory, the fundamental distinction would no longer be between sexual drives and ego-drives, but between the death drives and the life drives (Eros). Philosophical readings, however, reveal that harmonising the various perspectives and ideas on the death drive[1] in particular proves to be difficult. One often finds that an author decides to highlight specific passages as most significant for Freud's overall view of the death drive. This death drive is then for example defined in terms of auto-aggression, of organic elasticity and inertia, or of the compulsion to repeat. These different interpretations, however, are difficult to reconcile with each other, and often only seem to have plausibility when disregarding other passages in the text that threaten to undermine or contradict a certain interpretation. The fact that in many readings the focus is indeed on the concept of the death drive reveals an important problem: the tendency to reflect on the concept from an supposed consistency between Freud's elaborations of it in different texts.

We have known since the 1990s that Freud did not write the published version of *Beyond the Pleasure Principle* in one go. Ilse Grubrich-Simitis found

* This text is a modified and extended version of an article published in *Tijdschrift voor filosofie*: P. Van Haute (2022), 'Tussen driftmonisme en conflict'. This article in its turn was largely composed of material from a book chapter on *Beyond the Pleasure Principle* in a monograph on Freud's metaphysics of trauma: H. Westerink & P. Van Haute (2022), *Verleiding, drift en herhaling: Freuds metafysica van het trauma*, pp. 181–227.

1 We note here that Freud in *Beyond the Pleasure Principle* speaks of 'death drives' (plural) and does not mention 'death drive' (singular) or 'Thanatos'. It is only first in *The Ego and the Id* from 1923 that he turns to the singular, 'death drive'.

in Freud's estate an earlier version of *Beyond the Pleasure Principle* that he had already completed in April 1919.[2] For a while, Freud did not work on the manuscript. Only in May 1920 did he take it up again and concluded the revision in July that year. Save for a few interventions, this second draft is the text that was published later in 1920. In the reprints of 1921 and 1923, a few short but meaningful passages were added.[3]

The second version of *Beyond the Pleasure Principle* is an extension of the first. It contains *grosso modo* the first five chapters that, bar a few added passages, remained unaltered in the second version. The entire sixth chapter was added between the fifth and the original sixth and final chapter. In this way, the original sixth chapter became the seventh in the second version. This seventh chapter is a thoroughly revised version of the original chapter six.

When one compares the two main versions of *Beyond the Pleasure Principle*, one can hardly dismiss the conclusion that these two versions articulate two positions that cannot easily be harmonised. Notably, it appears that Freud laid the first version from early 1919 aside, because the line of argumentation in the fifth chapter had led to a conclusion Freud himself found difficult if not impossible to accept. If so, the sixth chapter written a year later should not be read as a continuation of the line of argumentation in the previous chapter, but as an answer to and correction of the ideas and insights developed in the first version. Freud indeed puts in perspective and undermines the classical distinction (or opposition) between sexual drives and ego-drives, claiming that *all* drives are characterised by the same conservative and regressive tendency. Fundamentally, *all* drives aim at restoring an earlier state of things and are ultimately aimed at restoring the initial state from which the first living entity departed – the inorganic state, death.[4] Subsequently, in chapter six Freud reintroduces a new drive dualism that counters the conclusion of an – implicit – drive monism in chapter five of the first version. At all costs, Freud wanted to save his dualistic conflict theory – fundamental for his study of the psychoneuroses – and avoid a Jungian drive monism.[5] A comparative study of the two text versions also reveals that Freud went some way in smoothing out the theoretical differences between the first version and the new drive theory introduced in the sixth chapter. At the same time, we can ascertain that Freud did not bother to rewrite the whole text or produce a completely new

2 I. Grubrich-Simitis (1996), *Back to Freud's Texts: Making Silent Documents Speak*, pp. 182ff.
3 See the critical edition of Freud's text in this volume, pp. 29–80, and Ulrike May's extensive commentary on the various editions of *Beyond the Pleasure Principle*, pp. 81–164.
4 S. Freud (1920g), *Beyond the Pleasure Principle*, *SE* 18, pp. 36, 38.
5 Ibid., p. 53.

manuscript, but chose to maintain the different perspectives in the published text – just like he had done in some of his other key publications.[6]

In this contribution we will argue that the different perspectives on the drives and 'the beyond' of the pleasure principle cannot be harmonised and that every attempt to deliver such a harmonised reading of *Beyond the Pleasure Principle* ultimately falls short. Instead, we argue that these different theoretical perspectives not only characterise Freud's text – and beyond that, possibly also a large part of his oeuvre – but also reveal the kind of theoretical problems Freud was confronted with in this text, and in several other texts from the same period. In order to substantiate our arguments, our starting point for a philosophical reading of *Beyond the Pleasure Principle* is the very fact of the two versions – the one from 1919 and the one from 1920. We will therefore in what follows first discuss the main ideas and trains of thought in the first version of the text, before turning our attention to introduction of the new drive theory.

Traumatic neurosis and the problem of repetition

For Freud and psychoanalysis, the effects of the First World War posed a challenge. With the outbreak of the war in 1914, however, Freud was again strongly confronted with the problematic of traumatic neurosis. Not a single army was spared from an epidemic psychiatry would name 'shell shock'.[7] What to make of soldiers who suddenly lost their ability to speak or hear, who claimed to be blind, who teetered through life and were unable to control their emotional expressions? The same soldiers suffered from insomnia or had the most terrifying nightmares.

The discussions on the status of the war neuroses to a large extent echo the discussions in the second half of the nineteenth century on the traumatic neuroses resulting from, for example, railway and industrial accidents, and what Charcot had named traumatic hysteria. In both discussions, the majority of psychiatrists first of all defined trauma in terms of the effect of external shock damaging the molecular or histological structure of the nervous system and/or brain, while taking also into account possible psychological factors

6 We notably refer here to *Three Essays on the Theory of Sexuality*, which was first published in 1905. In the various later editions of that text (1910, 1915, 1920 and 1924) Freud inserted several new sections and paragraphs adding new theoretical components that partly contradict and undermine the first theory. For a detailed reading of the various editions of *Three Essays*, see P. Van Haute & H. Westerink (2021), *From Pleasure to the Object: Reading Freud's Three Essays on the Theory of Sexuality.*

7 A. Scull (2009), *Hysteria: The Disturbing History.*

in the aetiology of the traumatic neuroses, notably reactions of fright.[8] In line with Charcot, Freud in the 1880s–1890s would interpret the traumatic neuroses in terms of traumatic hysteria, and radically proceeded to explain this hysteria from strictly psychological factors. This line of clinical inquiry eventually led to the formulation of the seduction theory, stating that (all forms of) hysteria – and by extension all psychoneuroses – originated from memories of sexual traumas in early childhood that were unacceptable for the ego and were therefore repressed.

One can think here for example of the case of Emma Eckstein as discussed by Freud in his 'Project for a Scientific Psychology' from 1895.[9] At the age of eight Emma had gone into a small shop where the shopkeeper had "grabbed at her genitals through her clothes". This experience at first had little or no effect. However, when she at the age of twelve enters a shop to buy clothes, she sees two shop-assistants laughing, one of whom she finds attractive, and she runs away in fright. The assistant's laughter apparently reminds her of the shopkeeper's grin which had accompanied his assault. Emma, now being in puberty, only now understands the sexual meaning of the remembered scene. From this moment onwards she develops a phobia and is not able to go into shops on her own. The conclusion Freud draws is that Emma's neurosis is the result of an inner conflict associated with an infantile sexual trauma. If such a conflict and sexual trauma are not present, a neurosis will not develop. The primacy of sexuality in the aetiology of the neuroses we find here is at the heart of Freudian metapsychology.

In this context the 'classical' traumatic neuroses found in patients suffering from the effects of severe industrial accidents, disappear from Freud's studies. It is only first in *Beyond the Pleasure Principle* that this problematic returns when Freud is faced with the urgent question of a psychoanalytic perspective on the war neuroses and the possibilities for treatment of shell-shock patients. For Freud, this problematic confronts him with a deeply puzzling riddle. After all, from the time of the seduction theory onwards he had always assumed that psychic life is automatically regulated by the pleasure principle, that is to say, the avoidance of unpleasure and the reduction of tension to a minimum.[10] Clinical findings from the study of the war neuroses, however,

8 See for example Hermann Oppenheim's 1889 classic study on the traumatic neuroses, *Die traumatische Neurosen*. For an overview of the theories of traumatic neuroses, see E. Fischer-Homberger (2004), *Die traumatische Neurose*; M. Micale & P. Lerner (2010), *Traumatic Pasts: History, Psychiatry and the Trauma in the Modern Age*; and Westerink & Van Haute (2022), *Verleiding, drift en herhaling*, pp. 21–59.

9 S. Freud (1950c), 'Project for a Scientific Psychology', *SE* 1, pp. 353–356.

10 For example S. Freud (1985), *The Complete Letters of Sigmund Freud to Wilhelm Fliess*, pp. 165ff.; Freud

contradict this principle. Shell-shock patients and patients suffering classical traumatic neurosis notably in their dreams constantly relive and repeat their traumas – highly disturbing, unpleasurable experiences in which there was absolutely no pleasurable sensation.[11] Hence, these dreams could not be seen as wish fulfilments. In other words, the traumatic and war neuroses confront Freud with a clinical phenomenon that fundamentally challenges his premises and theories: a compulsion to repeat (*Wiederholungszwang*) unpleasurable experiences that points towards a principle or tendency 'beyond' the pleasure principle.

With regard to the question of what trauma is, Freud's first answer is that trauma can be seen as a psychic shock without any meaning. Psychic traumas are events that out of the blue make a shocking impact. They are events that for this reason cannot be given any meaning or situated in a meaningful chain of events. According to Freud, the lack of meaning can be defined in terms of a lack of preparedness, more specific "preparedness for anxiety" (*Angstbereitschaft*).[12] Indeed, Freud argues that anxiety is a "particular state of expecting the danger" and as such the first and basic "protective shield" (*Reizschutz*) against a traumatic neurosis. Anxiety (*Angst*), after all, prepares for an incoming danger, even if this danger is as yet unknown. Fright (*Schreck*) stands in opposition to anxiety in the sense that it is the name for a situation of running into danger without being prepared for it.[13] Fright is characterised by the element of complete surprise. Freud concludes from this that the traumatic neurosis can be seen "as a consequence of an extensive breach being made in the protective shield against stimuli".

> It is caused by lack of any preparedness for anxiety, including lack of hypercathexis of the systems that would be the first to receive the stimulus. Owing to their low cathexis those systems are not in a good position for binding the inflowing amounts of excitation.[14]

Anxiety prepares for inflowing amounts of excitation (*Erregung*), and because of this, the incoming stimuli (*Reize*) can be processed in binding (*Bindung*) the incoming stimuli to a representation or a chain of representations. In this way the event can gain a meaningful place in psychic life – an event to which

(1950c), 'Project for a Scientific Psychology', p. 312; S. Freud (1900a), *The Interpretation of Dreams, SE* 4–5, pp. 564–565, 595ff.

11 Freud (1920g), *Beyond the Pleasure Principle*, p. 13.

12 Ibid., pp. 31–33.

13 Ibid., p. 12.

14 Ibid., p. 31.

an adequate response is possible, and as consequence the traumatic effect is less severe. Moreover, "the preparedness for anxiety and the hypercathexis of the receptive systems constitute the last line of defense of the shield against stimuli".[15]

From this perspective we can begin to understand the returning fright-dreams of traumatised and shell-shocked patients. These dreams are 'endeavouring to master the stimulus retrospectively', that is, to develop and reinstall the preparedness for anxiety that was absent or breached in the traumatic event. These dreams then can be seen as having the 'function' or 'task' of putting in place a first shield against stimuli. And the completion of this 'task' is the condition for the dominance of the pleasure principle. After all, in and through the repetition of the traumatic experience in the fright-dream, the patient retroactively attempts the preparedness for anxiety that would allow the 'binding' of the stimulus to representations. The traumatic or war neurosis results from a lack of anxiety: the omission of anxiety was the cause of the traumatic neurosis.[16] Being anxious – even when anxious about an unknown danger – means that one will not be caught by surprise, not be thrown into a state of fright, but it also means being able to bind incoming stimuli and sums of excitation to representations in time and space.[17] The binding of "inflowing amounts of excitation" makes it possible to adequately – i.e. in agreement with the pleasure principle – react to these excitations. As long as this binding is not established, as is the case in the war neuroses, a traumatic event cannot become a memory, but will instead be constantly and compulsorily repeated.[18]

In the classic descriptions of traumatic neuroses, a non-sexual trauma has an immediate and devastating effect causing organic damage and fright. The way in which Freud approaches the traumatic neuroses in the first chapters of *Beyond the Pleasure Principle* seem to confirm this. The shell-shock patients in their dreams return to and repeat non-sexual traumatic scenes. This is a remarkable fact in itself, since Freud in his early writings interpreted the traumatic neuroses from the perspective of his seduction theory, in which it is always a memory with a sexual content that produces the suffering from

15 Ibid.

16 Ibid., p. 32.

17 Freud's view of dreams as attempts to restore preparedness for anxiety in order to be able to bind stimuli to chains of representations, and in doing so preparing for a reconstruction of a normal relation with reality, echoes his view on delusions in psychosis as attempts to restore the relation with reality. Compare S. Freud (1911c), 'Psycho-Analytic Notes on an Autobiographical Account of a Case of Paranoia', *SE* 12.

18 Freud (1920g), *Beyond the Pleasure Principle*, pp. 34–35.

trauma. Does this mean that 'beyond' the pleasure principle implies thinking 'beyond' the sexual? The traumatic neuroses confront Freud with the limits of his theories of sexual trauma, and one of the open questions at the end of the first version of the text will be how to think the relation between the excitation caused by mechanical impact and the sexual excitation, i.e. how to relate traumatic neurosis to a theory of sexuality.

Repetition and drive

The problematics of repetition is, according to Freud, not only apparent in traumatic neuroses, but also in transference as an essential part of the analytic therapeutic process.[19] The analysand in the relation with the analyst repeats drive representations that are rooted in the past and are the source of the neurotic suffering. Such repetitions or 'reproductions' show that "the earlier neurosis has now been replaced by a fresh 'transference neurosis'".[20] Such a transference neurosis does not necessarily contradict the dominance of the pleasure principle. After all, through repetition in transference, the analysand tries to avoid the unpleasure that the remembering and bringing into consciousness of repressed drive impulses would cause for the ego. Any successful avoidance of unpleasure must be considered pleasurable ("for one system"). But Freud adds to this that the compulsion to repeat in the analytic process includes the reproduction of past experiences which held no possibility of pleasure and which never produced any satisfaction.[21] This short elaboration of transference leads Freud not only to conclude that there really exists a compulsion to repeat that can override the pleasure principle, but also that the "manifestations of a compulsion to repeat exhibit to a high degree an instinctual [*triebhafter*] character".[22] Freud's argument for this is as follows. Nothing in the unconscious resists the becoming conscious and actualisation of unconscious drive impulses. The resistance against these impulses stems from the ego and the higher psychic functions. Since the unconscious consists of representation invested with drive impulses, the compulsion to repeat must have an instinctual character. The compulsion to repeat, Freud writes, is "more

19 Compare: "Transference uses specific objects and operates in the framework of a specific relationship established with these objects. Its context par excellence is the analytic situation. In the transference, infantile prototypes *re-emerge* and are experienced with a strong sensation of immediacy." J. Laplanche & J.-B. Pontalis (1988), *The Language of Psychoanalysis*, p. 455, italics P.V.H./H.W.

20 Freud (1920g), *Beyond the Pleasure Principle*, p. 18.

21 Ibid., p. 20.

22 Ibid., p. 35.

primitive, more elementary, more instinctual" than the pleasure principle.[23] Transference, in which the repetition becomes manifest, is an expression of the unconscious and therefore of the drives. Freud thus concludes that compulsion to repeat is a fundamental characteristic of man as an instinctual (*triebhafter*) being. In this way Freud can confirm an essential aspect of his earlier ideas on trauma: trauma cannot be traced back to impacts from external forces, but stems from internal sources. And in order to understand trauma we must ask what is *in the drives* that is or leads 'beyond' the pleasure principle.

In the fourth chapter of *Beyond the Pleasure Principle* Freud further elaborates on this issue, adding a new step in his argumentation. He writes that we could perhaps still prepare for external stimuli but not for the drives that well up from within our bodies. He refers in this regard to the distinction between 'quiescent' ('bound') and 'mobile' ('free') energy, which Breuer had introduced in the theoretical part he wrote for *Studies on Hysteria* and that Freud had already used in his seventh meta-psychological chapter of his *Interpretation of Dreams*.[24] Freud identifies 'mobile energy' (*frei beweglicher Besetzungsenergie*) as the primary process that dominates unconscious processes. In the unconscious, cathectic energy can freely pass from one representation to the next (the energy is not fixed or coupled to any one representation), thus creating links that to the waking life appear to be senseless. But at the same time, it is precisely this 'mobility' that makes it possible for the unconscious to penetrate consciousness, in this way taking the shortest possible route to satisfying or discharging the libidinal energy it carries. Dreams are a good example. An unacceptable representation can pass its cathectic energy to one or more innocent representations (displacement), or different representations can concentrate their cathectic energy in a single one (condensation) in order to circumnavigate the censorship of the ego. These shifts in cathectic energy do not in any way consider the reality and the prevailing order, like, for example, the chronology. Therefore, the mental formations ruled by the unconscious sometimes seem very bizarre in waking life. In a dream one can be urinating against a wall while behind oneself the urine gathers into an entire lake, but in waking life this is absurd.[25] This primary process aims only at achieving satisfaction at any cost, as quickly as possible and eventually in a hallucinatory way.

---

23 Ibid., p. 23.

24 Ibid., p. 26; J. Breuer & S. Freud (1895d), *Studies on Hysteria, SE* 2, p. 194 – in note; Freud (1900a), *The Interpretation of Dreams*, pp. 601–603.

25 Ibid., pp. 367–368.

Freud distinguishes this primary process from the secondary process that characterises the (pre-)conscious. In the secondary process the mobile flow of cathectic energy is contained by binding this energy in a more stable way to a network of representations. Representations are occupied in a more stable way, taking account of, for instance, the ordering relationships of time and space.[26] The representations can subsequently no longer be linked to each other freely and without limits or simply act as each other's replacement. It is perhaps particularly important that Freud also links the pleasure principle with the secondary process. Considering the explanation above this seems obvious. We previously called binding a condition for the 'dominance' of the pleasure principle.[27] This binding now appears to be characteristic of the secondary process. The pleasure principle and the secondary process therefore go hand in hand.

All this results in Freud equating the pleasure principle to the reality principle, at least implicitly, from the fourth chapter of the text. Earlier in the text, Freud had already introduced the distinction between the pleasure principle and the reality principle.[28] As we know, the pleasure principle refers to the tendency of the psychic apparatus to discharge the tension as quickly as possible or keep it as low as possible. From the perspective of the material and the cultural outside world, this principle is useless from the start and often even dangerous to the organism. Therefore, according to Freud, the original pleasure principle is succeeded by the reality principle, which

> does not abandon the intention of ultimately obtaining pleasure, but it nevertheless demands and carries in to effect the postponement of satisfaction, the abandonment of a number of possibilities of gaining satisfaction and the temporary toleration of unpleasure as a step on the long indirect road to pleasure.[29]

---

26 In this instance Freud refers to Immanuel Kant's *a priori* forming of sensoriness. Freud links these forms with the structuring and binding of unconscious presentations in the (pre-)conscious system. It is understandable since it structures the sensory relationship to the world according to Kant. This relationship is as it were suspended in the unconscious. Freud (1920g), *Beyond the Pleasure Principle*, p. 28.

27 Ibid., p. 35.

28 A systematic discussion of the distinction and relation between the pleasure principle and reality principle can be found in S. Freud (1911b), 'Formulations on the Two Principles of Mental Functioning', *SE* 12.

29 Freud (1920g), *Beyond the Pleasure Principle*, p. 10. The reality principle is thus also part of the secondary process. After all, this principle implies that the free movement of energy is inhibited or called to a halt, and that satisfaction is postponed in order to be able to meet the demands of reality.

Here, a tension can be traced that is important for a good understanding of Freud's argument in *Beyond the Pleasure Principle*. Freud talks about a pleasure principle that is specific to the 'primary' psychic process.[30] By this he is referring to the spontaneous tendency to discharge the tension, at least to as low a level as possible.[31] For such a discharge, however, the mobile energy must first be 'bound'. From what we know so far, it seems obvious that this 'binding' can be understood in relation to the reality principle. After all, the binding of energy to representations can hardly imply anything else but binding the energy to a network of representations organised in space and time and in which external reality is also considered. If we follow Freud's reasoning, we may have to conclude that the opposition between the (sexual) unconscious and the higher ego functions is merely the opposition between varieties of the same principle. This seems to undermine the conflict models so typical of Freudian metapsychology.

In this way, the question of how trauma can also, in the case of traumatic neurosis, come from within and have an 'instinctual' base remains unresolved. In addition, the association with sexuality that Freud had postulated in his seduction theory remains as yet unclear. In the 1919 version of the text, Freud limits himself to arguing that the traumatic neurosis may result from a conflict in the ego – more specifically, between a narcissistic (hence libidinally invested) peace-ego and a war-ego that fundamentally questions the values and ideals of the peace-ego.[32] In some passages he added to the end of the fourth chapter in the 1920 edition, he alludes to what he wrote about the sources of sexuality in *Three Essays on the Theory of Sexuality*.[33] There he stated that mechanical shocks could cause sexual excitation. He also already associated this phenomenon with traumatic neurosis there. This is at least a decidedly speculative (and not very convincing?) point of view: from the fact

30 Ibid.

31 Freud identifies the tendency to keep the tension as low as possible with Fechner's principle of constancy. It is remarkable. After all, the constancy principle implies that 'too much' as well as 'too little' tension can be unpleasurable. For Fechner, this principle implies that the organism wants to keep the tension within certain upper and lower limits. On this point, see F.J. Sulloway (1979), *Freud: Biologist of the Mind.*

32 Freud (1920g), *Beyond the Pleasure Principle*, p. 33. Freud refers here to 'Introduction to *Psycho-Analysis and the War Neuroses*', a lecture he gave in September 1918 that was published as an introduction to a volume on psychoanalytic perspectives on the war neuroses. In this article, he states that the war neuroses can be interpreted in terms of an ego-conflict between a peace-ego and a war-ego. The fundamental issue Freud raises in his short text concerns the unresolved question of how this ego-conflict is to be related to the libido theory, i.e. the question whether and how traumatic neuroses the sexual drives are involved in the conflict. S. Freud (1919d), 'Introduction to *Psycho-Analysis and the War Neuroses*', *SE* 17.

33 Freud (1920g), *Beyond the Pleasure Principle*, p. 33.

that the rocking of a train could lead to sexual excitation, it is hard to gather that a train accident must represent the same thing to an extreme degree.[34] In *Beyond the Pleasure Principle*, Freud confirms this viewpoint without further commentary.[35] This means that, according to Freud, the mechanical shock that comes with the accident generates huge quantities of sexual energy that must be bound, that is, subjugated to the power of the secondary process and thus of the pleasure principle. In this way, trauma is again genuinely understood as an essentially 'internal event'. The external event on its own does not have any explanatory value for the pathology, according to Freud.[36]

Drive and phylogenesis

In the 1919 version of the text, Freud associates repetition with the drives, but without mentioning the sexual drives. In the fifth chapter Freud introduces a new definition of *all* drives. Here, Freud defines drive as "*an urge inherent in organic life to restore an earlier state of things* which the living entity has been obliged to abandon under the pressure of external disturbing forces".[37] He compares this drive with "a kind of organic elasticity, or, to put it another way, the expression of the inertia inherent in organic life". For a proper understanding of this definition, it is best to start from the concept of drive that Freud wants to avoid or at least amend here. We have become accustomed, Freud says, to viewing drive as "a factor impelling towards change and development".[38] But does this depiction allow for an adequate understanding of repetition as an essential expression of the drive? After all,

34 This hypothesis is connected to the complete reformulation of the paragraph about the chemical theory in the fourth edition of *Three Essays on the Theory of Sexuality*, which Freud was working on at the same time and that appeared in 1920. Freud seemed to think that through the shock, "special chemical substances are produce in the interstitial portion of the sex-glands; these are then taken up in the blood stream and cause particular parts of the central nervous system to be charged with sexual tension. (We are already familiar with the fact that other toxic substances, introduced into the body from the outside, can bring about a similar transformation of a toxic condition into a stimulus acting on a particular organ.)". Freud (1905d), *Three Essays on the Theory of Sexuality*, *SE* 7, p. 215.

35 The idea that just as rhythmic vibrations evoke moderate sexual excitation, mechanical violence produces a huge quantity of sexual excitation that overwhelms the ego results from the fact that Freud does not make qualitative distinctions between forms of excitation, but only takes into account quantitative differences.

36 In reaction to this point, in *Les nouveaux blessés* Catherine Malabou attempts to develop a general trauma theory that includes a Freudian psychoanalytic perspective (as notably articulated in *Beyond the Pleasure Principle*) while criticising Freud's primacy of sexuality and the sexual conflict. She argues that in Freud's theories the possibility of a damaging impact from a traumatic experience on the brain or nervous system is unthinkable. C. Malabou (2012), *The New Wounded: From Neurosis to Brain Damage*.

37 Freud (1920g), *Beyond the Pleasure Principle*, p. 36.

38 Ibid.

repetition is diametrically opposed to change and development. Those who repeat do not change and are not really included in progressive development.[39] If repetition expresses an essential aspect of drive, then the latter must have a conservative character according to Freud. All drives have a conservative character – Freud is very explicit on this matter.

In this section and the next, we shall see that the new determination of drive can only be fully understood from the perspective of the growing importance of phylogenetic theories. Indeed, Freud founds this new drive theory in reflections that immediately connect with psycho-Lamarckism and Ernst Haeckel's recapitulation theory. Only in this way can it become clear what exactly defines the conservative character of the drives. The arguments for this entails several steps, which we discuss one by one for the sake of good order.

First, Freud defines life itself as an effect of "the action of a force of whose nature we can form no conception" – a force that has generated life in matter.[40] He thus considers the origin of life according to the model of a trauma. And as the individual trauma generates libidinal energy that needs to be discharged, so the impact of an incomprehensible force created tension in the inorganic substance that needed to be discharged again. Freud concludes: "the tension which then arose in what had hitherto been an inanimate substance endeavoured to cancel itself out. In this way the first instinct [*Trieb*] came into being: the instinct to return to the inanimate".[41] This instinctual force that determines organic life is not directed at change or development. This first drive is in essence conservative and regressive, that is, it wants to return to its *status quo ante*. It pursues only one thing: to undo as quickly as possible the imposed modifications and the tensions that accompany it. This is also what Freud means when he states that the drive is governed by an inertia principle: it manifests the inertness inherent in organic life.[42] The drive does not want to move forward, it only wants to return to its (inorganic) origin.

The problem Freud faces is as follows. The opposition between drives of self-preservation and sexual drives had until now been the cornerstone of Freudian psychoanalysis. Even in the first chapters of *Beyond the Pleasure Principle*, Freud worked according to this plan. His reflections on the compulsion to repeat, however, forced him to at the same time introduce a new definition of drive and the instinctual. Drive as such is in essence conservative and regressive. Freud must now explain how this definition applies to self-preservation or

[39] That is also why Freud, as we noted earlier, is in this regard concerned with the "perpetual recurrence of the same thing". Ibid., p. 22.
[40] Ibid., p. 38.
[41] Ibid.
[42] Ibid., p. 36.

ego-drives as well as to sexual drives. This provision is already rather odd in terms of the drives of self-preservation, of which it is indeed at first glance difficult to assume that they aim to return to the inorganic. And the latter actually applies even more to sexual drives, which aim at the continuation of life through reproduction. In other words, in the 1919 version of the text Freud does not introduce an opposition between life drives and death drives. The drive dualism is only first introduced in 1920. When Freud in chapter five of his text mentions 'life drives', he refers to sexual drives that stand opposed to drives of self-preservation, and hence not to death drives.

How can we speak about drives of self-preservation at all when the aim of all life is the inanimate or the inert?[43] When drives only want to return us to the inorganic, why do we then not all jump out the window together? In other words, if there is an urge to move back to the inanimate, what explains the further development of organic life into forms that no longer "die so smoothly and easily" and do not have such a "short lifespan" as the first living organisms (protists)?[44] In the first edition of *Beyond the Pleasure Principle* from 1919, Freud argues the following in this regard. That, despite the urge for the inanimate, there is life, and that this life has further developed in more complex organisms is determined by organic life being subject to an endless series of imposed modifications and adjustments to circumstances. What we call evolution, development or progress does not originate from the drive. On the contrary, it is, Freud argues in line with Lamarck's view of evolution, a set of changes that determine the lifecycle of organisms as acquired characteristics and that are repeated in subsequent generations.[45] In successive developments in increasingly complex organisms, the set of imposed and acquired changes has obliged "the still surviving substance to diverge ever more widely from its original course [*Ablenkungen*] of life and to make ever more complicated *détours* [*Umwege*] before reaching its aim of death".[46] This "aim of death" is

43 Ibid., p. 39.
44 Ibid., pp. 38–39.
45 Ibid., p. 37.
46 Ibid., pp. 38–39. In much of the literature on the development of Freud's psychoanalytic theories it is claimed that Freud abandoned his seduction theory (*Verführungstheorie*) in 1897. See e.g. J. Masson (1984), *The Assault on Truth*; R. Leys (2000), *Trauma: A Genealogy*; G. Izenberg (2006), 'Seduced and Abandoned: The Rise and Fall of Freud's Seduction Theory'; A. Philips (2014), *Becoming Freud: The Making of a Psychoanalyst*; J. Whitebook (2017), *Freud: An Intellectual Biography*. This position neglects the fact that Freud never dismissed the role of accidental factors in the aetiology of the psychoneuroses, merely questions their exclusive significance: constitutional factors also have to be taken into account. In his inquiries into these constitutional factors, Freud goes back to the concept of seduction in its most original meaning – *ver-führen*, to lead astray, to divert from a normal course, to derail, to swing out of alignment. Freud's Lamarckian explorations (from *Totem and Taboo* onwards) lead him to conclude that constitution can be seen as the sum of effects of acquired characteristics through traumatic experiences in the past. The constitution, in other words, is the effect of a series of

here to be understood as the reduction of internal tension to an absolute minimum and hence the return to the inanimate. The evolution from single cell to increasingly complex organism thus makes the journey back to the inanimate longer and more laborious but does not change its fundamentally conservative and regressive character. Every organism of every kind has developed a kind of 'détour' from life's aim and wants to "die only in its own fashion", that is, to preserve itself up until it dies a "natural death".[47] Every other route will be unacceptable for the organism.

This insight can, as we know, only be understood from the perspective of Haeckel's biogenetic law. Not only does the embryo go through the various stages of the evolutionary line in a transient and abbreviated fashion,[48] but the episodes that determine our subsequent life are also repetitions of the 'traumatic' events in the life of the species.[49] Indeed, this can help explain why we cling to life yet are driven by urges that want to discharge all tension and thus aim for a return to the inorganic. We only want to die once our life is completed 'naturally'. More concretely, this means that humans and all organic life are directed only toward the inorganic through the repetition of the history of the species. In other words, every organism wants to die from *internal* causes and therefore tries to avoid every external event that would make this impossible by artificially shortening life. Accidents, illnesses at an early age and suicide, to name but some examples, are contrary to the 'natural' lifecycle, and so they are resisted with all instinctual (*triebhafter*) force. The drives of self-preservation were also originally "myrmidons of death".[50]

The association of the constancy principle with the recapitulation theory changes the meaning of the latter. Haeckel was an enthusiastic adherent of the idea of progression throughout evolution. In his view, evolution could be seen as a tree with a trunk that reaches its greatest height in the appearance of man. Haeckel is a representative of theories that assume a drive for perfection in nature: primitive life forms are repeated in advanced organisms in an ever more condensed and rapid way in order to make a next progressive step possible. The constancy principle cuts off this optimistic perspective on evolution. According to Freud, the evolution from unicellular to multicellular

Verführungen, or in terms Freud uses in *Beyond the Pleasure Principle*, of *Ablenkungen* and *Umwege*. For a more detailed discussion see Westerink & Van Haute (2022), *Verleiding, drift en herhaling*.

47 Freud (1920g), *Beyond the Pleasure Principle*, p. 39.

48 Ibid., p. 37.

49 For example, in *Inhibitions, Symptoms and Anxiety*, Freud writes that the latency period, and thus the fact that the formation of sexuality in humankind takes place in two distinct periods (infancy and puberty), must be the historical sediment of disturbing events in the vicissitudes of the human species. S. Freud (1926d), *Inhibitions, Symptoms and Anxiety*, *SE* 20, p. 155.

50 Freud (1920g), *Beyond the Pleasure Principle*, p. 39.

complex organisms merely produces a longer détour before reaching their aim of death.[51] The drive does not aim for change but is controlled through an inertia principle: whatever the meaning we bestow upon our existence, drive is a constant force that leads us to death via a path imposed upon us from the history of the species.[52] What we call progress is, incidentally, fully dependent on the perspective we take towards a given series of modifications.[53] Progress for one person may be something completely different for another. Consequently, there is no such thing as a "drive to perfection" (*Trieb zur Vervollkommnung*).[54]

Although at first glance, the sexual drives are opposed to the drives of self-preservation, we already pointed out that Freud also attributes a conservative character to them in the first version of the text. According to Freud, the sexual drives are aimed at preserving, protecting and fusing elementary organisms – germ-cells – which are the actual carriers of life. These germ-cells are the carriers of inherited and newly acquired drive dispositions. The sexual drives in this sense guard the emergence of more and more *new individuals* who nevertheless still *repeat the same kind of organic life*. According to Freud, they are conservative "in the same sense as the other drives in that they bring back earlier states of living substance", but they are in a way even more conservative "in that they are peculiarly resistant to external influences" and also because "they preserve life itself for a comparative long period".[55] The efficacy of the ego- and sexual drives is formally analogue. Both drives are profoundly conservative and regressive. They answer *to the same inertia principle and principle of repetition.*

Freud is now able to rewrite the relationship between drives of self-preservation and sexual drives in a way that takes account of his new general definition of drive:

51 Although Haeckel was seen by his contemporaries as an adherent of Darwinism, his views of a teleological principle in nature are far from Darwinian. In fact, Freud's rejection of a drive for perfection and his emphasis on adaptation to coincidental circumstances shows that Freud is closer to Darwin than Haeckel is.

52 It is at least noteworthy that none of the recent philosophical interpretations of *Beyond the Pleasure Principle* that we mentioned at the beginning of this chapter refer to Freud's psycho-Lamarckism. If our interpretation is correct, these interpretations thereby deny themselves the possibility of understanding exactly what Freud understands by drive as characterised by an 'inertia principle'. Freud's revival of the drive theory in 1919 is directly connected to his turn to psycho-Lamarckism.

53 Ibid., p. 41.

54 "The present development of human beings requires, as it seems to me, no different explanation from that of animals. What appears in a minority of human individuals as an untiring impulsion towards further perfection can easily be understood as a result of the instinctual repression upon which is based all that is most precious in human civilization." Ibid., p. 42.

55 Freud (1920g), *Beyond the Pleasure Principle*, p. 40.

> It is as though the life of the organism moved with a vacillating rhythm. One group of instincts rushes forward to reach the final aim of life as swiftly as possible; but when a particular stage in the advance has been reached, the other group jerks back to a certain point to make a fresh start and so prolong the journey.[56]

The sexual drives repeatedly create individuals who want to reach the end of life, or of every tension, as quickly as possible – according to the historical determination that characterises the life of the drive. They repeatedly establish the passage to death that determines life. The drives of self-preservation and the sexual drives thus become two sides of *the same instinctual process* that is essentially conservative and regressive.

Restoration of an earlier state of things and the problem of monism

In the first version of *Beyond the Pleasure Principle*, chapter five is the central chapter in which Freud seeks to answer the question of the 'beyond' of the pleasure principle through an inquiry into the instinctual character of the compulsion to repeat. We have seen that Freud put to ore a new definition of the drive. It is "*an urge* [Drang] *inherent in organic life to restore an earlier state of things* which the living entity has been obliged to abandon under the pressure of extenal disturbing forces".[57] This definition follows from the question of the relation between the compulsion to repeat in concrete (clinical) phenomena – the child's *fort-da*-play,[58] the traumatic neurosis, the transference and negative therapeutic reactions – and the instinctual. This question marks the step from clinical examples of the compulsion to repeat to what can be called the metaphysics of the drive. From this point onwards Freud is concerned with the conceptualisation of the drives as such and defines the compulsion to repeat in terms of an urge of regression (restoration, return) to an earlier state.

We can raise the question as to how this new definition of the drive provides new insights in the compulsion to repeat unpleasurable experiences. After all, this was the starting point in *Beyond the Pleasure Principle*: the

56 Ibid., pp. 40–41.

57 Ibid., p. 36.

58 In chapter two of *Beyond the Pleasure Principle* Freud presents a detailed analysis of a play he had observed in his own one-and-a-half-year old grandson. The child would repeatedly throw away a small wooden reel with a piece of string tied around it over the edge of his curtained cot (*fort*), and pull the reel by the string out of the cot again (*da*). Freud interprets the play as repeated staging of an unpleasurable experience – the departure of the mother. Ibid., pp. 14–17.

psychic apparatus was supposed to be automatically regulated by the pleasure principle, i.e. automatically aim at the reduction of tension. If so, how then to explain the repetition of unpleasurable experiences? How and why would shell-shock patients repeat the highly traumatic experiences in the trenches of the war? It appears that there must be another 'principle' at work – a principle that is now traced back to the 'conservative' and regressive character of all drives. But is this a convincing step? Has Freud indeed convincingly shown that the 'demonic' compulsion to repeat traumatic experiences and relive traumatic events can be traced back to the drives?

If we take the war neuroses as our starting point, the new definition of the drive could maybe be applied as follows. The shell-shock patients in their repeated – and tragically failing – attempts to produce preparedness for anxiety as the first protective shield against the inflow of huge quantities of excitation return in their dreams to the moment of traumatisation. The return or regression to the traumatic experience is then basically still an attempt to bind the excitation to representations in space and time. Accomplishing such a binding in its turn would be the precondition for the dominance of the pleasure principle and the reduction of tension: "the binding of an instinctual impulse would be a preliminary function designed to prepare the excitation for its final elimination in the pleasure of discharge". It is a 'preparatory act' for the dominance of the pleasure principle.[59] It is because of this necessary preparation that the patient would have to return to the moment of traumatisation, i.e. to the moment where he was obliged to abandon a certain state under the pressure of external disturbing forces. He therefore returns to a situation of high vulnerability – helplessness – and an absent or insufficient protective shield. This can be seen as defining for the tragic character of the war neuroses: to repeatedly return to a situation in which the disturbing forces are so massive that no protective shield can be erected. And yet, according to Freud, this tragic fact confirms that the repeated traumatic experiences would be desperate attempts to bind excitation and install the pleasure principle. At this point, one might expect Freud to elaborate on this issue in relation to the new definition of the drive as an urge pushing towards the restoration of an earlier state, even if that state is highly disturbing.

However, having presented his new definition of the drive, Freud does not return to his clinical examples. On the contrary, one of the striking aspects of the text is that the clinical examples presented in the first chapters are no longer discussed after the introduction of the new drive definition. This may

[59] Ibid., p. 62.

come as a surprise, and yet from the further course of the argumentation in the text we can begin to understand why Freud did not return to his clinical examples, notably the cases of traumatic neuroses. After Freud introduces his new definition of the drive, he continues his elaborations by turning his attention to evolutionary biology and the question of the origins and further development of organic life. Freud argues – in line with a Lamarckian perspective – that the conservative character of the drives is "historically acquired" in reaction to disturbing and diverting external influences.[60] The evolution and development of organic life is to be seen as an endless series of modifications due to such influences. This leads Freud to speculate on the first of all such modifications and "historically acquired" characteristics: the conservative character of the drive appears as the first reaction to the first modification, i.e. the disturbing 'force' that evoked "the attributes of life" in "inanimate matter".[61] In this context, the traumatic neuroses deliver the model for Freud's view of the origin of life and its further development. Life is disturbance of inanimate matter, that is, of matter in which there is no tension – life is matter infused with tension. It is in this first organic life that the conservative character of the drive manifests itself as an urge to return to the first original state of things, i.e. inanimate matter, dead matter – "the aim of all life is death".[62] Where the first new definition of the drive could still possibly be associated with the return to a traumatic unpleasurable experience, the further elaborations of the conservative character of the drive lead to a conclusion that the drives aim to return to an inanimate state. This state is not unpleasurable; on the contrary, it is a pleasurable state in which, after all, there exists no tension and excitation. In other words, the aim of all drives now de facto coincides with the pleasure principle – the reduction of all tension. The aim of the drive – the inanimate, death – is nothing other than the automatic regulation of the decrease of tension, i.e. the pleasure principle.

It is this second definition of the drive in chapter five that leads to an unexpected conclusion: there is no 'beyond' the pleasure principle. The inquiries into the compulsion to repeat unpleasurable experiences lead Freud to speculate on an urge in all life to return to the ultimate pleasurable state of things – the inanimate. All drives seek the reduction of tension.[63]

---

[60] Ibid., p. 37.

[61] Ibid., p. 38.

[62] Ibid.

[63] On this issue see also Malabou (2012), *The New Wounded*, pp. 8, 189ff.; A. Zupančič (2017), *What is Sex?*, pp. 98–99; and A. Allen (2021), *Critique on the Couch*, p. 40. Hans Loewald and more recently Benjamin Fong have argued that Freud's claim that the drives' aim of removing the state of stimulation – a claim that is elaborated in *Beyond the Pleasure Principle* and finds its zenith in the idea that all drives

If this is so, how then to answer the question why the shell-shock patient in his dreams repeatedly returns to the scenes of trauma, to the experience of disturbing forces? The idea that all life aims at the inanimate and hence at pleasure does not provide much insight into this question. Seen from this perspective, we cannot be surprised that Freud in chapters five and six (in the first version; chapter seven in the second version) does not return to his clinical examples. The speculations in chapter five do not shed light on the clinical phenomena he wanted to explain. This is likely one of the reasons why Freud did not publish the first version.

But there are more problems produced by the new definitions of the drive. In the first version of *Beyond the Pleasure Principle*, Freud had not introduced the notion of the death drives as distinct from the life drives. All drives are conservative, that is, both the ego-drives and the sexual drives. And this leads Freud to elaborate and confirm the conservative character of the sexual and ego-drives.[64] This inevitably leads to an undermining of his initial drive dualism and, as a consequence of this, the undermining of his conflict model (based on the study of the psychoneuroses) and the primacy of sexuality. In other words, Freud's speculations on the conservative character of the drive lead him to conclusions that contradict the pillars – the 'shibboleths' – of psychoanalytic theory. Does it still make sense to make a distinction between sexual and ego-drives when all drives are conservative and aim at the death? At the end of chapter five, Freud stares drive monism in the face – enough reason not to publish the text and to think through the drive theory.

Intermezzo: Freud discovers Eros

In his introduction to the English translation of *Massenpsychologie und Ich-Analyse* James Strachey writes that "there is little direct connection between the present work and its close predecessor, *Beyond the Pleasure Principle*".[65] This statement is likely based on the fact that the concept of death drives is

aim at death – is situated in a shift towards a biological model for understanding psychic life. This biological model can be distinguished from a physiological model in which on the hand the drives are seen as constant forces and on the other hand the psyche is defined as an apparatus regulated by the pleasure principle aiming at discharge of stimuli. In the biological model, the drives are no longer seen as 'external' to the psychic apparatus, but as an integral part of the psychic organisation. H. Loewald (1971), 'On Motivation and Instinct Theory', pp. 116–124; B.Y. Fong (2016), *Death and Mastery*, pp. 8–12.

[64] Freud (1920g), *Beyond the Pleasure Principle*, pp. 40–41.

[65] See Strachey's 'Editor's Note' in S. Freud (1921c), *Group Psychology and the Analysis of the Ego*, *SE* 18, p. 67.

not mentioned in the text on group psychology. But is this all there is to say about a text Freud was writing in the period between the first and second versions of *Beyond the Pleasure Principle*? We know that he finished the first version of *Beyond the Pleasure Principle* in April 1919 and started working on group psychology a month later. From correspondences we know that Freud was delving into "group psychology and death drives" in the winter of 1919–1920.[66] In the period of May–July 1920 Freud finishes the second version of *Beyond the Pleasure Principle*. A month later he composes a draft of *Group Psychology and the Analysis of the Ego* in which, according to Freud, all the important elements of that text, which he finishes in spring 1921, were already present.[67]

In two texts extensively referenced in *Group Psychology and the Analysis of the Ego* – Gustav Le Bon's *The Crowd* (1895) and Wilfred Trotter's *Instincts of the Herd in Peace and War* (1916) – Freud finds an idea that will be at the heart of his new drive theory (see next section). On the central question of how individuals are 'bound' (*Bindung*) together in a mass, Freud first quotes Le Bon: "The psychological group is a provisional being formed of heterogeneous elements, which for a moment are combined, exactly as the cells which constitute a living body form by their reunion a new being".[68] And in his critical discussion of Trotter and the dismissal of the notion of a herd instinct or social drive, Freud again voices a similar idea: what binds people together in masses is "biologically [...] an analogy to multicellularity". He adds: "In terms of the libido theory it is a further manifestation of the tendency which proceeds from the libido and which is felt by all living beings of the same kind, to combine in more and more comprehensive units".[69]

As we will see in the next section, these ideas on the binding of cells into a cell state and the formation of comprehensive units will be conceptualised by Freud as 'Eros'.[70] Hence, there is a direct connection between *Beyond the Pleasure Principle* and *Group Psychology and the Analysis of the Ego*. It is through the study of the literature on masses and the reflection on 'binding' in masses that Freud will be able to conceptualise a new perspective on the

66 The concept of 'death drives' first appears in a letter dated 8.3.1920 to Max Eitingon. S. Freud & M. Eitingon (2004), *Briefwechsel*, p. 194 (Letter 168 F).

67 For a more detailed study of the chronology see Ulrike May's text in this volume.

68 Freud (1921c), *Group Psychology and the Analysis of the Ego*, p. 73.

69 Ibid., p. 118.

70 We note here that Freud's concept of *Bindung* in the 1919 edition of *Beyond the Pleasure Principle* is used to describe the process of binding quantity of excitation to representations in space and time. In *Group Psychology*, *Bindung* is used to describe the affective relations between individuals to each other (i.e. to objects) – *Gefühlsbindungen*, notably identification. In other words, the concept describes two very different processes.

drives. If there is a tendency in all living organisms to combine into more and more comprehensive units, then this tendency must reflect characteristics of the drives. But Freud also learns something else from this study: the binding between individuals in masses is merely provisional and 'for a moment' – hence, there must also be forces at work unbinding what can be bound.

A new drive theory: life drives versus death drives

In the sixth chapter of his text, which was not written until 1920, Freud completely changes his reasoning. From the beginning of this chapter, he states that the sexual drives are profoundly non-conservative. Moreover, in the second version of the text, Freud added an interjection towards the end of the fifth chapter to prepare us for this change of perspective. Where in the first version the question was raised whether "there are no instincts that do not seek to restore an earlier state of things", Freud now adds "apart from the sexual instincts".[71] Moreover, in the second published version from 1921, Freud italicised this short addition, further emphasising its importance. This interjection from 1920 contradicts the 1919 paragraph that precedes it, in which Freud calls sexual drive conservative "to a higher degree" in comparison to the drives of self-preservation.[72] These passages should be read together with the already mentioned additions to the text at the end of chapter four, in which Freud associates the traumatic neurosis with the sexual drive. In this passage Freud also reintroduces the distinction between ego-drives and sexual drives, and the significance of psychic conflict.

In the sixth chapter Freud argues – contrary to his line of reasoning in the fifth chapter – that the sexual drive should not be defined in relation to repetition. The sexual drives, so he writes, do not aim for a return to the inorganic but to the "immortality of the living substance" and are characterised by a tendency of binding cells together into enduring units to prolong life. This is a different perspective from that which has dominated the text so far. We see, at the same time, that the sexual drives are placed in the service of self-preservation here. It is directed to the "immortality of the living substance" and prolonging life. Freud will therefore further in the sixth chapter see both

71 Freud (1920g), *Beyond the Pleasure Principle*, p. 41.

72 Ibid., p. 40. At the beginning of the sixth chapter, Freud confirms that the preceding fifth chapter of his text culminated in an opposition between the ego-drives and sexual drives (ibid., pp. 44 and 52–53). Thus, he presents his position as if drive dualism were never in danger and then as if it were only a matter of replacing one dualism with another. We believe, however, that the sixth chapter is about 'saving' drive dualism.

the sexual and self-preservation drives as expressions of the life drives or Eros. These life drives that manifest themselves in the ego-drives and the sexual drives are now opposed to the death drives. This means that Freud saves his drive dualism not through a return to the initial distinction between ego- and sexual drives, but through the identification of the tendency to return to the inanimate state with a separate set of drives – the death drives.

Freud connects these insights with a new perspective on the origin of life: the force that produced life to emerge in the inanimate matter caused the substance just brought to life to be "torn apart into small particles".[73] In response to this fragmentation, the life drives arise that aim to unite the particles into a living cell. These life drives, seen in this way, arise spontaneously in response to the fragmentation, but at the same time also continue a persistence of "the chemical affinity of inanimate matter", that is, of the ability of atoms and various chemical elements to enter into compounds (chemical reactions) with other atoms and elements.[74] This perspective also implies that the dynamics of the animate are no longer understood exclusively from or as inertia (or repetition). The life drives underpin the later development into multicellular organisms and the possibility of prolonging life.[75] From this perspective, the development of organisms into increasingly complex forms is not so much the result of "imposed and acquired modifications" or of protection against externally induced stimuli, but of drives aimed at binding particles together into a cell, from cells to a "cell-state" (multicellular organism) and from individuals to groups (culture). Life drives seek to integrate into larger units what is "torn apart" and fragmented.[76] Since then, binding into larger units is all about protection against the constant threat of fragmentation and destruction of the unit by external forces (e.g. natural disasters) and from within. Freud assigns the internal force opposing the tendency to unite to the death drives. He also views the death drives, in their urge to restore the inanimate, as the urge to again undo union and coherence. The death drives tend to fragment into separate particles without mutual 'affinity' and thus without mutual tension. It is from this perspective that we can comprehend why Freud will be able to associate the death drives with aggression (primarily masochism, sadism) and violence. The death drives tend towards a violent fragmentation of that which has become a unit.

73 Ibid., p. 58.
74 Ibid.
75 Ibid., pp. 50–51.
76 Ibid., p. 43.

How does this reaffirmation of dualism concretely come about in the sixth chapter of *Beyond the Pleasure Principle*? Freud attempts to ground this dualism primarily in insights from biological science. For this purpose, he takes the work of August Weismann as a starting point. In the fifth chapter Freud had already briefly referred to Weismann's distinction between a mortal and immortal half of living substance. The mortal half (the soma) is the body in the narrow sense. The germ-plasm (the sexual and genetic substances), on the other hand, is potentially immortal. It has a purely instrumental relationship to the soma. The fusion of germ-cells creates a new carrier (soma) every time, which, before dying off, is at the origin of yet another fusion (reproductive function).[77] Sexual drives are dynamic forces that bring about this fusion. Freud takes up this distinction again at the beginning of the sixth chapter. He now argues that the opposition between the ego-drives that seek death and sexual drives that want to retain life are at first glance a dynamic equivalent to Weismann's morphological theory of organic life.[78]

But can we sustain this equivalence, Freud wonders.[79] After all, it assumes that the opposition between germ-plasm and soma is as original as that between death and sexual drives. The latter does not seem to be the case since, according to Weismann, this opposition only applies to multicellular organisms.[80] In single-celled organisms, the individual and the reproductive cell, on the other hand, are still one and the same.[81] When they multiply by division, not only do they remain the same as themselves, but in principle they also lose nothing to vitality. The study of protists further teaches us that fusion, the copulation of two individuals without a resulting division, has a rejuvenating effect on both.[82] Single-celled organisms, or protists as Freud calls them, are in this sense immortal. The latter would also necessarily imply that only reproduction (multiplication) is an original characteristic of living matter, whereas death is rather a matter of adaptation to the external conditions of life. Death "cannot be regarded as an absolute necessity with its basis in the very nature of life".[83] The idea that there is in the living

77 The death of this body is, according to Weismann, "expedient" because after a certain duration it is "worn out" (*Abnutzung*) and thus can no longer fulfil any function for the germ-cell and the survival of the species. A. Weismann (1884), *Über Leben und Tod*, pp. 20 and 36; Freud (1920g), *Beyond the Pleasure Principle*, pp. 45ff; F.B. Churchill (2015), *August Weismann*.

78 A. Weismann (1892), *Das Keimplasma*. Here again we see how sexuality is placed in the service of self-preservation. Freud's statement that germ-cells are narcissistic fits into this view. We will return to this below.

79 Freud (1920g), *Beyond the Pleasure Principle*, pp. 46–47.

80 Weismann (1894), *Über Leben und Tod*, p. 36.

81 Ibid., pp. 16ff; Freud (1920g), *Beyond the Pleasure Principle*, p. 46.

82 Ibid., p. 55.

83 Ibid., p. 46.

substance originally a force directed at the return to the inorganic thus loses its ground.

Yet things are more complicated here than they might seem at first. Woodruff showed, Freud writes, that single-celled organisms, upon division alone, do not lose any vitality or show signs of ageing when – and only when – every new generation is immersed in fresh nutrient medium. I fact, organisms were harmed by metabolic products which they extruded into the surrounding fluid, and Woodruff could show that only products of their own metabolism have this effect of leading to the death of the generation.[84] This confirms the suspicion that the thesis that death is a later acquisition applies only to its manifest expressions, and that single-celled substances also do die for internal reasons. Thus, according to Freud, biology provides no compelling reasons to abandon the idea of an original opposition between two drive forces. Freud concludes: "The striking similarity between Weismann's distinction of soma and germ-plasm and our separation of the death instincts from the life instincts persists and retains its significance".[85]

Freud will now go a step further. When biology does not provide compelling or ultimate arguments against the hypothesis of the drive dualism, he writes, then we can perhaps conversely transpose the psychoanalytic drive theory to all the living substances.[86] Psychoanalytic drive theory will, in other words, be employed here to develop a comprehensive philosophy of life. Freud first recalls the history of his libido theory.[87] The initial contradiction between drives of self-preservation and sexual drives was put into perspective to a large extent through the introduction of narcissism. The study of homosexuality and psychoses led Freud to the insight that not only could the ego be the object of libidinal energy, but that it must itself be thought of as a libidinal construct. The ego arises through the pooling of libidinal energy that for the first time objectifies the body as a whole: "There must be something added to auto-erotism – a new psychical action – in order to bring about narcissism".[88] This ego is the original reservoir of the libido.[89] It is the starting point of the libidinal object relations, of which the energy can also be drawn back into the ego. In this way, the original opposition between ego- or self-preservative drives and sexual drives is replaced by an opposition between ego- or narcissistic libido and object libido. Freud understands the relation between these two

84 Ibid., p. 48.
85 Ibid., p. 49.
86 Ibid., p. 50.
87 Ibid., pp. 50–53.
88 S. Freud (1914c), 'On Narcissism', *SE* 14, p. 77.
89 Freud (1920g), *Beyond the Pleasure Principle*, p. 52.

poles as communicating vessels. The more energy is invested in the object, the less in the ego and vice versa.[90] From here, these drives can be interpreted as two sides of a more general life drive that Freud now identifies with the "Eros of the poets and philosophers".[91] This Eros is a fundamental force that works in everything that is alive. The germ-cells, for example, on the one hand behave completely narcissistically. They are fully focused on their own survival. But simultaneously and profoundly, for the same reason, they also, on the other hand, take other germ-cells as their objects to guarantee this survival. It comes as no surprise to see that Freud sometimes identifies Eros with sexual drives,[92] which is understandable since it unites object libido and ego-libido.[93]

Concerning Freud's depictions of Eros, it is difficult not to think of Jung's theory of primal libido. As in Jung's theory, the Freudian Eros is a force that urges all organic life to further complexity – a force of which the human sexual life is but one manifestation. Freud surely recognised this: in a few sentences added in 1921, Freud explicitly distances himself from Jung's monism and pansexualism.[94] Seen from this perspective, the introduction of the death drives was necessary to maintain drive dualism.[95]

What does Freud mean with death drives? As already mentioned, Freud first of all defines the death drives in terms of the force or urge to return to an inanimate state, that is, to return to a state of minimal tension. However, in chapter six this inertia principle is no longer associated with a compulsion to repeat or repetition as such, with Haeckel's biogenetic law (recapitulation theory) or with Lamarckian repeated attempts at acquiring new characteristics. In fact, Freud raises the question as to whether he had not overestimated the significance of the "facts of the compulsion to repeat".[96] Freud instead opts for another perspective. The death drives are defined in terms of a violent fragmentation of the unities and bindings established by Eros. According to Freud, this violent fragmentation should first and foremost be regarded as

90 Freud (1914c), 'On Narcissism', p. 76.
91 Freud (1920g), *Beyond the Pleasure Principle*, p. 50.
92 Ibid., p. 58.
93 Freud explored this in detail in his analyses of *Gefühlsbindungen* in *Group Psychology and the Analysis of the Ego*.
94 Freud (1920g), *Beyond the Pleasure Principle*, p. 53.
95 On this issue see also P. Moyaert (2022), *De doodsdrift revisited: een breuklijn tussen Freud en Deleuze*, pp. 57–61.
96 Freud (1920g), *Beyond the Pleasure Principle*, p. 59. Instead of references to Haeckel and Lamarckism, Freud in chapter six puts Weismann's theories to the fore – theories that bluntly contradict Lamarckism. After all, according to Weismann, the germ-cells are immune to change through external causes. Weismann (1892), *Das Keimplasma*, pp. 45ff.

a tendency towards reduction of tension. The union of different substances through Eros increases internal tensions and 'vital differences', and the death drives aim at the reduction of these tensions. But since the death drives operate against the increase of tension produced by Eros, the issue of repetition and compulsion to repeat indeed loses much of its significance. Contrary to what is often assumed, Freud in chapter six opts for a biological perspective that is very different from the one in chapter five.

To which manifest phenomena, Freud now asks, can the death drives be linked to make the necessity of their affirmation plausible? For this, Freud now does not refer to the problematic of repetition in traumatic neurosis or transference like in the first version of the text but to a polarity with which psychoanalysis is more familiar: the opposition between love and hate.[97] In this way, he hopes to give the opposition between life and death drives more specific content that is simultaneously its expression. In *Three Essays on the Theory of Sexuality* Freud had already assumed a sadistic component in the libido.[98] This sadistic component can individuate itself in the sexual perversion of the same name and usurp the entire sexual life. According to Freud in the text we are discussing here, it cannot be derived from Eros.[99] After all, unlike Eros, it is not oriented to the formation and maintenance of ever larger connections. Freud concludes:

> Is it not plausible to suppose that this sadism is in fact a death instinct which, under the influence of the narcissistic libido, has been forced away from the ego and has consequently only emerged in relation to the object? It now enters the service of the sexual function.[100]

Here Freud introduces the perspective of two opposing drives that are usually fused but that can also separate themselves so that they can show themselves in a 'pure' form. How this fusing and defusing can be thought of and described Freud pretty much disregards in *Beyond the Pleasure Principle*. It can be said,

---

97 Freud (1920g), *Beyond the Pleasure Principle*, pp. 53–54. In *The Ego and the Id* Freud makes this point even more explicit: "For the opposition between the two classes of instincts we may put the polarity of love and hate". S. Freud (1923b), *The Ego and the Id*, *SE* 19, p. 42.

98 Freud (1905d), *Three Essays*, pp. 157–158.

99 In *The Ego and the Id* Freud writes: "Over and over again we find, when we are able to trace instinctual impulses back, that they reveal themselves as derivatives of Eros. If it were not for the considerations put forward in *Beyond the Pleasure Principle*, and ultimately for the sadistic constituents which have attached themselves to Eros, we should have difficulty in holding to our fundamental dualistic point of view". Freud (1923b), *The Ego and the Id*, p. 46.

100 Freud (1920g), *Beyond the Pleasure Principle*, p. 54.

however, that the notions of fusion and defusion of drives replaces the train of thought from chapter five in which the ego-drives and sexual drives are referred to as a conservative tendency to return to an inanimate state.

Of particular interest to us here is that the death drives are explicitly connected to aggression in the sixth chapter. Not only was there no mention of the term 'death drives' in the first version of our text, but Freud also drew no connection between inertia of the drive and aggression. This connection is also not so obvious. This changes when the dynamic of organic life is bound to the reunion of an original fragmentation. The death drives can then be thought of in opposition to this dynamic. They are, as we indicated earlier, aimed at the disbandment of what was bound. They envisage undoing the 'chemical tensions' and 'vital differences' that accompany Eros as drives to union. This is a specification of the inertia principle that in the first version belonged to all drives and that from there was thematised from the repetition and recapitulation principle. This specification allows the inertia principle (tendency to reduce all tension) to be connected to aggression (towards the self and external objects). This aggressiveness is original and has its own purpose: destroy, fragment. It therefore does not owe its emergence to life, even though it can be placed in service of life.

From this perspective, we are from the outset bearers of an aimless aggression that only seeks destruction and needs no external frustrations to be unleashed.[101] At first, at the beginning of our existence, we are too weak to direct this aggression that rages within us outward. This aggression then attacks the still undeveloped organism from within. In his text 'The Economic Problem of Masochism', Freud later calls this process 'primary masochism'.[102] We can only defend ourselves against this by blending this aggression with the life drives to direct them outward. However, this does not prevent an aggression from raging within us that can never completely be nullified or overcome.

We have seen that towards the end of chapter five Freud stared a drive monism in the face – a conception of the drives in which the tendency to return to an inanimate state coincided with the pleasure principle. There appears not to be any 'beyond' the pleasure principle. All drives aim at the reduction of tension.

[101] H. Westerink (2015), 'De problematische plaats van de woede in het denken van Freud over agressiviteit'.

[102] S. Freud (1924c), 'The Economic Problem of Masochism', *SE* 19, pp. 160–161; P. Moyaert (2014), *Opboksen tegen het inerte: De doodsdrift bij Freud*, pp. 151–153.

Is this also the case in the new drive theory? At first sight, it may appear that the death drives aiming at violent fragmentation inevitably produce excitation and thus increase tension. However, the opposite is the case. The death drives are no 'trouble makers', but silent forces that seek reduction of tension through fragmentation and the unbinding of unities. After all, it is Eros that produces time and again new tensions between the various elements in union, and hence causes increase of unpleasure. It is with good reason that Freud refers to 'chemical tensions' and 'vital differences': the union of different living substances results in the influx of fresh amounts of stimulus and increases tensions between the substances.[103] The death drives – and the death drives only – coincide with the pleasure principle. On the question of the 'beyond' of the pleasure principle, only one answer is possible: Eros, the life drives.[104]

Final remarks

In most readings of Freud's *Beyond the Pleasure Principle* we can recognise the tendency either towards harmonising the oppositions and tensions in the text, or towards privileging one perspective over another in function of the author's own views of the drives. We started our reading of the text with the hypothesis that the contradictions, tensions and shifts *Beyond the Pleasure Principle* attests to can best be elucidated from the genesis of the text. Specifically, we argued that the sixth chapter should be read as a response to the difficulties to which the development in the first five chapters led. In the first part of the text, Freud initially relied on clinical phenomena, particularly on the compulsion to repeat in the dreams of war neurotics and in transference. Inspired by psycho-Lamarckism and Haeckel's recapitulation theory, he interprets this compulsion to repeat as a manifestation of the regressive and conservative character of all drives as such. However, this tragic view is in danger of culminating in a drive monism that Freud rejects. He replaces the clinical premise of his text in the sixth chapter with a speculative question: does death belong intrinsically to life? August Weismann's distinction between germ-

103 Freud (1920g), *Beyond the Pleasure Principle*, p. 55.

104 Freud elaborates the consequence of this train of thought – namely the idea that the sexual drives do not seek and produce pleasure but unpleasure – in 'The Economic Problem of Masochism' from 1924. In that text Freud argues that the identification of the pleasure principle with Fechner's tendency to stability and Barbara Low's Nirvana principle needs to be corrected. Pleasure cannot be reduced to the decrease of excitation to zero. After all, from the study of sexuality we know that sexual excitation is experienced as pleasurable. In other words, beyond the pleasure principle we find sexual excitation in sexual activities as pleasurable. S. Freud (1924c), 'The Economic Problem of Masochism', pp. 159–161.

plasm and soma should help answer this question. This distinction removes us from the psycho-Lamarckism that was the central point of reference in the first part. Germ-plasm is the sole bearer of heredity. It cannot change under the influence of what the soma acquires or what happens to it during its existence. Thus, the germ-plasm Weismann assumes is not traumatisable. Weismann explicitly rejects psycho-Lamarckism.[105]

Freud calls the opposition between the ego-drives and the sexual drives the dynamic correlate of Weismann's morphological distinction. This means that Freud from now on does not, in line with psycho-Lamarckism and the recapitulation theory, understand particularly the sexual drives from the repetition of the primal history of humankind. He broadens these drives to the life drives (Eros), which also include ego-drives. This has important implications regarding the status and meaning of sexuality. The reference to biology as the study of all living substances situates the problematic of sexuality in the context of reproduction. Human sexuality is immediately and structurally thought of as sexual reproduction, which is in itself a special case of reproduction. This perspective is at odds with the insights Freud addresses in his *Three Essays on the Theory of Sexuality*. Here, Freud discusses human sexuality in connection and sometimes in confrontation with animal sexuality. Sexuality is thus approached here primarily from an anthropological perspective and not from the perspective of a philosophy of organic life or even a cosmology. In *Three Essays*, sexuality is understood from the problematic of infantile sexuality. This is, according to Freud, essentially autoerotic and focused only on the acquisition of pleasure. The idea that sexuality should be described from the perspective of and as procreation was therefore dismissed as a "poetic fable".[106]

In the sixth chapter, Freud first introduces the concept of death drives, which he thematises as a tendency to fragmentation in opposition to Eros. The reference to this tendency specifies the notion of reducing tension through which drives are generally characterised in the first five chapters. This specification makes it possible to contrast the death drives with the life drives. Drive dualism, which was under pressure in the first part of the text, is thus restored. At the same time, the issues of repetition and trauma – including the problematic of the war neuroses – fade into the background at the expense of the problematic of aggression. After all, the relationship between the death

[105] Weismann (1884), *Über Leben und Tod*, pp. 45–46. It for instance already became apparent in a letter to Jones from 1912 – thus long before the publication of *Beyond* – that Freud's Lamarckism is irreconcilable with the theories of Weismann. S. Freud & E. Jones (1993), *The Complete Correspondence*, p. 150 (Letter 82 J).

[106] Freud (1905d), *Three Essays*, p. 135.

drives and fragmentation makes it easier to place aggression as an essential dimension of the drives in opposition to sexuality. Freud thus solves a problem that has haunted his work since the first edition of *Three Essays on the Theory of Sexuality* and the study of the Rat Man: sexuality and aggression are opposed to each other, and yet can also be 'fused'.[107]

Bibliography

Allen, Amy (2021), *Critique on the Couch: Why Critical Theory needs Psychoanalysis.* New York: Columbia UP.

Breuer, Joseph & Freud, Sigmund (1895d), *Studies on Hysteria*, in: *Standard Edition of the Complete Psychological Works of Sigmund Freud, Vol. 2*, transl. James Strachey. London: Hogarth Press, 1953–1974.

Churchill, Frederick B. (2015), *August Weismann: Development, Heredity, and Evolution*, Cambridge (MA) & London: Harvard UP.

Fischer-Homberger, Esther (2004), *Die traumatische Neurose. Vom somatischen zum sozialen Leiden.* Gießen: Psychosozial-Verlag.

Fong, Benjamin Y. (2016), *Death and Mastery. Psychoanalytic Drive Theory and the Subject of Late Capitalism.* New York: Columbia UP.

Freud, Sigmund (1900a), *The Interpretation of Dreams*, in: *Standard Edition of the Complete Psychological Works of Sigmund Freud, Vol. 4–5*, transl. James Strachey. London: Hogarth Press, 1953–1974.

Freud, Sigmund (1905d), *Three Essays on the Theory of Sexuality*, *SE* 7, pp. 130–243.

Freud, Sigmund (1911b), 'Formulations on the Two Principles of Mental Functioning', *SE* 12, pp. 218–226.

Freud, Sigmund (1911c), 'Psychoanalytic Remarks on an Autobiographically Described Case of Paranoia (Dementia paranoids)', *SE* 12, pp. 9–82.

Freud, Sigmund (1914c), On Narcissism: An Introduction', *SE* 14, pp. 73–102.

Freud, Sigmund (1915c), 'Instincts and Their Vicissitudes', *SE* 14, pp. 117–140.

Freud, Sigmund (1919d), 'Introduction to *Psycho-Analysis of the War Neuroses*', *SE* 17, pp. 207–210.

Freud, Sigmund (1920g), *Beyond the Pleasure Principle*, *SE* 18, pp. 7–64.

Freud, Sigmund (1921c), *Group Psychology and the Analysis of the Ego*, *SE* 18, pp. 69–143.

Freud, Sigmund (1923b), *The Ego and the Id*, *SE* 19, pp. 12–66.

[107] In 'The Economic Problem of Masochism' Freud contrasts a death or destruction drive that primarily seeks to "disintegrate" (fragment) the own organism with the libido that is tasked with defusing this death drive by directing it largely outwards. "A portion of the instinct," he argues, "is placed directly in the service of the sexual function, where it has an important part to play. This is sadism proper." Freud (1924c), 'The Economic Problem of Masochism', p. 163. Sexual sadism is thus a hybrid product of sexuality and the externally oriented death drive.

Freud, Sigmund (1924c), 'The Economic Problem of Masochism', *SE* 19, pp. 159–170.

Freud, Sigmund (1926d), *Inhibition, Symptom and Anxiety*, *SE* 20, pp. 87–174.

Freud, Sigmund (1950c), 'Project for a Scientific Psychology', *SE* 1, pp. 295–387.

Freud, Sigmund (1985 [1986]), *The Complete Letters of Sigmund Freud to Wilhelm Fliess, 1877–1904*, transl. & ed. Jeffrey M. Masson. Cambridge (MA) & London: The Belknap Press of Harvard UP.

Freud, Sigmund (2015), 'Beyond the Pleasure Principle', *Psychoanalysis and History* 17(2), pp. 151–203 (in this volume pp. 29–80).

Freud, Sigmund & Eitingon, Max (2004), *Briefwechsel 1906–1939*, 2 vols., ed. Michael Schröter. Tübingen: Edition Diskord.

Freud, Sigmund & Jones, Ernest (1993), *The Complete Correspondence 1908–1939*, ed. R. Andrew Paskauskas. Cambridge (MA) & London: The Belknap Press of Harvard UP.

Grubrich-Simitis, Ilse (1993), *Back to Freud's Texts: Making Silent Documents Speak*. New Haven & London: Yale UP.

Izenberg, Gerald N. (2006), 'Seduced and Abandoned: The Rise and Fall of Freud's Seduction Theory', in: ed. Jerome Neu, *Cambridge Companion to Freud*. Cambridge: Cambridge UP, pp. 25–43.

Laplanche, Jean & Pontalis, Jean-Bertrand (1988), *The Language of Psycho-Analysis*. New York: Routledge.

Leys, Ruth (2000), *Trauma. A Genealogy*. Chicago & London: Chicago UP.

Loewald, Hans W. (1971), 'On Motivation and Instinct Theory', in: *Papers on Psychoanalysis*. New Haven & London: Yale UP, 1980, pp. 102–137.

Malabou, Catharine (2012), *The New Wounded: From Neurosis to Brain Damage*. New York: Fordham UP.

Masson, Jeffrey M. (1984), *The Assault on Truth: Freud's Suppression of the Seduction Theory*. Cambridge (MA): Harvard UP.

May, Ulrike (2015), 'The Third Step in Drive Theory: On the Genesis of *Beyond the Pleasure Principle*', *Psychoanalysis and History* 17(2), pp. 205–280 (in this volume, pp. 81–164).

Micale, Mark S. & Lerner, Paul (eds.), *Traumatic Pasts, History, Psychiatry and the Trauma in the Modern Age, 1870–1930*. Cambridge & New York: Cambridge UP, pp. 115–139.

Moyaert, Paul (2014), *Opboksen tegen het inerte. De doodsdrift bij Freud*. Nijmegen: Vantilt.

Moyaert, Paul (2022), *De doodsdrift revisited. Een breuklijn tussen Freud en Deleuze*. Amsterdam: Boom.

Oppenheim, Hermann (1889), *Die traumatische Neurosen*. Berlin: Verlag von August Hirschwald.

Philips, Adam (2014), *Becoming Freud: The Making of a Psychoanalyst*. New Haven & London: Yale UP.

Scull, Andrew (2009), *Hysteria: The Disturbing History*. Oxford: Oxford UP.

Sulloway, Frank J. (1979), *Freud: Biologist of the Mind.* New York: Basic Books.
Van Haute, Philippe (2022), 'Tussen driftmonisme en conflict: Freuds *Aan gene zijde van het lustprincipe* herlezen', *Tijdschrift voor filosofie* 84, special issue, pp. 39–66.
Van Haute, Philippe & Westerink, Herman (2021), *From Pleasure to the Object: Reading Freud's 'Three Essays on the Theory of Sexuality'.* London & New York: Routledge.
Weismann, August (1884), *Über Leben und Tod. Eine biologische Untersuchung.* Jena: Gustav Fischer Verlag.
Weismann, August (1892), *Das Keimplasma. Eine Theorie der Vererbung.* Jena: Gustav Fischer Verlag.
Westerink, Herman (2015), 'De problematische plaats van de woede in het denken van Freud over agressiviteit', *Tijdschrift voor Filosofie* 77(4), pp. 719–746.
Westerink, Herman & Van Haute, Philippe (2022), *Verleiding, drift en herhaling. Freuds metafysica van het trauma.* Amsterdam: Boom.
Whitebook, Joel (2017), *Freud: An Intellectual Biography.* Cambridge: Cambridge UP.
Zupančič, Alenka (2017), *What is Sex?* Cambridge (MA) & London: MIT Press.

Traumatic Neuroses and Psychoneuroses in (and) *Beyond the Pleasure Principle*[*]

Ulrike Kistner

Introduction: 100 Years and Beyond

The year 2020 marked the centenary of Freud's essay *Beyond the Pleasure Principle*. This gives us pause and cause to consider what the text has given to its readers in the hundred years since its appearance in print, and how the hundred years of its reception have cast the text.

The signs of the times embedded in this text point to the First World War and the upheavals of the immediate post-war period – revolution and new political orders, the pandemic popularly referred to as the Spanish Influenza, economic hardship, supply shortages, and concern over the continued existence of the psychoanalytic movement. These signs have become inscribed in the history of psychoanalysis – not only in the biographies of its figureheads and their respective positions, in the directions, schools and institutions, but also in the questions, orientations, approaches, debates, and in the concepts and theories.

Under pressing conditions at the end of the First World War, Freud had decided to abandon the Lamarck project that he had planned together with his erstwhile close collaborator, Sándor Ferenczi – without, however, entirely abandoning its central themes. Elements of the conjectures on archaic adaptive responses to external threats and traumatogenic events (traces of which Freud presumes in narcissistic neuroses[1] and transference neuroses[2]) remain in elements.[3]

* The research and writing of this chapter was facilitated by a fellowship awarded by the Netherlands Institute for Advanced Studies, which I hereby would like to gratefully acknowledge.

1 For Freud, narcissistic neuroses include *dementia praecox* (this category coined by Emil Kraepelin would correspond to the category of schizophrenia elaborated by Eugen Bleuler), paranoia and melancholia-mania. See A. Hoffer & P.T. Hoffer (1987), 'Foreword', pp. ix, x.

2 In Freud's conceptualisation, transference neuroses include anxiety hysteria, conversion hysteria and obsessional neuroses. Ibid.

3 For the fundamental importance of the phylogenetic dimension in Freud's trauma theories, see H. Westerink & P. van Haute (2022), *Verleiding, drift en herhaling*.

Phylogenetically inscribed traumatic experiences continue to have effects, whether in times of war or in times of peace. Considered in this bigger picture, it becomes clear that traumatic experiences in the world cannot be neatly separated from psychoneuroses or transference neuroses; nor can they be excluded from the domain of psychoanalysis without theoretical loss. In the psychic processing of overwhelming stimuli crashing in from outside, and those bubbling up from the inside of the psychic apparatus, there are connections and interfaces that have often gone unnoticed in the reception of Freud's text.

Among the adversities of the time were illness and death – during the years 1918–1920 related specifically to the so-called Spanish flu, which swept over the globe in three waves, with an estimated 500 million infections and 50 million deaths. The idea that Freud had penned *Beyond the Pleasure Principle* under the shadow cast by the death of his beloved daughter Sophie, and that of his friend Anton von Freund (both of whom passed away towards the end of January 1920), was decisively refuted by its author in response to a contemporary biographer.[4] However, this does not diminish the significance of the reflections on mortality and immortality of organic life featuring in the fifth and sixth chapters of *Beyond the Pleasure Principle.* Freud's partner Martha was struck down by the flu, from which she did not manage to recover for months.[5] Four children in the family also fell ill with the flu, Sophie fatally. The notice of Sophie's death, dispatched to his friend Oskar Pfister, resonates uncannily with the experiences of another pandemic one hundred years later:

> [W]e received the news that our sweet Sophie in Hamburg had been snatched away by influenzal pneumonia, snatched away in the midst of glowing health, from a full and active life as a competent mother and loving wife, all in four or five days, as though she had never existed. Although we had been worried about her for a couple of days, we had nevertheless been hopeful; it is so difficult to judge from a distance. And this distance must remain distance; we were not able to travel at once, as we had intended, after the first alarming news; there was no train, not even for an emergency. *The undisguised brutality of our time* is weighing heavily upon us.[6]

---

4 Letter by Sigmund Freud to Fritz Wittels, 18 December 1923. S. Freud (1924g), 'Letter to Fritz Wittels', *SE* 19, p. 287 n. 1.

5 J. Wolff-Bernstein (2020), 'Spanische Grippe – Covid 19 und Sigmund Freud'.

6 Letter to Oskar Pfister, 27 January 1920. S. Freud & O. Pfister (1963), *Psychoanalysis and Faith: Letters*, pp. 327–328; italics U.K.

Initially, Freud seems inclined to ascribe deadly illness to natural necessity – as the notices of Sophie's death sent to his mother and to his friend indicate; but then he comes to view the idea of 'natural death' as an illusion acquired later in human history. Clearly alluding to the death of his beloved daughter, he notes in the sixth chapter inserted into the *Beyond* text, revised at the beginning of 1920, "that all living substance is bound to die from internal causes". This is probably of some comfort, Freud surmises, for

> If we are to die ourselves, and first to lose in death those who are dearest to us, it is easier to submit to a remorseless law of nature, to the sublime ἀνάγκη [Necessity], than to a chance which might perhaps have been escaped. It may be, however, that this belief in the internal necessity of dying is only another of those illusions which we have created '*um die Schwere des Daseins zu ertragen*'. It is certainly not a primal belief. The notion of a 'natural death' is quite foreign to primitive races; they attribute every death that occurs among them to the influence of an enemy or of an evil spirit.[7]

War, illness, death, trauma, the history of humankind and of organic life as a whole, and psychic processes are inextricably interwoven, taking us far beyond the hundred years of *Beyond.*

'Traumatic neuroses' as a challenge to psychoanalysis

In order to be able to test the "belief in the internal necessity of dying", Freud ventures onto the frontier between exogenous and endogenous sources of excitation and their psychophysical interaction. In the course of searches for explanations at the interfaces between psychoanalysis, cultural history and biological sciences, the text pegs psychic processes to anthropogenesis and to contemporary history.

In the historiography on 'traumatic neuroses'[8] from the end of the nineteenth century until the 1930s, we can identify a trajectory from 'accidental

7 S. Freud (1920g), *Beyond the Pleasure Principle*, *SE* 18, p. 44.

8 'Traumatic Neurosis' is presumably a concept introduced by Hermann Oppenheim – see H. Oppenheim (1888), 'Wie sind diejenigen Fälle von Neurasthenie aufzufassen, welche sich durch Erschütterungen des Rückenmarkes insbesondere nach Eisenbahnunfällen entwickeln?'; also H. Oppenheim (1889), *Die traumatischen Neurosen.*

neuroses' through hysteria and actual neuroses[9] to war neuroses and neuroses supposedly developed for the purpose of obtaining pension pay-outs. This is how the history of trauma and neuroses is generally presented. Considered in broad strokes, this corresponds, in a first step, to the change from accidental to psychological-aetiological explanations of neuroses;[10] and in a second step, to the question, posed anew in the course of the First World War, of traumatic neuroses, featuring at the time also as 'war neuroses'.[11] In her comprehensive conceptual-historical investigation of 'traumatic neuroses', Esther Fischer-Homberger notes the recession of the concept of 'traumatic neurosis' in the aftermath of the First World War; or, to put it more specifically, the exclusion of neuroses related to exogenous trauma from the domain of psychoanalysis.[12] Fischer-Homberger concludes:

> The more Freud formulated his theory psychologically, the more questionable the concept of 'trauma' became for him. He did subsequently still refer to sexual trauma, and to the traumatic scenes of early childhood, etc. But the more he defined trauma psychologically, the less remained of trauma.'[13]

What tends to get eclipsed in summary overviews of the history of psychoanalysis are the controversies, interventions and disagreements, some of which I would like to take up here, insofar as they became consequential for conceptual clarifications, explanations and theoretical orientations in Freud's *Beyond the Pleasure Principle*. In doing so, I am relying on the study by Esther Fischer-Homberger on traumatic neurosis (cited above), on the well-ploughed field of the psychiatric-historical debates on war neuroses, and on the detailed and differentiated text-critical edition of Freud's essay compiled by Ulrike May and Michael Schröter, as well as other articles by Ulrike May on the subject of Freud's *Beyond*. In a second step, I would like to take up further questions related to the third formulation of Freud's drive theory which

9 The term 'actual neuroses' designates neuroses whose symptoms are related to current experiences, rather than experiences of early childhood. R. Kloocke, H.-P. Schmiedebach & S. Priebe (2010), 'Psychische Ereignisse – organische Interpretationen', pp. 78–79; E. Fischer-Homberger (1975), *Die traumatische Neurose*, p. 77.

10 Thus Freud declares in *The Interpretation of Dreams* not to have any truck with anxiety dreams beyond those emanating 'from sexual sources', by virtue of which they become amenable to analysis. See S. Freud (1900a), *The Interpretation of Dreams*, *SE* 4–5, p. 582.

11 The concept of 'war neurosis' had been coined long before the First World War – in 1907 – by Wiesbaden-based internal medicine specialist and medical historian Georg Honigmann. See G. Honigmann (1929), 'Arzt und Unfall', pp. 29–30.

12 See also C. Malabou (2012), *The New Wounded*, pp. 79, 144, 145.

13 Fischer-Homberger (1975), *Die traumatische Neurose*, p. 79; transl. U.K.

continue to make waves in psychoanalytic theory, but which have hitherto been largely ignored by the bird's-eye view taken by some general histories of psychoanalysis. In short, the focus will be on the fundamental question of the relation between traumatic neuroses and psychoneuroses, which I believe has not been put to rest with the end of the First World War but has made a comeback in a new form.

To be able to get there, I will first have to briefly step onto the well-ploughed field of the 'war neuroses'.

About twenty-five years after Freud had gradually elaborated the sexual aetiology of neuroses, trauma-centred explanations of hysteria[14] unexpectedly presented renewed challenges to psychoanalysis. Nothing could have prepared Freud and his colleagues in the International Psychoanalytical Association for the vortex of the politically charged debates on the role of psychoanalysis in war psychiatry, into which they were drawn. Psychoanalysis of the war neuroses found itself between the Scylla of its irrelevance to the socio-political upheavals of the time, and the Charybdis of its capture by and selective application in military psychiatry.[15] Psychogenic explanations of neuroses were taken up and set to sail 'under false colours', as it were,[16] by military psychiatry – as for instance in descriptions and diagnoses of 'flight into illness', (primary) 'gain from illness' and 'purposive neurosis', while the sexual aetiology of neuroses was eclipsed. The debates at the International Psychoanalytical Congress in Budapest at the end of September 1918 brought the controversies to a head in what was to become a turning point – albeit with delayed effect, as by that time military defeat was a foregone conclusion. Now it was Freud's colleagues who sought to defend the foundations of psychoanalysis in opposition to military psychiatry in the service of war; the former tended to seek explanations for war neuroses in analogy to the sexual aetiology of neuroses (that is, in terms of the first and in some respects also in terms of the second formulation of Freud's drive theory).

14 Freud had extended the organic and accidental-traumatogenic explanations of Charcot, and distanced himself from Janet's explanations of 'splitting of consciousness' in cases of hereditary 'degeneracy', 'innate weakness of the capacity for psychical synthesis', and 'psychasthenia'. S. Freud (1893), 'On the Psychical Mechanism of Hysterical Phenomena', *SE* 3, pp. 27–39; S. Freud (1894a), 'The Neuro-Psychoses of Defence', *SE* 3, pp. 45–61; J. Breuer & S. Freud (1895d), *Studies on Hysteria*, *SE* 2.

15 After an initial Austrian patriotic enthusiasm for war, it did not take long for Freud to bemoan (in February 1915, in an address entitled '*Wir und der Tod*') the turmoil of war and its impact on scientific research: "Science herself has lost her passionless impartiality; her deeply embittered servants seek for weapons from her with which to contribute towards the struggle with the enemy". S. Freud (1915b), 'Thoughts for the Times on War and Death', *SE* 14, p. 275.

16 See S. Ferenczi (1921 [1919]), 'First address at the Symposium held at the Fifth International Psycho-Analytical Congress in Budapest, September 1918', p. 6.

Sándor Ferenczi, for one, insists on the important role of psychoanalysis in processes of social and political transformation. It entails a psychoanalytic explanation of and therapeutic intervention in the "enormous number of nervous disorders".[17] Yet Ferenczi distances himself from the psychogenic explanations of some of his opponents – for instance, from those of Adolf Strümpell who seeks the causes of traumatic neuroses in a combination of organic-mechanical and psychic elements, foregrounding the aim of *primary* gain from illness motivated by the expectation of an insurance pay-out. Ferenczi holds against this view, pointing out that the primary motive of illness is an entirely legitimate need for protection, security, and self-preservation. He comes up with a different psychogenic explanation: "an unconscious contrary wish puts itself in the way of the consciously wished act", to counteract the repetition of an unpleasant occurrence.[18]

What Ferenczi introduces into the discussion of the war neurosis here is the factor of narcissism – the motive force of the second formulation of Freud's drive theory. Entailed in it is an element that is to become the pivot of the third formulation of Freud's drive theory (in the second version of the *Beyond* essay):

> The war neuroses, according to psycho-analysis, belong to a group of neuroses in which not only is the genital sexuality affected, as in ordinary hysteria, but also its precursor, the so-called narcissism, self-love [...] [T]he sexual foundation of these so-called narcissistic neuroses is less easily apparent, particularly to those who equate sexuality and genitality and have neglected to use the word 'sexual' in the sense of the old platonic *Eros*. Psycho-analysis, however, returns to this extremely ancient standpoint when it treats all tender and sensual relations of the man to his own or to the opposite sex, emotional feelings towards friends, relatives and fellow-creatures generally, even the affective behaviour towards one's own ego and body, partly under the rubric 'erotism', otherwise 'sexuality'.[19]

There are two reasons why Ferenczi is looking over his shoulder, behind which he suspects the opponents of psychoanalysis to be lurking: he stands up to the representatives of war psychology who are intent on invalidating the psychoanalytically established sexual aetiology of neuroses (such as Max Nonne); and he argues against those who want to reduce sexuality to genitality.

17 Ibid.
18 Ibid., p. 15.
19 Ibid., p. 17.

Similarly to Ferenczi, but for different reasons, Karl Abraham finds that academic neurology differs significantly from psychoanalytical approaches.[20] Neurology largely relies for its findings on the reaction of ego impulses to the trauma – that is, on manifest expressions of the neuroses, excluding the role of unconscious factors, and particularly of sexual factors.

Without directly referring to the presentations of his colleagues, Ernst Simmel's address combines the positions of Ferenczi and Abraham: it is only through psychoanalysis that some light can be shed on the psycho-pathogenesis of the war neuroses.[21] The 'flight into illness' is not to be countered with a 'flight into health' enforced through torturous treatment.[22]

In their contributions to the Budapest Congress, Freud's colleagues thus clearly underline the libido theory of neurosis,[23] the sexual aetiology of neuroses, and the first formulation and in elements also the second formulation of Freud's drive theory.[24]

Just at the point at which his colleagues effectively style him as a pioneering thinker in the field and encourage him to declare himself on the subject, Freud remains hesitant and reserved. His own presentation at the Congress does not deal with the war neuroses, at least not in the first instance. Under the apparently nondescript title 'Lines of Advance Psycho-Analytic Therapy', Freud announces new lines of thought to his audience:

---

20 Ibid., p. 10; K. Abraham (1921 [1919]), 'Second address at the Symposium held at the Fifth International Psycho-Analytical Congress in Budapest', p. 22.

21 E. Simmel (1921 [1919]), 'Third address at the Symposium held at the Fifth International Psycho-Analytical Congress in Budapest', pp. 30–31.

22 Ibid., p. 43.

23 Two months after taking up his appointment in the Budapest military hospital in 1916, Sándor Ferenczi described "war hysteria" in terms of either anxiety hysteria or conversion hysteria, while at the same time introducing considerations of narcissistic injury. S. Ferenczi (1919), 'Über zwei Typen der Kriegsneurose', pp. 70, 77.

24 Freud inserts a summary of the different formulations of his drive theory in a footnote at the end of the sixth chapter of the *Beyond* essay, which only appears in the second version of that essay. Freud (1920g), *Beyond the Pleasure Principle*, p. 61 n. 1. The three steps in the conceptualisation of the drives can be summarily sketched as follows:
1. The drive groups that are of central importance are the sexual drives (libidinal, striving for the continuation of life, directed toward the object) and the self-preservative or ego-drives (rushing toward death).
2. After the elaboration of the phenomenon of narcissism, in which the ego-drive is libidinal and the ego becomes a sexual object, the opposition between narcissistic ego-drives and libidinal object drives becomes the prominent structure.
3. The opposition of Eros (effecting fusion, unification, integration, binding, characterised as 'life-drives', encompassing both ego and object) and death drive (characterised by the actions of breaking down, unbinding, dissolving, destroying). Ibid., pp. 44–53, 61 n. 1; also U. May (2015), 'Der Todestrieb im Kontext von Freuds Erkenntnisinteressen', p. 211.

> Now that we are met together once more after the long and difficult years of separation that we have lived through, I feel drawn to review the position of our therapeutic procedure – to which, indeed, we owe our place in human society – and to take a survey of the new directions in which it may develop.[25]

In the following, I would like to trace some of these "new directions", but not before lingering in the ambit of the Budapest Congress for a bit.

Steps towards the third formulation of the drive theory

Freud bundles the contributions of his colleagues (presented to the Budapest Congress on 28 and 29 September 1918) and prefaces them with a short Introduction, penned in February 1919. He re-states his sexual aetiology of neuroses, but attenuates its applicability to the war neuroses:

> [T]his portion of the theory has not yet been proved to apply to the war neuroses. The work that might prove it has not yet been taken in hand. It may be that the war neuroses are altogether unsuitable material for the purpose.[26]

---

25 S. Freud (1919a), 'Lines of Advance in Psycho-Analytic Therapy', *SE* 17, p. 159.

26 S. Freud (1919d), 'Introduction to *Psycho-Analysis and the War Neuroses*', *SE* 17, p. 208. Already in the eighteenth of his *Introductory Lectures on Psychoanalysis* (1917) entitled 'Fixation to Trauma,' Freud remarks: "Traumatic neuroses are not in their essence the same thing as the spontaneous neuroses which we are in the habit of investigating and treating by analysis; nor have we yet succeeded in bringing them into harmony with our views [...]. But in one respect we may insist that there is a complete agreement between them. The traumatic neuroses give a clear indication that a fixation to the moment of the traumatic accident lies at their root. These patients regularly repeat the traumatic situation in their dreams [...]. It is as though these patients had not finished with the traumatic situation, as though they were still faced by it as an immediate task which has not been dealt with [...]. [This view] shows us the way to what we may call an *economic* view of mental processes. Indeed, the term 'traumatic' has no other sense than an economic one. We apply it to an experience which within a short period of time presents the mind with an increase of stimulus too powerful to be dealt with or worked off in the normal way, and this must result in permanent disturbances of the manner in which the energy operates". S. Freud (1916–1917a), *Introductory Lectures, SE* 16, pp. 275–276.
In the twenty-fourth lecture on 'The Common Neurotic State,' Freud turns his attention to war neuroses and extends the considerations on traumatic neuroses in the direction of narcissism (while still keeping the 'purposive neuroses' in mind): "in traumatic neuroses, and particularly in those brought about by the horrors of war, we are unmistakably presented with a self-interested motive on the part of the ego, seeking for protection and advantage [...]. This motive tries to preserve the ego from the dangers the threat of which was the precipitating cause of the illness and it will not allow recovery to occur until a repetition of these dangers seems no longer possible or until compensation has been received for the danger that has been endured". Ibid., p. 382.

Instead, like Ferenczi, Freud tentatively adduces the second formulation of his drive theory, but modifies it: the serious conflict in the ego (also termed 'conflict between two ego-ideals') is drawn into the ambit of the narcissistic neuroses.[27] He also holds onto this view in his statements submitted to the commission investigating the war-time conduct of psychiatrist Julius Wagner-Jauregg in October 1920.[28] He considers the war neuroses to be traumatic neuroses shaped by responses to conditions of war, generating a conflict between a prior peaceful and a new war-like ego. The erstwhile peaceful ego protects itself against the threat of mortal danger through flight into traumatic neurosis. This insight shatters the frameworks of the first as well as of the second drive theory:

> The theory of the sexual aetiology of the neuroses, or, as we prefer to say, the libido theory of the neuroses, was originally put forward only in relation to the transference neuroses of peace-time, and is easy to demonstrate in their case by the use of the technique of analysis. But its application to the other disorders which we later grouped together as the narcissistic neuroses already met with difficulties.

And then comes the statement that is most instructive for the purposes of the argument developed here:

> The traumatic neuroses (of peace time) have always been regarded as the most refractory material of all in this respect; so that the emergence of the war neuroses could not introduce any new factor into the situation that already existed.[29]

Thus, Freud delimits the domain of the libido theory of neurosis as he had formulated it up to that point – that is, the first step in his drive theory – without giving it up; and he accords limited pertinence to the second formulation of his drive theory. In the bigger picture, he acknowledges the limits of psychoanalysis.

There is a further respect in which Freud's formulations sound very similar to those of Ferenczi. Both of them extend the concept of the sexual drive beyond genitality. At the time (in February 1919), though, Freud has not as

[27] See M. Schröter (2018), 'Die Psychoanalyse und die "Kriegsneurosen" des Ersten Weltkrieges', pp. 138, 140.

[28] See S. Freud (1955c), 'Memorandum on the Electrical Treatment of War Neurotics', *SE* 17, pp. 211–215.

[29] Freud (1919d), 'Introduction to *Psycho-Analysis and the War Neuroses*', 209.

yet mentioned Eros, whereas Ferenczi had adduced it in September 1918,[30] to extend the meaning of 'sexual' (to quote him again):

> [T]hose who equate sexuality and genitality and have neglected to use the word 'sexual' in the sense of the old platonic *Eros*. Psycho-analysis, however, returns to this extremely ancient standpoint when it treats all tender and sensual relations of the man to his own or to the opposite sex, emotional feelings towards friends, relatives and fellow-creatures generally, even the affective behaviour towards one's own ego and body, partly under the rubric 'erotism', otherwise 'sexuality'.[31]

Given the similarity between Freud's and Ferenczi's formulations of the conflict in the ego, and of 'Eros' (albeit, in Freud's case, only since the second version of the *Beyond* essay, in which 'Eros' appears for the first time), it does not appear surprising that, shortly after the Budapest Congress, Freud announces an idea ("*ein Traumgebilde*") reaching 'beyond' the first and the second formulations of his drive theory.[32] In a further letter to Ferenczi (17 March 1919), Freud confirms that he is working on a paper "with the mysterious heading Beyond the Pleasure Principle".[33] In fact, to be precise, Freud wrote the first version of the manuscript of *Beyond the Pleasure Principle* between March and April 1919. As Ulrike May's careful analysis of the different versions of the text shows, there was no mention of 'Eros', or of 'death drive' in a more narrowly defined sense, in the first version. As for the 'death drive', Freud only speaks of it in a letter to Max Eitingon dated 8 March 1920. Between May and June 1920, Freud revises the first (handwritten) version. The second version of July 1920 is a typewritten copy of the first version, with the sixth chapter and additional paragraphs and annotations inserted. It is in this second version that 'Eros' and 'death drive' appear in that form for the first time. At the end of November, the first edition appears in print with the Psychoanalytischer

30 Freud takes up Ferenczi's formulation (but references it to M. Nachmansohn, 1915) in the Preface to the fourth edition of *Three Essays on a Theory of Sexuality*, which was penned in May 1920, that is, at the time during which Freud revised the first version of the *Beyond* essay. Here he extends the realm of sexuality to take in the "the *Eros* of the divine Plato". S. Freud (1905d), *Three Essays on the Theory of Sexuality*, *SE* 7, p. 134.

31 Ferenczi (1921 [1919]), 'First address at the Symposium held at the Fifth International Psycho-Analytical Congress in Budapest, September 1918', p. 17. See also Freud's open letter to Einstein, published under the title 'Why War?' (1933). Here Freud talks of "erotic" drives "exactly in the sense in which Plato uses the word 'Eros' in his *Symposium*, or 'sexual', with a deliberate extension of the popular conception of 'sexuality'" to designate those drives which seek to preserve and unite (ibid.). S. Freud (1933b), 'Why War?', *SE* 22, p. 209.

32 May (2015), 'Der Todestrieb im Kontext von Freuds Erkenntnisinteressen', p. 215.

33 S. Freud & S. Ferenczi (1996), *Correspondence, Vol. 2*, p. 335.

Verlag. In the time period between the end of 1920 and mid-1925, three further revised, corrected and amended editions appear.[34]

Going beyond: *'thought of the outside'*

How does the death drive come alive, unseating the pleasure principle that had hitherto been thought to govern unconscious mental life? According dominance to the pleasure principle leaves open the question of how to make sense of unpleasure as a distinct psychic-motive force. *Beyond the Pleasure Principle* opens with the stipulation of a series of systematically negative conditions that limit the previously overarching sway of the pleasure principle. Sources of unpleasure that are of interest to Freud in this context are those that are not covered by previous explanations: they cannot be accounted for by the replacement of the pleasure principle with the reality principle; nor can they be related to the conflict and divisions between agencies within the psychic apparatus, whereby what is of pleasure to one agency is of unpleasure to the other one; nor can they be explained by the "pressure of unsatisfied instincts";[35] nor can they even be exemplified by the attempt of the eighteen-month-old child to actively master the distressing experience of the disappearance of the mother through a repetitious, staged *fort-da* game;[36] nor can they be fully explained by repression coming undone.[37] The first chapter concludes with a decisive comment – in the form of a concession – that validates the significance of the traumatic neuroses from a new perspective:

> Nevertheless the investigation of the mental reaction to external danger is precisely in a position to produce new material and raise fresh questions bearing upon our present problem [of determining the limits if not the de-activation of the pleasure principle].[38]

Freud's formulation at the end of the first chapter is instructive. "The investigation of the mental reaction to external danger" poses a new challenge to (psycho-)analysis. It heralds the thought of the outside in two related senses: firstly, in the sense of thought that does not seek its justification from

[34] See May (2015), 'Der Todestrieb im Kontext von Freuds Erkenntnisinteressen'.
[35] Freud (1920g), *Beyond the Pleasure Principle*, p. 11.
[36] Ibid., pp. 16–17.
[37] Ibid., p. 11.
[38] Ibid.

its positivities, but moves *beyond* itself, beyond the subject, "setting its limits from without";[39] and secondly, in the sense of the question as to what role external reality plays within the psychic economy or, more fundamentally, what role the external world plays in the constitution of the psyche.[40] In *Civilization and its Discontents*, Freud retrospectively highlights this 'outside' in both senses: "the frequent, manifold and unavoidable sensations of pain and unpleasure" enjoin us to recognise an external world independently of the ego – and be it for purposes of defence against unpleasure – the impact of which becomes consequential for the distribution of amounts of excitation and cathectic energy within the psychic economy.[41]

Thus, an economic explanation gains prominence here, of the kind that Freud had already adduced in the eighteenth of his *Introductory Lectures on Psychoanalysis*:

> Indeed, the term 'traumatic' has no other sense than an economic one. We apply it to an experience which within a short period of time presents the mind with an increase of stimulus too powerful to be dealt with or worked off in the normal way, and this must result in permanent disturbances of the manner in which the energy operates.[42]

Taking up this economic explanation again in his *Beyond* essay, Freud specifies the challenges that traumatic experiences pose to the psychic apparatus: the cortex receives stimuli from without as well as excitations from within; against externally impinging stimuli, it has to mobilise a protective shield to reduce their intensity by redirecting them; and the psychic apparatus has to transform them by binding them.[43]

The focus in this explanation is directed not to the *event* in the external world as the cause of the trauma (as had been foregrounded by Freud's teachers and predecessors Charcot and Janet, as a necessary condition for trauma), but to the effects triggered in the psychic apparatus, and to the question of how an external *event* becomes a psychic *experience*. Neither the one nor the other can itself be considered 'traumatic'; rather, it is the relation between event and experience, as it unfolds in anthropogenesis, psychogenesis and pathogenesis, that is of interest in Freud's explanation.

---

39 M. Foucault (1987), 'Maurice Blanchot', pp. 15–16.

40 M.M. Oliner (1996), 'Äußere Realität', p. 9; also S. Freud (1926d), *Inhibitions, Symptoms and Anxiety, SE* 20, p. 131.

41 S. Freud (1930a), *Civilization and Its Discontents, SE* 21, p. 67.

42 Freud (1916–1917a), *Introductory Lectures*, p. 276.

43 Freud (1920g), *Beyond the Pleasure Principle*, pp. 25–29.

In his 'Introduction to *Psychoanalysis and the War Neuroses*' (1919), Freud had emphatically stated that so-called accidental neuroses and war neuroses are 'refractory', posing limits to psychoanalytic therapy. But the ink had hardly dried on this publication when the war neuroses attained a different and no less significant – that is, systematic – status. Traumatic neuroses, previously bracketed as exceeding the scope and the possibilities of psychoanalytic theory and practice, turn into a starting point for the new theoretical orientation in Freud's metapsychology.[44]

Continuities and discontinuities in the third formulation of the drive theory

As decisive as the third formulation of Freud's drive theory is, and as decisively as it is differentiated from the first and the second formulation,[45] there are still noteworthy continuities that would not allow us to consider the first and the second formulation done and dusted. The formulation at the end of the 'Introduction to *Psychoanalysis and the War Neuroses*', which would at first glance seem contradictory, provides a first indication. Here Freud distinguishes the transference neuroses, in which the ego casts its own libido as the enemy, from traumatic and war neuroses, in which the ego protects itself against a danger threatening it from without, or against conflict within the ego. The two scenarios find a common denominator in the defensive stance of the ego fearing an injury. The next sentence corroborates this common denominator between the transference neuroses and the traumatic and war neuroses: "It might, indeed, be said that in the case of the war neuroses, in contrast to the pure traumatic neuroses and in approximation to the transference neuroses, what is feared is nevertheless an internal enemy".[46] This line of thought was not discontinued with the formulation of the third drive theory in *Beyond the Pleasure Principle.* Freud restates the common denominator between the transference neuroses and traumatic neuroses in the second version of *Beyond* – to be precise, at the end of the fourth chapter in an insert made into the typescript of July 1920. Here he introduces a consideration accounting for the assimilation of the accidental war- and traumatic neuroses to the psychoneuroses in more detailed but nonetheless controversial terms – namely,

[44] See Fischer-Homberger (1975), *Die traumatische Neurose*, p. 159; also U. May (2015), 'The Third Step in Drive Theory', p. 230 n. 48 (in this volume, p. 109).

[45] See Freud (1920g), *Beyond the Pleasure Principle*, pp. 51–53, 61 n. 1.

[46] Freud (1919d), 'Introduction to *Psycho-Analysis and the War Neuroses*', p. 210.

that (as previously mentioned in the *Three Essays on the Theory of Sexuality*) "mechanical agitation must be recognized as one of the sources of sexual excitation [...] which, owing to the lack of preparation for[47] anxiety, would have a traumatic effect".[48] Thus the "lack of preparation [through] anxiety", which Freud notes for cases of fright triggered by overwhelming stimuli impinging from without, also pertains to sexual excitation.[49] According to this view, both kinds of neuroses are related to overwhelming sexual excitation and perceived threats to life. More generally stated, frightening events battering the psychic apparatus from without will be experienced as traumatic, by virtue of what they unleash internally.[50] Trauma is being sexualised; and sexual excitation itself is traumatogenic. In this understanding, 'trauma' is removed from the conflict model of the drive theory in its first formulation – the conflict between the ego and the sexual drives repressed by it.[51] In further steps and subsequent writings (which revisit earlier case histories), this thought is developed further: sexual excitation is related phylogenetically and ontogenetically to the trauma of threats to life, and to the corresponding anxiety (as for instance in the case of the Wolf Man, and further reflections on it in *Inhibitions, Symptoms and Anxiety*). This line of thought raises a further problem, which Freud articulates retrospectively as a paradox:

47 "*infolge der mangelnden Angstvorbereitung*" – I would translate this as "owing to the lack of preparation *through* anxiety", because it is a matter of preparing *for* fright *through* anxiety. This translation is confirmed by the function of anxiety elaborated by Freud earlier on in the *Beyond* essay:
"'Fright' [...] is the name we give to the state a person gets into when he has run into danger without being prepared for it; it emphasizes the factor of surprise. I do not believe anxiety can produce a traumatic neurosis. There is something about anxiety that protects its subject against fright and so against fright-neuroses." Freud (1920g), *Beyond the Pleasure Principle*, p. 13.

48 Ibid., p. 33. The formulation of this statement is instructive: traumatic neuroses entail sexual excitations that are not subject to (failed) repression, but which become subject to repetition compulsion, so that preparation through anxiety can be retroactively instituted – see further elaborations below.

49 Ibid., pp. 31, 33.

50 This would require some explanation, which Freud supplies in the fourth and fifth chapters of his *Beyond* essay: in the case of overwhelming stimuli from without, which breach the protective shield, all defences are being mobilised. But a hypercathexis of the systems receiving stimuli withdraws cathectic energy from other systems, leaving them inadequate to the task of binding incoming amounts of stimulus; as a result, the pleasure principle is put out of action. From excitations from within, which emanate from the "the organism's instincts", the shield cannot protect the mental apparatus; their mastery depends on the capacity for psychic binding. Incapacity of the higher strata of the mental apparatus to bind the "instinctual excitation" would trigger "a disturbance analogous to a traumatic neurosis". This explanation indicates a new understanding of "traumatic neuroses": the "old, naïve theory of shock" resulting from direct injury to the molecular or the histological structure of elements within the nervous system is being developed into "a psychologically more ambitious theory" of the aetiological significance for the psyche of fright and threats to life. But even this expanded explanation proves inadequate; it is inflected, in turn, by the interaction between external "event" and psychogenic "experience". Freud (1920g), *Beyond the Pleasure Principle*, pp. 29, 31, 34, 35.

51 See E. Porge (1992), 'Introduction', pp. xvii–xviii.

> In view of all that we know about the structure of the comparatively simple neuroses of everyday life, it would seem highly improbable that a neurosis could come into being merely because of the objective presence of danger, without any participation of the deeper levels of the mental apparatus. But the unconscious seems to contain nothing that could give any content to our concept of the annihilation of life.[52]

As an experience analogous to the (impossible) experience of death, Freud posits castration anxiety, phylogenetically transmitted.[53]

Viewed in this light, it becomes clear that Freud modulated the libido theory of neurosis without, however, giving it up. Critics continue to raise the puzzling question as to where exactly the *Beyond* is to be located theoretically, and how even a charitable reader is to visualise this *Beyond* – impelling some to object, whether in resignation or in triumph, that there cannot be a 'beyond' of the pleasure principle.[54] On a closer reading of the first version of the *Beyond* essay, this objection appears short-circuited. It becomes clear that this version of the text diverges from the sexual aetiology of neuroses in important respects, and therefore also does not present any pivots for repression. There is mention of some processes (for instance the phenomenon of repetition of unpleasurable experiences in children's play, with the unconscious aim of mastering those powerful impressions) that do *not as yet* fall under the pleasure principle, but do *not stand in opposition* to it and are *not independent* of it.[55] But Freud explicitly distinguishes this kind of repetition from the repetition compulsion of "daemonic character" that acts in opposition to the pleasure principle.[56] The latter kind of repetition includes compulsive repetitions of experiences harking back to early psychic life, which could manifest themselves in negative therapeutic reactions; but in any case, the *Beyond* comprises experiences that are "incapable of obeying the secondary process".[57] More particularly, the *Beyond* pertains to instances of repetition compulsion that clearly override the pleasure principle, such as recurring dreams of accidents.[58] What requires explanation, Freud muses, is the fact that "the compulsion to repeat also recalls from the past experiences

52 Freud (1926d), *Inhibitions, Symptoms and Anxiety*, p. 129.
53 Ibid., p. 130.
54 See for instance J. Derrida (1987), 'To Speculate – On Freud', p. 402; also Malabou (2012), *The New Wounded*, pp. 8, 169, 189, 190, 196, 209.
55 Freud (1920g), *Beyond the Pleasure Principle*, pp. 32–33; italics U.K.
56 Ibid., pp. 32–33.
57 Ibid., p. 36.
58 Ibid., p. 23.

which include no possibility of pleasure, and which can never, even long ago, have brought satisfaction even to instinctual impulses which have since been repressed".[59]

For instance: dreams and nightmares

Although, therefore, the third step of the drive theory, variously associated with the end of the traumatic neuroses, is marked, it does not represent a clear, thoroughgoing break with the previous formulations. Freud turns the limits of previous explanations into the occasion to rethink previous suppositions and theses. Under the threshold of this 'step', elements of theories from various constellations come together, and are transformed in turn.

In the extension of the interpretation of dreams we can find an instance of such connections and transformations. With "the investigation of the mental reaction to external danger" programmatically announced at the end of the first chapter, the second chapter turns to the dreams of traumatic neuroses which repeatedly return to the situation of the accident. Parallel to the reformulation of the drive theory occasioned by accidental and war neuroses, the interpretation of dreams attains a new dimension that had already been indicated in twenty-ninth of the (*New*) *Introductory Lectures on Psychoanalysis,* entitled 'Revision of the Dream Theory':[60]

> The fulfilment of wishes is, as we know, brought about in a hallucinatory manner by dreams, and under the dominance of the pleasure principle this has become their function. But it is not in the service of that principle that the dreams of patients suffering from traumatic neuroses lead them back with such regularity to the situation in which the trauma occurred. We may assume, rather, that dreams are here helping to carry out another task, which must be accomplished before the dominance of the pleasure principle can even begin. These dreams are endeavouring to master the stimulus retrospectively, by developing the anxiety whose omission was the cause of the traumatic neurosis. They thus afford us

[59] Ibid., p. 19.

[60] S. Freud (1933a), *New Introductory Lectures*, *SE* 22, pp. 7–30. In the twenty-nineth of the *New Introductory Lectures*, Freud concedes the challenge to his previous 'Interpretation of Dreams' posed by the dreams of traumatic neuroses: "With the traumatic neuroses things are different [from the tendency of the dreamwork to denying unpleasure]. In their case the dreams regularly end in the generation of anxiety. We should not […] be afraid to admit that here the function of the dream has failed". Ibid., p. 29.

> a view of a function of the mental apparatus which, though it does not contradict the pleasure principle, is nevertheless independent of it and seems to be more primitive than the purpose of gaining pleasure and avoiding unpleasure.[61]

In the *Interpretation of Dreams*, Freud had stipulated the function of the dream as disguised fulfilment of a repressed wish.[62] The dreams of accidental and traumatic neuroses, in contrast, explicitly do *not* serve the purposes of wish fulfilment, at least not directly. In *The Interpretation of Dreams*, the mechanism of disguise operates in the tension between manifest dream content and latent dream thought; in cases of accidental and traumatic neuroses in *Beyond the Pleasure Principle*, in contrast, this tension largely falls away. In *The Interpretation of Dreams*, latent dream thoughts are disguised through impulsions to condensation, displacement, substitution, distortion and considerations of representability – to be deciphered in the interpretation of dreams; in *Beyond the Pleasure Principle*, in contrast, the manifest content of the dreams of traumatic neuroses subject to repetition compulsion are lying undisguised in full view. In the latter, trauma moves centre stage, and *The Interpretation of Dreams* fails with regard to the dreams of traumatic neuroses in *Beyond the Pleasure Principle*.[63]

However, these apparently irreconcilable theories of the dream do not remain opposed to each other, just as traumatic neuroses are not counterposed to psychoneuroses in absolute terms. To take up the previously cited statement of Freud's again:

---

61 Freud (1920g), *Beyond the Pleasure Principle*, p. 32.

62 Freud (1900a), *The Interpretation of Dreams*, p. 160.

63 Freud's revised understanding of the dreamwork, as far as the dreams of accidental and war neuroses are concerned, however, is in question. Clinical studies on trauma (for instance Lansky, 1995) did find discrepancies in the traumatic scene and in waking, indicating the screen function of the manifest dream content. M.R. Lansky (1995), *Posttraumatic Nightmares*; quoted in J. Levy (2011), 'The dream in *Beyond the Pleasure Principle* and beyond', p. 130. This intuition had occurred to Freud himself from early on: "How can unpleasurable dreams be unconscious wish fulfilment?", he asks in the seventh chapter of *The Interpretation of Dreams*. At the time, he answered this question partially and precipitately: "Analysis is able to demonstrate that these unpleasurable dreams are wish-fulfilments no less than the rest." Freud (1900a), *The Interpretation of Dreams*, p. 556. But this does not put the question to rest. The seventh chapter of the *Interpretation of Dreams* opens with the dream of the burning child, which continues to puzzle Freud. The dream, he says, "repeated these reflections unaltered, but it represented them in a situation which was actually present and which could be perceived through the senses like a waking experience". Ibid., p. 533. It is a dream "which raises no problem of interpretation and the meaning of which [...] nevertheless retains the essential characteristics that differentiate dreams so strikingly from waking life and consequently calls for explanation". This makes Freud realise "the incompleteness of our psychology of dreams". Ibid., p. 510.

> These dreams [of traumatic neuroses] are endeavouring to master the stimulus retrospectively, by developing the anxiety whose omission was the cause of the traumatic neurosis. They thus afford us a view of a function of the mental apparatus which, though it does not contradict the pleasure principle, is nevertheless independent of it and seems to be more primitive than the purpose of gaining pleasure and avoiding unpleasure.[64]

Pertinent to the repetition compulsion and the unconscious fixation on trauma observed in traumatic neuroses is what Freud had stated as a possibility in the twenty-ninth of his *New Introductory Lectures*: "the dream is an *attempt* at the fulfilment of a wish".[65] Here we see the double character of repetition compulsion: on the one hand, it is clear that the repetition of frightening dreams does not fall under the pleasure principle; on the other hand, repetition is not *beyond* or in opposition to the pleasure principle in every respect. Adducing the image coined by Ilse Grubrich-Simitis, we could visualise the role of repetition compulsion as a hinge operating between the model of the drive in the first version of *Beyond the Pleasure Principle*, which invokes a phylogenetically inscribed repetition compulsion (as "an urge inherent in organic life to restore an earlier state of things"),[66] and the model of trauma of the drive theory in its first formulation, from which the libido theory of neurosis is derived.[67]

Just as the repeated nightmares of traumatic neuroses could be understood as *attempts* at wish fulfilment, repetition in the trauma model of the drive theory in its first formulation could be understood as *endeavour* to master and bind powerful stimuli, so that they can be discharged.[68] This pertains to both stimuli coming from within and stimuli coming from without – and this is an additional reason not to draw the distinction between traumatic neuroses and psychoneuroses in absolute terms. Admittedly, Freud does "describe as 'traumatic' any excitations from outside which are powerful enough to break through the protective shield", mobilising all possible defences, as a result of which the pleasure principle is momentarily put out of action.[69] But this

64 Freud (1920g), *Beyond the Pleasure Principle*, pp. 32–33.
65 Freud (1933a), *New Introductory Lectures*, p. 29; italics Freud.
66 Freud (1920g), *Beyond the Pleasure Principle*, p. 36.
67 See I. Grubrich-Simitis (2007), 'Trauma oder Trieb', pp. 643, 647.
68 Freud (1920g), *Beyond the Pleasure Principle*, p. 29.
69 Ibid., p. 29. It would be consistent with Freud's earlier reflections on the subject to surmise that the drive entails the concept and the impact of trauma *ab initio*: "There is naturally nothing to prevent our supposing that the instincts themselves are, at least in part, precipitates of the effects of external stimulation, which in the course of phylogenesis have brought about the modifications in the living

does not apply only to stimuli impinging from without; the same applies to "internal excitations which produce too great an increase of unpleasure". These tend to be treated "as if they were acting, not from the inside, but from the outside".[70] But while there is a protective shield warding off and filtering stimuli from without, there is no such protection from excitations that emanate from the "organism's instincts" pressing from within.[71] They give rise to disturbances that are "comparable with traumatic neuroses".[72]

A question of binding – and what kind of binding

In the second version of the *Beyond* text, Freud adds a paragraph at the end of the last chapter, indicating some issues for further investigation. Having reinstated the pleasure principle, this time in a duel – and dualism – with the death drives, he makes the pleasure principle the guardian of stimuli impinging from without as well as of excitations pressing from within, and especially of "increases of stimulation from within, which would make the task of living more difficult".[73]

Does this mean that the pleasure principle favours the binding of excitations from within (over those impinging from without)? If that is the case, the distinction between and delimitation of psychoneuroses from traumatic neuroses does not lie in their particular manifestations, but in their specific aetiology, and especially in the capacity for binding stimuli specific to each. This supposition would be plausible insofar as the capacity for binding through psychic representation is possible in the case of psychoneuroses (as opposed to the case of traumatic neuroses, in which the possibility of binding is thwarted), as the sources of internal excitation are described as

substance." Freud (1915c), 'Instincts and Their Vicissitudes', p. 119.

70 Ibid. This phenomenon is what Freud associates with the mechanism of outward projection of instinctual danger. Freud (1920g), *Beyond the Pleasure Principle*, p. 29. That is, he associates it with a defensive mechanism, as for instance in cases of phobia: "The ego behaves as if the danger of a development of anxiety threatened it not from the direction of an instinctual impulse but from the direction of a perception and is thus enabled to react against this external danger with the attempts at flight represented by phobic avoidances." S. Freud (1915e), 'The Unconscious', *SE* 14, p. 184; see also Freud (1930a), *Civilization and Its Discontents*, p. 67. However, this direction turns out to be thwarted: "Attempts at flight from the demands of instinct are [...] in general useless"; but, more seriously, defences mobilised against internally arising unpleasure by means usually mobilised against unpleasure arising from external stimuli are bound to trigger pathological disturbances. Freud (1915e), 'The Unconscious', p. 184; Freud (1930a), *Civilization and Its Discontents*, p. 67.

71 Freud (1920g), *Beyond the Pleasure Principle*, p. 34; also Freud (1926d), *Inhibitions, Symptom and Anxiety*, p. 155.

72 Freud (1920g), *Beyond the Pleasure Principle*, p. 34.

73 Ibid., p. 63.

"the representatives of all the forces *originating in the interior of the body and transmitted to the mental apparatus*".[74] As the second version of *Beyond* would have it, in a concluding paragraph added in 1920, the life drives are connected to our internal perception, since they act as "breakers of the peace and constantly produc[e] tensions whose release is felt as pleasure".[75]

Thus, while impulses from somatic sources can principally be bound by representations, the reception and impact of external stimuli works differently.[76] How this difference pans out differently in the different versions of the *Beyond* text and subsequent reflections on the theme is what I would like to briefly and roughly sketch.

The first version of the *Beyond* text of 1919 takes up the central constellation of the first formulation of the drive theory[77] – the sexual drives, libido, aiming for the continuation of life and directed toward the object, in conflict with the self-preservation or ego-drives pushing towards death – but frames it differently: both are conservative in the sense that, even as they preserve life for a long period, they strive to "bring back earlier states of living substance"; they are all the more conservative insofar as "they are peculiarly resistant to external influence".[78] The sexual drive is tied into this drive mechanism. The 'driven' nature of the repetition compulsion that strives to get back to an earlier, anorganic state, corresponds to the death drive; and the sexual drive subject to it is itself traumatogenic, in phylogenetic as well as in ontogenic respects.

In the second version of the *Beyond* text of 1920 (and beyond), with the amendment at the end of the fifth chapter and the insertion of the sixth chapter, in contrast, it is no longer the repetition compulsion that characterises the working of the drives. The 'synthetic' character of drive elements attains central significance. Accordingly, the role of the repetition compulsion is much reduced, as it is redefined as repetition without 'compulsion'; along with libidinal (self-preservation) drives of the ego, and sexual drives, that is,

---

74 Ibid., p. 34; see also the third edition (1915) of Freud (1905d), *Three Essays*, p. 167; also Freud (1915c), 'Instincts and Their Vicissitudes', pp. 112–113, 117, 121; italics U.K. Exceptions to the possibility of binding internal excitations are cases such as infantile precocious traumatic experiences, sexual and otherwise, which impinge on an immature ego, thus deactivating the workings of the psychic apparatus, so that the pleasure-unpleasure series can no longer gain traction. See S. Freud (1937c), 'Analysis Terminable and Interminable', *SE* 23, p. 220; Freud (1926d), *Inhibitions, Symptoms and Anxiety*, pp. 87–172; also May (2015), 'Der Todestrieb im Kontext von Freuds Erkenntnisinteressen', p. 21.

75 Freud (1920g), *Beyond the Pleasure Principle*, p. 34.

76 This distinction would justify the notion that trauma requires an intervention different from the therapy indicated in the case of (intra-)psychic conflict. Ibid., p. 217.

77 See n. 24; also Freud (1920g), *Beyond the Pleasure Principle*, pp. 41 n. 2, 51, 61 n. 1.

78 Ibid., p. 41; italics U.K.

the life drives, it is now assigned to the realm of Eros. Based on the insight that repetition *qua* compulsion cannot be found to govern the sexual drive, the sixth chapter exempts the sexual drives from the repetition compulsion.[79] Phylogenetically, the role of repetition is assigned to the function of coalescence and fusion of cells, conjugation and reproduction in the development, renewal, continuity and preservation of the living organism.[80] In several instances of this line of argument, *the introduction of stimuli and substances from outside are said to be conducive to 'recuperation' and 'rejuvenation'.*[81]

In the second version of the *Beyond* text, Freud extends his phylogenetic speculations by adducing metaphors assimilating images of cell-physiological processes to human-libidinal actions. In the process, the focus of attention gets directed to object relations:

> [W]e might attempt to apply the libido theory which has been arrived at in psychoanalysis to the mutual relationship of cells. We might suppose that the life instincts or sexual instincts which are active in each cell take the other cells as their object.[82]

The process of 'binding' thus changes in the second version of the text, where it appears in a function different from that in the first one. In the second version, 'binding' is ambiguous. Alongside a fading economic-dynamic psychic function, the notion of 'binding' attains the role of 'fusion' and, in an extended sense, of an increase in complexity. According to the amended version of the text (with the paragraph at the end of the fifth chapter, inserted in 1923), it is the task of Eros to combine organic substances into ever greater unities (without thereby endorsing an evolutionary progressivism).[83]

In contrast to prior descriptions of partial drives combining in the process of the ontogenetic-developmental structuration of the libido (as elaborated in *Three Essays on the Theory of Sexuality*), what comes to the fore in the second version of the *Beyond* essay is the synthetic quality of the drives that fall under Eros – in a word, 'psychosynthesis'. For cases where Eros is found admixed with its duelling/dualistic counterpart – that is, the death drive and its manifestations in aggressivity and destructiveness – Freud resorts to the metaphorical terms of "fusion", "alloy" or "soldering of drive components".[84]

[79] Ibid., p. 55.
[80] Ibid., pp. 44–47.
[81] Ibid., pp. 48–50; italics U.K.
[82] Ibid., p. 50.
[83] Ibid., p. 43.
[84] S. Freud (1923b), *The Ego and the Id*, *SE* 19, p. 41; Freud (1930a), *Civilization and Its Discontents*,

'Binding' is the precondition for the rule of the pleasure principle – and not only within the psychic apparatus; in the extended sense in which it appears in the second version of *Beyond*, it becomes the basis for human community and society, for collective forms of human life.[85] Defusion of the drives, in contrast, is what characterises the death drives, which, in the second version of the *Beyond* text and subsequent writings, include aggressivity and destructiveness – on the part of the super-ego directed against the ego and the id, but also directed externally, against others.[86] It is not surprising to learn that Freud was working on *Group Psychology and the Analysis of the Ego* (1921) in tandem with his work on the *Beyond* essay.[87]

Dualism of the drives

The scope and prominence given to libidinally defined drives in the second version of the *Beyond* essay creates the impression of a monistic drive theory.[88] But beyond that, the relegation of the death drives to a secondary position in the second version raises the question of the 'beyond' of the pleasure principle anew. This time round, the death drive (as it is called in the second version), as mentioned above, is not invoked to explain the phenomenon of repetition compulsion, but to act as a counterpart to Eros. The reasons for Freud's postulation of death drives have changed: the introduction of the death drives is no longer motivated by the explanation of the phenomenon of repetition compulsion and the lack of preparedness for fright through anxiety, but by the challenge of formulating a counter-position to a monistic conceptualisation of the drive, as Freud attributes it to Jung. Freud is not prepared to sacrifice the dualism of the drives to a monism that considers the libido the sole drive force. Instead, Freud instantiates the dualism of the drives in the form of the polarity of love and hate in relation to an object. What comes to the fore in

pp. 120–121; Freud (1937c), 'Analysis Terminable and Interminable', p. 246.

85 See Freud (1930a), *Civilization and Its Discontents*, p. 122; also Freud (1933b), 'Why War?', pp. 203–215.

86 See S. Freud (1923a), 'Two Encyclopedia Articles', *SE* 18, p. 258; also Freud (1923b), *The Ego and the Id*, p. 41; Freud (1930a), *Civilization and Its Discontents*, pp. 119–120, 123; Freud (1933b), 'Why War?', p. 211.

87 The first remark on an "initial idea" on *Group Psychology* appears in April 1919. Freud (1921c), *Group Psychology and the Analysis of the Ego*, *SE* 18, p. 67; also U. May (2013), 'Das Ende der Psychoanalyse oder ihr Neubeginn?', p. 290.

88 Freud anticipates this objection from his critics: "If the self-preservative instincts too are of a libidinal nature, are there perhaps no other instincts whatever but the libidinal ones? At all events there are none other visible." Freud (1920g), *Beyond the Pleasure Principle*, p. 52.

relation to an object – hate, aggressivity, destructivity – is taken to furnish the evidence for the workings of the death drive, which had eluded him for a long time.[89] Thus, Freud moves the object-less drives rushing towards death, *phylogenetically* considered, of the first version into the relation to an object of the second version – as the drive's turn from the ego to the object (in the case of sadism) or as its return from the object to the ego (in the case of masochism).[90] Beneath the main dualism of life drives and death drives, the second version of the *Beyond* text thus installs a further division within the largely libidinally defined drives. Sadism aiming at injuring the object can possibly enter the service of the sexual function, or it can remain independent of the latter, in which case it manifests itself as unmitigated destructiveness.[91] The latter case would then correspond to the death drives as formulated in the first version of the *Beyond* text; and that case would motivate the reinstatement of the repetition compulsion in its original, albeit modified, meaning: the need to return to an earlier phase, in this case that of the *ontogenetically* considered pre-genital partial drives.[92] The same pertains to masochism.[93]

Traumatic neuroses and psychoneuroses between Diesseits *and* Jenseits

In the history of the diversifying theories based on a varied reception of *Beyond the Pleasure Principle*, the second version of the text has overshadowed the first version.[94] A reading that takes its cue from the shift of the death drive to object relations tends to conflate the specified delimitation of the 'beyond' highlighted in the first version of the text with other processes and functions, thereby obliterating the specificity of the conditions located 'beyond' the

89 See ibid., p. 55; also Freud (1937c), 'Analysis Terminable and Interminable', p. 242.
90 Freud (1920g), *Beyond the Pleasure Principle*, pp. 41, 54–55.
91 Ibid., pp. 54–55.
92 Ibid., p. 55.
93 Ibid.
94 The privileging of the second version is evinced in the conceptualisations of Kleinians and other object relations theorists, as well as proponents of ego psychology. J. Fernando (2012), 'Trauma und der Zeroprozess', p. 1047. Kleinian scholars tend to specify impulses derived from the death drive in terms of externally directed aggressivity and destructiveness. Freud himself provides a few pointers in this direction in the second and subsequent versions of the *Beyond* essay and related writings, as for instance in the case of the suggestion, formulated as a question, in the sixth chapter (inserted into the original version of the text), that sadism could plausibly be explained as "a death instinct which, under the influence of the narcissistic libido, has been forced away from the ego and has consequently only emerged in relation to the object". Ibid., pp. 54–55.

pleasure principle.[95] As a result, the findings of trauma research, pressed into the service of explaining the most diverse phenomena, become overly generalised.[96] At the same time, they are restricted in their scope, capturing mostly symptom formations, and structures and functions playing themselves out between primary and secondary processes and their interactions. They do not reach 'beyond'.

Conversely, the reduction of traumatic neuroses to externally impinging factors and reactions to 'events' such as catastrophes, accidents and violence of any description, on the basis of which traumatic neuroses have been excluded from the domain of psychoanalysis, obscures the dimension of unconscious processes. In the process, the aetiology of trauma is being pushed into the background.

Thus, Freud has good reason to reinstate the dualism of the drives in the second version, even at the risk of going against his intuitions, and of alienating his readers, among them his colleagues and students.[97]

The dividing line does not run between traumatic neuroses and the psychoneuroses, but within the dualism of the interrelated drives, into which traumatic neuroses and psychoneuroses are being tied; they draw their respective conditions of possibility from their contrary but combined interactions.[98]

---

95 See Fernando (2012), 'Trauma und der Zeroprozess', pp. 1055, also 1047. This pertains to certain directions taken by psychoanalytic theory after Freud, which attempt to merge the biphasic-pathogenetic trauma model with the dualistic drive model (among them Michael Balint, Donald Winnicott, Wilfred Bion and André Green). They tend to base their approaches partly on the significance accorded by Sándor Ferenczi to child sexual abuse and other traumatogenic experiences of the child at the hands of an adult, in structuring object relations. The object attains a central role in traumatic situations; and unconscious conflicts are considered important factors in triggering traumatic neuroses.

96 Ibid., p. 1058; W. Bohleber (2000), 'Die Entwicklung der Traumatheorie in der Psychoanalyse', p. 829.

97 See Freud (1920g), *Beyond the Pleasure Principle*, pp. 53–54; Freud (1930a), *Civilization and Its Discontents*, pp. 119–120.

98 Freud comments on this interaction of contrary forces in the context the negative therapeutic reaction which, in turn, he relates to the workings of the death drive, phylogenetically considered, and which manifests itself in aggression and destruction: "we shall no longer be able to adhere to the belief that mental events are exclusivey governed by the desire for pleasure. These phenomena are unmistakable indications of the presence of a power in mental life which we call the instinct of aggression or of destruction according to its aims, and which we trace back to the original death instinct of living matter. It is not a question of an antithesis between an optimistic and a pessimistic theory of life. Only by the concurrent or mutually opposing action of the two primal instincts – Eros and the death-instinct –, never by the one or the other alone, can we explain the rich multiplicity of life". Freud (1937c), 'Analysis Terminable and Interminable', pp. 242–243.

Bibliography

Abraham, Karl (1921 [1919]), 'Second Address at the Symposium held at the Fifth International Psycho-Analytical Congress in Budapest, September 1918', in: Sándor Ferenczi, Karl Abraham, Ernst Simmel & Ernest Jones, *Psycho-Analysis and the War Neuroses*. London, Vienna & New York: The International Psychoanalytical Press, pp. 22–29.

Bohleber, Werner (2000), 'Die Entwicklung der Traumatheorie in der Psychoanalyse', *Psyche. Zeitschrift für Psychoanalyse und ihre Anwendungen* 54, pp. 797–893.

Breuer, Josef & Freud, Sigmund (1895d), *Studies on Hysteria*, in: *Standard Edition of the Complete Psychological Works of Sigmund Freud, Vol. 2*, transl. J. Strachey. London: Hogarth Press, 1953–1974.

Derrida, Jacques (1987), 'To Speculate – On "Freud"', in: *The Postcard*, transl. Alan Bass. Chicago: University of Chicago Press, pp. 259–409.

Ferenczi, Sándor (1919 [1916]), 'Über zwei Typen der Kriegsneurose', in: *Hysterie und Pathoneurosen*. Leipzig & Vienna: Internationaler Psychoanalytischer Verlag, pp. 59–78.

Ferenczi, Sándor (1921 [1919]), 'First Address at the Symposium held at the Fifth International Psycho-Analytical Congress in Budapest, September 1918', in: Sándor Ferenczi, Karl Abraham, Ernst Simmel & Ernest Jones, *Psycho-Analysis and the War Neuroses*. London, Vienna & New York: The International Psychoanalytical Press, pp. 5–21.

Fernando, Joseph (2012), 'Trauma und der Zeroprozess', *Psyche. Zeitschrift für Psychoanalyse und ihre Anwendungen* 66, pp. 1043–1073.

Fischer-Homberger, Esther (1975), *Die traumatische Neurose. Vom somatischen zum sozialen Leiden*. Bern: Huber.

Foucault, Michel (1987 [1966]), 'Maurice Blanchot: The Thought from Outside', in: *Foucault – Blanchot*, transl. Brian Massumi. New York: Zone Books, pp. 7–58.

Freud, Sigmund (1893h), 'On the Psychical Mechanism of Hysterical Phenomena', in: *Standard Edition of the Complete Psychological Works of Sigmund Freud, Vol. 3*, transl. James Strachey. London: Hogarth Press, 1953–1974, pp. 27–39.

Freud, Sigmund (1894a), 'The Neuro-Psychoses of Defence', *SE* 3, pp. 45–61.

Freud, Sigmund (1900a), *The Interpretation of Dreams*, *SE* 4–5.Freud, Sigmund (1905d), *Three Essays on the Theory of Sexuality*, *SE* 7, pp. 135–243.

Freud, Sigmund (1915b), 'Thoughts for the Times on War and Death', *SE* 14, pp. 275–300.

Freud, Sigmund (1915c), 'Instincts and Their Vicissitudes', *SE* 14, pp. 117–140.

Freud, Sigmund (1915e), 'The Unconscious', *SE* 14, pp. 166–204.

Freud, Sigmund (1916–1917a), *Introductory Lectures on Psychoanalysis*, *SE* 15–16.

Freud, Sigmund (1919a), 'Lines of Advance in Psycho-Analytic Therapy', *SE* 17, pp. 157–168.

Freud, Sigmund (1919d), 'Introduction to *Psycho-Analysis and the War Neuroses*', *SE* 17, pp. 207–210.

Freud, Sigmund (1920g), *Beyond the Pleasure Principle*, *SE* 18, pp. 7–64.
Freud, Sigmund (1921c), *Group Psychology and the Analysis of the Ego*, *SE* 18, pp. 69–143.
Freud, Sigmund (1923a), 'Two Encyclopedia Articles', *SE* 18, pp. 235–259.
Freud, Sigmund (1923b), *The Ego and the Id*, *SE* 19, pp. 13–66.
Freud, Sigmund (1924c), 'The Economic Problem of Masochism', *SE* 19, pp. 159–170.
Freud, Sigmund (1926d), *Inhibitions, Symptoms and Anxiety*, *SE* 20, pp. 87–172.
Freud, Sigmund (1930a), *Civilization and Its Discontents*, *SE* 21, pp. 64–145.
Freud, Sigmund (1933a), *New Introductory Lectures on Psychoanalysis*, *SE* 22, pp. 5–182.
Freud, Sigmund (1933b), 'Why War?' (Letter to Albert Einstein, September 1932), *SE* 22, pp. 203–215.
Freud, Sigmund (1937c), 'Analysis Terminable and Interminable', *SE* 23, pp. 216–253.
Freud, Sigmund (1950c [1895]), 'Project for a Scientific Psychology', *SE* 1, pp. 283–387.
Freud, Sigmund (1955c [1920]),'Memorandum on the Electrical Treatment of War Neurotics', *SE* 17, pp. 211–215.
Freud, Sigmund & Ferenczi, Sándor (1996), *The Correspondence of Sigmund Freud and Sándor Ferenczi, Vol.2: 1914–1919*, ed. Eva Brabant, Ernst Falzeder & Patrizia Giampieri-Deutsch under the supervision of André Haynal, transcr. Ingeborg Meyer-Palmedo, transl. Peter T. Hoffer. Cambridge (MA) & London: The Belknap Press of Harvard UP.
Grubrich-Simitis, Ilse (2007), 'Trauma oder Trieb – Trieb und Trauma: Wiederbetrachtet', *Psyche. Zeitschrift für Psychoanalyse und ihre Anwendungen* 61, pp. 637–656.
Hoffer, Axel & Hoffer, Peter T. (1987), 'Foreword', in: Sigmund Freud, *A Phylogenetic Fantasy. Overview of the Transference Neuroses*, ed. Ilse Grubrich-Simitis, transl. Axel Hoffer & Peter T. Hoffer. Cambridge (MA) & London: The Belknap Press of Harvard UP, pp. vii–xiv.
Honigmann, Georg (1929), 'Arzt und Unfall', in: ed. Walter Riese, *Die Unfallneurose als Problem der Gegenwartsmedizin.* Stuttgart, Leipzig & Zürich: Hippokrates Verlag, pp. 25–39.
Kloocke, Ruth, Schmiedebach, Heinz-Peter & Priebe, Stefan (2010), 'Psychische Ereignisse – organische Interpretationen: Traumakonzepte in der deutschen Psychiatrie seit 1889', *Gesnerus* 67(1), pp. 73–97.
Lansky, Melvin R. (1995), *Posttraumatic Nightmares: Psychodynamic Explorations.* Hillsdale (NJ): Analytic Press.
Levy, Joshua (2011), 'The Dream in *Beyond the Pleasure Principle* and beyond', in: ed. Salman Akhtar & Mary Kay O'Neil, *On Freud's Beyond the Pleasure Principle.* London: Karnac, pp. 128–153.

Malabou, Catherine (2012), *The New Wounded. From Neurosis to Brain Damage*, transl. Steven Miller. New York: Fordham UP.

May, Ulrike (2015), 'The Third Step in the Drive Theory: On the Genesis of *Beyond the Pleasure Principle*', *Psychoanalysis and History* 17(2), pp. 205–280 (in this volume, pp. 81–164).

May, Ulrike (2013), 'Das Ende der Psychoanalyse oder ihr Neubeginn? Zur Entstehung und Bedeutung von Freuds *Jenseits des Lustprinzips*', in: ed. Ludger Hermanns & Albrecht Hirschmüller, *Vom Sammeln, Bedenken und Deuten in Geschichte, Kunst und Psychoanalyse. Gerhard Fichtner zu Ehren*. Stuttgart: Frommann-Holzboog Verlag, pp. 287–304.

May, Ulrike (2015), 'Der Todestrieb im Kontext von Freuds Erkenntnisinteressen', in: *Freud bei der Arbeit. Zur Entstehungsgeschichte der psychoanalytischen Theorie und Praxis, mit einer Auswertung von Freuds Patientenkalender*. Gießen: Psychosozial-Verlag, pp. 211–227.

Oliner, Marion M. (1996), 'Äußere Realität. Die schwer faßbare Dimension der Psychoanalyse', *Jahrbuch der Psychoanalyse* 37, pp. 9–43.

Oppenheim, Hermann (1888), 'Wie sind diejenigen Fälle von Neurasthenie aufzufassen, welche sich durch Erschütterungen des Rückenmarkes insbesondere nach Eisenbahnunfällen entwickeln?', *Die medizinischen Wochenschrift* 14, pp. 194–196.

Oppenheim, Hermann (1889), *Die traumatischen Neurosen nach den in der Nervenklinik der Charité in den letzten 5 Jahren gesammelten Beobachtungen*. Berlin: Verlag von August Hirschwald.

Porge, Erik (1992), 'Introduction', in: Kurt R. Eissler, *Freud sur le front des névroses de guerre*, transl. Madeleine Drouin, Anne Porge, E. Porge & A.-M. Vindras. Paris: Presses universitaires de France, pp. iv–xviii.

Schröter, Michael (2018), 'Die Psychoanalyse und die "Kriegsneurosen" des Ersten Weltkrieges. Eine zweideutige Probe aufs Exempel', *Psyche. Zeitschrift für Psychoanalyse und ihre Anwendungen* 72(2), pp. 122–145.

Simmel, Ernst (1921 [1919]), 'Third Address at the Symposium held at the Fifth International Psycho-Analytical Congress in Budapest, September 1918', in: Sándor Ferenczi, Karl Abraham, Ernst Simmel & Ernest Jones, *Psycho-Analysis and the War Neuroses*, London, Vienna & New York: The International Psychoanalytical Press, pp. 30–43.

Westerink, Herman & Van Haute, Philippe (2022), *Verleiding, Drift en Herhaling. Freuds metafysica van het trauma*. Amsterdam: Boom.

Wolff-Bernstein, Jeanne (2020), 'Spanische Grippe – Covid 19 und Sigmund Freud. Was können wir aus der Geschichte lernen?', *Wiener Arbeitskreis für Psychoanalyse*, 1 May 2020. Available at: https://psychoanalyse.or.at/nachrichten/artikel/2020/05/spanische-grippe-covid-19-und-sigmund-freud/

Neurotic Evolution: Bioanalysis against Biologism in *Beyond the Pleasure Principle**

Jenny Willner

Humoristic Withdrawal: Freud, Ferenczi and the Arena of Bioanalysis

> Without metapsychological speculation and theorizing – I had almost said 'phantasying' – we shall not get another step forward.[1]

Beyond the Pleasure Principle proceeds from a crisis and refrains from any attempt at closure. The "general enfeeblement and disturbance of the mental capacities"[2] in soldiers returning from the trenches of the First World War serves Freud as an occasion to integrate the traumatic aspects of the aetiology of neuroses into metapsychology. The traumatic disintegration of normal psychic processes, as it were, opens the view on underlying structures. Freud hopes for his "investigation of the mental reaction to external danger" to "produce new material and raise fresh questions bearing upon our present problem".[3] As we know, these "fresh questions" shook the foundations of Freud's own theory at a moment when Europe lay in ruins following the First World War and the International Psychoanalytic Association was being rocked by crises. The Habsburg monarchy had disintegrated, and in Hungary Béla Kun had proclaimed a soviet republic in March 1919, followed in June 1920 by the establishment of an authoritarian 'ethnic nation' under Miklós Horthy.

* This chapter is based on an article published in German in the journal *Psyche* (2020, Vol. 11(74)): 'Neurotische Evolution. Bioanalyse als Kulturkritik in "Jenseits des Lustprinzips"'. The article was translated to English by Michael Thomas Taylor and revised for the present volume.

1 S. Freud (1937c), 'Analysis Terminable and Interminable', *SE* 23, p. 225.

2 S. Freud (1920g), *Beyond the Pleasure Principle*, *SE* 18, p. 12.

3 Ibid., p. 11.

During this period, Freud remained closely connected to Budapest. In his lively correspondence with the Hungarian analyst Sándor Ferenczi, he first mentions the title 'Jenseits des Lustprinzips' in a letter on 17 March 1919, soon after he began working on the study.[4] Barely two weeks later, he writes to Ferenczi:

> In the meantime, don't think that I am worried or shocked. I have acquired a secure indifference. Even the lack of meat and chronic hunger contributes to the amelioration of affect in me. And in the end we are still grandees of Spain and are permitted to cry proudly before our execution:
>
> Nos têtes ont le droit
>
> De tomber *couvertes* devant de toi
>
> I am amusing myself greatly with a work, Beyond the Pleasure Principle, which I will then have copied in order to hear your opinion about it.[5]

"Our heads, oh! King, / Have right to fall before thee covered thus",[6] exclaims the noble bandit Hernani, anticipating his execution after being convicted of plotting to overthrow his sovereign. By quoting these two lines from Victor Hugo's play *Hernani* in his letter, Freud draws a connection from food shortages and other crisis-related deprivations to a study he had composed fourteen years earlier. In *Jokes and Their Relation to the Unconscious* the same two lines serve as an example for how humour, in contrast to jokes, is fundamentally to be understood in the sense of gallows humour: as a solipsistic withdrawal from a world which has become unbearable.[7] Presenting himself in his letter to Ferenczi as an observer of his own shielding mechanisms, Freud uses the gallows humour of Hernani as a hinge – between the state of 'safe indifference' on the one hand, and the source of a new amusement on the other, namely his ongoing work.

How are we to imagine this amusement? Should we look for gallows humour in *Beyond the Pleasure Principle*? Indeed, Freud's most sinister study provides reasons to take playfulness seriously. In Hugo's play, Hernani stubbornly insists on appropriate headgear for his execution: the hat goes on, the head comes off. It is as though the obstinacy of the soon-to-be-felled

4 U. May (2015), 'The Third Step in Drive Theory', p. 210 (in this volume, p. 84).

5 Freud to Ferenczi, 28 March 1919, in: S. Freud & S. Ferenczi (1996), *The Correspondence of Sigmund Freud and Sándor Ferenczi, Vol. 2*, pp. 339–340 (Letter 799 F).

6 V. Hugo (1894 [1830]), *Hernani*, p. 119.

7 S. Freud (1905c), *Jokes and Their Relation to the Unconscious*, *SE* 8, p. 229.

head (*Haupt*) were to be echoed in *Beyond the Pleasure Principle* when Freud rejects the common assumption that the organism is determined to "maintain its own existence in the face of every obstacle". The organisms are not as forward-striving and self-assertive as it seems: according to Freud, the notion of such a striving (Bestreben, sich zu be*haupt*en) may be dropped (ent*fällt*).[8] This crucial sentence is immediately followed by darkest phrase in the entire study: "What we are left with is the fact that the organism wishes to die only in its own fashion".[9]

This strange view of organic stubbornness resonates not only with Hernani's ceremonious wish to die in his own fashion (in noble headgear), but also with Ferenczi's description of the departure of a transport of Hussars off to war, in a letter to Freud written in the spring of 1915: "Things were very jolly; no trace of the fear of death, everybody sang and danced, everybody volunteered to go".[10] Such were the scenes in the beginning of the First World War, at the end of the epoch of progressive optimism which came to its end in the horrors of attrition warfare. Large parts of *Beyond the Pleasure Principle* read as though the entire history of development, from the emergence of organic life onwards, would need to be retold in the light of such baroque-like scenes. Perhaps gallows humour in the face of death is the alternative to cheerful disavowal.

Freud's speculations on the origin and development of organic life are born out of a crisis and can be read against the background of a long history of discursive borrowings between biology and politics. Both the Franco-German War and the founding of the German Empire had a formative effect on the language of biology and the early German-language reception of Darwin.[11] In the run-up to the First World War, this semantic transfer was happening in both directions: the political developments were increasingly rationalised biologistically.[12] A striking example of this is the book *Weltkriegsgedanken* (*World War Thoughts*), published in 1915 by the biologist and best-selling author Ernst Haeckel, who claimed to explain scientific, cultural, and technological progress, even war itself, "according to the laws of natural development".[13] In Haeckel, there is a drastic line leading from "unicellular

8 Freud (1920g), *Beyond the Pleasure Principle*, p. 39, italics J.W.
9 Ibid.
10 Freud & Ferenczi (1996), *Correspondence*, p. 60 (Letter 546 Fer).
11 K. Bayertz (1998), 'Darwinismus als Politik. Zur Genese des Sozialdarwinismus in Deutschland 1860–1900', pp. 244–253.
12 C. Gradmann (2007), 'Unsichtbare Feinde. Bakteriologie und politische Sprache im deutschen Kaiserreich', p. 332.
13 E. Haeckel (1915), *Ewigkeit. Weltkriegsgedanken über Leben und Tod, Religion und Entwicklungslehre*, p. 10.

protists"[14] to the necessity of a German victory in the interest of the human species: the German and Austrian soldiers, he argues, are racially, morally and culturally superior, whereas their opponents "build their giant army for the most part out of members of the uneducated lower classes, out of hired mercenaries and of coloured men of wild and half-wild races from all parts of the world".[15]

Freud's biological speculations bear political implications worth exploring. In the same year in which Haeckel published *Weltkriegsgedanken*, Freud published 'Thoughts for the Times on War and Death' and argued that the disenchantment following the brutal behaviour of nation states as well as individuals stemmed from an illusion: "In reality our fellow-citizens have not sunk so low as we feared, because they have never risen so high as we believed".[16] In *Beyond the Pleasure Principle*, Freud goes even further in dismantling illusions of completion, retelling not just the history of civilisation within a new framework, but the developmental history of organic life. In doing so, he rejects assumptions that large parts of his own generation took for granted: "There is unquestionably no universal instinct towards higher development observable in the animal or plant world, even though it is undeniable that development does in fact occur in that direction".[17] It is crucial that Freud, here, establishes a relationship of opposites: he suggests that development unfolds in one direction, towards more complex forms of life, while the underlying drives aim in the opposite direction. The drives cannot be observed, only speculatively inferred: Freud presupposes unknown forces, directed backwards, that somehow determine what at least seems to be moving forwards or upwards ("higher development").

Beyond the Pleasure Principle advises us not to follow our intuitions regarding organic life. In contrast to the morphological paradigm represented by Haeckel, Freud assumes that what can be empirically observed or viewed under a microscope leaves the last, universal questions unanswered. This epistemological challenge forms a common denominator between Freud's speculation on organic matter and his more well-known approach towards unconscious activity: both demand speculation, construction and counter-intuitive interpretation. Freud articulates a new narrative of the origin of life which, though arrived at counter-intuitively, is far from irrational. His speculation holds that precisely those processes usually interpreted as an

14 Ibid., p. 27.
15 Ibid., pp. 35–37.
16 S. Freud (1915b), 'Thoughts for the Times on War and Death', *SE* 14, p. 285.
17 Freud (1920g), *Beyond the Pleasure Principle*, p. 41.

"impulsion towards further perfection"[18] are to be understood as an escape from repressed tendencies pushing in the opposite direction:

> The processes involved in the formation of a neurotic phobia, which is nothing else than an attempt at flight from the satisfaction of an instinct, present us with a model [*Vorbild*] of the manner of origin of this supposititious 'instinct towards perfection'.[19]

How would the developmental narrative proceed if the assumption of an innate, primordial striving towards completion were to be replaced by an assumed originary neurosis? Methodologically, what Freud pursues here is the opposite of a biologistic argument. He does not borrow his 'model' from biology; rather, the clinical picture of neurotic phobia serves as a model for reinterpreting organic processes. As a result, an entire set of popular scientific commonplaces are defamiliarised. Freud's speculation disturbs the biological narratives of progression in a way that resembles his intervention in *Totem and Taboo*: there Freud countered the illusions of cultural origin with a new myth according to which a patricidal and cannibalistic primal horde established law and civilisation out of moral indigestion. Freud's speculations about the primal cell unfold in the same arena, under similar epistemological circumstances as his theoretical fiction about the primal patricide and the primal scene in the parental bedroom. The relation between these scenes and the manifest obsessions of patients is far from simple.[20]

In *Beyond the Pleasure Principle*, commonly presupposed "instincts of self-preservation, of self-assertion and of mastery",[21] appear phantasmatic if not delusional and must according to Freud be viewed as '*Trabanten des Todes*'.[22] The word 'trabants' can either refer to medieval military lifeguards or to planetary satellites, but instead of clarifying the enigmatic image, Freud violently interrupts his own train of thought – "But let us come to our senses!"

18 Ibid., p. 42.

19 Freud (1920g), *Beyond the Pleasure Principle*, p. 42.

20 The case study on the Wolf Man was written during the same period as Freud's first bioanalytical drafts. According to Laplanche and Pontalis, Freud's transition from a realist conception of the primal scene to the notion of a primal fantasy must be seen as an insistence on the prevalence of a pre-subjective structure: "Whatever reservations may be justified as regards the theory of an hereditary, genetic transformation, there is no reason, in our view (a), to reject as equally invalid the idea that structures exist in the phantasy dimension (*la fantasmatique*) which are irreducible to the contingencies of the individual's lived experience". J. Laplanche & J.-B. Pontalis (1973), *The Language of Psycho-Analysis*, p. 333.

21 Freud (1920g), *Beyond the Pleasure Principle*, p. 39.

22 Ibid., though both the alliteration and the military meaning of '*Trabanten des Todes*' are lost in translation here: 'myrmidions of death'.

(translation modified) – as though his own speculation were senseless, as though he had to break its spell. Looking back at *Beyond the Pleasure Principle*, Freud was later to recall how he first fiercely fended off the idea of a destructive drive, only to find himself unable to let go of it: "in the course of time they have gained such a hold upon me that I can no longer think in any other way".[23] Despite Freud's later revisions and retractions, it is precisely this thesis which forms the 'heart' of *Beyond the Pleasure Principle*: setting the death drive above the self-preservative and sexual drives, above narcissism too, and endowed with an equally regressive counterpart, the life drives.[24]

When Ferenczi received the letter discussed above, where Freud quoted *Hernani*, he could not have read the study Freud was only then in the process of writing. Nevertheless, it can be safely assumed that Ferenczi found the notion of a regressive impulse expressing itself in the form of progression to be immediately intelligible: it corresponds with his own work. The passage in Freud's letter plays on key concepts of the phylogenetic parallel which the two men worked out together. Shortly before the beginning of the war, in 'Stages in the Development of the Sense of Reality', Ferenczi argued that the imminent dangers of the Ice Age "compelled [in primitive man] the repression of favourite habits and thus 'development'".[25] According to Ferenczi, "misery of the glacial period", permanent lack of meat and hunger resulted in a dampening of affect and in acquired indifference,[26] a starting point for unconscious regressive longings and for neuroses. In a footnote Ferenczi broadened this thesis to encompass a "tendency of preservation, or regression-tendency, also dominating organic life", which, as a result of disturbances, turns into the opposite and expresses itself as "the tendency to further development, adaptation, etc.".[27]

The idea of development and of evolution structured like a neurosis runs through the phylogenetic speculations Freud and Ferenczi exchanged with each other during the First World War. In a next step, in the winter of 1914–1915, Freud wrote 'A Phylogenetic Fantasy: Overview of the Transference Neuroses', which remained a fragment. This text speculates on how the lack of food and the increased frequency of danger during the Ice Age, as postulated by Ferenczi, triggered a psychic dynamic to which all neuroses of the present individual bear witness.[28] According to this account, the development from

23 S. Freud (1930a), *Civilization and Its Discontents*, *SE* 21, p. 119.
24 May (2015), 'The Third Step in Drive Theory', p. 250 (in this volume, p. 131).
25 S. Ferenczi (1994 [1913]), 'Stages in the Development of the Sense of Reality', p. 237.
26 Ibid.
27 Ibid., n. 26.
28 S. Freud (1987 [1985a]), *A Phylogenetic Fantasy: Overview of the Transference Neuroses*, pp. 13–14.

the primal human animal to the human being began as a reaction to extreme need and resulted in a compromise "between what is primeval and the claims of what is new".[29]

Ilse Grubrich-Simitis, who discovered and edited Freud's phylogenetic fantasy about the Ice Age, declared: "He did not, would not ever have published it".[30] It is true that not only Freud but also Ferenczi seemed to take a certain other-worldliness of their phylogenetic speculations for granted. While this material is on the one hand centred around notions of shock and trauma, the most striking feature in their correspondence on the subject lies in the employment of playful registers. While drafting the first version of *Thalassa: A Theory of Genitality* in 1915, Ferenczi notes that the idea had come to him "at first as a bad joke", continuing: "but I forced myself to take it seriously, but I am ready for the eventuality that the whole thing will turn out to be nonsense".[31] Freud, in turn, attributes his 'Overview of the Transference Neuroses' to "phantasies" which "are disruptive and will hardly produce anything for the public".[32] During the same period, Ferenczi's reflection on the war as a trigger makes the phylogenetic speculation appear not only as a joke or as a fantasy, but as a symptom:

> It is interesting to observe the regularity [*Gesetzmäßigkeit*] which manifests itself in both of our reactions to the inactivity brought about by the war. One now understands the speculative biologists and philosophers who, always moving far from reality – would like to build the entire world edifice [*Weltgebäude*] on the few facts that are known to them.[33]

Ferenczi seems to associate Freud's and his own work on the phylogenetic parallel with nonsense and even a certain proximity to madness, almost as if these speculations had developed as an extension of their engagement with the cosmology of Daniel Paul Schreber. Is bioanalysis a joke, a symptom, a delusion or a daydream? While Freud used to stress that the arena of dreams is separated from the arena of the waking life, the same can perhaps be said of the arena of bioanalysis in relation to the canonised psychoanalytic theory.

29 Ibid., p. 79.

30 I. Grubrich-Simitis (1987), 'Trauma oder Trieb – Trieb und Trauma', p. 995. In a series of publications (1985, 1987, 2007), Grubrich-Simitis has demonstrated how the phylogenetic parallel nevertheless forms the site where Ferenczi and Freud continue to reflect on the role of the traumatic aetiology of neuroses – a role that was only seemingly abandoned with his theory of desire – even in the years before *Beyond the Pleasure Principle*.

31 Freud & Ferenczi (1996), *Correspondence*, pp. 44–45 (Letter 532 Fer).

32 Ibid., p. 65 (Letter 551 F).

33 Ibid., p. 47 (Letter 535 Fer).

Thalassa, the very text whose origin Ferenczi himself traced to a bad joke, sketches an evolutionary history of genital organs following the temporal structure of traumatic hysteria.[34] The basic hypothesis is that organs and tissues attest to traumatic processes which escape observation and require a theory based on speculation. This holds that prehistoric traumas have triggered a compulsion to regress, which manifests itself in a distorted form as further development: "the same force which impels to regression operates, when it is prevented therefrom by a censorship, in a progressive sense – in the sense, that is, of adaptation and constructiveness".[35]

The search for a title for the phylogenetic project remained unfinished:[36] in the correspondence between Ferenczi and Freud, we find terms such as 'metabiology', 'deep biology', the 'Lamarck project' and 'bioanalysis'.[37] The term 'bioanalysis' is connected to the most succinct explanation of the project's epistemological claim: in *Thalassa*, Ferenczi defines 'bioanalysis' as a speculative science that would "carry over into the field of the natural sciences in a systematic manner the knowledge gained and the technique used by psychoanalysis".[38] Ferenczi presents an organology based on the premise that organs, tissues and tissue elements – in this regard structurally analogous to psychosomatic symptoms – have a distorted, expressive character and are determined by multiple causes and layers of meaning. He arrives at the conclusion that "the explanation of physiological processes" must profit from "the idea of the overdetermination of one and the same process, as psychoanalysis teaches us".[39] This overdetermination is essentially related to

34. See J. Willner (2022), 'The Problem of Heredity: Ferenczi's Organology and the Politics of Bioanalysis'; for a more extensive version see J. Willner (2023), 'Catastrophes and Genitality. Ferenczi's *Thalassa* and the Politics of Bioanalysis'.
35. S. Ferenczi (2005 [1924]), *Thalassa: A Theory of Genitality*, p. 89.
36. For a first reconstruction of Freud's and Ferenczi's engagement with metabiology and bioanalysis, see I. Grubrich-Simitis (1985), 'Metapsychologie und Metabiologie. Zu Sigmund Freuds Entwurf einer Übersicht der Übertragungsneurosen'; I. Grubrich-Simitis (1987), 'Trauma oder Trieb – Trieb und Trauma'; I. Grubrich-Simitis (2007), 'Trauma oder Trieb – Trieb und Trauma: Wiederbetrachtet'. See also May in this volume.
37. In the correspondence between Ferenczi and Freud, the discussion culminates in Ferenczi's letter of 26 October 1915, in which he announces a "series of essays under the title 'Bio-analytical essays'". He mentions fifteen to twenty studies taking a "metapsychological and metabiological approach" as well as studies on the "phylogeny of genitality". Freud & Ferenczi (1996), *Correspondence*, p. 84 (Letter 572 Fer).
38. Ferenczi (2005), *Thalassa*, p. 82. Stephen Jay Gould's discussion of Ferenczi contains a misreading that has persisted in subsequent interpretations. In his summary, Gould writes: "Ferenczi states explicitly his desire to import biological conclusions into psychology, particularly Haeckel's version of evolutionary theory". S.J. Gould (1977), *Ontogeny and Phylogeny*, p. 163. Ferenczi, however, speaks of a transmission in the opposite direction.
39. Ferenczi (2005), *Thalassa*, p. 347. The epistemological implications of Ferenczi's method have been elaborated by R. Soreanu (2019), 'Sándor Ferenczi's Epistemologies and Their Politics: On Utraquism and the Analogical Method'.

the structure of *Nachträglichkeit,* of deferred action or belatedness. According to Ferenczi, organs crave interpretation: they are driven by regressive forces and they testify to bygone catastrophes which elude empirical observability.

Ferenczi's *Thalassa* has recently been referred to as "the silent partner" of *Beyond the Pleasure Principle.*[40] Freud's text is indeed framed by Ferenczi's book: *Thalassa* was drafted in the winter of 1914 to 1915 and completed in 1924 with several references to *Beyond the Pleasure Principle.*[41] The narrative of neurotic evolution, crucial for Ferenczi's theory of genitality, drafted by Ferenczi before *Beyond the Pleasure Principle*, is formative for Freud when he writes:

> The backward path that leads to complete satisfaction is as a rule obstructed by the resistances which maintain the repressions. So there is no alternative but to advance in the direction in which growth is still free – though with no prospect of bringing the process to a conclusion or of being able to reach the goal.[42]

If the idea of a neurotic cell seems absurd, then *Beyond the Pleasure Principle* draws our attention to the fact that more established assumptions regarding organic life are no less so. Compared to the rumbling pathos and rhetoric of combat found in Haeckel's popular Darwinism, the bioanalytic account of organic life possesses a certain comic quality. It seems that for the earliest organisms, Bartleby's words apply: "I would prefer not to".[43] According to Freud, a disturbance from outside has set a queer dynamic in motion which is however "bound to give a deceptive appearance of being forces tending towards change and progress".[44] At a closer look, the life-path of an organism observed in this way, is full of deprivation, leading to "ever more complicated *detours*".[45] What may appear as a goal-oriented striving thus reveals itself as the result of the effort to avoid any kind of effort. This shift of perspective makes dominant biological fantasies of striving and perfection appear ridiculous.

40 T. Dufresne (2017), *The Late Sigmund Freud: Or, The Last Words on Psychoanalysis, Society, and All the Riddles of Life*, p. 11.

41 It is not possible to completely reconstruct the authorship of individual bioanalytical ideas between Ferenczi and Freud. The first outlines of Ferenczi's study were written while he was stationed as a military doctor in Pápa in the winter of 1914–1915. The correspondence suggests that Ferenczi presented these ideas to Freud when Ferenczi was in Pápa in late September/early October 1915. Freud & Ferenczi (1996), *Correspondence*, pp. 80–82 (Letters 569 F, 570 Fer).

42 Freud (1920g), *Beyond the Pleasure Principle*, p. 42.

43 H. Melville (2016 [1856]), 'Bartleby, the Scrivener', p. 25.

44 Freud (1920g), *Beyond the Pleasure Principle*, p. 38.

45 Ibid., p. 41.

Herein lies the dark humour of *Beyond the Pleasure Principle*, an element which is essential precisely because trauma and survival, life and death are the subject matters at stake. The laughter provoked is however subject to historical change: knowing as we do the extent of the crimes that would be committed in the name of allegedly natural progression towards completion, the echoes are jarring.

In *Thalassa*, Ferenczi envisions a future science of bioanalysis. This vision is both a swan song and a retrospective theorisation of the by then crisis-ridden collaboration with Freud. Conflicts between Ferenczi and Freud became rife, and in 1932 the two men finally broke with each other.[46] Despite the deep rift between them, Freud emphasised the potential future of bioanalysis in his obituary of Ferenczi in 1933. Writing of Ferenczi's *Thalassa*, he concludes:

> It is a vain task to attempt already to-day to distinguish what can be accepted as an authentic discovery from what seeks, in the fashion of a scientific phantasy, to guess at future knowledge. We lay the little book aside with a feeling: 'This is almost too much to take in at a first reading; I will read it again after a while'. But it is not only I who feel like this. It is probable that some time in the future there will be a 'bio-analysis', as Ferenczi has prophesied, and it will have to cast back to the *Versuch einer Genitaltheorie*.[47]

It is doubtful whether there ever "really will be a science of 'bio-analysis' one day". Nonetheless, the experiment of reading Freud's speculation on unicellular organisms through the lens of Ferenczi's *Thalassa* proves to be fruitful. As though aiming to break open the usual way of thinking, Freud and Ferenczi create a counter-narrative with conceptual implications that are still worth exploring.

But how can we read further with bioanalysis in mind? While several studies in recent years have focused on Derrida's activation of Freud's biological speculation, in particular pertaining to the implications of biological discourses on life and death,[48] the following sections will follow a similar impulse but take a few steps back: How precisely does Freud himself work with and against the natural scientific discourses of this time? The next section will focus on the organic, the inorganic and the cosmorganic in Gustav Theodor Fechner,

---

46 For a detailed reading of the rift, see J. Staberg (2023), 'Instead of Language: Confusion'.

47 S. Freud (1933c), 'Sándor Ferenczi', *SE* 22, pp. 228–229.

48 D. Will (2016), *Inanimation: Theories of Inorganic Life*; F. Vitale (2018), *Biodeconstruction. Jacques Derrida and the Life Sciences*; R. Trumbull (2022), *From Life to Survival. Derrida, Freud, and the Future of Deconstruction.*

after which the last section discusses Freud's more indirect treatment of the evolutionary discourse formed by Ernst Haeckel.

Fechner and the Prehistory of the Pleasure Principle

> From the standpoint of death, life is the production of a corpse. It is not only in the loss of limbs, not only in the changes of the ageing body, but in all the processes of elimination and purification that the corpselike falls away, piece by piece, from the body. And it is no accident that precisely nails and hair, which are cut away from the living body as something dead, continue to grow on the corpse. A memento mori wakes in the physis, in the *mnēmē* itself.[49]

"What follows is speculation, often far-fetched speculation",[50] is how Freud begins the fourth chapter of *Beyond the Pleasure Principle*. He proceeds to make an analogy between the psychic apparatus and the cell, the system of perception-consciousness and "an undifferentiated vesicle of a substance that is susceptible to stimulation".[51] According to his speculation, the psychic apparatus and organic life emerged under analogous external circumstances: in the beginning there was shock, agitation, concussion (*Erschütterung*). In order to survive "in the middle of an external world charged with the most powerful energies", the membrane of the unicellular organism had to become "to some degree inorganic",[52] it had to harden into a crust, let an outer layer die in order to "save[] all the deeper ones from a similar fate".[53] Only through this production of a deadened layer "resistant to stimuli", as a sediment of a defensive process, can life begin to evolve.

In the case of the mental apparatus, the correlate to the production of a cortical layer consists in a function aimed at providing a shield against stimuli. According to this analogy, consciousness is inherently defensive. It is structured like scar tissue, deadened, as it were, and the result of a function "which, though it does not contradict the pleasure principle, is nevertheless independent of it and seems to be more primitive than the purpose of gaining

49 W. Benjamin (2019 [1925]), *The Origin of the German Trauerspiel*, pp. 236–237, translation modified.
50 Freud (1920g), *Beyond the Pleasure Principle*, p. 24.
51 Ibid., p. 25.
52 Ibid., p. 27.
53 Ibid.

pleasure and avoiding unpleasure".[54] Freud argues that the principle of stability, manifesting itself in terms of lifeless and deadening repetition, plays a part in "the most universal endeavour of all living substance – namely to return to the quiescence of the inorganic world".[55] The pleasure principle merely serves this older function, which according to Freud nevertheless remains effective, independent from the pleasure principle. The purpose of the pleasure principle here is "to free the mental apparatus entirely from excitation or to keep the amount of excitation in it constant or to keep it as low as possible".[56]

Accordingly, consciousness owes its existence to a prior death at its edges; and to such a death the unicellular organism, too, owes its existence as a cell. Repetition in all its forms testifies to the lifeless structures that govern life. Where the psychic functions break down, the compulsion towards the inorganic can be glimpsed in the incessant recurrence with which trauma, pain or a crack in an organism's shield against stimulus makes itself felt. Through the failing of the pleasure principle it becomes possible to speculatively conjecture both what goes beyond it – and a time before.

Indeed, the word 'beyond' also figures as a time-bound category, as a transient state *before* the pleasure principle became operative. How did things function before "the whole of mental life had accepted the dominance of the pleasure principle"?[57] What can be investigated if we "grant that there was also a time before the purpose of dreams was the fulfilment of wishes"?[58] The assumption of a "time before" the pleasure principle is in itself remarkable. Freud not only presupposes the reader's willingness to understand the mental apparatus as a heuristically valuable structural model, as is usually the approach of metapsychology, but also does something even stranger: throughout his speculative scenario, he invites us to imagine this apparatus as a structure that has formed over time, with its own history of development.

The relation between the cell and the apparatus is anything but clear, the transitions are slippery: it is not always possible to decide whether a given formulation refers to a primitive organic being in murky waters or to the model of an apparatus in which one can "literally hear the 'rattling of the machine'".[59] Over the course of the study, the nature of the relation between Freud's speculative history of the development of the apparatus and the no

54 Ibid., p. 32.
55 Ibid., p. 62.
56 Ibid.
57 Ibid., p. 33.
58 Ibid.
59 M. Wegener (2004), *Neuronen und Neurosen. Der psychische Apparat bei Freud und Lacan. Ein historisch-theoretischer Versuch zu Freuds Entwurf von 1895*, p. 21.

less speculative history of the development of organisms remains unresolved, generating a fundamental uncertainty. Perhaps it is no coincidence that in his parallel study, 'The Uncanny', Freud highlights intellectual uncertainty about whether something is a living being or an automaton as an example of the feeling after which the study is named.[60] In *Beyond the Pleasure Principle*, not only is the ongoing tension between physicalism and evolutionism in natural sciences at stake, but with it also the status of what is living and what is dead.

This is where Gustav Theodor Fechner comes into the picture: Fechner, who coined the term 'pleasure principle',[61] and from whom Freud famously borrowed the image of the dream occupying a different arena than the arena of waking life. In his most famous work, *Elemente der Psychophysik* (1860), Fechner proposed that the senses act as a measuring device of the mind, arguing that there is a non-linear relationship between the intensity of a measurable stimulus on the one hand and the psychological sensation in the mind on the other. Fechner is credited for introducing a basic mechanistic view into the German natural sciences, in accordance with the ideal of the exact sciences. But Fechner has two faces:[62] he is not only the author of physio-psychological studies relevant for physicalism, but also a bizarre mystic, inspired by the natural philosophy of Oken and Schelling, wildly speculating on the relationship between the external world and the soul life of everything from plants to planets.[63] While it may appear obvious that Fechner the physicalist, not Fechner the mystic, is relevant for *Beyond the Pleasure Principle*, a closer look will complicate the relation between the two.

Freud is generally fond of concealing quotations. And yet, in the first chapter of *Beyond the Pleasure Principle* he makes a complete bibliographical reference to Fechner, not in a footnote, but noticeably placed in the main text. He mentions Fechner's "small work, *Einige Ideen zur Schöpfungs- und Entwicklungsgeschichte der Organismen*, 1873, 1873 (Section XI, Supplement, 94)".[64] It is strange that this particular title is highlighted. Fechner's ideas about evolution are not relevant for the context in this passage and there would have been far more obvious titles to quote for Fechner's theory of correlation. The emphasis on the title seems to anticipate that Freud will indeed later explicitly engage with something other than physicalism: questions pertaining to the

60 S. Freud (1919h), 'The Uncanny', *SE* 17, p. 239.
61 G.T. Fechner (1846), *Ueber das höchste Gut.*
62 M. Wegener (2005), 'Das psychophysische Unbewusste. Gustav Theodor Fechner und der Mond', p. 240.
63 G.T. Fechner (1984), *Das unendliche Leben.*
64 Freud (1920g), *Beyond the Pleasure Principle*, p. 8.

origin and development of organisms.[65] What happens if we read Fechner's book beyond the passages quoted by Freud?

Indeed, in the "small work" quoted by Freud, Fechner does begin by emphatically affirming the theory of evolution. He praises Ernst Haeckel's *Natürliche Schöpfungsgeschichte* as his own road-to-Damascus experience: "I myself confess to having been converted to the doctrine of descent after long resisting it".[66] Fechner proceeds to declare an important reservation: he excludes one of Haeckel's central presuppositions from his new-found belief, namely the well-established view that all organic life arose from inorganic matter. Instead, Fechner argues that the initial state was organic rather than inorganic, and that organic life in the sense commonly understood today was split off from this original, cosmorganic state, which all in all – and this is where it becomes relevant for Freud – tends towards the inorganic. In Fechner's pantheist universe, there is however no such thing as truly inanimate matter: what is usually considered inanimate is instead thought of as capable of consciousness inasmuch as it is physically mobile.[67] According to Fechner, the state of absolute stability in inorganic matter can be attained only approximatively.

"The aim of all life is death",[68] Freud writes in agreement with Fechner. In the following sentence, and without marking this break in any way, he contradicts Fechner's main thesis: "inanimate matter [*das Leblose*] existed before living matter".[69] There is a particular irony in the fact that Freud derives his concept of the death drive from a study predicated on a universe in which death is only theoretically possible but practically unreached: Fechner evades the concept of death.

While obviously reading Fechner against the grain, Freud's account in *Beyond the Pleasure Principle* also contains a delocalised echo of Fechner's textual universe: Freud adopts, from Fechner, the fascination for ossified matter as an inherent part of the living, albeit strictly detached from Fechner's animistic enlivening of the inorganic. To give an example, Fechner makes the compelling argument that we have never witnessed life arising from inorganic

---

65 This is supported by the observation that Freud added the discussion with Fechner only after writing the passages containing his biological speculations. May (2015), 'The Third Step in Drive Theory', p. 225 (in this volume, p. 103).

66 G.T. Fechner (1873), *Einige Ideen zur Schöpfungs- und Entwicklungsgeschichte der Organismen*, p. III.

67 Documenting the discrepancies between Freud and Fechner, Manfred Riepe concludes that the "system of the professor of physics in Leipzig [Fechner], itself reminiscent of a paranoid hermeticism", stands in a relationship of mutual exclusion to psychoanalysis and that this "apparently eluded" Freud. M. Riepe (2001), 'Freud und Fechner. Zur Rekonstruktion eines Paradigmenwechsels', p. 344. I assume that Freud must have noticed the difference but agree with Riepe that Freud gives a meaning to the Fechnerian terms that is incompatible with their function in the discourse of Fechner. Ibid., p. 367.

68 Freud (1920g), *Beyond the Pleasure Principle*, p. 38.

69 Ibid., translation modified.

matter, whereas we can observe daily how organisms excrete inorganic substances such as carbon dioxide, urea, etc.[70] Fechner calls it absurd to assume that organic life could ever develop from inorganic matter, "as though one were to believe that flesh and nerves had developed from bones during a certain period of foetal life, and could still do so under favourable conditions".[71] The idea of an inanimate skeleton in the womb that is only gradually covered with flesh exemplifies a morbid excess in Fechner's writing that never quite aligns with his optimistic conclusions.

For Fechner, the skeleton of the living organism marks the presence of death even while the surrounding body is still alive and breathing: he emphasises that in living beings "a more or less inorganic structure underlies all bones, solid shells, hooves, and skins".[72] In this sense, the processes of life, from growth to ageing, amount to a gradual ossification governed by the principle of stability, even before this tendency emerges triumphant. While we age, the proportion of calluses and sclerotic hardenings increases; the skin becomes drier; the parts of the body become "firmer and more rigid"; and its movements slow down "until at last the whole organism lapses into an inorganic state".[73] Fechner repeatedly refers to the positioning of the body, ashes and dust in the tomb as "fitting together".[74] In the peaceful eternal rest, earth and the organism have finally converged and reached the goal of all life.

Fechner is present in *Beyond the Pleasure Principle* wherever crusts and skins are formed, as well as in the associative link established between repetitive phenomena of any kind and the repeated impact or collision (*Aufprall*) to which Freud speculates the unicellular organism was subjected. From Fechner's little study comes the consideration according to which every periodicity, even the heartbeat, testifies to the functioning of the principle of constancy within life: "sleep and waking, circulation of the blood, peristaltic movements of the viscera, the rhythm of respiration, the more or less periodical intake of food and sexual intercourse".[75] Following Fechner, Freud abstracts rhythms from both psychic and organic processes, like the ticking of a clock.[76] Approaching

70 Fechner (1873), *Einige Ideen zur Schöpfungs- und Entwicklungsgeschichte der Organismen*, p. 34.
71 Ibid., p. 41.
72 Ibid., p. 38.
73 Ibid., p. 39.
74 Ibid., p. 89f.
75 Ibid., p. 38.
76 Mai Wegener argues that Freud's reception of Fechner heralds what Lacan later made explicit: what emerges in the model of the psychic apparatus is the skeleton of the symbolic structure. Here, a structure is peeled out of the flesh of speaking beings, and this symbol as such is brought into circulation in machines. Wegener (2004), *Neuronen und Neurosen*, p. 60. This does not entail dematerialisation; on the contrary, what materialises and becomes operative is the symbolic. Ibid., p. 21.

Freud's arguments via Fechner makes it more plausible why Freud calls the infant's insistence on the identity of repetition "daemonic".[77] If rhythms suggest automatic periodicity in organic processes and if repetition testifies to the lifeless structures that govern life, it is not all that far-fetched to perceive an uncanny machine-like element in a child insisting on the same bedtime story.

Such images are evoked by Freud and Fechner alike. But while the ageing Fechner argues that inorganic matter, from crystals to planets, is in principle capable of consciousness since absolute stability cannot be attained, Freud withdraws the animism from Fechner's edifice. Fechner's animism indeed fits into a broad spectrum of strategies for coping with crises which are specific to the epoch and approached by Freud with utter scepticism. In his essay 'On Transience' Freud presented the "demand for immortality"[78] as a revolt in the mind against mourning.[79] In 'Thoughts for the Times on War and Death' he stressed that "[i]n our civilized attitude towards death we are once again living psychologically beyond our means",[80] and noted "an unmistakable tendency to put death on one side, to eliminate it from life",[81] "to exclude death from our calculations in life".[82] He concluded the essay with the famous lines:

> We recall the old saying: *Si vis pacem, para bellum.*
>
> If you want to preserve peace, arm for war.
>
> It would be in keeping with the times to alter it: *Si vis vitam, para mortem.*
>
> If you want to endure life, prepare yourself for death.[83]

In 1915 Freud called for death to be given "the place in reality [...] which is its due",[84] since denial has become too costly. It appears that four years later, this is where *Beyond the Pleasure Principle* sets off to inscribe death into different discourses of organic life. This pertains in particular to the different Darwinisms of the time.

77 Freud (1920g), *Beyond the Pleasure Principle*, p. 36.
78 S. Freud (1916a), 'On Transience', *SE* 14, p. 305.
79 Ibid., p. 306.
80 S. Freud (1915b), 'Thoughts for the Times on War and Death', *SE* 14, p. 299.
81 Ibid., p. 289.
82 Ibid., p. 291.
83 Ibid., p. 300.
84 Ibid., p. 299.

"'Out-Haeckeling' Haeckel":[85] *Freud and Darwinisms around 1900*

> For in this man [Ernst Haeckel], who resembled a young Teutonic king, there had always been a trembling desire of impatience, expectation, and readiness for bold actions. And then came [...] the meeting in Stettin, and its first speaker was Haeckel, young and handsome and bright, and this radiating man, exuding youth, gleaming like the morning, said aloud what Darwin was.[86]

In his 'Outlines of a Poetics after Darwin', the literary theorist Anselm Haverkamp noted that the last pages of *On the Origin of Species* "nearly proclaimed a 'Beyond the Pleasure Principle'" – in finally calling "extinction" by its name.[87] With this observation in mind, it is worth re-reading Darwin, particularly passages such as:

> Judging from the past, we may safely infer that not one living species will transmit its unaltered likeness to a distant futurity. And of the other species now living very few will transmit progeny of any kind to a far distant futurity; for the manner in which all organic beings are grouped, shows that the greater number of species of each genus, and all the species of many genera, have left no descendants, but have become utterly extinct.[88]

Perhaps the greatest shock associated with Darwin is related to such formulations: the number of living species is vanishingly small in relation to those that have long been extinct. Since Darwin, then, the story of organic life would primarily have to be told as a process of dying, in which the extent of extinction exceeds any imagination. In the distant future, Darwin notes, most species that exist today will not only be dead and gone but "utterly extinct".[89] Added to this comes an epistemological problem: as Darwin himself emphasised, only a fraction of all extinct life forms have left behind fossils, and of these fossils, only a fraction are ever found, and these often in

85 I borrow this formulation from Frank J. Sulloway, who relates it to Ferenczi's treatment of recapitulation theory in *Thalassa*. Freud, too, out-Haeckels Haeckel by assuming regressive drives as the impetus of what Haeckel himself interprets as forward-directed striving for perfection. F.J. Sulloway (1979), *Freud: Biologist of the Mind*, p. 380.

86 H. Bahr (1912), 'Natur', p. 127.

87 A. Haverkamp (2015), 'Undone by Death. Umrisse einer Poetik nach Darwin', p. 37.

88 C. Darwin (1964 [1859]), *On the Origin of Species: A Facsimile of the First Edition*, p. 489.

89 Ibid.

fragmentary form. Accordingly, the course of evolution can only be inferred through retrospective construction: as a brittle genealogy of the present, faced with the fact that most empirical material has been erased.[90]

On the Origin of Species causes a narrative crisis which can be understood in terms of the 'blow' (*Kränkung*, humiliation) that Freud associated with Darwin.[91] In her now-classic study *Darwin's Plots*, Gillian Beer highlighted the role of natural selection in this context by pointing out the near-impossibility of eliminating notions of intention, progress and higher development from the narrative of development. In formulating the principle of chance that governs natural selection, she writes, "[Darwin] was telling a new story, against the grain of the language available to tell it in".[92] Accordingly, she argues, even in Darwin we find that an intentionalistic language creeps in, creating throughout his account a tension with the paradigm shift of his own theory.[93] Another dimension of the blow lies in the fact that Darwin does not paint a clear picture but rather calls on his readers to marvel at the presumption of imagining they might ever be able to gain an overview of the complex contingencies on which the origin of any species depends:

> The mind cannot possibly grasp the full meaning of the term of a hundred million years; it cannot add up and perceive the full effects of many slight variations, accumulated during an almost infinite number of generations.[94]

This constitutive opacity, which Darwin further emphasised through the breaks in his genealogical sketches, was to prove the "most fragile part of his legacy".[95]

Darwin's reception is marked by a re-teleologisation.[96] Whereas Darwin pursues epistemological criticism and speaks in the linguistic register of mourning, his followers express "evolutionist enthusiasm"[97] driven by progressive

90 G. Beer (2009), *Darwin's Plots: Evolutionary Narrative in Darwin, George Eliot and Nineteenth-Century Fiction*, p. 79f.

91 S. Freud (1917), 'A Difficulty in the Path of Psycho-Analysis', *SE* 17, p. 139.

92 G. Beer, *Darwin's Plots*, p. 3.

93 Ibid., p. 19.

94 Darwin (1964), *On the Origin of Species*, p. 481.

95 J. Voss (2007), 'Das erste Bild der Evolution. Wie Charles Darwin die Unordnung der Naturgeschichte zeichnete und was daraus wurde', p. 78.

96 P.J. Bowler (1983), *The Eclipse of Darwinism: Anti-Darwinian Evolution Theories in the Decades around 1900*; E.-M. Engels & T. Glick (2008), *The Reception of Charles Darwin in Europe*.

97 W. Michler (1999), *Darwinismus und Literatur. Naturwissenschaftliche und literarische Intelligenz in Österreich 1859–1914*, p. 100.

as well as epistemological optimism. It was above all Ernst Haeckel who contributed to the fact that Darwinism was received in the German-speaking world as a worldview claiming totality.[98] In a famous speech delivered in Stettin in 1863, Haeckel speaks of a "natural law [...] of progressive development" which he also applies to society. This "continual process of perfection", he argues, is the natural consequence of natural selection's "war of all against all".[99]

The Darwinian reception associated with Haeckel is typical of the broader phenomenon of the biologisation of social theory. Haeckel's writings enjoyed immense popularity across the entire political spectrum at the time.[100] And yet, the spread of Haeckelian Darwinism can in no way be taken to disprove the Freudian paradigm of a 'blow' against anthropological narcissism; on the contrary, this 'blow' is affirmed in the mode of restorative defence, in an act of fetishistic disavowal. A main tendency of *Weltanschauungsliteratur* around 1900 is particularly evident in Haeckel's worldview:[101] the claim to totality combined with the effort to establish semantic hermeticism.[102] The defensive structure of his edifice stands in relation to the aggressive undertones of his progressive optimism. The vitalism in Haeckel's work – never explicitly admitted but consistently present below the surface[103] – goes hand in hand with a fear of degeneration. From 1905 Haeckel was an honorary member of the German Society for Racial Hygiene,[104] and in his *Weltkriegsgedanken* he explains why "newborns with defects" should, in cases of doubt, be killed for the benefit of society as a whole.[105]

After the First World War, Haeckel's optimism went out of fashion and seemed naive. Haeckel is not mentioned in *Beyond the Pleasure Principle*, and yet it seems that an entire strand of Freud's text is driven by the contradictions associated with his name and the notions coined by him: ontogeny, phylogeny and the biogenetic law. When Freud speaks, in *Beyond the Pleasure Principle*, of "embryology, in its capacity as a recapitulation of developmental history",[106] Haeckel is present. His concepts are at work in Freud's biological

98 K. Bayertz (1998), 'Darwinismus als Politik', p. 239.

99 E. Haeckel (1968 [1863]), 'Die Jungfernrede [Stettiner Rede]. Über die Entwicklungstheorie Darwin's', p. 24.

100 Michler (1999), *Darwinismus und Literatur*; Bayertz (1998), 'Darwinismus als Politik'; A. Kelly (2011), *The Descent of Darwin: The Popularization of Darwinism in Germany, 1860–1914*.

101 H. Thomé (2004), 'Weltanschauungsliteratur. Vorüberlegungen zu Funktion und Texttyp'.

102 J. Willner (2019), 'Weltanschauung'.

103 B. Kleeberg (2005), *Theophysis. Ernst Haeckels Philosophie des Naturganzen*, p. 220.

104 Ibid., p. 201.

105 Haeckel (1915), *Ewigkeit*, p. 34.

106 Freud (1920g), *Beyond the Pleasure Principle*, p. 26.

speculation.[107] At least since Frank Sulloway's comprehensive study, it has become a commonplace that Haeckel's biogenetic law exerted a "hypothetico-deductive influence upon Freud's thinking".[108] Indeed, it formed the starting point for Freud's parallelisation of infantile psychosexual stages with the early developmental stages of human beings and pre-human species. What has been largely overlooked so far is, however, Haeckel's presence *ex negativo*. By subtle means, and yet in striking consistency, Freud demarcates his use of the phylogenetic parallel from the worldview (*Weltanschauung*) with which it is inseparably connected in Haeckel.[109]

When Freud speaks pejoratively of those who "demand that science shall be a substitute for the catechism",[110] it is not difficult to detect a reference to Haeckel's catchphrase of the "catechism of the monistic worldview".[111] The etymological sense of 'catechism' – as a guideline (*Leitfaden*) – was central to Haeckel's rhetoric: "The Ariadne's thread (*Ariadnefaden*) we follow as our sure guide is our modern theory of development".[112] Haeckel's interpretation of recapitulation theory played a substantial part in softening the Darwinian blow, among other things by claiming to make evolution visible in miniature: "[O]ntogenesis [is] a short and rapid recapitulation of phylogenesis".[113] This miniaturisation and acceleration suggests that it is possible to register a process that is constitutively inaccessible to experience: evolution perceived as a metamorphosis within the span of our own lives, in the uterus of every pregnant woman. "Metamorphosis bypasses death",[114] Gillian Beer writes in reference to the mythically exaggerated circular structure which, in Haeckel, is always configured as an internal element of an upward movement.

Haeckel's recapitulation theory furthermore presupposes an evolutionary temporality that can be reliably perceived by the senses in the form of an unbroken flow reflecting the beauty and symmetry of nature.[115] For Freud,

107 For an overview of theoretical accounts of recapitulation before and beyond Haeckel, see Gould (1977), *Ontogeny and Phylogeny*, and I. Müller (1998), 'Historische Grundlagen des Biogenetischen Grundgesetzes'. Kleeberg demonstrates in an extensive study how Haeckel teleologises recapitulation theory. Kleeberg (2005), *Theophysis*, pp. 136, 143–144.

108 Sulloway (1979), *Freud: Biologist of the Mind*, p. 200.

109 Freud's years in *Gymnasium* (1865–1873) coincided with Haeckel's breakthrough as a populariser of the theory of evolution. It was only after he began studying under Ernst Wilhelm Brücke that physicalism came to have a decisive influence on his thinking. Until then, he was most likely not averse to Haeckel's interpretation of Darwin along the lines of natural philosophy. L.B. Ritvo (1990), *Darwin's Influence on Freud: A Tale of Two Sciences*, p. 10.

110 Freud (1920g), *Beyond the Pleasure Principle*, p. 64.

111 E. Haeckel (1914), *Gott-Natur (Theophysis). Studien über monistische Religion*, p. 48.

112 Ibid., p. 57.

113 E. Haeckel (1866), *Generelle Morphologie der Organismen*, p. 300.

114 Beer (2009), *Darwin's Plots*, p. 104.

115 S. Ferguson (2010), 'The Face of Time between Haeckel and Bergson: Or, toward an Ethics of Impure

by contrast, evolutionary time has no flow; it is broken. In place of Haeckel's conception of nature as a miracle of creation, continuously manifesting itself morphologically, being fundamentally accessible to perception, bioanalysis assumes catastrophe at the point of origin, a state which can at best be speculatively reconstructed, by means of counter-intuitive, intellectual operations. Freud's focus on compulsion, need and surviving catastrophes stands in striking contrast to the notion of an inherent, progressive tendency: The "germ of a living animal" is "obliged" to "recapitulate [...] the structures of all the forms from which it sprung";[116] organisms develop by means of detours which external circumstances have compelled them to take again and again.

Above all, Freud's concept of the 'compulsion to repeat', as developed in parallel in 'The Uncanny', contributes to the psychoanalytic hijacking of recapitulation theory.[117] Repetition, for Freud, is thoroughly pervaded by *Nachträglichkeit*: what becomes manifest in the present is fundamentally overdetermined and serves as the starting point for retrospective conjectures about processes which can only be constructed in the mode of interpretation and speculation. The logic of deferred action categorically excludes linear determinism.[118] Bioanalysis introduces repression and recurrence, desire, defence and compromise-formation into the narrative of organic life, with the clinical image of traumatic neurosis replacing the Bismarckian rhetoric of combat (*Kampf*) as the frame of reference.

Last but not least, the systematic proximity of Freud's concept of repetition to that of the symptom is essential.[119] This blurs the distinction between normalcy and pathology which was so essential for the late Haeckel. With his view of organic life, Freud produces an alienation effect: he estranges the "monumentalisation and illumination"[120] which characterises both Haeckel's narrative and his visual representation of protists. Later, Ferenczi would

Vision', p. 124.

116 Freud (1920g), *Beyond the Pleasure Principle*, p. 37.

117 Grubrich-Simitis describes the compulsion to repeat as a concept connecting the model of trauma and the model of drives, prepared already in the phylogenetic fantasies. Grubrich-Simitis (2007), 'Trauma oder Trieb – Trieb und Trauma: Wiederbetrachtet', p. 647. Raluca Soreanu sees in the relationship between the death drive and the compulsion to repeat a problem which is bypassed by Freud and only later conceptualised more precisely, in metapsychological terms, by Ferenczi: especially in his *Klinisches Tagebuch* (Clinical diary). As Soreanu argues, Ferenczi goes further than Freud with his theory of splitting and fragments, outlining a metapsychology of post-traumatic forms of survival in the abandonment of ego or self-preservation instincts. R. Soreanu (2017), 'Something Was Lost in Freud's "Beyond the Pleasure Principle": A Ferenczian Reading', pp. 224f., and Jakob Staberg in this volume, pp. 271–273.

118 Laplanche & Pontalis (1973), *The Language of Psycho-Analysis*, pp. 111–112.

119 U. Hock (2012), *Das Unbewußte Denken. Wiederholung und Todestrieb*, p. 138.

120 D. Grünbein (2001), 'Das grandiose Bilderbuch. Ernst Haeckels Kunstformen in der Natur', p. 16.

find, "in the hysterical and pathoneurotic type of reaction, a prototype of the energy displacements that take place in the accomplishment of every adaptation and development".[121] Freud analogously draws on the neurotically structured psychic apparatus as a model for speaking in a different way about the developmental history of organisms. This patho-analysis[122] of unicellular organisms becomes apparent when Freud compares the inner cortical layer of the vesicle with consciousness and speaks of the unicellular organism's tendency to projection: the vesicle treats stimuli from the inside "as though they were acting [...] from the outside, so that it may be possible to bring the shield against stimuli into operation as a means of defence against them".[123] With this reference to the clinical picture of paranoia, he suggests that a similar process in unicellular organisms is the "origin of *projection*, which is destined to play such a large part in the causation of pathological processes".[124] There is no pure origin, there are no vitalist strivings in *Beyond the Pleasure Principle.*

Like Haeckel, Freud and Ferenczi refer to Lamarck. But whereas in Lamarck the satisfaction of desires, efforts and intentions results in abilities and achievements which are passed on to future generations, the bioanalytic narrative regards the descendants as encumbered with burdens. In bioanalysis, the object of transgenerational transference consists of displaced reaction formations in the face of unrememberable shocks that elude empirical knowledge. Bioanalysis subverts Lamarckism via the psychoanalytic theory of pathoneuroses, psychoses, and above all hysteria. Ferenczi makes this intervention explicit:

> When, for example, Lamarck makes the use or non-use of an organ responsible for its further development or its retrogression, he overlooks the fact that he evades the very problem [...]. The observations made by us on hysteria and pathoneuroses make clear for the first time how, under the influence of the wish for the restoration of the equilibrium which had been disturbed [...] there is directed toward the disturbed part of the body an excessively strong countercathexis which acts on the one hand

---

121 Ferenczi (2005), *Thalassa*, p. 91.

122 Drawing upon by Jacques Schotte's notion of patho-analysis, Philippe Van Haute and Thomas Geyskens have highlighted that Freud, at least between 1895 and 1905, treats the pathological manifestations of hysteria as excessive expressions of anthropological phenomena. P. Van Haute & T. Geyskens (2012), *A Non-Oedipal Psychoanalysis? A Clinical Anthropology of Hysteria in the Works of Freud and Lacan*, pp. 17–18, 25. It can be argued that the project of bioanalysis forms a hidden continuation of such a patho-analytic line of thought.

123 Freud (1920g), *Beyond the Pleasure Principle*, p. 29.

124 Ibid.

> as a protection to the rest of the body against the noxa in question and on the other as a source of curative and regenerative power.[125]

Ferenczi reformulates the process of biological inheritance as follows: "What we call heredity is, perhaps, therefore, only the displacing upon posterity of the bulk of the traumatically unpleasurable experiences".[126] This is because mnemic traces operate "in the same way as in Freud's account of disturbing stimuli of traumatic neuroses which have not been disposed of: they compel the perpetual recapitulation of the distressing situation".[127] This eccentric combination of Lamarckism and the Freudian theory of neurosis opens up a broad field of inquiry. The bioanalytic foray into the Lamarckian discourse of heredity is echoed in Freud's much later intervention into the theory of cultural transmission. In *The Man Moses and Monotheistic Religion*, neither tradition nor inheritance are understood as positively representable; rather, they are conceptualised as the result of repression and recurrence, as fractured transmissions across generations.

With the structure of neurosis, a destabilising feature is placed into the centre of the narrative of development. It is precisely that from which C.G. Jung wanted to purify the psychoanalytic notion of origin. Unlike Jung, Freud rejects both the notion of a pure origin and the claim of psychoanalysis to be a *Weltanschauung*. Development as Freud understands it is also not compatible with Teutonic glorification as we find in Jung at the latest in 1934.[128] When Freud reinterprets the unicellular organism, he also subjects the human belief in progressive evolution to an analysis. The narrative of development towards completion seems to be driven by unconscious, destructive desires:

125 Ferenczi (2005), *Thalassa*, p. 91.

126 Ibid., p. 66.

127 Ibid.

128 In 1934, in an attempt to legitimise his own form of therapy vis-à-vis the Nazi regime, Jung resorted to the image of an energetic seed [*Keim*] in order to promote the potential of the Germanic people. In contrast to the Jewish unconscious, he writes, "the 'Aryan' unconscious [...] contains explosive forces and seeds of a future yet to be born, and these may not be devalued as nursery romanticism without psychic danger. The still youthful Germanic peoples are fully capable of creating new cultural forms that still lie dormant in the darkness of the unconscious of every individual – seeds bursting with energy and capable of mighty expansion. [...] In my opinion it has been a grave error in medical psychology up till now to apply Jewish categories – which are not even binding on all Jews – indiscriminately to Germanic and Slavic Christendom. Because of this the most precious secret of the Germanic peoples – their creative and intuitive depth of soul – has been explained as a morass of banal infantilism, while my own warning voice has for decades been suspected of anti-Semitism. This suspicion emanated from Freud. He did not understand the Germanic psyche". C.G. Jung (1970 [1934]), 'The State of Psychotherapy Today', pp. 165–166. For a commentary on this passage, see Y.H. Yerushalmi (1991), *Freud's Moses: Judaism Terminable and Interminable*, pp. 48–49.

> It may be difficult, too, for many of us, to abandon the belief that there is an instinct towards perfection [*Trieb zur Vervollkommnung*] at work in human beings, which has brought them to their present high level of intellectual achievement and ethical sublimation and which may be expected to watch over their development into supermen. I have no faith, however, in the existence of any such internal instinct and I cannot see how this benevolent illusion is to be preserved. The present development of human beings requires, as it seems to me, no different explanation from that of animals. What appears in a minority of human individuals as an untiring impulsion towards further perfection can easily be understood as a result of the instinctual repression upon which is based all that is most precious in human civilization.[129]

The reference to the grey zone between sublimation and repression, and to its significance for "all that is most precious in human civilization" invites us to read *Beyond the Pleasure Principle* within the framework of psychoanalytic cultural theory. Freud's speculation on unicellular organisms indicates that he was no cryptobiologist. His engagement with biology is bioanalytical, that is, psychoanalytical; it aims beyond biology. In its application to organic life, the concept of the death drive can serve as a vehicle for analysing ideologically deeply rooted views of nature. It also holds the possibility of introducing negativity as a category necessary for a critique of civilisation, in the face of the catastrophic entanglement of biology and politics. It remains necessary to continue to spell out implications that remained unwritten in the bioanalytical speculation but which impose themselves on readers with historical distance. While Freud accepts the inevitability that his text will remain unfinished, the notion of the death drive remains a foreign body, posing to all subsequent psychoanalytic theorisation the ongoing task of establishing its significance within metapsychology.

129 Freud (1920g), *Beyond the Pleasure Principle*, p. 42.

Outlook

> *Let us beware.* – Let us beware of thinking that the world is a living being. Where should it expand? [...] The living is merely a type of what is dead, and a very rare type. Let us beware of thinking that the world eternally creates new things.[130]

In *Beyond the Pleasure Principle,* Freud inscribes death at every level. This tendency forms a common denominator for his approach to most diverging biological concepts, even beyond Haeckel's Lamarckism, even in the most vocal opponent of Lamarckism. It can be observed when Freud discusses August Weismann's thesis of the immortality of germ-cells. Weismann describes the mortal body as a "secondary appendage" (*nebensächliches Anhängsel*),[131] arguing that the germ line is theoretically immortal. According to Weismann, both the first single-cell organisms and later the germ-cells pass on their bodies completely through division, leaving no corpses behind.[132] Weismann is fascinated by the immortality of the germ-line and considers death to be a secondary phenomenon, the price paid for the specialisation of cells. Freud shows little interest in the notion of immortality, he reverses the direction of vision altogether and turns away from the idea of future generations as *telos,* towards the aspect of dissolution and fusion that accompanies procreation. His focus lies on destruction as the result of fusion, with a firm interest in what Weismann deems a secondary appendage: the psychosoma subjected to mortality. Seen from this perspective, Freud's concept of life drives appears as the result of reading Weismann against the grain, informed by Sabina Spielrein.[133]

Bioanalysis can serve to defamiliarise a set of rationalisations that were formative for the decades to come. For the reading presented here, the question was not whether or not the bioanalytically formulated scenes describe reality. The topic at stake was not whether something *really* drives – or pulls – the organisms, or whether such forces tend towards the organic, the inorganic, upwards, downwards or into the sea. Instead, attention was drawn to the concepts overwritten by bioanalytical speculations. Bioanalysis in *Beyond the Pleasure Principle* can be read as a psychoanalysis of biological

130 F. Nietzsche (1974 [1882]), *The Gay Science,* § 109, pp. 167–168.
131 A. Weismann (1892 [1884]), 'Über Leben und Tod', p. 165.
132 A. Weismann (1885), 'Zur Frage nach der Unsterblichkeit der Einzelligen', p. 690.
133 S. Spielrein (1994 [1912]), 'Destruction as the Cause of Coming into Being'.

narratives, opening up the broader question of unconscious motivations behind politically influential fantasies of progression and immortality.

Ernst Haeckel died on 5 August 1919, during the period in which *Beyond the Pleasure Principle* was being written. Two years earlier, the World War had become an occasion for him to think about inorganic matter.[134] In his 1917 book *Kristallseelen: Studien* über *das anorganische Leben* (*Crystal Souls: Studies on Inorganic Life*), he more explicitly articulated a tendency we can already find in his early work: an extension of the concept of the soul to the entire universe, as part of a belief that all matter is ensouled. In Haeckel's late writing, the *bios* generally figures as an episode in "the immeasurable history of Anorgon, of dead nature, as it is falsely called".[135] This is where Haeckel and Fechner meet.

By eliminating all references to eternal life and conscious matter in his reading of Fechner, Freud undoes, for *Beyond the Pleasure Principle,* the bypassing of death which is found in both Haeckel and Fechner. And yet years later, in a letter to Lou Andreas-Salomé in the spring of 1925, he still depicts ageing in terms that resonate with Fechner:

> The pleasure it provides me is no longer intensive enough. A crust of insensitivity is slowly enveloping me; I state this without complaint [*klaglos*]. It is also a natural progression, a way of beginning to become inorganic. 'The sereneness of old age' is what it is called, I believe.[136]

Freud's realisation of his own insensitivity holds a particular pathos. He notes that he is stating this fact without complaint – thus subjecting his lack of sensation to a moment of reflection. What is lost in the process of hardening cannot be mourned. And with this, we have arrived at the concept of melancholia, which the late Freud was to regard as fundamental to the structure of the individual. The phrase "without complaint", *klaglos*, the negated lament, comes close to admitting that there are indeed reasons for lamentation. In oceanic feeling, in animism, in evolutionist enthusiasm and in fantasies of the immortal germ line, this is disavowed.

---

134 M.A. Di Gregorio (2005), *From Here to Eternity: Ernst Haeckel and Scientific Faith*, p. 539.
135 Haeckel (1914), *Gott-Natur (Theophysis)*, p. 46.
136 S. Freud & L. Andreas-Salomé (1966), *Briefwechsel*, p. 169.

Bibliography

Bahr, Hermann (1912), 'Natur', in: *Essays*. Leipzig: Insel, pp. 127–136.

Bayertz, Kurt (1998), 'Darwinismus als Politik. Zur Genese des Sozialdarwinismus in Deutschland 1860–1900', in: ed. Erna Aescht, Gerhard Aubrecht, Erika Krausse, Franz Speta, Werner Michler & Bernd Lötsch, *Welträtsel und Lebenswunder. Ernst Haeckel – Werk, Wirkung und Folgen*. Linz: OÖ Landesmuseum, pp. 229–289.

Beer, Gillian (2009 [1983]), *Darwin's Plots: Evolutionary Narrative in Darwin, George Eliot and Nineteenth-Century Fiction*. Cambridge: Cambridge UP.

Benjamin, Walter (2019 [1925]), *The Origin of the German Trauerspiel*, transl. Howard Eiland. Cambridge (MA): Harvard UP.

Bowler, Peter J. (1983), *The Eclipse of Darwinism: Anti-Darwinian Evolution Theories in the Decades around 1900*. Baltimore & London: Johns Hopkins UP.

Darwin, Charles (1964 [1859]), *On the Origin of Species: A Facsimile of the First Edition*. Cambridge (MA): Harvard UP. https://doi.org/10.2307/j.ctvjf9xp5.

Di Gregorio, Mario A. (2005), *From Here to Eternity: Ernst Haeckel and Scientific Faith*. Göttingen: Vandenhoeck & Ruprecht.

Dufresne, Todd (2017), *The Late Sigmund Freud: Or, The Last Words on Psychoanalysis, Society, and All the Riddles of Life*. Cambridge: Cambridge UP.

Engels, Eve-Marie & Glick, Thomas F. (2008), *The Reception of Charles Darwin in Europe, Vol. 1–2*. London: Continuum.

Fechner, Gustav Theodor (1846), *Ueber das höchste Gut*. Leipzig: Breitkopf & Härtel 1846.

Fechner, Gustav Theodor (1873), *Einige Ideen zur Schöpfungs- und Entwicklungsgeschichte der Organismen*. Leipzig: Breitkopf & Härtel.

Fechner, Gustav Theodor (1984), *Das unendliche Leben. Mit Zeichnungen von Leonardo da Vinci und einem Nachwort von Gert Mattenklott*. Munich: Matthes & Seitz.

Ferenczi, Sándor (1994 [1913]), 'Stages in the Development of the Sense of Reality', in: Sándor Ferenczi, *First Contributions to Psycho-Analysis*, transl. Ernest Jones. London & New York: Karnac, pp. 213–239.

Ferenczi, Sándor (2005 [1924]), *Thalassa: A Theory of Genitality*, transl. Henry A. Bunker. London & New York: Karnac.

Ferguson, Scott (2010), 'The Face of Time between Haeckel and Bergson: Or, toward an Ethics of Impure Vision', *Qui Parle* 19, pp. 107–151.

Freud, Sigmund (1905c), *Jokes and Their Relation to the Unconscious*, in: *Standard Edition of the Complete Psychological Works of Sigmund Freud, Vol. 8*, transl. James Strachey. London: Hogarth, 1953–1974, pp. 3–236.

Freud, Sigmund (1915b), 'Thoughts for the Times on War and Death', *SE* 14, pp. 273–302.

Freud, Sigmund (1916a), 'On Transience', *SE* 14, pp. 303–308.

Freud, Sigmund (1917a), 'A Difficulty in the Path of Psycho-Analysis', *SE* 17, pp. 135–144.

Freud, Sigmund (1919h), 'The Uncanny', *SE* 17, pp. 217–256.
Freud, Sigmund (1920g), *Beyond the Pleasure Principle, SE* 18, pp. 7–64.
Freud, Sigmund (1930a), *Civilization and Its Discontents, SE* 21, pp. 59–148.
Freud, Sigmund (1933c), 'Sándor Ferenczi', *SE* 22, pp. 227–232.
Freud, Sigmund (1937c), 'Analysis Terminable and Interminable', *SE* 23, pp. 209–244.
Freud, Sigmund (1937d), 'Constructions in Analysis', *SE* 23, pp. 255–270.
Freud, Sigmund (1985a), *A Phylogenetic Fantasy: Overview of the Transference Neuroses*, ed. Ilse Grubrich-Simitis, transl. Axel Hoffer & Peter T. Hoffer. Cambridge (MA) & London: Harvard UP.
Freud, Sigmund & Andreas-Salomé, Lou (1966), *Briefwechsel*, ed. Ernst Pfeiffer. Frankfurt a.M.: Fischer.
Freud, Sigmund & Ferenczi, Sándor (1996), *The Correspondence of Sigmund Freud and Sándor Ferenczi, Vol. 2: 1914–1919*, ed. Eva Brabant, Ernst Falzeder & Patrizia Giampieri-Deutsch. Cambridge (MA) & London: The Belknap Press of Harvard UP.
Gould, Stephen Jay (1977), *Ontogeny and Phylogeny*. Cambridge (MA): Harvard UP.
Gradmann, Christoph (2007), 'Unsichtbare Feinde. Bakteriologie und politische Sprache im deutschen Kaiserreich', in: ed. Philipp Sarasin, Silvia Berger, Marianne Hänseler & Myriam Spörri, *Bakteriologie und Moderne. Studien zur Biopolitik des Unsichtbaren, 1879–1920*. Frankfurt a.M.: Suhrkamp, pp. 327–353.
Grubrich-Simitis, Ilse (1985), 'Metapsychologie und Metabiologie. Zu Sigmund Freuds Entwurf einer Übersicht der Übertragungsneurosen', in: Sigmund Freud, *A Phylogenetic Fantasy: Overview of the Transference Neuroses*, ed. Ilse Grubrich-Simitis. Cambridge (MA) & London: Harvard UP, pp. 83–119.
Grubrich-Simitis, Ilse (1987), 'Trauma oder Trieb – Trieb und Trauma. Lektionen aus Sigmund Freuds phylogenetischer Phantasie von 1915', *Psyche. Zeitschrift für Psychoanalyse und ihre Anwendungen* 41, pp. 992–1023.
Grubrich-Simitis, Ilse (2007), 'Trauma oder Trieb – Trieb und Trauma: Wiederbetrachtet', *Psyche. Zeitschrift für Psychoanalyse und ihre Anwendungen* 61, pp. 637–656.
Grünbein, Durs (2001), 'Das grandiose Bilderbuch. Ernst Haeckels Kunstformen in der Natur', in: ed. Hendrik Röder & Maren Ulbrich, *Welträtsel und Lebenswunder. Der Biologe Ernst Haeckel (1834–1919)*. Potsdam: Vacat, pp. 13–18.
Haeckel, Ernst (1866), *Generelle Morphologie der Organismen. Allgemeine Grundzüge der organischen Formen-Wissenschaft, mechanisch begründet durch die von C. Darwin reformirte Descendenz-Theorie*. Berlin: Georg Reimer.
Haeckel, Ernst (1903), *Die Welträthsel. Gemeinverständliche Studien über monistische Philosophie*. Bonn: Strauß.
Haeckel, Ernst (1914), *Gott-Natur (Theophysis). Studien über monistische Religion*. Leipzig: Kröner.
Haeckel, Ernst (1915), *Ewigkeit. Weltkriegsgedanken über Leben und Tod, Religion und Entwicklungslehre*. Berlin: Georg Reimer.

Haeckel, Ernst (1917), *Kristallseelen. Studien über das anorganische Leben*. Leipzig: Alfred Kröner.

Haeckel, Ernst (1968 [1863]), 'Die Jungfernrede [Stettiner Rede]. Über die Entwicklungstheorie Darwins', in: ed. Gerhard Heberer, *Der gerechtfertigte Haeckel*. Stuttgart: Gustav Fischer, pp. 45–59.

Haverkamp, Anselm (2015), 'Undone by Death. Umrisse einer Poetik nach Darwin', in: ed. Carolin Blumenberg, Alexandra Heimes, Sophie Witt & Erica Weitzmann, *Suspensionen. Über das Untote*. Paderborn: Fink, pp. 33–50.

Hock, Udo (2012), *Das Unbewußte Denken. Wiederholung und Todestrieb*. Gießen: Psychosozial-Verlag.

Hugo, Victor (1894 [1830]), 'Hernani', in: *Dramatic Works of Victor Hugo*, transl. Frederick L. Slous & Camilla Newton Crosland. New York: P.F. Collier.

Jung, Carl Gustav (1970 [1934]), 'The State of Psychotherapy Today', in: *Collected Works of Carl Jung, Vol. 10: Civilization in Transition*, transl. Richard F.C. Hull. Princeton: Princeton UP.

Kelly, Alfred (2011), *The Descent of Darwin: The Popularization of Darwinism in Germany, 1860–1914*. Chapel Hill: University of North Carolina Press.

Kleeberg, Bernhard (2005), *Theophysis. Ernst Haeckels Philosophie des Naturganzen*. Cologne, Weimar & Vienna: Böhlau.

Laplanche, Jean & Pontalis, Jean-Bertrand (1973), *The Language of Psycho-Analysis*, transl. Donald Nicholson-Smith. New York: W.W. Norton.

May, Ulrike (2015), 'The Third Step in Drive Theory: On the Genesis of *Beyond the Pleasure Principle*', *Psychoanalysis and History* 17(2), pp. 205–280 (in this volume, pp. 81–164).

Melville, Herman (2016 [1856]), 'Bartleby, the Scrivener', in: *Billy Budd, Bartleby, and Other Stories*. New York: Penguin, pp. 17–54.

Michler, Werner (1999), *Darwinismus und Literatur. Naturwissenschaftliche und literarische Intelligenz in Österreich 1859–1914*. Cologne, Weimar & Vienna: Böhlau.

Müller, Irmgard (1998), 'Historische Grundlagen des Biogenetischen Grundgesetzes', in: ed. Erna Aescht, Gerhard Aubrecht, Erika Krausse, Franz Speta, Werner Michler & Bernd Lötsch, *Welträtsel und Lebenswunder. Ernst Haeckel – Werk, Wirkung und Folgen*. Linz: OÖ Landesmuseum, pp. 119–130.

Nietzsche, Friedrich (1974 [1882]), *The Gay Science*, transl. Walter Kaufmann. New York: Vintage Books.

Riepe, Manfred (2001), 'Freud und Fechner. Zur Rekonstruktion eines Paradigmenwechsels', in: ed. Georg Christoph Tholen, Gerhard Schmitz & Manfred Riepe, *Übertragung – Übersetzung – Überlieferung. Episteme und Sprache in der Psychoanalyse Lacans*. Bielefeld: Transcript, pp. 343–370.

Ritvo, Lucille B. (1990), *Darwin's Influence on Freud: A Tale of Two Sciences*. New Haven: Yale UP.

Soreanu, Raluca (2017), 'Something Was Lost in Freud's "Beyond the Pleasure Principle": A Ferenczian Reading', *American Journal of Psychoanalysis* 77, pp. 223–238.

Soreanu, Raluca (2019), 'Sándor Ferenczi's Epistemologies and Their Politics: On Utraquism and the Analogical Method', in: ed. Ferenc Erős, Anna Borgos & Júlia Gyimesi, *Psychology and Politics: Intersections of Science and Ideology in the History of Psy-Sciences*. Budapest: Central European UP, pp. 95–106.

Spielrein, Sabina (1994 [1912]), 'Destruction as the cause of coming into being', *Journal of Analytical Psychology* 39, pp. 155–186.

Staberg, Jakob (2023), 'Instead of Language: Confusion. Sigmund Freud / Sándor Ferenczi', in: ed. Raluca Soreanu, Jakob Staberg & Jenny Willner, *Ferenczi Dialogues. On Trauma and Catastrophe*. Leuven: Leuven UP, pp. 23–71.

Sulloway, Frank J. (1979), *Freud, Biologist of the Mind: Beyond the Psychoanalytic Legend*. Cambridge (MA) & London: Harvard UP.

Thomé, Horst (2004), 'Weltanschauungsliteratur. Vorüberlegungen zu Funktion und Texttyp', in: ed. Lutz Danneberg, Friedrich Vollhardt, Hartmut Böhme & Jörg Schönert, *Wissen in Literatur im 19. Jahrhundert*. Tübingen: Niemeyer, pp. 338–380.

Trumbull, Robert (2022), *From Life to Survival. Derrida, Freud, and the Future of Deconstruction*. New York: Fordham UP.

Van Haute, Philippe & Geyskens, Thomas (2012), *A Non-Oedipal Psychoanalysis? A Clinical Anthropology of Hysteria in the Works of Freud and Lacan*. Leuven: Leuven UP.

Voss, Julia (2007), 'Das erste Bild der Evolution. Wie Charles Darwin die Unordnung der Naturgeschichte zeichnete und was daraus wurde', in: ed. Kurt Bayertz, Myriam Gerhard & Walter Jaeschke, *Weltanschauung, Philosophie und Naturwissenschaft im 19. Jahrhundert, Vol. 2: Der Darwinismus-Streit*. Hamburg: Meiner, pp. 47–82.

Vitale, Francesco (2018), *Biodeconstruction. Jacques Derrida and the Life Sciences*, transl. Mauro Senatore. Albany: State University of New York Press.

Wegener, Mai (2004), *Neuronen und Neurosen. Der psychische Apparat bei Freud und Lacan. Ein historisch-theoretischer Versuch zu Freuds Entwurf von 1895*. Paderborn: Fink.

Wegener, Mai (2005), 'Das psychophysische Unbewusste. Gustav Theodor Fechner und der Mond', in: ed. Michael B. Buchholz & Günter Gödde, *Macht und Dynamik des Unbewussten. Auseinandersetzung in Philosophie, Medizin und Psychoanalyse, Vol. 1*. Gießen: Psychosozial-Verlag, pp. 240–261.

Weismann, August (1885), 'Zur Frage nach der Unsterblichkeit der Einzelligen', *Biologisches Zentralblatt* 4, pp. 650–691.

Weismann, August (1892 [1884]), 'Über Leben und Tod', in: *Aufsätze über Vererbung und verwandte biologische Fragen*. Jena: Gustav Fischer, pp. 123–190.

Will, David (2016), *Inanimation: Theories of Inorganic Life*. Minneapolis: University of Minnesota Press.

Willner, Jenny (2019), 'Weltanschauung', in: ed. Thomas Erthel & Robert Stockhammer, *Welt-Komposita. Ein Lexikon*. Paderborn: Fink, pp. 15–25.

Willner, Jenny (2020), 'Neurotische Evolution. Bioanalyse als Kulturkritik in Jenseits des Lustprinzips', *Psyche. Zeitschrift für Psychoanalyse und ihre Anwendungen* 11(74), pp. 895–921.

Willner, Jenny (2022), 'The Problem of Heredity: Ferenczi's Organology and the Politics of Bioanalysis', *Psychoanalysis and History* 24(2), pp. 205–2018.

Willner, Jenny (2023), 'Catastrophes and Genitality: Ferenczi's *Thalassa* and the Politics of Bioanalysis', in: ed. Raluca Soreanu, Jakob Staberg & Jenny Willner, *Ferenczi Dialogues. On Trauma and Catastrophe*. Leuven: Leuven UP, pp. 91–130.

Yerushalmi, Yosef Hayim (1991), *Freud's Moses: Judaism Terminable and Interminable*. New Haven & London: Yale UP.

Ferenczi Thinking Beyond the Pleasure Principle

Jakob Staberg

Beginnings

When during the 1920s Walter Benjamin sought to understand why poetry no longer mattered by considering how Charles Baudelaire's poems from the middle of the preceding century indicated the end of poetry as such, he reached the conclusion that experience had undergone a structural change. Since, for Benjamin, neither philosophy nor science provided the means to understand this change, he turns elsewhere: first to literature, specifically Marcel Proust, and eventually to psychoanalysis. When he approaches Freud, whose theoretical discoveries were still at that time new and somewhat uncertain, he does so from a work that can be considered part of the very problem he seeks both to clarify and resolve. The essay *Jenseits des Lustprinzips*, published in 1920, established in Benjamin's view a new correlation between memory (for him, following Proust, *mémoire involontaire*) and consciousness. It did so in the form of a radical hypothesis that Benjamin sought not to prove, but rather to test its applicability in contexts far removed from those relevant to the site of Freud's original discovery.[1] Benjamin's way of working with *Beyond the Pleasure Principle* is part of a discourse I want to seek the contours of in the following. The steps we shall take are suggested by the Italian writer Roberto Calasso, who saw the Freudian endeavour as a sober and analytic approach to the symptoms of Western history. He writes: "In the tangled structure of *Beyond the Pleasure Principle*, Freud outlines the insurmountable cosmogony of modernity".[2] The uncanny conclusion – "the pleasure principle seems actually to serve the death instincts"[3] – derives in his view from a syndrome of

[1] W. Benjamin (1939), 'Über einige Motive bei Baudelaire' ['On Some Motifs in Baudelaire'].

[2] R. Calasso (1994), *The Ruin of Kasch*, p. 206.

[3] S. Freud (1920g), *Beyond the Pleasure Principle*, *SE* 18.

repetition-compulsion empowering this culture's desire to obtain order from nature, thereby commencing a vicious circle leading back to the cancellation of itself.

In what follows, I would like to read the *Beyond the Pleasure Principle* project as part of a discourse intrinsic to modernity, hovering on the verge of catastrophe in which nature and death are given new meaning within the field of culture. What I seek to formulate takes the form of essayistic reflections, gravitating toward a reformulation of the notion of a death drive that can be found in the late works of the Hungarian psychoanalyst Sándor Ferenczi. Ferenczi was for decades involved in a complicated dialogue with Freud, sharing his endeavour to develop the theories of psychoanalysis, in particular the link to other fields of culture and the sciences, such as biology. My argument will, in particular, interpret certain entries from his posthumously published *Clinical Diary.* Here the death drive shimmers as a *Fremdkörper*, that is, a foreign body, in Ferenczi's outlines of a metapsychology that evolves around the notion of psychic fragments – the existence of dead split-off parts of the psyche, – but first and foremost around the capacity for survival.[4] The themes that over the years Ferenczi developed emerged while he was exploring the psychoanalytic setting and the role of transference. He thus created a theoretical framework that was anticipated by Freud's elaboration of psychoanalytic concepts, entangled with notions drawn from contemporary biology. If it can be said that with a 'Ferenczian' metapsychology the organs themselves begin to think we must recognise that Ferenczi reaches this unknown terrain, admittedly embedded within Freud's bioanalytical speculation, through a refined ability to pay attention to transference phenomena.

A guiding thread in Freud's speculation is the conclusion that 'progress' can only be understood as an 'illusion'.[5] This radical assumption breaks with the politics of nationalism and authoritarianism that in late nineteenth and early twentieth centuries saw biological science as the legitimisation of its own project of exploitation of nature and man. Freud's assumption places his analysis in the context of an intellectual culture that extends beyond psychoanalysis. Rather, modern culture is characterised by a "lack of any idea of historical progress".[6] Instead, a theory of catastrophe emerges from the experience of exile and oppression, of historical discontinuity, whose representatives include both Walter Benjamin and Sándor Ferenczi. In Buci-Glucksmann's words:

---

4 R. Soreanu (2018), 'The Psychic Life of Fragments'.

5 Freud (1920g), *Beyond the Pleasure Principle*, p. 42.

6 C. Buci-Glucksmann (1994), *Baroque reason: the aesthetics of modernity*, p. 63.

> Unlike Christianity and the conservative Judaism of the Book, the mystical-messianic Jewish culture which circulated from 1900 to 1920 throughout Central Europe and the German-language area always referred to a history marked by radical insecurity an element of instability and catastrophe, a consciousness of rupture and utopianism.[7]

With the founder of psychoanalysis, Benjamin shares not only an attention to detail, but an interest in the dream as a self-organising system in which catastrophes and their effects can be captured in some form of pictorial writing: *Bildschrift*. They both attach themselves to this awakening, even though they draw equally different and critical conclusions from the need to dissolve the dream image into meaningful utterances. In Benjamin's, as well as in Freud's writing, a methodological principle can be uncovered that could be described as dissolving uncanny experiences and contexts into mobile semantic configurations. However, the analytical method of uncovering meanings must always operate at the level of specific details, all the while remaining cognisant of the interface along which such analysis is working. For example, the concept of drive connects psyche and soma, such that Freud's art of representation, like the *Jugendstil* ornament, connects body and technology.[8] These analyses create amalgams between language and other artificial semiotic systems, whereby processes of meaning activate fields where culture and biology communicate. How can we think about this relationship today? And how did these interfaces appear at the threshold of the first industrial war that resulted in mass death and general suffering? What shaped bodies in the wake of the death drive of colonial projects? What happens to mental life with the emergence of the modern disenchanted positivist society that was increasingly based on a new radical biopolitics? Freud's entire project hovers, indeed dances, on that threshold. Guided by Ferenczi's late work, we will in the following dwell on these questions further.

Beyond the Pleasure Principle was written in two phases, one in early 1919, in parallel with the article 'The Uncanny', and a second in which the fourth section was completed and the central sixth section added in the early summer of 1920.[9] Some difficulties along the way had caused the project to stall. During this period, Freud was in close contact with his Hungarian colleague

7 Ibid.

8 K. Thonack (1997), *Selbstdarstellung des Unbewussten: Freud als Autor*, p. 58.

9 I. Grubrich-Simitis (1993), *Back to Freud's Texts: Making Silent Documents Speak*, pp. 182ff. See also Ulrike May's contribution in this volume, pp. 86ff.

with whom he explored the possibility of relating psychoanalysis to the science of biology. Some passages in 'The Uncanny' show that one phenomenon in particular set Freud on the track of this speculation, which would lead to a reassessment of twenty-five years of psychoanalytic practice and theoretical discourse: repetition. He had encountered this phenomenon in clinical practice as well as in his own experience, in his encounter with war neurosis and in the dreams of those suffering from these painful conditions. In his desire to understand these phenomena, he finds a purely neurological model of explanation unsatisfactory, so he superimposes on it reasoning directly emerging from a biological framework. Concepts that were earlier elaborated in an abandoned draft for a psychology focusing on how energy is handled by the internal system according to an inertial principle that seeks to relieve tensions created by internal and external stimuli are now actualised in a tentative theory of operation at work at the level of psychic quantities.[10] The phenomena of repetition had led Freud to assume that there is a tendency in all living things to move from the organic to the inorganic. The conundrum Freud faces here – and which is why the whole project falters for a moment – is this: if all drives are subject to the same tendency, the conflictual understanding of the drives on which his theory was at that point based must be abandoned. The genesis of the text, the fact that something makes the work halt for a moment is carefully outlined by Ulrike May, Philippe Van Haute and Herman Westerink in their contributions to this volume. Their aim is to define the problem Freud faces and the solution he proposes. When realising that the pleasure principle is at the service of the death drives, subordinated to an all-encompassing effort to cancel all tension, Freud turns to the biological sciences in order to disentangle his theory from the monism into which it was threatened to fall. As a result, in a speculative gesture he sketches the outlines of something beyond the pleasure principle on the level of germ-cells where life instincts operate and where there persists the violent fragmentation of the death drives.[11]

Through the phenomenon of repetition Freud had stumbled on an urge to return to the non-living as a matrix for a theory of modernity oriented around the notion of catastrophe. Thus the compulsion to repeat can be read as arising from a fear of an origin to be sought in the non-human, expressed in 'demonic' coincidences and in the incomprehensible monotony of nature. Modernity's great project of extracting order from nature can thus only be fulfilled on condition that it adopts such an order as the endless

10 S. Freud (1950c), 'Project for a Scientific Psychology', *SE* 1.
11 Freud (1920g), *Beyond the Pleasure Principle*, p. 49.

envelopment of repetition in a vicious circle of self-annihilation. Freud's "hallucinatory vision of primordial times" reflects a view of civilisation as a merely temporarily postponed death; while culture can choose an increasingly complicated 'detour' toward it, the individual organism can be assured that it will "die only in its own fashion".[12] Against that background, and in a desire to rescue the dualism of his drive theory, Freud explores in the sixth chapter, written in late spring 1920, the possibility of understanding the sexual drives through contemporary biology's notion of an unknown force that produced life from inanimate matter. This specific tension thus indicated constitutes, in my view, the very area of tension between Freud and Ferenczi, as it informs their bioanalytical speculation. This unknown force that has given life to inanimate matter causes, for Freud, the same substance to be "torn apart into small pieces".[13] Thus, fragments, split-off parts, conciliatory drives and impulses come to the fore in these speculations. "In response to this fragmentation, the life drives arise that aim to unite the particles into a living cell".[14] In other words, the urge to live seems to emerge spontaneously in response to this fragmentation, persistently progressing "the chemical affinity of inanimate matter",[15] that is, chemical relations forming assemblages of atoms and elements. However, when Ferenczi develops these themes, a new set of notions will be put in play, which will eventually provoke a conflict between him and Freud concerning therapeutic techniques and, by extension, the conditions for a metapsychology. In the following we will view these domains of psychic life, which bioanalytic speculation investigates, from the perspective of this conflict. This can, according to my argument, be outlined through notions that Ferenczi explores in his clinical work, particularly in the form of the figure of an archaic mother aligned with nature threatening the individual with extinction, yet as if by magic capable of summoning conciliatory impulses and powers – a notion woven into his thought, the importance of which we can deduce from his late clinical notes.

12 Ibid., p. 39; Calasso (1994), *The Ruin of Kasch*, pp. 206–207; R.M. Rilke (1966), *Sämtliche Werke, Bd. 6*.

13 Freud (1920g), *Beyond the Pleasure Principle*, p. 58.

14 P. Van Haute & H. Westerink in this volume, p. 186.

15 Freud (1920g), *Beyond the Pleasure Principle*, p. 58.

A conflictual relationship

> The model of repetition is not just the rotation of the stars, but physiology: breathing, sleep, hunger. For Freud, everything bears the mask of death – like the number on the cloakroom ticket he is given.[16]

The genesis of *Beyond the Pleasure Principle* has been shown in the work of Ilse Grubrich-Simitis and Ulrike May to rest on a radical rupture – a sudden caesura during which the work is interrupted for more than a year.[17] This allows Freud's disparate approaches to the elusive subject matter to be understood as separate emerging parts.[18] Its genesis can be understood in a context of the continuous and ultimately increasingly conflictual relationship between Freud and the Hungarian psychoanalyst Sándor Ferenczi, and their joint project involving the notion of a bioanalysis.[19] This project resonates in the form of a dialogue that appears in their correspondence to each other, and can also be traced in their different theoretical presentations. Their relationship, however, constitutes an event which, as a missed encounter, finally took the form of an inevitable catastrophe.[20] Bioanalysis seems to mean for Ferenczi a certain method of transferring psychoanalytic concepts such as "repression, symbol formation and the like" to organic phenomena.[21] When Ferenczi returns to the project in the clinical diary he kept during the last year of his life, essential themes emerge that once constituted the common approach to a bioanalysis; in particular, the question of trauma comes to the fore.[22] Around this key concept cluster sometimes fragmentary statements: notions of overdetermined organs; the presence of dead parts in the psyche; survival in the form of previously unsuspected psychic processes, and so on. It is as if, toward the end of his life, he was collecting disparate traces and entities that did not fit into Freud's speculative essay, yet belong to its core. I would like to argue that here we can sense a radical re-reading of the bioanalytical speculations based on the question of survival; we stumble on a thinking *Beyond the Pleasure Principle.* What we find arches toward a psychoanalytic understanding of an archaic

16 Calasso (1994), *The Ruin of Kasch*, p. 213.
17 Grubrich-Simitis (1993), *Back to Freud's Texts*, pp. 182ff.; H. Westerink & P. Van Haute (2022), *Verleiding, drift en herhaling: Freuds metafysica van de het trauma*, pp. 181–227. See also May in this volume, p. 86.
18 See also Van Haute & Westerink in this volume, pp. 165–196.
19 J. Willner (2020), 'Neurotische Evolution. Bioanalyse als Kulturkritik in Jenseits des Lustprinzips'.
20 J. Staberg (2022), 'Anstatt Sprache: Verwirrung'.
21 S. Ferenczi (2018 [1924]), *Thalassa. A Theory of Genitality*, p. 102.
22 S. Ferenczi (1988), *The Clinical Diary of Sándor Ferenczi*.

mother: life-giving, and yet inseparable from what Freud suggests lies beyond the pleasure principle.

In a final meeting between Ferenczi and Freud, at the latter's summer residence, in 1932, the former insists on presenting his findings, the result of long clinical experience and theoretical work, which Freud sees as contradicting everything he had achieved.[23] Ferenczi reads a paper he is due to deliver at an upcoming conference in Wiesbaden, the content of which is met with suspicion. The text would be published many years later under the title 'Confusions of Tongues between Adults and the Child', and appears today as central in understanding of Ferenczi's later development. Its publication was for political reasons long delayed by Freud's trusted colleague Ernest Jones, Ferenczi's former analysand. For Ferenczi, at this point suffering from a fatal illness unfamiliar to those around him, the confrontation was painful. The aftermath was also to be ugly. After Ferenczi's death, in letters exchanged between Freud and Jones, the image of Ferenczi took shape as someone mentally unstable, indeed, tormented by "degeneration".[24] His work was declared invalid, referring to his illness, which they believed had impaired his mental faculties.

However, recent decades have witnessed a tremendous renaissance and re-evaluation of Ferenczi's work, including his late fragmentary speculations. With his discoveries of phenomena such as introjection, seduction, and the 'psychic fragments' that analytic work can uncover, Ferenczi makes visible the force field of transference. Ferenczi realised early on that the methods of psychoanalysis could in fact renegotiate the techniques of contemporary psychiatry, methods perhaps still resonating within its institutions – such as suggestion and hypnosis, the use of medication and, not least, the authoritarian role of the physician. Psychoanalysis shifted attention toward an encounter between the physician and the patient where symptoms ideally dissolved into meaningful images through the free associations of the talking cure. But this encounter, in Ferenczi's view, also proves to be dangerous, in a sense. Indeed, psychoanalysis has often been described as a dangerous method insofar as it invites a re-enactment of traumatic experience; that is, an uncanny repetition.[25] More pressingly, it possessed a strange continuity with psychiatric power, in withholding a firm sense of the authoritarian role of the doctor, and yet unleashing disturbing psychic forces barely contained within its

23 J. Staberg, 'Instead of language: Confusion. Sigmund Freud / Sándor Ferenczi'.

24 S. Freud & E. Jones (1996), *The Complete Correspondence of Sigmund Freud and Ernest Jones 1908–1939, Vol. 2*, p. 721 (Letter 612 F).

25 S. Ferenczi (1933), 'Confusions of Tongues between Adults and the Child', pp. 156–167.

framework. Following the basic rules and outlines of techniques stipulated by Freud, Ferenczi acknowledged that mental processes are approached through peculiarities that had, up to that point, not been the object of scientific or medical attention – for example, slips of the tongue, wit, momentary forgetfulness and dreams, as it were, harmless things, certain oddities. But at the same time, through these peculiarities, curious events arose once the analytic process stumbled on more disturbing notions: uncanny states of mind; more frightening conditions; reminiscences, perhaps of scenes of a sexual nature, certainly involving notions beyond the life-preserving drives. As a consequence, Ferenczi felt obliged to develop and experiment with the setting itself, calling into question some of the fundamental techniques of psychoanalysis. In Ferenczi's writing, a notion of something beyond the pleasure principle emanates from the psychoanalytic experience itself.

Although these phenomena had long been well known at the psychiatric institutions, at the turn of the last century they were seen as disturbing elements in the treatment of hysteria. This in particular speaks to the patient's resistance to the physician's authority and to the sexual nature of the symptoms, phenomena that, with the genesis of psychoanalysis, became the very core of the treatment. Freud's early case study 'Fragment of an Analysis of a Case of Hysteria' (1905), known for the Dora case, is proof of that. On the basis of this case study, Ferenczi understands the techniques of suggestion and hypnosis as an alien will imposed upon the subject. For him, this is the reason why the mental states the techniques in the therapeutic relation generate evoke traces of previous relations and experienced traumas. In response, Ferenczi developed a certain sensitivity toward hitherto unknown phenomena, unsettling states of mind, such as deep trances or dreamlike experiences, to which the analytic situation seemed to give rise, phenomena that Freud in his 1920 essay struggled to fit into the psychoanalytic discourse.

Based on this, Ferenczi came to a notion of psychic fragments, which would anticipate Melanie Klein's notion of partial objects, but which arguably articulated the phenomena more radically.[26] Ferenczi was unable to disclose to Freud his manner of working, i.e. the techniques that brought these notions to the fore – something that Freud complains about in a letter to his daughter, Anna.[27] However, the *Clinical Diary* Ferenczi kept at the time of their last encounter, and which was unknown to Freud, can now shed some light on the matter.[28] Here he sketches, with certain complex insights, the results of

[26] Soreanu (2018), 'The Psychic Life of Fragments', pp. 421–444.
[27] S. Freud & A. Freud (2006), *Briefwechsel 1904–1938*, 3 September 1932, p. 527.
[28] Ferenczi (1988), *The Clinical Diary*.

his investigations, developing themes that had preoccupied him for decades. Based on these insights, Ferenczi presents in a new way the importance of transference in the psychoanalytic process. The notion of transference is viewed as essentially traumatic, involving a possible reliving of the dead child within the adult. Here, death becomes an ambivalent and unsettling notion constantly present in the psychoanalytic situation. If for Freud the need to explore the existence of something beyond the pleasure principle led him from clinical experiments to biological speculation, Ferenczi came to integrate these speculations into a new and innovative way of experiencing the psychoanalytic situation, opening up for the development of clinical techniques.

Transference

Let us examine the notion of transference a little more before we move further in our argument. The question of transference haunts psychoanalytic theory. The term was used in the early work *Studies of Hysteria*, in which Freud, together with Joseph Breuer, had laid the foundation for a new practice and science.[29] In *The Interpretation of Dreams*, transference still denotes a range of different psychic phenomena.[30] With the first longer case study however, the aforementioned 'Fragment of an Analysis of a Case of Hysteria', which was based on analytical work that dates to 1901, but written in 1905, Freud specifically draws attention to the significance of the phenomenon for the psychoanalytic process, thereby giving the concept a more clearly defined meaning.[31] At this point, transference refers to the productive ability of neurosis to create a specific form of unconscious figures of thought: new formations of affects and fantasies evoked by the analytic situation where the impressions of past persons are transferred to the analyst. The case study, referred to as the Dora case, depicts an interrupted psychoanalytic process where a young female patient's decision to end the analysis is provoked precisely by the inability of the analyst to acknowledge and thereby handle the forces developed through transference. On the basis of this case study, Ferenczi – in his first major contribution to the psychoanalytic literature, the article 'Introjection and Transference' (1909) – treats the phenomenon in a way that highlights the proximity to and the delimitation from the psychiatric techniques and notions

[29] J. Breuer & S. Freud (1895d), *Studies on Hysteria*, *SE* 2.
[30] S. Freud (1900a), *The Interpretations of Dreams*, *SE* 4–5.
[31] S. Freud (1905e), 'Fragment of an Analysis of a Case of Hysteria', *SE* 7.

of the time.[32] The alleged tendency of the hysteric to simulate, to imitate – 'psychic contagion' so frequently observed at the institution and sometimes referred to as hysterical identification – is here ascribed to phenomena that, understood as symbolic means of representation, must in fact be considered to be results of the effect of transference. Michel Foucault has, in his lectures on psychiatric power, analysed hysteria on the basis of this simulation as a phenomenon conditioned by the psychiatric institution and the authority of the doctor.[33] The question of the doctor's authority would as it were become a crucial point in the conflict between Freud and Ferenczi.

Toward the end of his life, Ferenczi returned to and developed these themes in the clinical diary he kept, resignedly formulating his view of Freud's observation of the authority of the psychoanalyst protected by the allegedly *neutral* attitude prescribed by technical writings. These notes – long viewed as utter madness – today open up new fields for thinking about the therapeutic settings, not least foregrounding the experience of the child. Thus, experiencing the overwhelming power that emerges from within the analytic situation, when feeling lost in helplessness, Ferenczi reaches beyond individuals simply occupying the positions of doctor and patient, rather letting themselves be receptive toward strange phenomena, such as the particular idea of a presence of a 'guardian angel'.[34] Ferenczi, either unafraid of or protecting himself from the feeling of helplessness, uses such an idea as a tool with an almost magical quality. I believe the insights achieved through the guidance of transference phenomena establish a way of thinking about psychoanalysis beyond the notion of the pleasure principle. In an illuminating entry in his diary, from 1 May 1932, this theme is introduced under the headline: "Who is crazy, we or the patients? (the children or the adults)." Here we encounter Ferenczi going against what he saw in Freud as a tendency "to cling too strong to theory". He writes: "[Freud] must have been first shaken and disenchanted, however, by certain experiences, rather like Breuer when his patient had a relapse and when the problem of countertransference opened up before him like an abyss".[35] Ferenczi proposes a quite different approach: "yielding to Orpha's proposal, I tried to allow myself to be analyzed by the patient", which means "to place myself in the patient's power". Thus, to acknowledge this terrifying power means also confronting a patient who is "unconscious of his own malicious

32 S. Ferenczi (1909), 'Introjection and Transference'.
33 M. Foucault (2006), *Psychiatric Power: lectures at the Collège de France*, 1973–1974, pp. 133–139, 304, 322f.
34 Ferenczi (1988), *The Clinical Diary*, p. 9.
35 Ibid., p. 92.

impulses", who may well "abuse this situation".[36] In the following we will deepen this understanding of what Ferenczi calls 'Orpha', a fragment of the psychic activity acting as this protective angel. For now, though, we note that while Ferenczi puts himself at risk in his practice, he also takes a leap beyond theoretical orthodoxy, casting him beyond established norms.

Clinical Diary

What was really at stake concerning therapeutic technique in the conflict raised between Freud and Ferenczi? In a letter dated 25 December 1929, Ferenczi summarises the theoretical disagreement as a result of an "overestimation of the imagination" and an "underestimation of traumatic reality" in Freud's thinking.[37] The insights to which the clinical diary testifies have consequences for clinical techniques: here Ferenczi returns to the necessity of opposing rigid standards of work. Instead, according to Ferenczi, psychoanalysis always has as its aim a "dismantling of the father image".[38] Ferenczi developed certain aspects of trauma hinted at in Freud's *Beyond the Pleasure Principle*, on the basis of his clinical experience. A crucial example is the understanding of nature as an excessive threat, which leads Freud to recognise that by necessity dead parts exist within the living organism. Indeed, to save itself from the rampant spread of nature, the psychic apparatus even kills a part of itself to create within it an insensitive 'protective shield', a last defence against the murderous fury of external nature. This 'protective shield' is the "outer layer" of the apparatus itself, which consents to die, becoming to "some degree inorganic" in order to save "all the deeper [layers] from a similar fate".[39] By investigating how parts of the individual appear to be split off – even dead – Ferenczi is led further toward a way of thinking based on such fragments. He wants to explore "a state which – continuing the picture of fragmentation – one would be justified in calling atomization", going on to note that "one must possess a great deal of optimism not to lose courage when facing such a state".[40] Ferenczi thus develops a certain attention toward phenomena, a sensitivity,

---

36 Ibid.

37 S. Freud & S. Ferenczi (1993–2000), *The Correspondence of Sigmund Freud and Sándor Ferenczi Correspondence, Vol. 3*, p. 376 (Letter 1173 Fer).

38 Ibid., *Vol. 1*, p. 417 (Letter 331 Fer). On the case studies as a "re-interpretation of masculinity at the dawn of personal life", emphasising "male vulnerability in the age of mechanisation", see E. Zaretsky (2005), *Secrets of the Soul: A Social and Cultural History of Psychoanalysis*, p. 57.

39 Calasso (1994), *The Ruin of Kasch*, p. 214.

40 S. Ferenczi (1933), 'Confusion of Tongues', p. 165.

perhaps, that makes him perceptive to the presence of these fragments or images of mental states in the analytic work. The clinical diary testifies to this work, while the results are outlined in the 'Confusion of Tongues' article he insisted on reading to Freud during that last meeting, in the summer of 1932. As we have seen, when trauma becomes crucial for understanding transference, repetition comes into play. In the article, he takes as his point of departure "the almost hallucinatory repetitions of traumatic experiences which have begun to accumulate in my practice."[41] This finding enforces a new understanding of what transference contains. Ferenczi now realises that the analyst "invited the patient to a reproduction of the trauma within the frames of an analytic situation".[42] Only by recognising and admitting how "docile patients secretly experienced impulses of hatred and anger" directed at him in his capacity as analyst, and thus "explore repressed or suppressed criticism of us", can the effect of the trauma be revealed.[43] The possible recognition of the patient's dislike of the analyst makes a crucial difference. Indeed, if the repetition of the trauma is forced by the analytical encounter, "the contrast between the present and the unbearable, traumatogenic past" has to crystallise.[44]

In the clinical diary he kept during the last year of his life, Ferenczi sought to reconsider certain theoretical foundations central to psychoanalysis, documenting his clinical exploration of the psychoanalytic method toward a new understanding of the phenomenon of transference. As mentioned, the diary remained a secret for a long time, and once it was published after some resistance, it came to be regarded within the established psychoanalytic milieu as the work of a questionable figure. It is only in recent years that his findings have become the subject of serious interpretive interest.[45] The article Ferenczi insisted on reading at that last meeting with Freud, 'Confusions of Tongues', has certainly long since received some acknowledgement,[46] but in relation to the main corpus of psychoanalytic literature, it stills awaits full recognition.

41 Ibid., p. 156.
42 Ibid., pp. 157f.
43 Ibid.
44 Ibid., p. 160.
45 L. Aron & A. Harris (1993), *The Legacy of Sándor Ferenczi*; P.L. Rudnitzky, A. Bókay & P. Giampieri-Deutsch (1996), *Ferenczi's Turn in Psychoanalysis*. T. Keve and J. Szekacs-Weisz edited two further volumes: *Ferenczi and His World: Rekindling the Spirit of the Budapest School*, 2012 and *Ferenczi for Our Time: Theory and Practice*, 2012. In 2015, Harris and Kuchuck published the Routledge anthology *The Legacy of Sándor Ferenczi: From Ghost to Ancestor*. The most recent extensive anthology on Ferenczi is A. Dimitrijević, G. Cassullo & J. Frankel (2018), *Ferenczi's Influence on Contemporary Psychoanalytic Traditions. Lines of Development. Evolution of Theory and Practice over Decades.*
46 M. Bálint (1968), 'The Disagreement Between Freud and Ferenczi and Its Repercussions', pp. 149–158; A. Haynal & J.E. King, *Controversies in Psychoanalytic Method. From Freud and Ferenczi to Michael Bálint.*

The clinical diary thus deepens our understanding of phenomena that had preoccupied Ferenczi throughout his life-long practice. Suggestion, seduction and trauma are recurring motifs explored here through the ability, cultivated in his own clinical work, to listen to the child – the child dormant in the unconscious of the adult – whose voice is inaccessible to the waking self, except in certain dreamlike states. The psychoanalytic experience that Ferenczi unearths thus reveals a *fragmented* individuality. His work will increasingly focus on the ability of the psychoanalytic situation to recall split-off parts of the self, or, as he writes in a late diary entry, "ashes of earlier mental sufferings".[47] Not until much later, after years of negotiations with Freud's daughter Anna, who finally approved its publication, would the diary be published and translated into English, which in the years after the war had become the dominant language of the international psychoanalytic movement. Thus, a documentation of Ferenczi's therapeutic 'experiments' – which, according to Freud's polemical statement in 'Analysis Terminable and Interminable' (1937), did not result in anything[48] – was eventually made available. Together with the correspondence, the clinical diary provides an important source of understanding of the conflict areas between the two men, between whom a driving tension in the praxis of psychoanalysis can be discerned. It is this tension that has been the starting point for the present reflections, and I have sought so far to approach the project of bioanalysis manifested in *Beyond the Pleasure Principle* as re-read in Ferenczi's late work, based on the last encounter between Ferenczi and Freud, contemplated in light of the long-lasting relationship that developed between them. I will now seek to deepen this analysis by offering a close reading of some entries from the *Clinical Diary.*

Through the diary it is possible to follow, at least fragmentarily, a number of psychoanalytic processes Ferenczi records in it. Some of these fragments are also drafts of what would become the article 'Confusion of Tongues'. We get to read first-hand about his experimental attitude, especially regarding the psychoanalytical method; it is important to underline how this is, so to speak, inscribed on the body itself. The diary notes follow what happens in the therapeutic encounter, wherein Ferenczi reads his own reactions symptomatically. He makes himself very much the sensitive instrument of which Freud spoke in his technical writings. We notice his desire to achieve what he considered a relaxed stance in the encounter, one mirroring the relationship between child and adult. It is, however, only when he gives up –

47 Ferenczi (1988), *The Clinical Diary*, p. 10.
48 S. Freud (1937c), 'Analysis Terminable and Interminable', *SE* 23, p. 230.

something that naturally shocked the psychoanalytic establishment and the circle around Freud – the supposed 'superiority' of the psychoanalyst that he can lead the analysis toward a notion of mutuality. Ferenczi is here quite open about acknowledging the feelings of discomfort that his submission to the analysand admits, feelings the diary notes in the form of "symptoms: headache, sleep disturbances; the feeling of fatigue and sleepiness during analytic sessions, also during lengthy theatre performances".[49]

Forces active in analysis thus become discernible on many levels, and from the standpoint that Ferenczi takes up, his exploration of the analytical approach will lead him into unknown territories. Ferenczi's investigations of what he calls the mutual approach to analysis – first by giving up "temporarily, the role of 'watchman'" – unleashes psychic forces. Certainly the observation about a time when the analysand was allowed, so to speak, to take over the analytic position has contributed within the psychoanalytic world to the image of Ferenczi's experiment as the work of a 'degenerate' man, with reference to Freud's correspondence and Jones's smear in his biography. A more sober reading would suggest that Ferenczi here opens analytic work up to the "dialogue of unconsciousness",[50] something Freud also recognised in his technical writings as the most valuable level of the analytic process, albeit that Ferenczi's exploration of Freud's approaches in fact implies a hitherto unattained "manifestation of receptivity".[51]

In Ferenczi's writings, the notion of repetition demonically emerges: "The ill will of an insane person can transcend time and space as well, and persecute one even in one's dreams", thus disturbing sleep, "annihilating potency", even "destroy[ing] one demonically". In other words, what he exposes himself to helps him to reach the dramatic conclusion in the form of an imperative question: "why then should he, the patient, place himself blindly in the power of the doctor?" The investigation forces him to rethink the analytic setting and its power-relations beyond the pleasure principle. Insofar as transference can be understood as being fostered by a certain matrix, understood as a parent–child relationship, then the therapeutic method is at risk of becoming increasingly repressive: "the poor patient, reduced to the status of a mere child [...] as transference is artificially provoked by this kind of behavior".[52] Ferenczi's questions and proposals threaten the Freudian concepts of the doctor's position in the psychoanalytic relation in a way the psychoanalytic

[49] Ferenczi (1988), *The Clinical Diary*, p. 73.
[50] Ibid., p. 84.
[51] Ibid., p. 85.
[52] Ibid., p. 93.

establishment could not accept. Along these lines, his criticism of Freud's alleged neutrality becomes severe:

> [I]f the doctor does not watch himself he will remain longer than necessary in this situation, comfortable for him, in which, his patients spare him the unpleasure of self-criticism and give him the opportunity to enjoy his superiority, and to be loved without any reciprocity (a situation of almost infantile grandeur).[53]

Thus: "A patient is quite justified in describing part of the behavior of such an analyst as crazy". Ferenczi seeks instead a psychoanalyst "sobered from scientific delusion", an analyst allowing a "sinking back to the traumatic past, and from this a recovery can be expected that will be definitive, spontaneous, and no longer based on authority".[54] This traumatic past seems to touch on how Calasso identifies that the "dark vision of the repetition-compulsion spring[s] from a single source: a terror at the nonhuman origin of meaning, expressed in the demonic whim of coincidences and in the relentless monotony of nature" that we find in Freud's *Beyond the Pleasure Principle*.[55]

Psychic fragments

Ferenczi never systematised his metapsychology oriented around psychic fragments, rather he conjures, in a way that is unique to psychoanalysis, a theory of catastrophe. Ferenczi's exploration of psychic fragments suggests a new map of the mental landscape that goes beyond Freud's model of the self, the id and the superego. The forms of splitting Ferenczi discovered in his clinical practice suggest a revision of metapsychology. In a number of articles Raluca Soreanu has provided psychoanalytic theory with a mapping of these mental spaces in an attempt at offering a metapsychology of fragments. To this end, she is engaged in a mapping of the 'new' types of psychic fragments Ferenczi uncovers, where in particular the aforementioned Orpha fragment, understood as a female Orpheus oscillating between the urges of life and death, plays a crucial role in turning attention to the forces or forms that help an individual to survive. She writes: "Ferenczi was much more curious about how subjects survive, in fragments, through the action of intrapsychic

53 Ibid., pp. 93–94.
54 Ibid., p. 94.
55 Calasso (1994), *The Ruin of Kasch*, p. 206.

forces, rather than how they are held together by the environment".[56] This helps direct our tentative investigation into how, internal to Ferenczi's world of thought, we find an ongoing re-reading of *Beyond the Pleasure Principle*.

It is possible to trace a line from Ferenczi's thinking in terms of atomisation and fragments to Melanie Klein's concept of partial objects. Soreanu crystallises Ferenczi's work in contrast to Klein's notion of the good and the bad breast. "Psychic life", according to Ferenczi, "is from the onset based on *qualities*, and not on sheer polarities".[57] Ferenczi's observations open a different mental landscape: "We can certainly be frustrated or satisfied, by the object or in the imagination, but the question of importance that should be formulated is: 'in which particular way does frustration/satisfaction occur?'".[58] Posing the question in this way points to an 'eventful' form of splitting that leaves more stable fragments as its traces. The analysis goes beyond Klein's detailed depiction of a first type of splitting, performed by the self in relation to the object and resulting in the polarity of the bad and the good object. In Soreanu's view, Ferenczi explores the forms of change or transformation that take place through the body, even within organs themselves. We are at the heart of bioanalysis. Instead of considering binary couples of good and bad, Ferenczi in his *Clinical Diary* invites an exploration of qualities. He conceives an investigation into a new kind of splitting within psychic life, which is at once stable and potentially irreversible. Suddenly, new areas of the unconscious can be uncovered, populated by terrifying fragments, beyond or untouched by the development of the self and with the capacity to overwhelm it. It is an integrated psychic life of fragments, split off from the self and the superego. Thinking such a life of fragments is a thinking beyond the pleasure principle.

The receptivity Ferenczi approaches reveals phenomena that cut through and go beyond the hitherto constructed theoretical models and dogmas. Beyond the abandonment of control, beyond the strict observance of a supposedly neutral analytic subject – but also beyond his own notion of a possible reciprocal analysis – Ferenczi, confronted with his own helplessness in the role of analyst, as a subject in the encounter with the other, discovers the presence of surprising forces and energies. Not unlike how Freud once allowed himself to be guided by his 'hysterics' in his exploration of the field of the unconscious, Ferenczi accounts for processes in which analytic work is confronted with unexpected forces: "Under the pressure of helplessness, the patient split off fragments of intelligence to give me directions about how

56 Soreanu (2018), 'The Psychic Life of Fragments', p. 426.
57 Ibid., p. 430.
58 Ibid.

and what I should do or should have done at that particular moment".[59] The discovery of this life of psychic fragments is perhaps the most important innovation Ferenczi leaves as his legacy. The most central, as mentioned, he calls 'Orpha,' a kind of female Orpheus, who takes the form of a guardian angel.[60] An angel, as it were, that we can think of not unlike Rilke's confrontation with the immense, or the angel, deeply enmeshed in Jewish mysticism, with which Walter Benjamin was confronted in an image by Paul Klee, and which played such a role for his thinking, *Angelus Novus*.[61]

Bioanalysis and the *Beyond the Pleasure Principle* project stumble on the limits of psychoanalysis. What occurred to Freud relatively early was the possibility that psychoanalysis as a technique and a science might one day be abolished in favour of the ability of a scientifically based practice capable of acting directly on perception and cognition by chemical means, thus doing away with the unconscious as an interpretive construct. Its clearest manifestation can be found in the posthumously published outline for a scientific psychology.[62] This was an idea he never gave up on. For several years, however, the interface was brought to life in an equally speculative project, sometimes presented as a joke, sometimes as a radical reassessment of values: the invention of bioanalysis. The project dwells as a secret correspondence between Freud and his younger colleague and is fundamental to the text that still appears like a 'foreign body' within psychoanalytic theory: *Beyond the Pleasure Principle*. In the work of Ferenczi, biology and psychoanalysis form a floating amalgam. This does not suggest that he sought some sort of ground for psychoanalysis in biology or in the natural sciences – quite the contrary. As Jenny Willner writes in a recent study:

> Freud's and Ferenczi's engagement with 19th century biology has often been read as an attempt to provide psychoanalysis with a natural scientific foundation. However, at a closer look, Ferenczi's genital theory deconstructs precisely what claims such a founding status: He reads his sources against the grain.[63]

---

59 Ferenczi (1988), *The Clinical Diary*, p. 85.

60 Soreanu (2018), 'The Psychic Life in Fragments'.

61 R.M. Rilke, *Duino Elegies*, p. 8–13; W. Benjamin (1972), 'Agesilaus Santander, p. 57–59; Scholem (1972), 'Walter Benjamin and his Angel'; G. Scholem (1965), *On the Kabbalah and Its Symboliosm*; Buci-Glucksmann (1994), *Baroque Reason*, pp. 82–89.

62 Freud (1950c), 'Project for a Scientific Psychology'.

63 J. Staberg (2023), 'Reading against the Grain: On How Organs Crave Interpretation', p. 131; Willner (2020), 'Neurotische Evolution'; Willner (2023), 'Catastrophes and Genitality: Ferenczi's *Thalassa* and the Politics of Bioanalysis', p. 114.

When it comes to the place of biology in Ferenczi's project, the relationship can thus be turned around. Contrary to previous notions, recent studies show that his 'bioanalysis' does not seek a basis or find justification in bio-politics rooted in the natural sciences. In fact, he directs the tools of psychoanalysis against contemporary discourses on biological processes themselves. In *Thalassa*, Ferenczi delivers the most elaborate reflection on the method in question. He defines bioanalysis as a speculative science that would "carry over into the field of the natural sciences in a systematic manner the knowledge gained and the technique used by psychoanalysis".[64] Ferenczi's speculative manoeuvres now appear to be precisely effective deconstructions of a world of imagination, according to which developmental optimism and the idealisation of progress understood as biological necessity could nurture an aggressive nationalism as well as affirm the interpretive primacy of natural science. Ferenczi's series of catastrophes, the notice of shock, convulsion and ubiquitous trauma, replace the slogan 'wonders of nature', which was seminal both for Haeckel's reception of Darwin and for Bölsche's narrative.[65] Following Willner's analysis, it is possible to dismantle the supposed notion within the psychoanalytic milieu that Ferenczi's critique of Freud could be undermined by reducing his thought to the product of a certain biologism. Willner has shown how Ferenczi's psychoanalytic work contains speculative models in which Freud's world of thought, especially thoughts oriented around the notion of the death drive, is at once challenged and taken to its extreme, as a re-evaluation of all values.

This analysis invites a plurality of images and landscapes; in particular, Ferenczi's work invites possible ways of thinking about catastrophes and transformations. *Thalassa*, one could say, echoes shipwrecks, losses, transitions between oceans and land, sudden openings of biological possibilities. Reading Ferenczi's work in such a way takes the themes established with *Beyond the Pleasure Principle* onto multiple paths, engaging new understandings that perhaps resonate with the looming catastrophes of our time, and the challenges we are facing. It could be said, with Soreanu, that Ferenczi's concepts of catastrophe, trauma and event constitute a vocabulary for making sense of an "eventfulness of our time".[66] Psychoanalytic thinking thus becomes eventful, in this sense, since it revolves around the question: 'What does it mean to have survived a psychic catastrophe?' Thus, imagining the catastrophe not as a singular, unitary event, but as a *scene* where qualitative forces are held

---

64 Ibid.; S. Ferenczi (2018), *Thalassa*, p. 82.
65 Staberg (2023), 'Reading Against the Grain', p. 133.
66 R. Soreanu (2023), 'Catastrophe and the Creativity of Fragments: Toward a Phenomenology of the Scene of Trauma', p. 148.

together, the whole world of fragments becomes intense, vibrating with particular elements of becoming.

Referring to a lived experience resonates with aesthetics, in the way it can shape our understanding of the psychoanalytical situation. In Soreanu's words, what had hitherto constituted a phenomenological gap in the understanding of psychic fragments, is now being addressed in recent research, opening up a new understanding of the field, for which both Ferenczi and Melanie Klein paved the way: "The images that predominate here are those of fractures, splits, atomisations, pulverisations, leakages, detritus, but also new formations, protective membranes, expansions, contagions, and inner growths".[67] We find ourselves brought into strange environments and mental states, landscapes of cut-off parts, of fragments. With the help of Ferenczi we can experience forms of psychic life that go beyond ego, even beyond consciousness, perhaps emanating from the organs themselves. It is against this background that I have viewed Ferenczi's re-reading of *Beyond the Pleasure Principle*.

Thinking organs

Ferenczi's analysis is prompted by certain questions. What does it mean to think the psychic life of a fragment? How should we understand its forces? What in this sense are organs, and most of all, what do they do? What are they capable of? With the death drive, Freud establishes processes of fragmentation that Ferenczi takes further. We have moved from the neat binary coupling of the good and bad of the world of partial objects to something that at first seems strange and perhaps uncanny. Ferenczi forces us through his elaborate reading of the psychoanalytic situation to deepen the concept that Freud in his writing developed regarding unconscious processes. Such a view contributes to the renewed interest in Ferenczi we have seen over the last few decades, and that insists on rethinking the psychoanalytic environment and its theoretical apparatus. While this comes close to a certain genealogical method, such an analysis of metapsychology must always be rooted in a strong insight extracted from the clinical work of Ferenczi. Thus, his *Clinical Diary* shows how closely Ferenczi's thoughts about metapsychology are related to his work with patients, always following leads from them. We experience it in the whole process of mutual analysis, in his way of scrutinising himself, constantly exploring the possibilities and failures of the psychoanalytical situation.

[67] Ibid., p. 145.

Returning to our initial question: is there a radical rethinking of *Beyond the Pleasure Principle* in the work of Ferenczi and how does it support a certain theory of catastrophe and survival? *Beyond the Pleasure Principle* brings us below the Acheron, which Freud in his *Interpretation of Dreams* had promised to obscure. In Calasso's words we enter "the region of blind germinations, the vast inorganic silence that is sometimes broken by improbable life", and indeed Ferenczi beguiles us to stay in "this fathomless place, well 'beyond the pleasure principle'".[68] "Ferenczi", according to Soreanu, "discusses these primal substrates in the first pages of his *Clinical Diary*, pointing to a process when different organs or body parts produce effects of thinking".[69] All along there is this agonising concern: what is this *stuff* that constitutes psychic life? Leading us through this complex field, Ferenczi underlines the importance of discovering this psychic stuff as it appears in registers, in different and separate languages, in different modes of arranging things and objects, parts and connections. In my view it not only brings us back to thinking fragments, but involves creating entanglements, linkages, assemblages.

In his late work, Ferenczi reports the results of his explorations of the psychoanalytic situation in general, and transference in particular – what he calls autoplastic reaction patterns.[70] That shock or horror – phenomena which bear traces of a split in personality – can produce a regression to an event-state that, he argues, is at the same time strange and familiar. When his patients confront him with death and anxiety, Ferenczi experiences a "sudden, surprising rise of new faculties after a trauma, like a miracle that occurs upon the wave of a magic wand".[71] Trauma and its effects exist virtually like an ancestor and can develop a kind of "coming ability" through "the pressure of traumatic necessity".[72] For Ferenczi, the fact that shock can help the maturation of a part of the personality is not limited to the cases he worked with in the psychoanalytic situation, although these invariably opened his eye to phenomena he describes as, for instance, a "precocious maturation" or traumatic progression, through which the whole emotional register of a full-grown person is produced.[73] Ferenczi is thinking in "register",[74] acknowledging the will and ability to survive. If this will has the strength to create changes,

---

68 Calasso (1994), *The Ruin of Kasch*, p. 202.

69 Soreanu (2023), 'Catastrophe and the Creativity of Fragments', p. 165; Ferenczi (1988), *Clinical Diary*, p. 6.

70 Ferenczi (1988), *The Clinical Diary*.

71 Ferenczi (1933), 'Confusion of Tongues', p. 164.

72 Ibid. See also E. Glissant (1997), *Poetics of Relation*, pp. 8–9.

73 Ferenczi (1933), 'Confusion of Tongues', p. 165.

74 Soreanu (2023), 'Catastrophe and the Creativity of Fragments', p. 146.

then metapsychology seems, in light of the death drive, to be cast in a new way.

Thinking Beyond the Pleasure Principle

> [W]hile Freud argues that the erection provides an opportunity to analyse hysteric reactions in women, Ferenczi treats the erection itself as a hysterical phenomenon, the example *par excellence* of hysteria understood as psychosomatic conversion.[75]

The body's capability of transformation and survival as a response to an overwhelming experience is a guiding principle in Ferenczi's writing. The clinical diary explores, for example, neoformations in the self from fragmented parts.

> 'Concussion', reaction to an 'unbearable' external or internal stimulus in an autoplastic manner (modifying the self) instead of an allo-plastic manner (modifying the stimulus). A neoformation of the self is impossible without the previous destruction, either partial or total, or dissolution of the former self. A new ego cannot be formed directly from the previous ego, but from fragments, more or less elementary products of its disintegration. (splitting, atomization.)[76]

In Ferenczi, a manifestation of forces is present, informing a new way to think about bodily organs. Such a manifestation allows us to see how Ferenczi connects to a certain art of interpretation, where, by activating such Freudian notions as overdetermination and deferred action, the body, organs and organisms themselves are approached, whereby the transformations intersecting them can now be articulated. Resonating here with Deleuze, we can note how "consciousness is essentially reactive; this is why we do not know what a body can do, or what activity it is capable of".[77] I would like to argue that, following the intricate way that Ferenczi opens up for thinking about bodily

---

75 Willner (2023), 'Catastrophes and Genitality', p. 114–115 (on Ferenczi's *Thalassa* and Freud (1905e), 'Fragment of an Analysis of a Case of Hysteria', p. 32).

76 Ferenczi (1988), *The Clinical Diary*, p. 181.

77 G. Deleuze (1983), *Nietzsche and Philosophy*, p. 41.

organs, hysterical fits of the body, we are led to a specific art of interpretation. As Willner argues, "Ferenczi stresses that there is no neutral, transparent language that can represent the organic [...] Ferenczian organs do not come clear, but demand interpretation".[78] This involves a radical reassessment in which what were thought of as so-called active forces are revealed as reactive, and where evolution itself, i.e. development, must suddenly be understood as effects of catastrophes producing trauma. Understanding bodies, psychic life, microscopic processes in this way involves the recognition of changes, mutations and, indeed, the play of chance and coincidences. What appear to be stable entities, products of a given evolution, appear as neurotic responses to chaotic, unknowable events imbued with the hidden Darwinian insight, namely *complete extinction* as an ever-forming principle. Here, the death drive is at hand.[79]

At the core of the matter we encounter a psychoanalyst who looks at his material, at the metamorphoses and tensions created within the psychoanalytic situation, with a certain astonishment. With this in mind I shall pursue some final reflections on the presence of *Beyond the Pleasure Principle* in Ferenczi's late writing.

The possibilities I would like to sketch concern not only Ferenczi's re-evaluation of the contemporary popular science idealisation of violence and progress, but his relationship to Freud, and in particular the restructuring of the death drive he outlines toward the end of his life. If *Beyond the Pleasure Principle* constitutes an alien body in metapsychology that subsequent psychoanalytic theory has sought either to incorporate or displace, it is important for us to see how it operates, so to speak, in the very thinking that Ferenczi's work invites us to follow. The death drive haunts Ferenczi's theoretical and clinical models right up to the crucial articles written during the last few years of his life, and the clinical diary he kept. These discursive elements can be used to suggest the outlines of a potential discourse within psychoanalytic metapsychology, a thinking yet to be realised. In other words, the question concerns how the impact of this alien body can be read in Ferenczi's work – perhaps in particular the later texts – in a way that, I suggest, borders on something *untimely*, in Nietzsche's sense of the word. By following the reformulations and displacements of the death drive and its effects that the clinical diary in particular makes possible, I would argue that we can still discern new layers in Ferenczi's intellectual and clinical legacy. Ferenczi's thinking about bodies,

78 Willner (2023), 'Catastrophes and Genitality: Ferenczi's *Thalassa* and the Politics of Bioanalysis', p. 112; S. Ferenczi (2018), *Thalassa*, p. 34.
79 See Willner's contribution to this volume, p. 241.

organs and active forces invite new readings of how the death drive works as an alien body in the psychoanalytic corpus, itself the object of unimagined transformations. In this sense a reassessment of Ferenczi's relation to biology opens up certain trajectories in which questions of body, organs and thought can be raised.

On 21 and 23 February 1932, Ferenczi makes some interesting remarks that may function as a conclusion to the argument I have sought to make on how Ferenczi's work might imply a thinking beyond the pleasure principle. The context is the analytical task of working with traumatised patients in whom parts of the self have been split off, and where the analytical approach is, in Ferenczi's words, to "remove this split". The reasoning concerns the exploration of how "a destructive process results in productivity".[80] In this way, as we have noted, a mental landscape is uncovered. The aim of psychoanalytic work is described by Ferenczi as a method 'to revive tactfully yet energetically the 'ghost'.'[81] In other words, the psychoanalytic process strives 'slowly to persuade the dead or split-off fragment that it is not dead after all'.[82] In this way, the project revolves around issues of death and survival, exploring psychic life in the form of encrypted fragments, ghosts, haunting dead parts but also the capacity for life within these processes. The note made on 23 February develops this notion, and deals subsequently with processes of awakening and 'transformation' that are explored in greater depth.[83] As so often in Ferenczi's clinical diary, we notice how the analysis follows "a conscious lead by the patient". Here he states how, temporarily, certain 'principles' embodied in nature crystallise, which he designates on the basis of differences, and for this reason may be analysed qualitatively. What is at stake here can be related to the death drive, specifically how something in "the female organism" can be contrasted with "the egoism and self-assertion of the male".[84] This leads the analysis to a re-evaluation of forces, as well as to a modification of the notion of the death drive.

> Ferenczi interprets the forces at stake as an expression of a 'maternal willingness to suffer and capacity for suffering'. Ferenczi's mode of interpretation grasps organs qualitatively as forces: Whenever a force or substance has been 'subjected' to the changing, modifying, destructive influence of another force [...] one must also reckon equally with the

80 Ferenczi (1988), *The Clinical Diary*, p. 42.
81 S. Ferenczi & J. Dupont (1988), *The Clinical Diary of Sándor Ferenczi*, p. 39.
82 Ibid., p. 39f.
83 Ibid., p. 41.
84 Ibid.

> influence of the feminine principle, which we must assume to exist as a potential everywhere.[85]

What Ferenczi's argument amounts to is a new way of thinking the models that Freud elaborated in *Beyond the Pleasure Principle*: "All this would represent only a slight modification of Freud's assumption of life and death instincts. I would give the same thing other names".[86] Ferenczi here presents a haunting insight that connects the death drive with the perception of an archaic mother. 'Egoism is the impulse to rid oneself of a quantity of unpleasure-producing tension at all costs'.[87] Against this ability stands the feminine principle, which can seem frightening and overwhelming to the individual. "Death=feminine, mother".[88] Against the background of the death drive, the forces Ferenczi explores and associates with a feminine principle function as a capacity for life, bordering on death at the same time as they acknowledges life beyond the individual: "Conciliatory drives and impulses are mobilized from everywhere and summoned as if by magic: just as in human society the feminine principle clusters in the strongly masculine principle".[89] The prime example Ferenczi gives is the maternal function understood as "a toleration of parasitic beings, which develop a completely egoistic manner at the expense of the mother's own body".[90] Perhaps it is in light of this capacity that his conception of masculinity as a hysterical fit should be understood: "That masculinity only takes its place for traumatic reasons (primal scene), as a hysteric symptom".[91] An exploration of Ferenczi's reading against the grain leads us to the brink of an understanding of the re-evaluation of the theory of the death drive encapsulated in the late notes on the *Beyond the Pleasure Principle.* In contrast to the assumption that Ferenczi turns to biology in search of a scientific foundation, he instead directs the tools of the psychoanalytic method against orthodoxy. What results is a new way of thinking trauma and catastrophe, deriving from an interpretation of organs as charged with meaning.

85 Ibid.
86 Ibid.
87 Ibid., p. 42.
88 Ibid., p. 183.
89 Ibid., p. 42.
90 Ibid., p. 42.
91 Ibid., p. 188.

Bibliography

Aron, Lewis & Harris, Adrienne (eds.) (1993), *The Legacy of Sándor Ferenczi*. London: The Analytic Press.

Bálint, Michael (1968), 'The Disagreement Between Freud and Ferenczi and Its Repercussions', in: *The Basic Fault. Therapeutic Aspects of Regression*. London: Tavistock, pp. 149–158.

Benjamin, Walter (1939), 'Über einige Motive bei Baudelaire', in: *Selected Writings, Vol. 4: 1938–1940*, ed. Howard Eiland & Michael W. Jennings. Cambridge (MA): Harvard UP, 1996–2003, pp. 313–355.

Benjamin, Walter (1976), 'Agesilaus Santander', transl. Werner J. Dannhauser, in: Gershom Scholem, *On Jews and Judaism in Crisis*. New York: Schocken, pp. 204–208.

Breuer, Josef & Freud, Sigmund (1895d), *Studies on Hysteria*, in: *Standard Edition of the Complete Psychological Works of Sigmund Freud, Vol. 2*, transl. James Strachey. London: Hogarth Press, 1953–1974.

Buci-Glucksmann, Christine (1994), *Baroque Reason: The Aesthetics of Modernity*. London: Sage.

Calasso, Roberto (1994), *The Ruin of Kasch*. Cambridge (MA): Belknap Press of Harvard UP.

Deleuze, Gilles (1983), *Nietzsche and Philosophy*. London: Athlone Press.

Dimitrijević, Aleksandar, Cassullo, Gabriele & Frankel, Jay (eds.) (2018), *Ferenczi's Influence on Contemporary Psychoanalytic Traditions. Lines of Development. Evolution of Theory and Practice over Decades*, London & New York: Routledge.

Ferenczi, Sándor (1955 [1933]), 'Confusions of Tongues between Adults and the Child', in: *Final Contributions to the Problems & Methods of Psycho-Analysis*, ed. Michael Balint, transl. Eric Mosbacher. London: The Hogarth Press, pp. 156–167.

Ferenczi, Sándor (1988), *The Clinical Diary of Sándor Ferenczi*, ed. Judith Dupont. Cambridge (MA): Harvard UP.

Ferenczi, Sándor (2018 [1924]), *Thalassa. A Theory of Genitality*. London & New York: Routledge.

Foucault, Michel (2006), *Psychiatric Power: Lectures at the Collège de France, 1973–1974*, ed. Jacques Lagrange, transl. Graham Burchell. Basingstoke: Palgrave.

Freud, Sigmund (1900a), *The Interpretations of Dreams*, in: *Standard Edition of the Complete Psychological Works of Sigmund Freud, Vol. 4–5*, transl. James Strachey. London: Hogarth Press, 1953–1974.

Freud, Sigmund (1905e), 'Fragment of an Analysis of a Case of Hysteria', *SE* 7, pp. 15–122.

Freud, Sigmund (1920g), *Beyond the Pleasure Principle*, *SE* 18, pp. 7–64.

Freud, Sigmund (1937c), 'Analysis Terminable and Interminable', *SE* 23, pp. 216–253.

Freud, Sigmund (1950c), 'Project for a Scientific Psychology', *SE* 1, pp. 295–397.

Freud, Sigmund & Freud, Anna (2006), *Briefwechsel 1904–1938*, ed. Ingeborg Meyer-Palmedo. Frankfurt a.M.: Fischer.

Freud, Sigmund & Ferenczi, Sándor (1993–2000), *The Correspondence of Sigmund Freud and Sándor Ferenczi, Vol. 1–3*. Cambridge (MA): The Belknap Press of Harvard UP.

Freud, Sigmund & Jones, Ernest (1993), *The Complete Correspondence of Sigmund Freud and Ernest Jones 1908–1939*, ed. R. Andrew Paskauskas. Cambridge (MA): The Belknap Press of Harvard UP.

Glissant, Edouard (1997), *Poetics of Relation*. Ann Arbor: University of Michigan Press.

Grubrich-Simitis, Ilse (1993), *Back to Freud's Texts: Making Silent Documents Speak*, transl. Philip Slotkin. New Haven & London: Yale UP.

Harris, Adrienne & Kuchuck, Steven (2015), *The Legacy of Sándor Ferenczi: From Ghost to Ancestor*. New York: Routledge.

Haynal, André & King, J.E. (1990), *Controversies in Psychoanalytic Method. From Freud and Ferenczi to Michael Bálint*. New York & London: New York UP.

Keve, Tom & Szekacs-Weisz, Judit (eds.) (2012a), *Ferenczi and His World: Rekindling the Spirit of the Budapest School*. London: Karnac.

Keve, Tom & Szekacs-Weisz Judit (eds.) (2012b), *Ferenczi for Our Time: Theory and Practice*. London: Karnac.

May, Ulrike (2015), 'The Third Step in the Drive Theory: On the Genesis of *Beyond the Pleasure Principle*', *Psychoanalysis and History* 17(2), pp. 205–280 (in this volume, pp. 81–164).

Rilke, Rainer Maria (1966), *Sämtliche Werke Bd 6. Malte Laurids Brigge, Prosa 1906–1926*. Wiesbaden: Insel.

Rilke, Rainer Maria (1975), *Duino Elegies*, transl. Elaine E. Boney. Chapel Hill: University of North Carolina P.

Rudnitzky, Peter L., Bókay, Antal & Giampieri-Deutsch, Patrizia (1996), *Ferenczi's Turn in Psychoanalysis*, New York & London: New York UP.

Scholem, Gershom (1965), *On the Kabbalah and its Symboliosm*. London: Routledge & Kegan Paul.

Scholem, Gershom (1972), 'Walter Benjamin and his Angel', in: ed. Gary Smith, *On Walter Benjamin. Critical Essays and Recollections*. Cambridge (MA) & London: MIT Press, 1991, pp. 51–89.

Soreanu, Raluca (2018), 'The Psychic Life of Fragments: Splitting from Ferenczi to Klein', *American Journal of Psychoanalysis* 78(4), pp. 421–444.

Soreanu, Raluca (2023), 'Catastrophe and the Creativity of Fragments: Toward a Phenomenology of the Scene of Trauma', in: ed. Raluca Soreanu, Jakob Staberg & Jenny Willner, *Ferenczi Dialogues. On Trauma and Catastrophe*. Leuven: Leuven UP, pp. 145–192.

Staberg, Jakob (2020), 'Anstatt Sprache: Verwirrung: Eine verfehlte Begegnung zwischen Sigmund Freud und Sándor Fernczi', *Psyche. Zeitschrift für Psychoanalyse und ihre Anwendungen* 74(5), pp. 321–343.

Staberg, Jakob (2023), 'Instead of Language: Confusion. Sigmund Freud / Sándor Ferenczi', in: ed. Raluca Soreanu, Jakob Staberg & Jenny Willner, *Ferenczi Dialogues. On Trauma and Catastrophe.* Leuven: Leuven UP, pp. 23–71.

Staberg, Jakob (2023), 'Reading Against the Grain: On How Organs Crave Interpretation', in: ed. Raluca Soreanu, Jakob Staberg & Jenny Willner, *Ferenczi Dialogues. On Trauma and Catastrophe.* Leuven: Leuven UP, pp. 131–136.

Thonack, Klaus (1997), *Selbstdarstellung des Unbewussten: Freud als Autor.* Würzburg: Königshausen und Neumann.

Westerink, Herman & Van Haute, Philippe (2022), *Verleiding, drift en herhaling: Freuds metafysicavan het trauma.* Amsterdam: Boom.

Willner, Jenny (2020), 'Neurotische Evolution. Bioanalyse als Kulturkritik in Jenseits des Lustprinzips', *Psyche. Zeitschrift für Psychoanalyse und ihre Anwendungen* 11(74), pp. 895–921.

Willner, Jenny (2023), 'Catastrophes and Genitality: Ferenczi's *Thalassa* and the Politics of Bioanalysis', in: ed. Raluca Soreanu, Jakob Staberg & Jenny Willner, *Ferenczi Dialogues. On Trauma and Catastrophe.* Leuven: Leuven UP, pp. 91–130.

Zaretsky, Eli (2005), *Secrets of the Soul: A Social and Cultural History of Psychoanalysis,* New York: Vintage.

On the Contributors

Ulrike Kistner is Professor Emerita in the Department of Philosophy at the University of Pretoria, South Africa, where her teaching and research has been focused on social theory and political philosophy. All along, she has been pursuing an interest in psychoanalytic theory, which has resulted in publications on psychoanalytic theory, especially on trauma, the death drive, and the psychology of (de-)colonisation. In the course of her work on psychoanalytic theory, she encountered issues in translation. This has led to work in and on philosophical translation, including the translation (2016) of the first edition of Freud's *Three Essays on a Theory of Sexuality*. Other issues of philosophical translation arose in discussions around Fanon's reading of Hegel, which resulted in a compilation of essays, edited together with Philippe Van Haute, under the title *Violence, Slavery and Freedom between Hegel and Fanon* (2020).

Ulrike May, Dr phil., is a practising psychoanalyst in Berlin, and a member of the Karl-Abraham-Institute Berlin, the German Psychoanalytic Association and the International Psychoanalytic Association. She has published four books: *Freuds frühe klinische Theorie (1894–1896). Wiederentdeckung und Rekonstruktion* (1996), *Edith Jacobson. Sie selbst und die Welt ihrer Objekte* (2005, together with Elke Mühlleitner), *Freud at Work. On the History of Psychoanalytic Theory and Practice, with an Analysis of Freud's Patient Record Books* (2018) and *Der Abschied vom Primat des Sexuellen. Zum Wandel der Psychoanalyse in Berlin und London zwischen 1920 und 1925* (2023). Of her numerous papers on the history of psychoanalytic theory and practice, the last one concentrated on the conversation between Freud, Abraham and Ferenczi on 'Mourning and Melancholia' (2019). In 2013, together with Michael Schröter, she presented a critical edition of Freud's *Beyond the Pleasure Principle* (1920), including a transcript of its first version from 1919 that had been not published before.

Jakob Staberg is a practising psychoanalyst and psychotherapist, and a member of the International Psychoanalytical Association. He is an Assistant Professor for Comparative Literature and a Lecturer in Aesthetics at Södertörn University, Sweden. Staberg works in the field of aesthetics, literature and psychoanalytic theory. He received his PhD in 2002 at Stockholm University. In 2009, Staberg published the monograph *Sjukdomens estetik* [*The Aesthetics of Illness*]. He is currently working on a project that seeks to rethink the genealogy of psychoanalysis. In particular, he has devoted himself to the relationship between Freud and Ferenczi from the perspective of the problem of transference and as it is expressed in dream interpretation. He has published on this topic in the journal *Psyche. Zeitschrift für Psychoanalyse und ihre Anwendungen* 5(74), 2020. He co-authored the book *Ferenczi Dialogues. On Trauma and Catastrophe* together with Raluca Soreanu and Jenny Willner (Leuven UP, 2023).

Philippe Van Haute was Full Professor of Philosophical Anthropology at Radboud University Nijmegen, the Netherlands, and Extra-ordinary Professor of Philosophy at the University of Pretoria, South Africa. He did his PhD at KU Leuven, Belgium. He was a psychoanalyst of the Belgian School for Psychoanalysis for many years. He has published numerous articles and books on Freudian psychoanalysis and philosophical anthropology, amongst others (both with Tomas Geyskens) *Confusion of Tongues: The Primacy of Sexuality in Freud, Ferenczi and Laplanche* (2004) and *A Non-Oedipal Psychoanalysis? A Clinical Anthropology of Hysteria in the Works of Freud and Lacan* (2012). Recently he edited (with Herman Westerink and Ulrike Kistner (translator)) the first English translation of Freud's *Three Essays on the Theory of Sexuality*, and wrote (with Herman Westerink) a monograph on the different editions of *Three Essays* (2021). The last major publication was a monograph published in Dutch on Freud's metaphysics of trauma (with Herman Westerink). This book will be published in English in 2025.

Herman Westerink is Endowed Professor and Associate Professor for Philosophy of Religion and Psychoanalysis at the Center for Contemporary European Philosophy, Radboud University Nijmegen, the Netherlands. He did his PhD at the University of Groningen and wrote his professorial dissertation (Habilitation) at the University of Vienna. He has published many books and articles on Freudian psychoanalysis, sexuality, subjectivity and religion. Amongst others, he has published a monograph on Freud's theories of the sense of guilt (2009), a monograph on and text editions of the first edition of Freud's *Three Essays on the Theory of Sexuality* (2016, 2021 – with Philippe Van Haute and Ulrike Kistner (translator)). He has also published a monograph on Michel Foucault's *History of Sexuality* (2019). His latest monograph is on Freud's metaphysics of trauma (2022 – with Philippe Van Haute). He is co-editor of the book series "Sigmund Freuds Werke: Wiener Interdisziplinäre Kommentare" (Vienna UP) and of the book series "Figures of the Unconscious" (Leuven UP).

Jenny Willner is an Assistant Professor for Comparative Literature and currently Deputy Professor at the Department for German Studies and at the Ludwig-Maximilians-University in Munich, Germany. She completed her PhD at Freie Universität Berlin with *Wortgewalt. Peter Weiss und die deutsche Sprache* (Konstanz UP, 2014) and has published in the area of literary studies in several international journals and anthologies. Her work on Freud and Ferenczi has been published in *Psyche. Zeitschrift für Psychoanalyse und ihre Anwendungen* (11, 2020), *RISS. Zeitschrift für Psychoanalyse* (94, 2021), *Psychoanalysis and History* (24, 2022) and *Imágó Budapest* (3, 2023). She co-authored the book *Ferenczi Dialogues. On Trauma and Catastrophe* together with Raluca Soreanu and Jakob Staberg (Leuven UP, 2023). In 2024 she completed her professorial dissertation (Habilitation) at the LMU Munich: *Unbehagen am Erbe. Psychoanalyse, Biologie und Neurologie bei Freud und Ferenczi.*

24W31770/ T2/ 9789462704091